When Fitness Went Global

When Fitness Went Global

The Rise of Physical Culture in the Nineteenth Century

Conor Heffernan

BLOOMSBURY ACADEMIC
LONDON • NEW YORK • OXFORD • NEW DELHI • SYDNEY

BLOOMSBURY ACADEMIC

Bloomsbury Publishing Plc, 50 Bedford Square, London, WC1B 3DP, UK
Bloomsbury Publishing Inc, 1359 Broadway, New York, NY 10018, USA
Bloomsbury Publishing Ireland, 29 Earlsfort Terrace, Dublin 2, D02 AY28, Ireland

BLOOMSBURY, BLOOMSBURY ACADEMIC and the Diana logo are
trademarks of Bloomsbury Publishing Plc

First published in Great Britain 2026

Copyright © Conor Heffernan, 2026

Conor Heffernan has asserted his right under the Copyright, Designs and
Patents Act, 1988, to be identified as Author of this work.

For legal purposes the Acknowledgements on pp. vii–viii constitute an
extension of this copyright page.

Cover design by Paul Smith
Cover image © mikroman6 via Getty Images

All rights reserved. No part of this publication may be: i) reproduced or transmitted in
any form, electronic or mechanical, including photocopying, recording or by means of
any information storage or retrieval system without prior permission in writing from
the publishers; or ii) used or reproduced in any way for the training, development or
operation of artificial intelligence (AI) technologies, including generative AI technologies.
The rights holders expressly reserve this publication from the text and data mining
exception as per Article 4(3) of the Digital Single Market Directive (EU) 2019/790.

Bloomsbury Publishing Plc does not have any control over, or responsibility for, any
third-party websites referred to or in this book. All internet addresses given in this
book were correct at the time of going to press. The author and publisher regret
any inconvenience caused if addresses have changed or sites have ceased
to exist, but can accept no responsibility for any such changes.

A catalogue record for this book is available from the British Library.

A catalog record for this book is available from the Library of Congress.

ISBN: HB: 978-1-3505-0078-5
       PB: 978-1-3505-0077-8
       ePDF: 978-1-3505-0080-8
       eBook: 978-1-3505-0079-2

Typeset by Integra Software Services Pvt. Ltd.
Printed and bound in Great Britain

For product safety related questions contact productsafety@bloomsbury.com.

To find out more about our authors and books visit www.bloomsbury.com
and sign up for our newsletters.

CONTENTS

List of figures vi
Acknowledgements vii

Introduction 1

1 The long durée of fitness 17

2 Globalizing local practices 53

3 Institutional and international gymnastics 95

4 Physical culture and selling fitness 133

5 Protected practices 171

Conclusion 205

Bibliography 214
Index 244

FIGURES

1.1	Standing statue of Hanuman, with Gada at the Ram Janaki Temple in Nepal	24
1.2	*De Arte* Gynmastica illustration	35
1.3	The Bikini Mosaic	40
2.1	'Daily Exercise, Mahratta Camp', 1813	58
2.2	Painting of 'Conjurer' show, *c.* 1740	73
2.3	Edith Garrud jujutsu demonstration, *c.* 1910	88
3.1	GutsMuths' depiction of rope climbing and gymnastics, 1793	101
3.2	Before and after images of MacLaren's initial student, *c.* 1860	113
3.3	Girls exercising on bars, *c.* 1899	123
4.1	Sandow in pose, *c.* 1902	139
4.2	Plasmon advertisement from 1903	150
4.3	Sandow and pupil	155
4.4	Indian strongman, *c.* 1915	160
4.5	Hornibrook and his Fijian Sandow trainees, *c.* 1900s	161
4.6	Martin Willis front double bicep pose	163
5.1	German weightlifter showcasing array of equipment, *c.* 1895	176
5.2	Franz Defregger painting depicting stone-lifting, *c.* 1898	186
5.3	Harrison's first image in *The Illustrated London News*	195
5.4	Club swinger at the 1896 India and Ceylon Exhibition, London	198
5.5	Club swingers in India, *c.* 1860	199

ACKNOWLEDGEMENTS

I am fascinated with fitness. From childhood memories of watching World's Strongest Man to recent trips to the west of Ireland to lift historic lifting stones, my research has, in many respects, been an effort to understand my passion better. This book is the culmination of a decade of research and a lifetime love affair with movement. There is then a debt of gratitude owed to fellow academics, athletes, training partners and family whose influence is dotted throughout this book. I will never be able to do justice to everyone who has supported me, shared resources or put up with my rambling.

There are, however, a few I would like to cite as responsible, hopefully for the better, for this work. Jan Todd and Terry Todd began as mentors and turned into friends. My love of fitness and strength pales in comparison to theirs and some of my most treasured memories are lunches and phone calls spent discussing obscure physical culturists or objects. I owe them more than I can express. I hold similar affection to John Fair and David Chapman whose work I hold to the highest standard and whose friendship surpasses even that. I am getting old, and further away from my original doctoral work, but my advisor Paul Rouse deserves mention. Paul encouraged me to explore the human motivations for physical culture, to look beyond the macro. He reminded me that history is fundamentally about people. Finally, I owe a debt of gratitude to Patrick Bernhard, who was the first historian to encourage me to study this field, and Jacqueline Hayden for being the first to encourage me to communicate with the world.

I am not stupid enough to cite six people and lay claim to the glory, or failure, that this book may entail. Institutionally I am blessed. My colleagues at Ulster University have shaped me as a researcher and instructor. Katie, Paul (s!), Deirdre, Rachael, Tandy, Ben, Simon, Ryan, Sinead and Mo show a level of dedication to their work that I struggle (but try) to match. This is true for my colleagues in the Sciences and History. Away from home, I have found friendships in societies like the British Society for Sport History, the North American Society for Sport History, the Irish Economic and Social History group, among others, the Irish Association of Professional Historians and the Zombie Studies Network (yes really). The work found here was presented, over the course of many years, at various conferences where I 'expertly' rambled through presentations and parasitically took questioners' expertise to pass off as my own.

Academia and well-being are not regular bedfellows but I have found and developed so many friendships whose value has, and continues to, sustained me. Thank you to Claire Warden, Conor Curran, Conor Murray, Tom Fabian, Julien Clenet, Aishwarya Ramachandran, Nevada Cooke, Philip Chipman, Lisa Taylor, Nick Piercy, Dave Day, Amanda Callan-Spenn, Raf Nicholson, Matt McDowell, Margaret Roberts, Alec Hurley, Max Portman, Lucy Boucher, Rachel Ozerkevich, Eric Helms, David Nolan, David Keohan, Juan Carlos Cassano, Omar Isuf, Arthur Lynch, Jason Shurley, Charles Stocking, Ian Miller, Sarah-Anne Buckley, Aidan Hughes, Kim Beckwith, Conor McClean, Broderick Chow, Scott Hamilton, Phillipa Levine, Brad Love, Sean Donnelly, Tim Ellis, Geoff Levett, Dill Porter, Gary James, Cormac Moore, Mike Cronin, Tom Hunt, Liam O'Callaghan, Helena Byrne, David Gentle, Carol Osbourne, Rob Lake, Tanya Evans, Matt Doherty, David Webster, Jarrett Hulse and the entire ironhistory.com family, Petter Sellberg, Jeff Russo, Simon Truesdale, Stevie Shanks, Marcus Kment, Broderick Chow and all those who I may have missed. I am an ass. Sorry. My thanks to those archivists at the Stark Center, British Library, Royal Army Physical Training Corps Museum, Wellcome Library, Olympic Studies Centre and various National Archives who helped track down texts on my behalf. Finally, Bloomsbury have been a delight to work with, and I extend a huge thanks to Megan Harris and Maddie Smith for believing in this project.

I would not be here without the support of my family. My parents Paul and Mary have sacrificed a great deal for me, and more than I am sure I realize. Thank you is not enough but I am who I am because of you. My wife Susan has been, and continues to be, my best supporter, and even better coach to **stop working**. She has helped by my son Cuán who began this project as an infant and is now capable of closing my laptop screen down while explaining that it is now 'his time' to work. How things change. Finally to the Carney family. Thank you for accepting me. During the course of this book, we lost Jack Carney, and his absence is felt daily. Jack, you are missed. *Níl cara ag cumha ach cuimhne.*

Introduction

In 1889 a man tore his clothes off in a packed auditorium to show off his muscular physique. Five years later he wrestled a lion, and the animal lost in a unanimous decision. In its defence, it was likely heavily sedated. Soon after the man created a magazine wherein men could send half-naked images of themselves to be evaluated by others who hailed from the British Empire and beyond.[1] What connects these stories is fitness. Specifically, a new turn in the fitness industry. We will return to our half-naked, lion-wrestling entrepreneur, whose name was Eugen Sandow, as this book is not about him. It is about the processes which made Sandow's life possible. That process was a globalization of fitness ideals and behaviours, which began in the early nineteenth century and continues to this present day. During the nineteenth and twentieth centuries, fitness practices around the world became incredibly similar. This meant that Indian exercisers began to use the same movements and equipment as counterparts in New Zealand or France. Likewise fitness authorities, and celebrities, became globally recognizable and popular. Take, for example, the lesser-known physical culturist, Tom Burrows, who engaged in tours in North and South America, Africa and Great Britain during the 1890s and early 1900s. Information about health, about training and about physical culture became increasingly homogenized. This book is centred then on a single question. Why did exercisers begin using the same movements and what impact did this have?

If the person reading this book is versed in global history, this last line about practices becoming the same is likely to cause some annoyance. Since the emergence of 'globalization' studies in the 1980s, academics have fought for nuance in studying global processes.[2] It is important, then, to sketch this book's argument, and understandings of globalization, before returning to the lion-wrestling entrepreneur with a penchant for ripping clothes off. This

---

[1]David Chapman, *Sandow the magnificent: Eugen Sandow and the beginnings of bodybuilding* (University of Illinois Press, 1994).
[2]Pamela Crossley, *What is global history?* (Polity, 2008).

book studies physical culture in the nineteenth century and argues that, for the first time in history, fitness practices around the world began to cluster around a clear set of ideas, movements, products and body ideals. Outside of academics, and a fringe community of gym-goers, the term 'physical culture' is not a popular one in modern language. Borrowing from the world's leading repository of physical culture materials, the term is used to describe 'the various activities people have employed … to strengthen their bodies, enhance their physiques, increase their endurance, improve their health, fight against aging, and become better athletes'.[3] For us, it will be used to describe gymnastic and callisthenic practices, including yoga, weight-training, self-defence, club-swinging and stone-lifting. In popular conversation the term was typically used from the 1890s to 1920s to refer to fitness activities.[4] Here we stretch its usage to the 'long' nineteenth century (1789–1914).[5]

Before returning to the global historians, whose ire is warranted, it is important to explain what physical culture is not. It is not, typically, sport. While some activities can have a sporting element such as competitions in weightlifting, bodybuilding, yoga, etc., it is typically a lifestyle. A comparison may be to say that physical culture is concerned with building biceps, as opposed to winning medals. It is a form of 'serious leisure'.[6] Yes the boundaries between sport and physical culture are blurry but physical culture is about 'purposive exercise' and not necessarily play. Thus this book is not concerned with the globalization of sport but the globalization of physical culture.[7] Studies on the globalization of physical culture are relatively few, and those that do exist are more concerned with the late twentieth century.[8] Thus a conversation about the globalization of fitness typically revolves around names like Arnold Schwarzenegger, Jane Fonda, Les Mills and Gold's Gym.[9] In one sense, that is a correct interpretation of the world. Fitness, and gym-going, burst into the mainstream from the 1970s and, with that, so did a 'McDonaldization' of fitness practices wherein the same workouts, supplements and chains emerged in diverse parts of the world.[10]

---

[3] 'About the Center', *The H.J. Lutcher Stark Center for Physical Culture and Sports*. Available at: https://starkcenter.org/about/. Visited 2 December 2024.
[4] Jan Todd, 'Reflections on physical culture: Defining our field and protecting its integrity', *Iron Game History*, 13 (2015): 2–8
[5] Eric Hobsbawm, *Age of empire: 1875–1914* (Hachette, 2010).
[6] Conor Heffernan, 'State of the field: Physical culture', *History* 107 (2022): 143–62.
[7] Matthew Taylor, *World of sport: Transnational and connected histories* (Taylor & Francis, 2024).
[8] Jesper Andreasson and Thomas Johansson, 'The fitness revolution: Historical transformations in the global gym and fitness culture', *Sport Science Review* 23 (2014): 91–112.
[9] Patrizia Gazzola, Enrica Pavione and Francesco Ferrazzano, *Evolution of the global fitness industry* (Taylor & Francis, 2024).
[10] Jesper Andreasson and Thomas Johansson, "Doing for group exercise what McDonald's did for hamburgers': Les Mills, and the fitness professional as global traveller', *Sport, Education and Society* 21 (2016): 148–65.

As so often happens, historians spoil a celebratory narrative. Charlotte McDonald's work on British physical culture in the 1930s outlined a legislative globalization wherein fitness acts in Britain were replicated in Australia and New Zealand.[11] Those studying the late nineteenth and early twentieth centuries have pinpointed global fitness ideas and practices permeating English, French, German, Irish, North American, South African and Asian fitness cultures.[12] Other research has discussed the migration of fitness instructors, and equipment, around the world from the 1820s.[13] Historians can and have dragged this globalization timeline further back than the 1970s. The issue, and niche that this book fills, is that such works have tended towards national histories, as opposed to international ones. My own work on Irish physical culture is an illustrative example. In it, I examined Irish physical culture first, and its international influences second.[14] I studied the development of gyms in Ireland by looking at local developments, and then noted that Irish gym-goers read American, British or French fitness magazines. This has largely been the approach within the field. We discuss global patterns but often leave them within the backdrop, just left of stage. Two scholars to buck this trend, Sebastian Conrad and Carey Watt, have focused on global processes, but focused on the 1890s and early 1900s.[15]

This book reverses this order and looks at global processes and histories of fitness to understand how and why so many countries exhibited the same receptiveness, to a narrow band of fitness practices. Now we return to the ire of global historians. I am aware that the above paragraphs have committed two cardinal sins. I have picked the late eighteenth and early nineteenth centuries as a starting point for this period of globalization, and second, I have confidently proposed that fitness practices became the same the world over, without consideration for local resistance or divergences. Many have noted the contentiousness with which 'starting points' of globalization are usually met.[16] For this reason historians have often discussed waves or prototypes of

---

[11] Charlotte Macdonald, *Strong, beautiful and modern: National fitness in Britain, New Zealand, Australia and Canada, 1935–1960* (UBC, 2013).
[12] Heffernan, 'State of the field'.
[13] Ibid.
[14] Conor Heffernan, *The history of physical culture in Ireland* (Palgrave, 2020).
[15] Sebastian Conrad, 'Globalizing the beautiful body: Eugen Sandow, bodybuilding, and the ideal of muscular manliness at the turn of the twentieth-century', *Journal of World History* 32 (2021): 95–125; Carey Watt, 'Cultural exchange, appropriation and physical culture: Strongman Eugen Sandow in colonial India, 1904–1905', *The International Journal of the History of Sport* 33 (2016): 1921–1942. Jürgen Martschukat, *The age of fitness: How the body came to symbolize success and achievement* (Wiley, 2021).
[16] C.A. Bayly, *Remaking the modern world 1900–2015: Global connections and comparisons* (Wiley, 2018); Jürgen Osterhammel, *The transformation of the world: A global history of the nineteenth-century* (Princeton University Press, 2015); Peter Stearns, *World past to world present: A sketch of global history* (Routledge, 2021).

globalization which can be found from the eleventh century onwards.[17] This book does not argue for a strict starting point and is not foolish enough to suggest that 1801 was different from 1800 from a global perspective. The book is foolhardy enough, however, to state that the 'long nineteenth century' (1789–1914) was seismic in fitness terms. More than any previous period fitness took an enhanced, and multifaceted role, within various societies. It became common for some individuals to set aside time from their normal routine to partake in physical culture. Simultaneously the exercises people used in different parts of the world began to resemble one another. While there was no one 'global workout', there were global workouts.

The reasons for this are expanded in this book but some will be familiar to many with a passing knowledge of world history. The industrialization of Europe and North America, deepening trade networks, increasing literacy, formalized schooling, etc., played a role.[18] So too did colonialism.[19] Countries had long engaged in trade with one another, and empires of conquest were globalized prior to this period.[20] Nevertheless the long nineteenth century of globalized fitness saw a deepening of European, and to a much lesser extent, American interest in African, Asian and Oceanic conquest. Colonialization was neither easy nor even across regions but its impact on our subject is clear. Many fitness patterns were moved across Empire, both from the colonizers to the oppressed and also from the colonized to the colonizers. I want to state, very clearly, that the globalization of fitness discussed in this book is not a celebratory story. Traditional forms of physical culture existed, but many were pushed to the margins thanks to the spreading of European and American systems. This mirrors the globalization of sport long discussed by historians of British and French histories.[21]

This brings us to my second *faux pas*. I continually refer to a levelling out of exercise practices, wherein Swedish gymnasts used the same exercises as British schoolchildren. Such an argument may have passed muster in the early 1990s when many discussed globalization with reference to similarities.[22] Later work has instead looked at the process of assimilation, contestation and rejection among communities.[23] The 'glocalization' of the world wherein local comments adapt global trends to their own sensibilities is arguably a

---

[17] Kevin O'Rourke and Jeffrey Williamson, *Globalization and history: The evolution of a nineteenth-century Atlantic economy* (MIT Press, 2001).
[18] Mokyr Joel, *A culture of growth: The origins of the modern economy* (Princeton University Press, 2016).
[19] Jane Burbank and Frederick Cooper, *Empires in world history: Power and the politics of difference* (Princeton University Press, 2010).
[20] Frank Trentmann, *Empire of things* (Penguin, 2016).
[21] J.A. Mangan, ed. *Sport in Europe: Politics, class, gender* (Routledge, 2013).
[22] Alan Scott, ed. *The limits of globalization: Cases and arguments* (Psychology Press, 1997).
[23] Christopher Bayly and Leila Fawaz, 'Introduction: The connected world of empires'. In Christopher Bayly and Leila Fawaz (eds.), *Modernity and culture from the Mediterranean to the Indian Ocean, 1890–1920* (Columbia University Press, 2002), 1–27.

truer story.²⁴ Where local assimilation will be discussed, the larger story is one of the global similarities as opposed to local idiosyncrasies. Again this book is not a celebratory one, and indeed, I welcome future studies which focus on global differences in far greater detail. A baseline is needed at this point, and this is where the focus on similarities lies.

What does a global history of fitness provide that the study of the individual nation does not? Put cruelly, *who cares*? We have discussed the centrality of fitness in many societies in the present age and, truthfully, such an answer is something of a cop-out. 'It's important because it's important. Trust me.' Instead I want to highlight three benefits which come from studying fitness in this way: changes in body practices, a greater understanding of fitness commerce, and nuance when it comes to issues of gender and race. Writing in 1914 in the *Dubliners*, James Joyce noted a Mr. Duffy, who was said 'to live just a short distance from his body'. Joyce's most famous character, and protagonist of the book *Ulysses*, Leopold Bloom, had no such trouble. Unlike Mr. Duffy, who was divorced from his body, Bloom owned a Sandow exerciser and, for a time, pushed and strained his way to a better awareness of his body.²⁵ Bloom was joined by millions of real, and imagined, men and women who took to physical culture to change their bodies, and outcomes.

How a body moves matters. During my undergraduate days, I chanced upon Iris Marian Young's essay, 'Throwing like a Girl'. In it, Young sought to show that her desire to throw a ball, and her body's inability to do so, was not down to innate biological differences, but rather to a socio-cultural system which denied female physicality and sport.²⁶ As my academic career, such as it is, continued, I gravitated towards the works of sociologist Pierre Bourdieu, whose idea of *habitus* promised to explain how bodies implicitly and explicitly learn mannerisms which, in turn, can reify social inequities.²⁷ Even something as simple as how men sat, or carried their bodies, could implicitly map gender or class hierarchies.²⁸ Some Bourdieusian scholars, like Loïc Wacquant and Chris Shilling, extended these insights into the sporting world wherein the body learned specific techniques and could replicate them without conscious effort.²⁹ In Wacquant's case, his boxing training allowed him to retrain his body to move on instinct during the chaos of battle.

---

²⁴Conor Heffernan, 'The Irish Sandow school: Physical culture competitions in fin-de-siècle Ireland', *Irish Studies Review* 27 (2019): 402–21.
²⁵Vike Martina Plock, 'A feat of strength in' Ithaca', *Journal of Modern Literature* 30 (2006): 129–39.
²⁶Iris Marion Young, 'Throwing like a girl: A phenomenology of feminine body comportment motility and spatiality', *Human Studies* 3, no. 1 (1980): 137–56.
²⁷Philip Gorski, ed. *Bourdieu and historical analysis* (Duke University Press, 2013).
²⁸Pierre Bourdieu, 'The peasant and his body', *Ethnography* 5 (2004): 579–99.
²⁹Loïc Wacquant, *Body & soul: Notebooks of an apprentice boxer* (Oxford University Press, 2006); Chris Shilling, *The body in culture, technology and society* (SAGE, 2005).

I was, however, left somewhat numb by these accounts. Bodily practices told of broader hierarchies and structures, but what of fleshy experience? Physical culture is about power struggles, as well as idealized bodies, but it is also about the fleshy and decaying, body. Physical culture involves movement which, as anyone who has ever exercised will attest, contains a certain element of introspection. This has both an individual and communal consequence. For individuals exercise can invite a sense of 'extra daily consciousness' which those studying theatre describe as a kind of 'third eye examining the internal workings of the self'.[30] Those in sport psychology may refer to this as 'flow'.[31] At an individual level, physical culture offers an opportunity to connect with one's body and, at a higher state, provide an alternative experience of the world, and even, enter a trance-like state.[32] Put bluntly, if I am lifting a heavy weight or struggling to catch my breath, I am present with my body. What about bodies moving together? William McNeill's *Keeping Together in Time* remains one of my favoured explorations of this question. Studying dance and drill cultures, McNeill posited that groups moving together can reach of point of 'muscular bonding' wherein relationships are strengthened without words. A modern comparison would be the solidarity often recorded in group exercise classes.[33]

This book is primarily about movements and less about the inner worlds inhibited by individuals. I do want to stress that although movements are the primary focus, we must remember that the bodies discussed were living bodies. Changes in movement patterns had the potential to impact individual and group ideas. This book's core argument then is twofold. First that fitness practices globalized and second that this globalization helped, in effect, to create a 'global body'. In 1996 George Mosse published *The Image of Man*, a book which continues to challenge my understanding of masculinity. In it Mosse put forward the idea of a masculine stereotype, born from middle-class cultures, which permeated Germany and surrounding countries. This 'national stereotype' was used by the State to assert its right to rule and was presented as unchanging.[34] It was a hegemonic ideal and one which can be understood as a fragile but seemingly unchanging sense of what a man 'should be'.[35] Self-controlled, dutiful, hard-working, courageous

---

[30]Phillip Zarrilli, 'Toward a phenomenological model of the actor's embodied modes of experience', *Theatre Journal* 56 (2004): 653–66. Broderick Chow, *Muscle works: Physical culture and the performance of masculinity* (Northwestern University Press, 2024).

[31]Susan Jackson and Mihaly Csikszentmihalyi. *Flow in sports* (Human Kinetics, 1999).

[32]Margaret Lock, 'Cultivating the body: Anthropology and epistemologies of bodily practice and knowledge', *Annual Review of Anthropology* (1993): 133–55.

[33]William McNeill, *Keeping together in time: Dance and drill in human history* (Harvard University Press, 1997).

[34]George Mosse, *The image of man: The creation of modern masculinity* (Oxford University Press, 1998), 5–23.

[35]R.W. Connell and James Messerschmidt, 'Hegemonic masculinity: Rethinking the concept', *Gender & Society* 19 (2005): 829–59.

and physically fit were the ideals of the time.[36] Emerging at a period when sciences began to deal with individuals as nameless groups, and the quest for the normative category challenged innumerable scientists, physicians and philosophers, the 'national stereotype' seemed to be an *a priori* sense of what man was.[37]

Here it is argued that a 'global body' emerged in fitness. This was a popular and scientific ideal of radiant health made possible through physical culture. The path to this body could differ across systems but the body itself was presented as unchanging. For men it was lean and muscular, but not overly so. For women it tended towards slimness with stricter physical dimensions.[38] Both, incidentally, were implicitly white bodies. Returning to the lion-taming physical culturist Eugen Sandow, his white body was celebrated in colonial India by many as physical perfection. Many even attempted to become Indian Sandows in their own right.[39] Global ideals met with local variances. Conrad has written about the globalization of male beauty during this period while Vigarello has discussed the shifting norms around obesity and slimness.[40] This work examines both the ideal body and critically the methods associated with its achievement. Contemporary work in fat studies and the sociology of fitness have stressed the moral and quasi-religious fervour long placed on the sacrifice needed to maintain ideal health.[41] To understand the allure of the global body, we need to understand its attainment and the messages associated with it.

The emergence of a global body marked a profound shift in how physicality was understood and shaped across cultures. This was not about the spread of specific exercises or equipment, but rather the creation of a standardized ideal of how bodies should look, move and be measured. Drawing on Bourdieu's concept of habitus, we can understand this global body as a set of deeply ingrained physical dispositions that transcended national boundaries while still being adapted to local contexts.[42] Military officers, physicians and physical educators across Europe, Asia and the Americas increasingly evaluated bodies against universal standards of posture, muscular development and movement. This standardization was made possible through new networks of knowledge circulation but also through the embodied experiences of millions who encountered similar

---

[36]Mosse, *The image of man*.
[37]Ibid.
[38]Heffernan, 'State of ... '.
[39]Conrad, 'Globalizing ... '; Watt, 'Cultural exchange ... '.
[40]Georges Vigarello, *The metamorphoses of fat* (Columbia University Press, 2013).
[41]Brian Pronger, *Body fascism: Salvation in the technology of physical fitness* (University of Toronto Press, 2002); Kimberly Dark, 'Exposure and erasure: Fat kids in gym class, fat adults as athletes', *Fat Studies* 8 (2019): 127–34.
[42]Lee Monaghan, 'Bodybuilding, drugs and risk: Reflections on an ethnographic study', in A. Smith and I. Waddington (eds.), *Doing real world research in sports studies* (Routledge, 2013), 93–106.

training regimens in schools, armies and recreational settings. The global body was an aesthetic ideal, visible in the muscled physiques celebrated from London to Tokyo, and a system of bodily discipline that reflected emerging forms of power. Yet this was not simply a case of Western practices being imposed elsewhere. As this book demonstrates, the global body emerged through complex processes of appropriation, and transformation across cultures, even as it ultimately served to establish new hierarchies of physical 'perfection' that often privileged white, male bodies.[43]

What then, about commerce, the prime way in which people attempted to achieve this body? At the time of writing it is estimated that the global market for nutritional supplements, workout equipment, personal training and workout apparel is in its trillions.[44] Despite this, we still know very little about the historical development of the fitness industry. Studies have been conducted, and they are wonderful, but they have tended to be studies of individual entrepreneurs.[45] We do not have a substantive framework for what a fitness entrepreneur is, what a fitness good is and how fitness commerce evolved.[46] Achieving a global body often meant the buying of supplements or equipment, subscribing to magazines, gymnasium memberships and much more. There was a new nineteenth-century fitness commodity market that we need to know more about.[47]

Contrast this with the study of sporting entrepreneurs which dates to at least the 1980s if not further. This book offers an opportunity to reflect on what a fitness good is but, more importantly, what defines a fitness industry.[48] Hardy, Porter and Vamplew have done much to unpack the concept of the sporting entrepreneur and sporting product.[49] Sporting entrepreneurs have been divided by Vamplew between those who manufacture equipment, sell entertainment, own grounds and act as professionals or as charitable promoters. Likewise Porter has divided between those sporting goods which 'piggyback' off the sport itself, those created to link non-sporting

---

[43]Shannon Walsh, *Eugenics and physical culture performance in the progressive era: Watch Whiteness Workout* (Springer, 2020).
[44]Sarah Rappaport, 'Global Wellness Industry Is Now Worth $6.3 Trillion', *Bloomberg News*, 5 November 2024. Available at https://www.bloomberg.com/news/articles/2024-11-05/global-wellness-industry-is-now-worth-6-3-trillion. Accessed 3 December 2024.
[45]Heffernan, 'State of ... '.
[46]Conor Heffernan, 'All muscle and no brains?: Contextualizing the fitness entrepreneur in sport history', *Sporting Traditions* 39 (2022): 13–32.
[47]Ibid.
[48]Jeroen Scheerder, Hanna Vehmas and Kobe Helsen, eds. *The rise and size of the fitness industry in Europe: Fit for the future?* (Palgrave, 2020).
[49]Wray Vamplew, 'Products, promotion, and (possibly) profits: Sports entrepreneurship revisited', *Journal of Sport History* 45 (2018): 183–201; Dilwyn Porter, 'Opportunistic, Parasitic, Strategic, Symbiotic: Entrepreneurship and the business of sport', *The International Journal of the History of Sport* 35 (2018): 641–58; Stephen Hardy, 'Entrepreneurs, organizations, and the sport marketplace: Subjects in search of historians', *Journal of Sport History* 13 (1986): 14–33.

and sporting businesses, and those created in tandem with the sport.[50] Fitness entrepreneurs, as this book shows in a global context, differ. Here, fitness goods are conceptualized into direct and indirect goods. Examples of direct goods include gymnasium memberships and exercise equipment. Indirect goods are classed as those which do not have an obvious impact on physical fitness and include books, magazines, lectures and some supplements. While this is a simple split, we can add nuance by adding a further distinction between legitimate and illegitimate goods.

Returning to Vamplew, he previously noted the existence of 'dark entrepreneurs' in sport.[51] Those being individuals who sell goods or services in questionable ways. We will use the terms 'legitimate' and 'illegitimate goods'. This recognizes that fitness and well-being spaces, in the period studied and in the present age, attract a great deal of 'snake oil' or illegitimate products.[52] One particularly interesting example of this was noted in 1908 when German strongman Arthur Saxon criticized his fellow strongmen for attributing their strength to a supplement which they knew to be false.[53] This came some years after Sandow claimed to have lived for several months consuming only a food supplement.[54] Rather than lose his strength, or achieving scurvy, he claimed that he was stronger. Questionable claims are made about sporting goods but they often pale in comparison to those found in fitness. Studying the globalization of fitness allows us an opportunity to track the evolution of this across countries, but also to help us understand the pervasiveness of fitness marketing.

Finally we come to identity, specifically, race and gender. The past half decade has seen an increasing number of studies focusing on race and physical culture.[55] Scholars have examined the privileging of white bodies and eugenic zeal physical culture was discussed about in many countries. A throughline in physical culture has been the faith that Western commentators have had in using physical culture to improve racial fitness. This could be found in the phrenology endorsements attached to American gymnast Dio L. Lewis' gymnastics in the 1860s, to early medical commentaries on Ludwig Jahn's workouts in the 1820s, and to the high point of physical culture in the early 1900s when Francis Galton, the man who coined the term eugenics, professed an admiration for physical culture.[56] Physical culture was not

---

[50]Porter, 'Opportunistic, ... '.
[51]Vamplew, 'Products, ... '.
[52]Heffernan, 'All muscle ... ?'
[53]Arthur Saxon, *The development of physical power* (Health & Strength, 1906), 3.
[54]Heffernan, 'All muscle ... ?'
[55]Heffernan, 'State of ... '. One exception is Chow, *Physical Culture and ...* .
[56]John Fair, 'Eugen Sandow and eugenics', *Sport in History* 44 (2024): 56–77; Conor Heffernan, 'The best developed man in Great Britain and Ireland? Eugen Sandow and the commercialization of Eugenics in twentieth-century Britain', *Journal of Victorian Culture* 28 (2023): 302–20. Jan Todd, *Physical culture and the body beautiful: Purposive exercise in the lives of American women, 1800–1870* (Mercer University Press, 1998).

just confined to white bodies, however, and while a handful of excellent studies have examined the interplay between white and non-white bodies in physical culture, more can be done.[57] Race will thus be studied here in two distinct, but intersecting ways. This book will examine conceptions of race in European and American physical culture, what their drivers were and how these messages were exported. An obvious example, found in Chapter 2, will be the British colonization of India and the desire among certain officials to use physical culture to uplift British soldiers but also to mould Indian bodies to fit British ideals.

The second, and to my mind, far more interesting discussion will focus on how white and non-white physical culture interacted within the global physical culture zeitgeist. Watt has led the way in this realm through a study of Eugen Sandow's 1904–5 Indian tour. Building on Watt's work, this book will examine how ideas about racial purity through physical culture were interpreted within individual countries and co-created in global communities.[58] This latter interest will become more apparent when discussing the end of the nineteenth century to 1914 as physical culture magazines opened up new spaces for global dialogue. It was thus common to see messages from African and Asian physical culturists appearing in British and American physical culture magazines. Studying race in this way, the book will also examine shifting gender norms in physical culture communities over this period. Bodies mattered in physical culture discourses. For men, certain body types were linked to sexual virility, a Protestant work ethic, discipline and social value. Likewise for women, physical culture and the ideal body type were contextualized with reference to issues of motherhood, domesticity and beauty. These messages endured over the period studied here but nuance existed. Messages changed over time, at times subtly, but the bodies praised as ideal changed rapidly for both genders. Conrad has discussed a global idea of beauty which crossed international borders.[59] The same observation can be made about body types. In many senses, physical culture allowed people to reinvent themselves through their physical forms. This had global appeal.

Finally, it is important to consider what happened when a product, or a practice, became globalized. Studying club-swinging, which originated in India and spread to much of the Western world, Joseph Alter cited an 'emptying process' whereby the clubs' origins, meanings and even traditional practices were cast aside in favour of new meanings and uses.[60] The globalization of fitness means an inherent change to those practices. A

---

[57]See footnote 54.
[58]Carey Watt, Strongman Eugen Sandow's world tour of 1904–1905: The 'Perfect Man' in colonial India and Afro-Asia (Anthem Press, 2025).
[59]Conrad, 'Globalizing … '.
[60]Joseph Alter, 'Indian clubs and colonialism: Hindu masculinity and muscular Christianity', *Comparative Studies in Society and History* 46 (2004): 497–534.

difference exists in the national use of a practice versus the international use. At a surface level the international practice, be it club-swinging, gymnastics, yoga or weightlifting, has to be somewhat superficial and emptied of its original meanings. It makes them less offensive, and more adaptable. The truer observation is that these practices were emptied of their original meanings, filled with international meanings and then, national meanings specific to each country. Examining gymnastics in the early 1800s, it is notable that Jahn's system, which was inherently tied to Prussian nationalism, was refitted in Ireland and England as a means of children to avoid illnesses.[61] In the later scenario, nationalism was absent and, in its place, more generalized concerns about growing generations existed.

The final chapter examines those practices, which did not become globalized during this period despite their popularity. One point to raise is that the practices which did travel around the world benefited from two factors. They had a print culture and often lent themselves to mass production. Those practices which entered the global marketplace were those which could be easily described through text. They were transmitted through magazines, books, training pamphlets and correspondences. While any practice is capable of being written about, the second point, about mass production, limited this scope. Those practices which were shared globally were those which could be easily exported. They were either bodyweight-only systems, required minimal equipment or the equipment promoted was easily manufactured. Indian clubs, although typically large in stature and size in India, were reshaped during the 1820s as smaller and lightweight clubs. Eighty years later, when Sandow began exporting equipment around the world from his base in Britain, he promoted lightweight and standardized goods. Addressing what makes a global fitness product or practice, the answer lies in its adaptability philosophically, textually and commercially.

Structure

This is a terribly difficult topic to approach, and I have debated whether or not I should write it chronologically or thematically. In the end, I have chosen a thematic approach for one simple reason. This history is chaotic. There was no even globalization process when it came to fitness. Practices and products emerged at different points and for different reasons. Because of this I have clustered the book into main themes be they individual practices, institutional practices, the physical culture movement or 'protected' practices. This, I believe, provides a clearer and cleaner method of studying the dissemination of fitness practices.

---

[61]Heffernan, *The history of physical culture ...*, 91–126.

To help us understand the shift from national to global fitness, Chapter 1 discusses the *long durée* of fitness prior to its globalization. The chapter looks at four defining elements of fitness from the ancient world to the seventeenth century: religious, medical, military and educational practices. These themes bring us into the world of ancient gymnasiums, the Middle-Age castles and Renaissance classrooms. This chapter draws on research conducted on Europe, Asia, the Americas and Africa, and serves as a needed contextualization for this book's 'pre-history'. The goal is not to provide an infallible account of fitness but to survey differences which existed across time and space. Is there an innate human desire for strength and fitness relative to the human desire for play? It is only by understanding previous regional differences and what underpinned fitness structures in the past that the relative collapsing of some of these differences can be understood.

Chapter 2 is the first to explore global fitness practices. It begins with one of the first exercise practices to experience globalization, Indian club-swinging. Originating in India, Iran and Pakistan, the practice of swinging clubs for exercise existed for millennia. During the 1820s it was adopted by the British military and, from the early 1830s, was popularized in nascent gymnastic circles. By the mid-century it was a global practice. While its early transfer was largely due to an institutional interest, it quickly spiralled into a commercial and popular enterprise. This chapter focuses on practices unique to a specific region which were reconceptualized and emptied for global audiences. The chapter is thus focused on 'local' practices. The second half of the century, and continuing to the outbreak of the Great War, witnessed the popularization of two more Asiatic practices within a global context. They were yoga and judo. Both were conceptualized as physical culture and systems applicable to various settings. Here the chapter focuses on the popular expression of global fitness. While the practices themselves represent an eclectic mix of movements, they were underpinned by the same processes of commercialization, knowledge transfer, entertainment and migration.

Chapter 3 focuses on institutional physical culture. That is, practices which spread around the globe through militaries, educational practices and groups like the Young Men's Christian Association (YMCAs). Institutional physical culture coincided with a burgeoning professionalization of fitness instructors across Europe and North America. The institutional spread of physical culture was driven by deepening trade networks around the world and the intensification of Asian and African colonialization. The chapter begins with 'light' institutional physical cultures at the dawn of the nineteenth century, primarily those advocated in Prussia and Sweden. Both systems revolutionized training in schools and militaries through the exportation of instructions and instructors. While many European nations had colonial empires, none, by the mid-century, matched the British Empire. At its height, it encompassed one-fourth of the world's population. For this reason the chapter's study of mid-century physical culture focuses on the institutionalization of physical culture in the British military from 1860. This decision not only impacted Great Britain but her empire and informal connections. The chapter ends by discussing the formalization of physical education courses and systems in the late nineteenth and early twentieth centuries. In some instances this meant the creation of teacher training colleges but in other countries meant the creation of a profession. What is compelling for us are the global enquiries and comparisons that occurred during this process.

The spread of local practices, combined with the institutionalization of physical culture, provided fertile ground for the eventual rise of the 'physical culture' movement. As a term, physical culture dates to the eighteenth century but it was only from the 1880s, to the outbreak of the Great War, that it began to denote a lifestyle and identity in popular settings.[62] Men and women could label themselves as physical culturists to denote their interest in gymnasiums, diets, exercise, etc. Physical culture, despite the grand proclamations of some of its keenest voices, did not emerge from a vacuum. It built on previous globalization trends and, through them, deepened fitness ties around the world. The chapter examines physical culture with reference to its global popularity, its communities and its bodies. It opens with a relatively well-known story of Sandow and other physical culture entrepreneurs who spread its influence around the globe. From here, and diverging from previous works, physical culture is examined with reference to commodities and communities. Physical culture was, in many respects, an 'empire of things'. New and renewed products and supplements drove behaviours towards attempts to consume perfect health. Through a focus on a select number of local and global products, the chapter places a fresh emphasis on physical culture commerce against the backdrop of global connections. During the writing of this book, and through several good-natured critiques of my students' social media consumption, it became apparent that distinct fitness communities exist in very specific forums.[63] These forums exist outside the gym and are repositories of information where trainees interact with one another. While research exists on online spaces in the fitness community, it became apparent that we have not studied their global precursor: the fitness magazine.[64] For this reason the chapter focuses on popular European and American physical culture magazines and readers' submissions. These submissions have often been alluded to but escaped serious attention. The consequence of this is that we have tended, as a field, to ignore the diversity of locations contained therein. Studying French,

---

[62]Todd, 'Defining ... '.
[63]James Brighton, Ian Wellard and Amy Clark. *Gym bodies: Exploring fitness cultures* (Routledge, 2020).
[64]Ibid.

British and American magazines allows us to scrutinize these informal print communities of global physical culturists.

This is, obviously, a book about global fitness and its deepening relations during the nineteenth century. Rather than end with the rise of physical culture and an observation about its aftermath, I wanted to explore those practices which did not globalize. Some of these practices, in fact, did not globalize until the late twentieth century, if at all. Studying what practices were not shared helps, I believe, to magnify the processes underpinning those that did spread. I am also conscious that owing to the trajectory of European and North American colonization and industrialization, this book has to walk a tightrope between reporting historical trends while avoiding the privileging of the century's cultural and economic victors. This chapter studies the other element to globalizing fitness – those practices which remained local or, in some cases, solely within isolated pockets. It does so in three separate, but inter-related case studies – weightlifting, stone-lifting and heavy club-swinging. Each of these practices had glimpses of globalization during our period but never globalized. Weightlifting in this context refers to competitive weightlifting which readers may watch every four years at the Olympics. As a sport, weightlifting was fractured during the late nineteenth and early twentieth centuries. Proof of this is the fact that between 1891 and 1914 there were over twenty 'world' weightlifting contests of some descript, all of which had different rules, exercises and organizers. Next, the chapter explores the practice of stone-lifting which, despite being a global practice, was not a *globalized* practice. This is despite the fact that at one point it appeared as if it may become an Olympic sport in the early 1900s. Stone-lifting is a practice found in Iceland, Scotland, Ireland, the Faroe Islands, Japan, China and India, among other regions. While it has become a global practice in the late twentieth century thanks to the popularity of the World Strongest Man competition, stone-lifting has tended to retain its local roots. Each nation has its own distinct method of lifting these stones (to the knees, to the waist, to the chest, overhead, etc.) and their own stories. Here particular emphasis will be given to Basque and Scottish stone-lifting as practices formalized to an extent without globalizing. Moving from Scotland and the Basque Region to India, the chapter explores 'traditional' club-swinging and its failure to transfer globally. The Indian clubs discussed in Chapter 2 were light-weight imitations of the heavier clubs used in India. While we have a handful of instances of Western strongmen using traditional Indian clubs in performances and training, the practice never transferred outside of Asia. This is despite the popularity of its lighter-styled cousin. Its failure to do so allows us to discuss the commercial, and at times racial, currents concerning what was, and was not, popularized.

This book is driven by a simple premise, physical culture practices became globalized and similar in nature over the long nineteenth century. For modern exercisers the global nature of fitness is unproblematic, and something perhaps taken for granted. Indeed during the course of this book, I followed a strength programme written by an American powerlifter, which had been translated into a smartphone app by a German developer. I reached out to them when the app stopped working during my workout in Ireland. Between trips to archives, conferences and a family holiday, I maintained my training despite visiting Europe and North America in two occasions. Italian, German, Swiss, British, Irish and American gyms differed in their cultures but the equipment I used, and the way I used it fit perfectly within these contexts. I was also fortunate to attend several high-level powerlifting, bodybuilding and strongman shows where I saw and spoke to athletes from Oceania, Asia, Africa, North and South America, and Europe, all of whom shared commonalities in how they trained, ate and exercised.

The trainee of the nineteenth century did not have the same level of connectedness, nor in my case the same problematic carbon footprint, but theirs too was a global world. Fitness, like sport, in the modern age, is global. Rather than take this for granted, I implore readers to study the origins of this development, consider which practices were globalized and why and, more importantly, to situate themselves and their interests within this process. The globalization of fitness in the nineteenth century was neither deliberate nor banal. It represented incremental changes across institutional and individual practices which transformed societies and bodies. Muscles matter, and this is true for global muscles and global bodies.

1

The long durée of fitness

Is there an innate desire for strength? Our physical bodies are built with the capacity to be strong. When faced with resistance, our muscles damage themselves under the burden of a weight but, by dint of physiological blessing, repair themselves, enlarge and return stronger.[1] Every trainee is familiar with this process when they enter a gym, or exercise class, only to realize that a weight which challenged them is now easier. For those engaged in physical labour, they too may find that tasks which used to challenge them are no longer feared. The human body is biologically designed to respond to external stimuli and evolve to match them.[2] We adapt to stresses over time. Is there, then, an innate human desire for strength? If desire is too strong a word, perhaps we could ask if the human body is predisposed towards strength or adaptive fitness? If we were not, it is likely humans would cease to exist and any difficult task would prove impossible. At the same time, our bodies are built to preserve energy and avoid unnecessary energy expenditure.[3] We are a bundle of playful contradictions. There is a distinction in these questions between whether individuals desire strength versus whether they have the capacity for it. The capacity for strength, and ability to increase our strength, exists before language and cultures. It is embedded in our DNA.[4]

Strength and fitness practices have a history dating to the ancient World and the evidence it left behind.[5] Is there an innate human desire for strength

---

[1] Priscilla Clarkson and Mary Dedrick, 'Exercise-induced muscle damage, repair, and adaptation in old and young subjects', *Journal of Gerontology* 43 (1988): M91–M96.
[2] Matthew Rhea, Brent Alvar, Lee Burkett and Stephen Ball, 'A meta-analysis to determine the dose response for strength development', *Medicine & Science in Sports & Exercise* 35 (2003): 456–64.
[3] James Levine, 'Non-exercise activity thermogenesis (Neat)', *Nutrition Reviews* 62 (2004): S82–S97.
[4] Mike Atkinson, 'Norbert Elias and the body', in Bryan Turner (eds.), *Routledge Handbook of Body Studies* (London: Routledge, 2012), 62–74.
[5] Russell Pate, 'The Evolving Definition of Physical Fitness', *Quest* 40 (1988): 174–9.

and health or is this simply a pre-requisite of living? This is a question I believe that is not asked enough in studies of physical culture. Why do some people, and, societies, engage in physical culture practices ranging from callisthenics and stretching to weightlifting? Is it for practical purposes? Aesthetic concerns? Out of medical necessity? Or somewhere in between? One of the first scholars to emphasize the importance of studying sport, John Huizinga cited play as an innate human desire. Writing in the 1930s, Huizinga observed that 'animals have not waited for man to teach them their playing' and so too, it is with humans that play is 'older than culture'.[6] At the heart of our desire for play was fun or spontaneous activity.[7] While Huizinga's study has been critiqued, his interest in understanding play remains admirable.[8] Physical culture is distinct from sport and many argue play. Physical culture has tended to be functional. It assisted in building, moving and fighting. Is there an innate human desire, even pre-verbal for physical culture? I am struck in many respects by those cultures' stone-lifting practices which were a rite of passage but also driven by a playfulness and childlike wonder to see who was strongest.[9] If this is a rosy-eyed view of physical culture, driven by my own practices forgive me. It is a question worthy of further study and even those who abhor physical culture will concede many societies have found use in it.[10] That is the purpose of this chapter – to study the 'long history' of physical culture across multiple continents and eras.

We have evidence of physical culture being used for 'practical' purposes for millennia. Why study them? Especially in a book about the nineteenth century? To understand how physical culture changed so dramatically in the nineteenth century it is important to understand its previous uses. Certainly those in the nineteenth century used history to advance their cause. Strongmen and women often posed mimicking Greco-Roman statues and used names like Samson to denote their strength.[11] Preachers turned to religious texts, Christian or otherwise, to contextualize the need for health.[12] Educators quoted classical texts while physicians returned

---

[6]Robert Anchor, 'History and play: Johan Huizinga and his critics', *History and Theory* 17 (1978): 63–93.
[7]Johan Huizinga, *Homo Ludens* (Amsterdam University Press, 2008).
[8]Samuel Duncan, 'The spirit of play: Fun and freedom in the professional age of sport', *Sport, Ethics and Philosophy* 16 (2022): 281–99.
[9]John Walton, 'Sport and the basques: Constructed and contested identities, 1876–1936', *Journal of Historical Sociology* 24 (2011): 451–71.
[10]Conor Heffernan, 'State of the field: Physical culture', *History* 107 (2022): 143–62.
[11]Peter Miller, 'The imaginary antiquity of physical culture', *The Classical Outlook* 93 (2018): 21–31.
[12]Nick Watson, Stuart Weir and Stephen Friend, 'The development of muscular Christianity in Victorian Britain and beyond', *Journal of Religion and Society* 7 (2005): 1–21.

to the same sources for inspiration.[13] This chapter focuses on the 'long history' of fitness, dating back to the earliest records and moving us to the sixteenth and seventeenth centuries. It argues that while physical culture practices have taken diverse forms across cultures and periods, they have consistently served four key societal functions: religious expression, medical treatment, educational development and military preparation. By examining these functions globally, we can understand the universality and cultural specificity of fitness. The theme for this chapter is one of similarities and distinctiveness. Prototypes of globalization or, as some might label it, 'archaic globalization', occurred prior to the nineteenth century.[14] There is a long history of cultural exchange in fitness practices, challenging the notion that globalization of physical culture began in the nineteenth century. It was the nineteenth century where globalization became the **norm**, as opposed to a sporadic occurrence. As this is not a chronological account, we shall be jumping across time and place with some regularity. Exercise and its various functions are our interest and not necessarily strict historical timelines. With that in mind, let's begin.

Exercise and religious practices

orandum est ut sit mens sana in corpore sano.

– Juvenal, second century CE[15]

The above text, taken from Roman philosopher Juvenal, translates roughly as 'you should pray for a healthy mind in a healthy body'. During the nineteenth century this phrase became repackaged as *mens sana in corpore sano* ('a healthy mind in a healthy body') and was used by countless officials, teachers and leaders as justification for sport and physical culture across Europe, the United States and beyond.[16] Its appropriation by those in Europe and further afield during this period was indicative of the longer history of fitness. Whereas other sections of this chapter are interested in protypes of globalization, I want to consider the cultural scripts provided by various religious texts, which themselves were products of sharing and appropriation.[17] During the nineteenth century, Christian, Judaic, Muslim and Hindu figures cited a religious component to the need for physical

---

[13]Jack Berryman, 'Exercise and the medical tradition from Hippocrates through Antebellum America: A review essay' in Jack Berryman and Roberta Park (eds.), *Sport and Exercise Science: Essays In the History of Sports Medicine* (University of Illinois Press, 1992), 3–15.
[14]Peter Stearns, *Globalization in world history* (Routledge, 2016), 35–90.
[15]Martin Madan, *A new and literal translation of Juvenal and Persius* (T. Tegg, 1829), 42.
[16]Watson et al., 'The Development ... '.
[17]Malcolm Hamilton, *The sociology of religion* (Routledge, 2002), 12–17.

culture. Swami Vivekananda linked the building of biceps to understanding the Hindu *Bhagavad Gita*.[18] The 'muscular Christian' movement of the same century saw innumerable clerics and laypeople link the strengthening of one's body with their faith in God.[19] This found parallels in what we may class as Muscular Judaic or muscular Hindu movements.[20] Many scholars, myself included, have downplayed or ignored religion in the spread and sustainment of nineteenth-century physical culture.[21] At times we view it in instrumental terms; that is, YMCAs helped spread gymnastics or drill in church halls. Other times we note the importance of the muscular Christian movement in superficial terms.[22] Religion helped add respectability to physical culture and provide a cultural script broader than individual desire, vanity or fun when describing one's exercise habits. For the individual, they may have added a valuable sense of meaning. The muscular Christian movement was not the first time that physical culture and religion intersected. This history is one which dates further back and can be traced in two ways – first through religious texts and second through devotional practices. The goal for this section is not to detail every instance of this but rather to build a case for, or more modestly to highlight, the human fascination with physical culture.

Regarding religious texts, I am aware that texts, and their interpretations, evolve over time.[23] Discussing the appearance of physical culture in religious texts is not meant to open a theological debate about scriptural accuracy but to discuss the meaning of exercise within societies. If we begin with an unproblematic approach that religion was/is often the explanatory framework used by people to understand their world, there is a philosophical value in discussing what has been included within them. To begin with the Abrahamic religions (those being Christianity, Judaism and Islam), all three branches have had long-running, explicit and implicit, discussions about the need for health and strength. They are also deeply intertwined, especially the Christian Old Testament which was either part of other religious doctrines in Judaism or alluded to in the *Quran*.

Eisen's work on physical culture in the Old Testament highlighted three key strains of thoughts concerning health and fitness. Dance played a keen role in exhibiting one's health.[24] In the *Book of Samuel*, David dances in the presence of God. There was also the matter of those imbued with strength

---

[18]Gopal Shrinivas Banhatti, *Life and philosophy of Swami Vivekananda* (Atlantic Publishers & Dist, 1995), 163.
[19]Watson, Weir, and Friend, 'The Development … '.
[20]Sander Gilman, 'Muscular Judaism: The Jewish body and the politics of regeneration', *Monatshefte* 100, no. 2 (2008): 320–1.
[21]Heffernan, 'State … ', 143–62.
[22]Ibid.
[23]Stig Hjarvard, 'The mediatization of religion: a theory of the media as agents of religious change', *Northern Lights: Film & Media Studies Yearbook* 6 (2008): 9–26.
[24]George Eisen, 'Physical activity, physical education and sport in the Old Testament', *Canadian Journal of History of Sport & Physical Education* 6 (1975): 44–65.

by God, such as Samson whose feats were indicative of God's power and blessing. Sport and physical fitness played a symbolic role. How else can one understand the Book of Genesis tale of Jacob, who spent an entire night wrestling with one of God's angels? Fascinating was Eisen's conclusion that the peoples described in the Old Testament 'did not engage systematically in sports, but with the intention of training and strengthening their bodies'. Similarly, Kotteck cited twelfth-century Jewish philosopher Maimonides (1138 CE–1204 CE) and his *Mishneh Thora* as a key text in understanding Judaism's approach to physical culture.[25] Written partly as a commentary on the *Talmud*, the *Mishneh* 'warns against a loss of strength that may result from living a sedentary life and from lack of exercise'.[26] Within the *Talmud* itself, prescriptions for activity are muted and indeed later originator of the 'muscular Jew' ideal in the nineteenth century Max Nordau criticized the 'enfeebled' reader of the *Talmud* versus those Judaic men who took sport and physical culture seriously.[27] Looking at *Mishneh*, one finds an exhortation to 'take utmost care and watch yourselves scrupulously' which later interpretations took it to be a 'mitzvah' (obligation) to remain healthy.[28] This passage later fuelled Maimonides' assertion that 'bodily health and wellbeing are part of the path to God'.[29] A similar pattern, although one with an obvious religious exhortation of strength, can be found in the Christian Bible wherein proverbs and stories speak of fitness. Scarpa and Carraro highlighted the spiritual and symbolic value of healthy bodies within the Christian Bible, countering claims that Christianity demeaned the physical body. While the Old Testament contains references to sport and strength, Scarpa and Carraro cited the New Testament as a place where spiritual salvation was believed to occur through the body.[30]

Looking at the New Testament, the duo cited multiple instances wherein Jesus Christ healed followers of deformities, bringing them back to 'perfect' health.[31] While this has been critiqued for its ableism, such stories highlighted a Christian belief in some form of good or heavenly body.[32] This idea is born out in biblical passages from the *Book of Isaiah* in the Old Testament, which reminded devotees that 'the Lord shall renew their strength'.[33] Insom

---

[25]Samuel Kotteck, 'Physical exercise and training in Ancient Jewish Lore', *Iron Game History* 4 (1996): 19–20.
[26]Ibid.
[27]Adam Sutcliffe, *What are Jews for?: History, peoplehood, and purpose* (Princeton University Press, 2020), 171–5.
[28]Todd Samuel Presner, 'Clear heads, solid stomachs, and hard muscles: Max Nordau and the aesthetics of Jewish regeneration', *Modernism/Modernity* 10 (2003): 269–96.
[29]Kotteck, 'Physical ... '.
[30]Stefano Scarpa and Attilio Nicola Carraro, 'Does Christianity demean the body and deny the value of sport?–A provocative thesis', *Sport, Ethics and Philosophy* 5 (2011): 110–23.
[31]Ibid., 116.
[32]Ibid., 116–18.
[33]Robert Higgs, 'Muscular Christianity, Holy play, and spiritual exercises: Confusion about Christ in sports and religion', *Aethlon* 1 (1983): 59.

has suggested that good or perfect health was taken to be divinely gifted to individuals.[34] This was notably seen in the story of Old Testament warrior Samson, whose strength was given by God. Samson's awesome strength, as scrutinized in Leonard-Fleckman's study, is initially at odds with its divine origin.[35] His feats, which included tearing a lion apart with his hands, killing thirty men and harming hundreds more, were driven by 'reaction, impulsivity and revenge'.[36] When Samson loses his strength he is captured by the Philistines. His story ends with Samson praying to God to grant him one last feat of strength and, imbued with divine inspiration, Samson uses his strength to collapse a temple on himself and the Philistines. The message from such a story was clear. Strength was in some way connected to the divine, and strength correctly directed in the way of God was honourable.[37] While it is true that some in later centuries created a split between the body and soul within the Christian faith, resigning the body to a secondary status, such passages were revived in the eighteenth and nineteenth centuries to invoke a form of muscular Christianity which linked spiritual and physical strength.[38]

The last of the Abrahamic religions, Islam, is generally dated to the seventh century CE. Its founding religious text, the *Quran*, does not explicitly discuss the use of sport and/or physical culture but does include passages on the need to eat healthily and maintain fitness. There is, for example, a passage from the Prophet Muhammad which advises that the 'strong believer is more beloved to Allah than the weak believer, but there is goodness in both of them'.[39] While some have taken this distinguish one of strong versus weak faith, others have cited it as a key direction to followers that sport and/or some form of physical culture is acceptable.[40] Certainly other passages in the *Quran* encourage devotees to 'prepare them [meaning Muslims] whatever you are able of power and steeds of war by which you may terrify the enemy of Allah'.[41] In this context, sport and training are acceptable provided they served one's religious devotion. Physical activity, as Kizar later expressed, was considered acceptable if it had noble intentions, adhered to Islamic regulations, preserved one's health and/or was necessary to obtain recourses

---

[34]Surachet Insom, 'The Bible and health: The Miracle of healing', *Human Behavior, Development & Society* 24 (2023): 71–80.
[35]Ibid.
[36]Ibid.
[37]Ibid.
[38]Brian Allred, 'Working out your salvation and just working out: Toward a biblical perspective on physical fitness', *Mid-America Journal of Theology* 29 (2018): 173–81.
[39]Wasim Khan, Asif Ali, Salahuddin Khan and Naveed Yazdani. 'Islamic perspective regarding the promotion of health and participation in sports activities', *Journal of Islamic Thought and Civilization* 10 (2020): 364–74.
[40]Ibid.
[41]Ahmet Şeyhun, *Islamist thinkers in the late Ottoman Empire and early Turkish Republic* (Brill, 2014), 94.

for one's family.⁴² Maintaining one's health was explicitly linked to devotion. There were also multiple mentions of the Prophet Muhammad's strength and fighting capabilities, especially archery, within the *Quran*. Within prayer it was noted that the Prophet asked Allah for 'protection from powerlessness, laziness, cowardice miserliness and weakness'.⁴³ Other passages find prescriptions that 'taking proper care of one's health is the right of the body' and that it was acceptable to 'entertain [yourselves] and play for indeed I dislike harshness to be seen in your religion'.⁴⁴ While there was not an explicit message to engage in physical activity, it is clear that maintaining one's health was embedded within Islam's religious teachings.⁴⁵

During my previous research on club-swinging (originating in what we now call India, Pakistan and Iran), I wrote about the inclusion of wrestling, archery and combat sports within the *Bhagavad Gita*, a key Hindu text written sometime between the fifth and second century BCE.⁴⁶ Part of the *Mahabharata,* the *Gita* focuses on a conversation between Prince Arjuna and Lord Krisha. Counselling Arjuna about an upcoming war, the text is an allegory for spiritual challenges. At several points Krishna implores Arjuna to maintain and focus upon his physical health.⁴⁷ When Arjuna threatens to do nothing, he is admonished that free from his duties he could not maintain his own body. There is a clear message that action is needed to stay strong and healthy. Hinduism is interesting for its inclusion of Lord Hanuman, a devotee of Lord Rama, and powerful gods. Mentioned in the *Mahabharata* and *Ramayana* Hanuman was praised for his strength and bravery. His strength was noted in several epics, most notably in a battle between Rama and Ravana, when Hanuman lifted a mountain to save Rama. This act of strength and devotion is often memorialized with images of Hanuman carrying a mountain in the palm of his hand.

This connection between a sporting practice and religious devotion has echoes in other regions as evidenced by the link between martial arts and certain forms of Buddhism or, say, yoga and Hinduism.⁴⁸ Accepting that we are limited to surviving texts, it is notable that many religious practices had Gods devoted to sport and/or strength. The ancient Greeks revered the

---

⁴²Oktay Kizar, 'The place of sports in the light of Quran, Hadiths and the Opinions of the Muslim Scholar in Islam', *Universal Journal of Educational Research* 6 (2018): 2663–8.
⁴³Yusuf Qaradawi, *Islam: An introduction* (The Other Press, 2010), 41.
⁴⁴Issah Wabuyabo, Edwin Wamukoya and Hannington Bulinda. 'Influence of Islam on gender participation in sports among Muslim students in Kenyan universities', *Journal of Physical Education and Sport Management* 6 (2015): 82–9.
⁴⁵Ibid.
⁴⁶Conor Heffernan, *Indian club-swinging and the birth of global fitness: Mugdars, masculinity and marketing* (Bloomsbury, 2023), 27–45.
⁴⁷Ibid.
⁴⁸Available from Wikipedia Commons. See https://commons.wikimedia.org/wiki/File:Standing_Hanuman.jpg.

FIGURE 1.1 Standing statue of Hanuman, with Gada at the Ram Janaki Temple in Nepal.[49]

gods of the gymnasium, athletics and Olympic games.[50] In Norse mythology, gods of sports existed, and research by Thorlindsson and Halldorsson on Icelandic physical culture traced the importance of strength in Nordic mythology with the primacy of movement.[51] This is to say nothing of the strength feats of a Herakles/Hercules or Thor. Without belabouring the point religion operates as an explanatory work for how the world works. It is pivotal for existential questions about the afterlife but also why the world one is born into operates the way it does.

I want to end this section by discussing some distinct religious physical culture practices. Those being the lifting of culturally significant objects

---

[49]Steven Trenson, 'Buddhism and martial arts in premodern Japan: New observations from a religious historical perspective', *Religions* 13 (2022): 440.
[50]David Lunt, 'The heroic athlete in Ancient Greece', *Journal of Sport History* (2009): 375–92.
[51]Thorolfur Thorlindsson and Vidar Halldorsson, 'The roots of Icelandic physical culture and sport in the Saga age', in Mikkel Tin, Frode Telseth, Jan Ove Tangen and Richard Giulianotti (eds.), *The Nordic Model and Physical Culture* (Routledge, 2019), 101–16.

in China and Japan, and gymnasium cultures of India and Persia. Other notable inclusions are the Olympic Games in Ancient Greece which were dedicated to the Gods or, in the case of the still ongoing Scottish Highland Games, the festival's roots trace to the Celtic calendar.[52] In Chinese and Japanese practices, some form of strength performance can be linked with devotion. In China, this took the form of *ding* (heavy cauldron) lifting.[53] Allen has cited their use as a cauldron for sacrificing animals to ancestor spirits. During the Warring States period (475–221 BCE), evidence exists of martial artists taking part in lifts of the three-legged *ding* in a quasi-spiritual/sporting tribute.[54] The practice was included in the *Records of the Grand Historian*, as well as the *Book of Han*, these being two major written historical texts in China (dating to the first and second centuries BCE).[55] It was also recorded in stone portraits in the Jiangsu Province and, indeed, Li's work highlights several instances in which the strength practices of Chinese men with the *ding*, as well as with other strength objects, were captured.[56] Unlike other practices, *ding* lifting appears to be one of the few instances in which a religiously significant object was lifted. As a practice it existed for hundreds of years before reaching something of an apogee during the Hàn漢 dynasty (202 BCE–220 CE) when it shifted more towards a popular form of strength.[57] Those who practised it ranged from normal citizens to monarchs. King Wu of Qin, the ruler of the Qin State in the west of China from 310 to 307 BCE, was such an admirer of strength that he was known for patronizing strongmen. His untimely death is traced to efforts to lift a heavy *ding*. Urged on by a strongman Wu lifted a heavy *ding* to demonstrate his vitality. While he succeeded, he broke his shin trying to carry it. That night he died.[58] His death was a commentary on the weight of the *ding* but also about the dangers of not treating these objects with respect.

Chikaraishi stone-lifting in Japanese cultures involves strength feats at religious sites. Defined as weighing stones, such stones, which number in their thousands, are commonly found at Shinto shrines.[59] Shintoism is a polytheistic religion centred on supernatural entities call *kami*. *Kami* are believed to inhabit all things, thus some rocks are revered.[60] Krüger and Ito's study on *Chikaraishi* in Tokyo found that lifting Shinto stones dated to at least

[52]Donald Kyle, *Sport and spectacle in the ancient world* (Wiley, 2014).
[53]Jeffrey Moser, 'Why cauldrons come first: Taxonomic transparency in the earliest Chinese antiquarian catalogues', *Journal of Art Historiography* 11 (2014): 1–5.
[54]Barbara Allen, *Animals in religion: Devotion, symbol and ritual* (Reaktion, 2016), 416–18.
[55]Fuhua Huang and Fan Hong, *A history of Chinese martial arts* (Routledge, 2018), 57–60.
[56]Xifan Li, *A general history of Chinese art: From the Prehistoric Era to the Zhou Dynasty* (De Gruyter, 2022), 283–90.
[57]Ibid., 50–5.
[58]David Keightley, *These bones shall rise again: Selected writings on early China* (SUNY Press, 2014), 262–4.
[59]Minoru Matsunami, 'Traditional sport in Japan', in Karl Spracklen, Brett Lashua, Erin Sharpe and Spencer Swain (eds.), *The Palgrave Handbook of Leisure Theory* (Palgrave, 2017), 169–86.
[60]Stephen Mansfield, *Japanese stone gardens: Origins, meaning, form* (Tuttle Publishing, 2012), 68–76.

the nineteenth century and stemmed from sporting and spiritual practices.[61] Regarding the former, there is an overlap with sumo wrestlers', many of whom lifted stones to increase their power. In Tokyo, some of the stones were dedicated or left at Shinto shrines by sumo wrestlers.[62] Concerning the spiritual side, Ito noted that *Chikaraishi* in Tokyo were also offered by local people in districts and part of *Hono-Chikaraishi* (roughly defined as stone-lifting contests dedicated to the God). Other research has indicated that the sporting element to *Chikaraishi* was most dominant in the eighteenth and early nineteenth centuries if not before (it was a noted practice during the late Edo period 1603–1868 CE).[63] The sport peaked in the early nineteenth century and, from there, continues to hold a religious focus. There is quite a lot of disagreement among scholars concerning the origin of this practice. Its recorded high point was in relatively contemporary times, but its origin point appears to have been much older. Some researchers have dated the practice of lifting *Chikaraishi* to the eighth century and others, like Matsunami, have traced its relevance in *Jinja* (Shinto) and Buddhist temples in Japan.[64] One hint as to its longevity is the Benkei stone, named after Saitō Musashibō Benkei, a Japanese warrior-monk who lived during the Heian Period (794–1185 CE). Known for his strength, Benkei was the first to supposedly lift the stone and leave it at a temple.[65] Weighing anywhere from 60 to 300 kilograms, *Chikaraishi* were used to demonstrate one's strength, to mark one's transition from adolescence into adulthood, or as a religious ritual.[66] Latter uses note making a wish prior to lifting. The easier the lift, the more likely it is to come true. One example of this is the *Omokaru-Ishi* wherein it is believed that the lighter the stone feels during lifting, the more fortunate one's life will be.[67] In other stone-lifting cultures such as Scotland or Ireland, it is common to find significant lifting stones in churchyards and graveyards. Japan differs in having such objects directly at the Shrines and inscribed with religious texts or messaging. The first of these descriptions dates to the mid-seventeenth century in Tokyo but written records are sparse about how this practice originated, and what its original significance was outside.[68]

The other side of this is, of course, gymnasium sites which held religious functions. While the Athenian gymnasium in Ancient Greece did hold religious relevance, the Indian *akhara* is a far more obvious example and

---

[61]Arnd Kruger and Akira Ito, 'On the limitations of Eichberg's and Mandell's theory of sports and their quantification in view of Chikaraishi', *Stadion*, 3 (1990): 103–13.
[62]Ibid.
[63]Matsunami, 'Traditional ... ', 180–4.
[64]Ibid.
[65]Richard Dorson, *Folk legends of Japan* (Tuttle, 2012), 52–6.
[66]Matsunami, 'Traditional ... '.
[67]Joseph Cali and John Dougill, *Shinto shrines: A guide to the sacred sites of Japan's ancient religion* (University of Hawaii Press, 2012), 102–3.
[68]Allen Guttmann and Lee Thompson, *Japanese sports: A history* (University of Hawaii Press, 2001), 48–52.

dates to the *Mahabharata* text (written sometime in 400 BCE).⁶⁹ The *akhara* evolved into a gymnasium for soldiers and wrestlers from around the sixth century onwards. Alter's work on Indian wrestling noted the many tributaries of the *akhara* system from its transformation thanks to the Moghul invasion of India in the sixteenth century to the later bifurcation between Hindu and Muslim *akharas*.⁷⁰ Places where men would meet, train and pray, *akharas* spread across the Indian landmass from the eighth century onwards.⁷¹ Many *akharas* were said to be founded by near superhuman men whose spiritual and physical strength was beyond comparison.⁷² Within these spaces shrines to various deities were found. Accepting that Indian Vedic texts like the previously mentioned *Mahabharata* included texts on wrestling and fighting, it is interesting to note the ascetic lifestyle expected of wrestlers in later wrestling manuals.⁷³

The *akhara* has a parallel in the Persian *zurkhaneh* (gymnasium). A place to practice *koshti* (wrestling), it dates to the *Shahnameh* epic written sometime between 977 and 1100 CE. A poem written to preserve the mythical and real history of the Persian empire, the *Shahnameh* included passages about Rostam, a warrior credited with inventing *koshti*.⁷⁴ Initially the *zurkhaneh* was inspired by Mithrasim, and spaces often contained gods and goddesses, either in sculpture or paintings. Following the spread of Shia Islam, and the Sufism lineage within Islam, the *zurkhaneh* gained the same sort of religious significance as the Indian *akhara*. Rituals within the *zurkhaneh* were, and continue to be, deeply aligned with the Sufi tradition beginning with the ethical behaviours expected within the training space.⁷⁵ Collaborative work by Mohammadi, Azizi and Deimary credited the *zurkhaneh* as a place of physical and moral strengthening.⁷⁶ This connection was further strengthened by tales of heroic soldiers and figures whose time in the *zurkhaneh* was retold in folk tales. In many *zurkhaneh* a *Murshid* existed whose role was to recite epic poetry, offer and encourage prayer

---

[69]Lakhveer Kaur and Rajesh Chander, 'Ancient Indian sports: A historical analysis', *International Journal of Humanities* 3 (2015): 75–8
[70]Joseph Alter, 'Somatic nationalism: Indian wrestling and militant Hinduism', *Modern Asian Studies* 28 (1994): 557–88.
[71]Nityananda Misra, *Kumbha: The traditionally modern mela* (Bloomsbury, 2019), 28–34.
[72]Joseph Alter, *The wrestler's body: Identity and ideology in North India* (University of California Press, 1992), 33.
[73]Ibid., 4–45.
[74]Hamid Reza Safari Jafarlou, Azim Jabareh Naserou and Mohammad Hossein Ghorbani, 'Koshti/Wrestling: A victory key for heroes in Shahnameh', *Sport, Ethics and Philosophy* 15 (2021): 522–45.
[75]Nima Deimary and Mohammad Mohammadi, 'Investigating the impact of ancient and heroic rituals on formation of Zurkhaneh architecture in Iran', *American International Journal of Research in Humanities, Arts and Social Sciences* 20 (2017): 40–5.
[76]Mohammad Mohammadi, Bisotoon Azizi and Nima Deimary, 'The role of ancient sports and Zurkhaneh in ethical promoting and religious virtues', *Sport, Ethics and Philosophy* 17 (2023): 162–71.

and play music as athletes moved from one exercise to the next.[77] Ridgeon's work on the *zurkhaneh* cited multiple instances in which the movements found therein were linked with a semi-meditative form of either Shi-ite or Sufi devotion.[78] Religion thus served three purposes. It legitimized devoting time/attention to health, it provided archetypes for strength be they Samson or Hanuman, and it provided a deeper meaning, in some contexts for physical culture.

Exercise as medicine

Here we will examine the inclusion of exercise within health paradigms from the Ancient World through to the seventeenth century. The first thing to note is that we are relying on written texts, rather than archaeological materials, and it is clear that many cultures in the Ancient World distinguished exercise between for health and for sport. Tipton's research on ancient Indian and Chinese medicine, supplemented by others, found that physicians who supported physical activity for health purposes often resisted training to excesses.[79] This latter form was associated with athletes. It is also important to stress that the idea of exercise as medicine was not necessarily commonplace. Equally important and influential was the idea that health was, in fact, something divined from the gods.[80]

One of the earliest written instances we have of a physician advocating exercise was 600 BCE Indian physician Susruta. Viewing health through the tridosha system, which conceived of health as a balance between the natural elements, exercise was depicted as a means of ensuring, or regaining, healthy functioning.[81] Interesting Susruta's prescriptions were often tailored to the age, strength and diet of patients. From a holistic perspective, he noted exercise's ability to make the body strong, lose weight, and increase energy. It was 'absolutely conducive to a better preservation of health'. Tipton positioned Susruta as one of the early forerunners of 'exercise and medicine'.[82] Defining exercise as a 'sense of weariness from bodily labour', Susruta distinguished between movement for health and sport. For the former, he encouraged walking, running, jumping and diving. For athletes

---

[77]Jafarlou et al., 'Koshti ... '.

[78]Lloyd Ridgeon, 'The Zūrkhāna between tradition and change', *Iran* 45 (2007): 243–65.

[79]Charles Tipton, 'The history of "Exercise is Medicine" in ancient civilizations', *Advances in Physiology Education* 38 (2014): 109–17.

[80]Ibid; Nikitas Nomikos, C. Trompoukis, Chris Lamprou and G. Nomikos, 'The role of exercise in Hippocratic Medicine', *American Journal of Sports Science and Medicine* 4 (2016): 115–19.

[81]Helen King, 'Comparative perspectives on medicine and religion in the ancient world', *Religion, Health, and Suffering* (1999): 276–94.

[82]Charles Tipton, 'Susruta of India, an unrecognized contributor to the history of exercise physiology', *Journal of Applied Physiology* 104 (2008): 1553–6.

he encouraged archery, wrestling and javelin.[83] A later Indian physician was Charaka (250–100 BCE). Charaka likewise promoted exercise in some capacity and their thoughts have been recorded in one of the foundation medical texts of Ayurvedic medicine.[84] He promoted daily exercise and left at least one hundred commentaries about health and exercise. Like Susruta, he warned against over-exertion and believed correct exercise was marked by 'perspiration, enhanced respiration, lightness of body ... ' etc.[85] The exercises of choice were marked by running, swimming, jumping, tumbling and wrestling. On this latter suggestion, Shephard cited Charaka's encouragement to wrestle those of great strength to improve one's health.[86]

For those seeking to expand on the pre-history of medical exercise, which has privileged Greco-Roman models, the next stop has typically been China where both mythical and recorded instances of physicians are found. Balaneskovic recorded the case of Hua Tuo, a legend from roughly 100 CE. Seeking to help improve individual's health, he recommended exercises based on animal movements.[87] Interestingly the idea of gaining inspiration from the natural world continued to be a theme in the world of physical culture in the nineteenth and twentieth centuries.[88] Nineteenth-century physical culturist Bernarr McFadden held a strong interest in cats and felines' ability to stretch and pounce.[89] Returning to Tuo, his system was referred as the Five Animals Practices/Play/Pattern. Part of his underlying logic was that exercise expelled 'bad air', thereby allowing greater circulation. Such understandings based on a system of balance characterized by Yang and Yin, terms being taken to represent life and death. Tuo's writings were spread by two of his 'disciplines' Wu Pu and Fan A, both of whom combined exercise with medical practices. While Hua Tuo was a recorded instance of exercise as medicine, some evidence exists of breathing practices being recommended existed as early as 2600 BCE.[90]

I want to pause here to discuss the importance of distinguishing between Indian, Chinese and soon-to-be-discussed European approaches. We find

---

[83]Jatinder Kumar and Abhishek Magotra, 'Role of Vyayama (Exercise) in Maintenance of Health-An Ay', *Journal of Ayurveda and Integrated Medical Sciences* 5 (2020): 489–93.
[84]Madhuri Hemant Wagh, 'Exercise in Health and Disease: Brief Review of Ancient Indian Ayurveda Perspective', *ICSSPE Bulletin (17285909)* 71 (2016): 64–71.
[85]Kshama Gupta and Prasad Mamidi, 'Pushpitakam of Charaka Indriya sthana–An explorative study', *Int J Ayu Alt Med* 7 (2019): 176–82.
[86]Roy Shephard, *An illustrated history of health and fitness, from pre-history to our post-modern world* (Springer, 2015), 120–5.
[87]Saša Balaneskovic, 'Hua Tuo's Wu Qin Xi (Five Animal Frolics) movements and the logic behind it', *Chinese Medicine and Culture* 1 (2018): 127–34.
[88]Jan Todd, 'Bernarr Macfadden: Reformer of feminine form', *Journal of Sport History* 14 (1987): 61–75.
[89]Ibid.
[90]Charles M. Tipton, 'Antiquity to the early years of the 20th century', *History of Exercise Physiology* (2014): 3–32.

in all an acceptance of some form of exercise. Differences existed in how individuals understand the body, and the machinations of how it works. The final, Greco-Roman lineage, to be discussed of the 'Ancient World' was informed by its own distinct understanding of the body: humoral theory which saw the body as a balance between different elements, natural and non-natural.[91] While Tipton and others have discussed early forerunners to exercise as medicine in Pythagoras (570–495 BCE), Berryman cited Hippocrates (460–370 BCE) and Galen (AD 129–210) as the most influential advocates for medical. Incidentally, one of Hippocrates's former teachers, Herodicus has been credited as the 'father of sports medicine', so it is important to allude to a broader cultural thinking about activity in Greek medical teaching.[92] Hippocrates, Galen and those inspired by them have been, for several centuries, held up as a definitive 'school' of exercise as medicine.[93] Hippocrates was the first 'recorded' physician to prescribe exercise for a patient. He recommends a holistic treatment of medication, baths, sleep and walking.[94] A similar approach was taken in Hippocrates' prescriptions for pregnant women. Malamitsi-Puchner's study of exercise during pregnancy cited Hippocrates and Aristotle, as well as later Roman physicians like Galen, as normalizing the idea of some form of moderate exercise for pregnant women.[95]

Preaching a moderation which classed excessive exercise and no exercise as harmful, Hippocrates associated exercise with physical and mental health. He was a forthright proponent of the idea that 'eating alone will not keep a man well; he must also talk exercise'.[96] Walking was not, however, the only activity Hippocrates supported and his was a mind clearly shaped by the *gymnastica* system in Greece. Writing in Book Three of the *Regimen*, Hippocrates listed walking, wrestling and gymnastic exercises to strengthen one's health.[97] On this latter point it is notable that nineteenth-century physical educationalists and physicians, such as James Chiosso, cited Hippocrates as the 'inventor of gymnastics as a medicinal agent'.[98] Tipton, Berryman and

---

[91] Ibid., 71–3.
[92] George Snook, 'The history of sports medicine. Part I', *The American Journal of Sports Medicine* 12 (1984): 252–4.
[93] Tipton, 'The ... '.
[94] Charles Tipton, 'Historical perspective: The antiquity of exercise, exercise physiology and the exercise prescription for health', in A.P. Simopoulos (ed.), *Nutrition and Fitness: Cultural, Genetic and Metabolic Aspects* (Karger, 2008), 218–22.
[95] Ariadne Malamitsi-Puchner, 'Recommendations of Ancient Greek and Byzantine physicians and philosophers on perinatal nutrition and care', *Acta Paediatrica* 110 (2021): 2344–7.
[96] Tipton, 'Historical ... ', 218–24.
[97] Nikitas Nomikos, C. Trompoukis, Chris Lamprou and G. Nomikos, 'The role of exercise in Hippocratic Medicine', *American Journal of Sports Science and Medicine* 4 (2016): 115–19.
[98] James Chiosso, *Gymnastics, an essential branch of national education, both public and private the only remedy to improve the present physical condition of man* (Walton & Maberly, 1854), 59.

others have cited Roman physician Galen (129–210 CE) as a 'descendent' from Hippocrates and an individual whose medical practices influenced European and Arabic thought.[99] Both Hippocrates and Galen ascribed good health to a balance between the body's humoral system. Maintaining equilibrium was not a case of divine intervention but good nutrition and regular exercise. For something to be classified as physical activity, it needed to involve laboured breathing. How best to exercise varied depending on the condition but Galen was steadfast in believing that sailing, wrestling, horseback riding and running were valuable. He saw health as necessary, arguing that 'even infants needed exercise'.[100] Galen also recommended the use of exercise equipment in the form of a small ball. This he described as the best possible form of physical activity. There has been a temptation, in the past, for writers to jump from Galen, to the 'rediscovery' of Greco-Roman culture in Renaissance Europe when discussing the medical use of exercise and physical culture more generally.[101] Previously, and in popular culture, some have ascribed to the idea of a 'dark ages' following the fall of Rome in the fifth century, and the Byzantine Empire in the fifteenth.[102] This narrative follows the line that during this period Europe was under the control of a Catholic Church which abhorred focusing on the body.[103]

Owing to a general bleeding between European and Arab cultures the idea of exercise as medicine continued to be promulgated in various guises. Pieterse's work on prototypes of globalization cited this period as one of cultural sharing, only surpassed by the Renaissance period as an early precursor of our nineteenth-century interest.[104] Writings by Byzantine physicians illustrate this melding. Here we rely on work which noted the medical and philosophical promotion of running, swimming, gymnastics and weight training.[105] Many Byzantine physicians, such as Oribasisus (320–403 CE) or Paul of Aegina (625–690 CE) used Galen as a reference point. In treating obesity, Paul recommended 'active exercise, an attenuated regimen, medicines of the same class ... ' and a series of other methods to keep the body lean. Belying his inspiration from Greece, Paul's prescriptions for boys' education involved the use of gymnastic exercises alongside academic endeavours.[106]

---

[99]Ibid; Berryman, 'Exercise ... '; Shephard, *An* ... .
[100]Tipton, 'Historical ... ', 218–24.
[101]Berryman, 'Exercise ... '.
[102]Janet Nelson, 'The Dark Ages', *History Workshop Journal* 63 (2007): 191–201.
[103]D.B. Van Dalen, 'The idea of history of physical education during the Middle Ages', in Earle Zeigler (ed.), *Sport & Physical Education in the Middles Ages* (Trafford, 2006), xx.
[104]Jan Nederveen Pieterse, 'Periodizing globalization: Histories of Globalization', *New Global Studies* 6 (2012): 7–30.
[105]N. Stavrakakis and E. Albanidis, 'The therapeutic use of sport during the Byzantine period', *Archives of Hellenic Medicine/Arheia Ellenikes Iatrikes* 32 (2015): 95–101.
[106]Ibid.

Concurrent with Paul's use of exercise were the writings of Sun Simiao (581–682 CE). Known as China's 'King of Medicine', Simiao works advanced and summarized the ideas of previous generations. It listed over 5,000 'recipes for health' which were later used in Asian, and to a lesser extent European medical writings. While his 'thirteen measures to keep health' included exercise, these were light-weight rhythmic movements akin to Qigong practices. Nevertheless he was clear that 'if people exercise their bodies, the hundred ills cannot arise'. Iranian physician, and philosopher during a high point of Muslim Science, Avicenna (980–1037 CE) likewise linked exercise to health. Displaying an interdependency of medical thought, he has been cited as a key figure in synthesizing Hippocrates and Galen's theories with Islamic medicine.[107] This blending was made possible by the general strength of humoral theory across cultures.[108] Concerning exercise, Avicenna noted its ability to tackle 'materialistic diseases'. Like others, he preached moderation and advocated for exercise across the life-cycle. While older patients were encouraged to indulge in walking or horse-riding, younger patients were prescribed vigorous activity.[109] For him, a person who systematically exercised did not need medicine.[110] Likely inspired, partly, by Persian gymnasium cultures (*zurkhaneh*), his prescriptions were wide-ranging and can be crudely divided between gentle and vigorous movements. Among recommendations for walking and horse-riding were endorsements of stone-lifting, javelin, tug-of-war and rowing.

It is at this point we return to Europe and the publication of the *Regimen Sanitatis Salernitanum*, a poem on the maintenance of health published sometime between the twelfth and thirteenth centuries. Produced in Italy, and written for an anonymous English king, the work was inspired by an Arab health text.[111] Published in Latin, it spread across Europe and was translated into several domestic languages.[112] Previous work on its importance has stressed the quality and quantity of these reproductions. Regarding the former, the poem contained several thousand stanzas. It has been estimated

---

[107] M.B. Siahpoosh, M. Ebadiani, GhR Shah Hosseini, M.M. Isfahani, A. Nikbakht Nasrabadi and H. Dadgostar, 'Avicenna the first to describe diseases which may be prevented by exercise', *Iranian Journal of Public Health* 41 (2012): 98–104.
[108] Christopher Bayly, 'From archaic globalization to international networks, circa 1600–2000', in Jerry Bentley, Renate Bridenthal and Anand Yang (eds.), *Interactions: Transregional Perspectives on World History* (University of Hawaii Press, 2005): 14–15.
[109] Sabriye Ercan and Aydan Örsçelik, 'Avicenna's Perspective of Exercise: Content Analysis of the "Canon of Medicine"', *Mersin Üniversitesi Tıp Fakültesi Lokman Hekim Tıp Tarihi ve Folklorik Tıp Dergisi* 12 (2022): 483–92.
[110] Ibid.
[111] Maria Pasca, 'The Salerno School of Medicine', *American Journal of Nephrology* 14 (1994): 478–82.
[112] Sandra Cavallo and Tessa Storey, 'Regimens, authors and readers: Italy and England compared', in Sandra Cavallo and Tessa Storey (eds.), *Conserving Health in Early Modern Culture* (Manchester University, 2017), 23–52.

that thousands of copies were reproduced in just one century.[113] This was the result of its popularity, but also the invention of the printing press in Europe during the 1440s. The press broke down barriers on the sharing of health tracts previously transcribed by hand.[114] On exercise, the *Regimen Sanitatis* placed it as a cornerstone of health. The preservation of health was linked to a balance between 'air, food, exercise, sleep, the excretions and the passions'. *Sanitatis* can be viewed as a palimpsest for European and otherwise, health prescriptions. It spread rapidly and could, in some senses, be viewed as an evolution in global health tracts.[115] Whereas previously writings spread through written reproductions, the printing press created greater ease of migration for texts.

While many domestic medical tracts were published after the *Regimen Sanitatis*, historians have credited Italian physician Hieronymus Mercuriale's *De Arte Gymnastica Aput Ancientes* as formative in shaping the European mind around physical culture.[116] It helped challenge and change body ideals concerning the male body and, to a lesser extent, the female body. Mercuriale (AD 1530–1606) was a professor of medicine for eighteen years prior to the publication of *De Arte Gymnastica* in 1569. *De Arte* is best considered a collection of previous works. In total it features the writings, or ideas of, 105 authors, the majority of whom were Greco-Roman. It was not just confined to European authors, as Arab physicians Avicenna and Ibn Rushd (or Averroes, 1126–98 CE) were included.[117] At one point Mercuriale disagrees with Galen's prescriptions on exercise and defers briefly to Avicenna.[118] *De Arte* sought to catalogue various medical thoughts on exercise and to convince readers of its utility. What was relatively unique was his focus on gymnastic systems rather than general exercise. Mercuriale distinguished between exercise for medical purposes, that to train soldiers and that pursued by athletes.

Exercise was presented as a defence against illness and the opening pages stated that the simple life needed no medicine. McIntosh described *De Arte* as less a health book, and one concerned with cataloguing gymnastics, athletics and sports.[119] Kavvadia in an ambitious reading of *De Arte*, asked less about its legacy and more about its creation.[120] Mercuriale's book was born from an engaging interest in physical culture, informed by Western

---

[113]Sabrina Minuzzi, '15th-century practical medicine in print: Beyond the profession, towards the miscere utile dulci', *Nuncius* 36 (2021): 199–263.
[114]Ibid.
[115]Ibid.
[116]Peter McIntosh, 'Hieronymus Mercurialis "De Arte Gymnastica": Classification and dogma in physical education in the sixteenth century', *The International Journal of the History of sport* 1 (1984): 73–84.
[117]McIntosh, 'Hieronymus ... ', 77–80.
[118]Ibid.
[119]Ibid.
[120]Maria Kavvadia, *Making medicine in post-tridentine Rome: Girolamo Mercuriale's 'De Arte Gymnastica': a different reading of the book* (PhD diss., European University Institute, 2015), 7–22.

and Arab texts, and focused on the best means of improving health.[121] Its prescriptions and descriptions were printed in the original 1569 book and enjoyed four reprints by 1601 (three in Vienna, one in Paris). It was edited and reprinted in Amsterdam in 1672 and circulated in Europe for over a century after its original publication.[122] It was referenced for even longer after that, sometimes fraudulently as happened when English physician John Blundell claimed to have translated it for his 1864 work but did nothing of the sort.[123]

What I want to focus on here is the illustrations accompanying *De Arte*. Without the illustrations, it is likely that *De Arte* would just have been 'another' health book. Indeed, Spanish physician Cristobal Méndez (1500–56 CE) published a similar book, *Libro del Exercicio* sixteen years before *De Arte* but never received the same fanfare.[124] The 1569 edition contained no illustrations but the second edition (the most popular version) featured reconstructions of athletes from the Ancient world playing ball games, engaging in rope-climbing and other activities. Without fail the bodies were presented as lean and muscular.[125] It is for this reason that people often focus on *De Arte* as a piece of male physical culture but, as Todd examined, Mercuriale was also interested in health practices for women.[126] It was one of the first popular medical texts to feature images of muscular individuals engaged in gymnastics. It has been cited as an early inspiration for later bodybuilding cultures and, more impactfully, as a text which promoted the Greco-Roman model of gymnastics in the mind of several sixteenth- and seventeenth-century educationalists.[127] The below image was one of many within the text.

Mercuriale proves a useful stopping point for the 'pre-history' or prototype of exercise as medicine. It contained global texts, discussed fitness, privileged Western and non-Western authors and sought to synthesize them. The figures listed in this history were those who proved most receptive to exercise as a form of medical practice or intervention. There were, of course, those physicians who either ignored it or viewed exercise as

---

[121]Ibid., 201–222.

[122]McIntosh, 'Hieronymus … ', 73.

[123]Ibid., 73–4.

[124]Luis Sánchez Granjel, 'La obra de un médico giennense: Cristóbal Méndez', *Seminario médico* 42 (1990): 13–36.

[125]Bill Hayes, *Sweat: A history of exercise* (Bloomsbury, 2022), 12–15.

[126]Jan Todd, 'As men do walk a mile, women should talk an hour … . Tis their exercise', and other pre-enlightenment thought on women and purposive training', *Iron Game History* 7 (2002): 56–70.

[127]Duygu Harmandar Demirel and Ibrahim Yildiran, 'The philosophy of physical education and sport from ancient times to the enlightenment', *European Journal of Educational Research* 2 (2013): 191–202.

FIGURE 1.2 *De Arte* Gynmastica illustration.¹²⁸

dangerous.¹²⁹ This, then, is a very one-sided chronology. The second point, which a cursory reading of the above history highlights, is that medical thought around exercise was porous prior to the nineteenth century.¹³⁰ Certainly texts in Latin travelled to many countries and, after the creation of the printing press, this process became easier. In time it extended to mass

---

¹²⁸ Available from Wellcome Library, https://wellcomecollection.org/works/e2bych65.
¹²⁹ R. Rost and W. Hollmann, 'Athlete's heart-a review of its historical assessment and new aspects', *International Journal of Sports Medicine* 4 (1983): 147–65.
¹³⁰ Roberta Park, 'Concern for health and exercise as expressed in the writings of 18th century physicians and informed laymen (England, France, Switzerland)', *Research Quarterly. American Alliance for Health, Physical Education and Recreation* 47 (1976): 756–67.

translations of texts published elsewhere. This book does not argue that the nineteenth century was the first ever period of globalization, but rather that it was the deepest and 'stickiest' form in terms of longevity. Borrowing from previous works, we could say that the history outlined above is about waves of globalization.[131] A final point to make is to stress the influence from the Islamic world on Western medical thought, especially in the *Arte Gymnastica* which has tended, in popular histories, to be remembered solely for its allusion to Greco-Roman thought. Avicenna and others prove that this was not the case.

Exercise and physical education

Physical education (PE), its philosophical development and institutional deployment, was a leading factor in the globalization of physical culture practices during the nineteenth century. Driven by Renaissance and Enlightenment philosophical texts, many educators began to propose, and implement, gymnastics and other activities for boys and girls. And yet, many in the nineteenth century drew encouragement from their counterpart the Ancient Athenian gymnasium.[132] We do have to be careful not to conflate what I am classing as PE for sport and vice versa. While many of the individuals to be discussed viewed the two in unison, we are interested in that stream of work which gave fruit to PE as a subject. It is important to realize that no definition will ever satisfy, or do justice, to all parties.[133] Instead it is useful to distinguish between desired outcomes of sport versus PE from a generalist perspective.

Whereas sport is primarily concerned with winning, points, medals and goals, physical education has ideologically been concerned with improving health or bodily function/movement. People obviously engaged in sport for health purposes but once a game began, this motive was obscured behind the playing of the event.[134] For keen-eyed readers this is similar to my distinction between sport and physical culture, the difference between physical culture and PE is that physical education has been an institutional phenomenon in that it was attached to schools, and physical culture has typically been a popular practice.[135] Tenuous as this is, it is notable that

---

[131] Stearns, *Globalization*, 69–72.
[132] Andrew Carter, *Games, Greek and pluck: Athleticism, classicism and elite British education, 1850–1914* (PhD diss., Manchester Metropolitan University, 2023), 45–58.
[133] David Kirk, *Defining physical education: The social construction of a school subject in postwar Britain* (Routledge, 2012), 15–30.
[134] Tristan Wallhead and Mary O'Sullivan, 'Sport Education: Physical Education for the New Millennium?' *Physical education and sport pedagogy* 10 (2005): 181–210.
[135] Jan Todd, *Physical culture and the body beautiful: Purposive exercise in the lives of American women, 1800–1870* (Mercer University, 1998), 6–10.

late nineteenth- and twentieth-century physical educators in Britain and the United States were often forthright in their view that PE was not physical culture.[136] Indeed the decline of the term 'physical culture' in the twentieth century was encouraged by the splitting of physical culture away from PE.[137] PE programmes often included sport over the past two millennia but this, I would argue, was more sport education than PE. Here I will be focusing on non-military forms of institutional exercise, across three critical moments in the history of PE. They are the teaching practices in Athens, China and India during the Ancient World, early institutional practices during the 'Middle Ages', and new turns in the European Renaissance and Enlightenment period. Here we are interested in the cultivation of distinctive practices and early forms of appropriation, that is, prototypes to the nineteenth-century globalization we are interested in.

I have deliberately chosen three starting points for the history of PE based on their legacy. Within European and North American histories, there is little doubt that Ancient Athenian physical culture/education influenced ideas of exercise for centuries. As this book is about global fitness, as opposed to European fitness, I have also decided to look at the institutionalization of PE in China and India during a comparable time to Athens. Because of a broader public and indeed scholarly discourse, I will divide this section between the Ancient world and then the Renaissance period in Europe, as well as developments within Asia. This is a large 'jump' temporally but for educators of the nineteenth century, they typically took privileged the Ancient world, or the Renaissance when looking for historical resonances.[138] Indeed, many educators in Europe and America, not to mention imperial hubs, used *mens sana in corpore sano* as a sort of mantra to sweep aside cultural objections to physical education.[139]

Writing in the *American Physical Education Review* in 1907, Leonhard Felix Fuld implored students of PE to study Athenian and Roman exercise practices.[140] The benefit, he prophesized, would be a full understanding in the use of exercise for the development of the body, and the training of the 'hardy' soldier. It is the former which engages us. Although other Greek city-states, notably Sparta, contained gymnasia, Miller noted that it was Athens

---

[136]Martha Verbrugge, *Active bodies: A history of women's physical education in twentieth-century America* (Oxford University, 2012), 14–25.
[137]David Kirk, 'Physical culture, physical education and relational analysis', *Sport, Education and Society* 4 (1999): 63–73.
[138]Andy Carter, 'At home at Oxbridge': British views of ancient Greek sport 1749–1974', *Sport in History* 41 (2021): 280–307.
[139]Tony Collins, 'Sport and physical culture at the edges of the imperial project', in Francois Cleophas (ed.), *Critical reflections on physical culture at the edges of empire* (African Sun Media, 2021), 209–13.
[140]Leonhard Fuld, 'Physical Education in Greece and Rome', *American Physical Education Review* 12 (1907): 1–14.

which provided the 'earliest evidence for the architecture of the gymnasium and its support by the State'.[141]

Depending on the time and context, the Athenian gymnasium operated as an offshoot of military training, a conduit to the athletic training, a branch of educational philosophy or some combination of the three.[142] Originally a space where wrestling and running occurred, these spaces eventually took a standard format. As per Scott, gymnasiums held a *palaestra* or open courtyard containing baths, changing rooms and rooms for informal teaching. There were also central areas for training. Strict rules existed on conduct, including who could, and could not participate in exercises, and who could, and could not, exercise nude (the word gymnasium being derived from the Greek words for naked exercise).[143] Kyle explained that gymnasiums were typically built outside city walls, as they required a large area for running, shade from the sun and a source of water.[144]

Rather than an institution on the periphery of Athenian society, gymnasiums played a key role in socializing men of the *polis* as to the expectations the Greek city-state had of them. 'Free' males up to the age of thirty were typically allowed to use gymnasiums while slaves, tradesmen, freedman, women or men of disrepute were excluded.[145] There is some evidence of city-states outside of Athens which were open to women, and Spears's work on ancient Greece is illustrative of women's physical culture being someway institutionalized albeit the scale was small compared to men.[146] This is not to say that women's sport and physical culture did not occur during this period and, on that, I happily direct readers to Kyle's study of Greek sport.[147]

Two of the most famous gymnasiums, the Academy, and the Lyceum, highlight the importance of these prototype PE systems in Athens.[148] Aside from being training spaces, they were known for the philosophical schools they hosted. During the fourth century BCE, Plato used the Academy as a teaching space. Even after the fall of Greece, and its annexation by the

---

[141] Peter Miller, *Sport: Antiquity and its legacy* (Bloomsbury, 2022), 26–35.
[142] Mark Golden, *Sport and society in ancient Greece* (Cambridge University Press, 1998), 22–34.
[143] Michael Scott, 'The social life of Greek athletic facilities (other than stadia)', in Paul Christesen (ed.), *A Companion to Sport and Spectacle in Greek and Roman Antiquity* (Wiley, 2013), 295–308.
[144] Kyle, *Athletics in ancient Athens*, 99.
[145] Betty Spears, 'A perspective of the history of women's sport in ancient Greece', *Journal of Sport History* 11 (1984): 32–47.
[146] John Mouratidis, 'Heracles at Olympia and the exclusion of women from the ancient Olympic Games', *Journal of Sport History* 11 (1984): 41–55.
[147] Donald Kyle, 'Greek female sport: rites, running, and racing', in Paul Christesen and Donald Kyle (eds.), *A Companion to Sport and Spectacle in Greek and Roman Antiquity* (Wiley, 2013), 258–75.
[148] Clarence Forbes, 'Expanded uses of the Greek Gymnasium', *Classical Philology* 40 (1945): 32–42.

Roman Empire in 146 BCE, the Academy continued to provide physical and mental education until 529 CE. The Academy was often held up by later European physical educationalists as a golden period wherein exercise was seen complementary to, if not commensurate with, higher learning.[149] The Lyceum was Athens' second most important gymnasium. Like the Academy, its origins lay in the fourth century BCE as a religious sanctuary. Under the guidance of Aristotle it became a culturally rich space. Kyle suggested that the Lyceum was 'a less prestigious or august athletic facility than the Academy' but it still held a civic function.[150] Under Aristotle, the Lyceum has been compared by Pellegrin to something which resembled a modern university.[151] Aristotle lectured to the public before conducting advanced conversations with regular attendees. Time was devoted during the day also to physical training.

Certainly Athenian gymnasium cultures experienced cultural transfer with the rise of the Roman Empire 27B CE–395 CE. As explained by Forbes, the gymnasium and sport facilities found in Greek city-states, but especially Athens, provided inspiration and a cultural script for Roman gymnasia.[152] Gymnasia became, at times, status projects for leaders, a point exhibited by Emperor Nero's construction of a great gymnasium in Rome in *c.* 60 CE.[153] Still a traditionally male space, many Grecian, or Grecian-inspired gymnasia were combined with, or morphed into, bath-houses.[154] The gymnasium also took on an arguably greater state function as, depending on the period, gymnasia were used to train troops or gladiators. What is arguably the most interesting element is the role of women within these spaces. There is some evidence of women in the eastern parts of the Empire, where the Greek influence was more strongly felt, participating in dedicated 'women only' spaces.[155] While we know women exercised in Greek city-states, it has oftentimes been difficult to envision what this meant. A fascinating example from the Roman Empire is the so-called 'bikini mosaic' discovered among the ruins of a fourth-century CE villa in Sicily. In the mosaic women are shown in running, throwing and dumbbell-lifting movements.[156]

Roman rhetorician Quintilian (35 BCE–*c.* 100 CE) in his work on rhetoric *Institutio Oratoria*, cited strength and fitness as key parts of a public

---

[149] Fuld, 'Physical ... '.
[150] Kyle, *Athletics*, 84.
[151] Pierre Pellegrin, 'The Aristotelian way', in Mary Louise Gill and Pierre Pellegrin (eds.), *A Companion to Ancient Philosophy.* Oxford: Blackwell (Wiley, 2006), 235–44.
[152] Forbes, 'Expanded ... '.
[153] John Mouratidis, 'Nero: The artist, the athlete and his Downfall', *Journal of Sport History* 12 (1985): 5–20.
[154] Forbes, 'Expanded ... '.
[155] Georgia Tsouvala, 'Women members of a Gymnasium in the Roman east (igiv 732)', in John Bodel and Nora Dimitrova (eds.), *Ancient Documents and Their Contexts* (Brill, 2015), 111–23.
[156] Ibid.

FIGURE 1.3 The Bikini Mosaic depicting various forms of physical culture.[157]

speaker's education.[158] Vitruvius (c. 80 BCE–15 BCE) in *De Architectura* noted the social function of the gymnasium while statesman Seneca the Younger (c. 4B CE–65 CE) spoke about the value of exercise as part of his Stoic worldview.[159] This is to say nothing of the previously mentioned Juvenal who, despite critiquing Rome's obsession with physicality, popularized *mens sana in corpore sano*.[160] As occurred in other parts of Roman social and political life, the gymnasium's purpose and importance were fuelled, in part, by a cultural transfer from Greece of ideas concerning education and health.[161]

Although not necessarily as structured, or funded, as the Athenian gymnasium, it is worth discussing the *gurukulam* education system in Ancient India. Existing during several waves of Indian history (beginning in some accounts in the period 5000 BCE), the *gurukula* system was a residential one wherein pupils stayed in teacher's home and were educated in art and

---

[157] Wiki Commons. Available at https://commons.wikimedia.org/wiki/File:Casale_Bikini.jpg.
[158] Quintilian and Harold Edgeworth Butler (ed.), *The Institutio Oratoria of Quintilian* (Heinemann, 1968), 253.
[159] Craig Williams, 'The Rhetoricity of Gender and the Ideal of Mediocritas in Vitruvius's de Architectura', *Arethusa* 49, no. 2 (2016): 245–6. Seneca, *Letters from a Stoic* (Xist, 2016), 33–4.
[160] Madan, *A New...*, 42.
[161] Ulrich Gotter, 'Cultural differences and cross-cultural contact: Greek and Roman concepts of power', *Harvard Studies in Classical Philology* 104 (2008): 179–230.

philosophy as well as sport and physical culture.¹⁶² Returning, briefly to religious tracts, the *Upanishads* contain several mentions of *gurukulam*.¹⁶³ Students were known as *Shishya* or disciplines and the practice was traditionally associated with Hinduism and, in later centuries, Buddhism. In Hindu *gurukulam*, Sanskrit and Vedic system of education was used, while Buddhist gurukulams used Pal and Buddhist systems.¹⁶⁴ Prominent *gurukulam* did exist, comparable to the Athenian Academy or Lyceum. We know of the Takshaila *gurukulam* which became an important centre in the sixth century BCE.¹⁶⁵ Under the Vedic system children typically entered a *gurukulam* between the ages of eight and twelve, before graduating in their mid-twenties. Students were required to remain celibate during their education and the system was largely financed through donations.¹⁶⁶

The difficulty of including gurukulams is the variety these forms could take. It is clear that some *gurukulam* were, in effect, places of spiritual learning wherein the focus was on esoteric matters. Other gurukulams were training schools for future kings. Other pipelines for military leaders. The variety and lack of centralization meant curricula differed.¹⁶⁷ Nevertheless it is clear that some form of physical education was practised be it yoga, military training or sporting activity. Scharfe's study made clear that the privileging of team sport or individual sport was relatively unknown in many gurukulams.¹⁶⁸ Focus was placed on the development of physical stamina and martial skills. For example, Mahapatra cited lessons on military tactics, weapons and callisthenics designed to prepare young men for battle. Additionally, students engaged in physical labour, such as chopping trees. Such work was part of the typical day and while not cited as physical culture was nevertheless physical activity.¹⁶⁹

In a comparative piece studying Athens and Chinese, Wooyeal and Bell discussed the fractured nature of PE in Ancient China which rarely held the longevity found elsewhere.¹⁷⁰ Chinese PE appeared to ebb and flow in importance due to a cultural distinction between military and educational

---

¹⁶²Vinod Kumar Shanwal, 'Development of the Gurukula education system in India', *Journal of Education and Teacher Training Innovation* 1 (2023): 60–7.
¹⁶³Krishna Mohan Shrimali, 'Knowledge transmission: Processes, contents and apparatus in early India', *Social Scientist* 39 (2011): 3–22.
¹⁶⁴P. Selvamani, 'Gurukul System – an ancient educational system of India', *International Journal of Applied Social Science* 6 (2019): 1620–2.
¹⁶⁵Veenus Jain, 'International study exchange: Glimpses from Indian history', *Perspective* 24, no. 2 (2016): 224–48. Hartmut Scharfe, *Education in ancient India* (Brill, 2018), 120.
¹⁶⁶Selvamani, 'Gurukul … '.
¹⁶⁷Ashok Kumar, 'Status of education system in ancient Indian society', *International Multidisciplinary Research Journal*, 4 (2017): 1–3.
¹⁶⁸Scharfe, *Education*, 55.
¹⁶⁹Achintya Mahapatra, 'Warfare and military history in ancient India – a case study', *RES MILITARIS* 13 (2023): 5649–53.
¹⁷⁰Paik Wooyeal and Daniel Bell, 'Citizenship and state-sponsored physical education: Ancient Greece and Ancient China', *The Review of Politics* 66 (2004): 7–34.

physical culture. During the Western Zhou period (1111–771 BCE) a tentative, but powerful, distinction was made by educators between the military and schools. So while PE disappeared in schools, it continued, if not intensified in military circles. Unlike Athenian or Indian schools, PE in China was directed on a seasonal basis. Physical activities were part of the curriculum in the spring and summer, while the arts were taught in autumn and winter.[171] This was informed by a Chinese medical framework which stressed the balancing of opposing forces. Focus was on students achieving excellence in the 'six arts' by the time they finished schooling as teenagers. Archery and charioteering were considered PE within this context. It was also during this period that the Emperor specifically ordered that soldiers were trained in these physical practices, as well as wrestling.[172]

The teaching of subjects, whose students were exclusively male, was staggered so that music, poetry, dance, etc., were the primary focus to the age of thirteen while archery and charioteering were taught from fifteen. This system remained for several centuries but PE fell out of favour. This is surprising given that military training in the Zhou period remained critically important, and military texts were clear on the need to engage in physical activities.[173] Shifting temporally and geographically, a few comments will be made about physical education during the medieval period, in Moghul, European and Sikh systems before finishing with a conversation about the European Renaissance and Enlightenment.

When discussing PE during the medieval period in Europe, many have advanced the idea that the Catholic Church's grip on power during the Middle Ages meant that many societies held a distrusting view of physical culture.[174] While sport and folk games thrived, the simplified thesis is that the Church's view of the body as sinful meant that time given to the body was wasteful.[175] While this narrative is false, it held a great deal of cultural power. The decision here to jump to the fifteenth century in Europe and Asia was not due to the Church's tyrannical repression, but rather the seismic regional and global shifts in physical culture which occurred during this period. This was driven by a wave of global texts which emerged. A key driver in this was the invention of the printing press.[176] Although not immediately obvious, the printing press democratized health knowledge through the transnational spread of texts.

Beginning with European physical culture, we move to fifteenth-century Florence in an Italian city-state in the throes of the 'Renaissance'. A time

---

[171]Ibid.
[172]Ibid.
[173]Ibid.
[174]Van Dalen, 'The ... ', xx.
[175]Ibid., vii–xx.
[176]Elizabeth Eisenstein, *The printing press as an agent of change* (Cambridge University Press, 1980), 3–42.

of social and artistic change, Renaissance Italy was characterized by a Humanist philosophy which advanced the value of education, civic virtue and individual development. This was partly fuelled by a rediscovery of Greco-Roman cultures made possible by a flourishing economy and global trade.[177] One example of this came in 1506 when the statue of *Laocoön and his Sons* was unearthed in Rome. Famed artist Michelangelo was given access to view the marble and was deeply impressed, if not influenced, by the sculpture's depictions of muscularity.[178] Looking at PE during this period McIntosh contrasted the renewal of medical gymnastics and a growth in school gymnastics in the schools of Vittorino da Feltre (1378–1446 CE) in Mantua and Gurrino da Verona (1374–1460 CE) in Ferrara.[179] Da Feltre was an Italian schoolmaster whose conception of education has been credited by some as the birth of the *l'uomo universal* (or 'whole man') ideal in Italy.[180] A professor at the University of Padua in the 1420s, da Feltre was offered the opportunity to teach the marquis of Mantua's children. This blossomed into an academy known as *La Casa Giocosa* or the 'house of joy'. Open to the children of the local nobility (and later those funded through scholarships), *La Casa* became an esteemed institution comparable to Eton in England or the Athenaeum Illustre in the Netherlands.[181]

McIntosh made a critical distinction about da Feltre's educational model. It was almost entirely divorced from military physical culture.[182] It was common during this time, and even several centuries after, for school PE to be influenced, if not outright copied, from military training. The reasons for this were practical, the military trained large numbers of men, some of whom could transfer their knowledge into schools.[183] At *La Casa* such training was absent and sport and physical culture was distinguished across ages and done in conjunction with nature for both genders. Teaching methods focused predominantly on the development of physical stamina, although ball games were included to increase students' skill and grace.

Guarino da Verona was a contemporary of da Feltre's based in Ferrara who in 1429 was hired by the Marquis to be a tutor for their heir. He did so

---

[177] Jan Todd, 'Bernarr Macfadden: Reformer of feminine form', *Journal of Sport History* 14 (1987): 61–75. John Stephens, *Italian renaissance, the origins of intellectual and artistic change before the reformation* (Routledge, 2014), 7–22.

[178] Giovanna Baldissin Molli, 'The sculpted body: Interferences between beauty and anatomy', in Renzo Pegoraro, Luciana Caenazzo, Lucia Mariani (eds.), *Introduction to Medical Humanities: Medicine and the Italian Artistic Heritage* (Springer, 2022), 69–89.

[179] Peter C. McIntosh, *Landmarks in the history of physical education* (London: Routledge, 2013), 60–80.

[180] Ibid.

[181] Angela Schattner, 'Putting sports in place: Sports venues in sixteenth- and seventeenth-century England and their social significance', in Rebekka von Mallinckrodt and Angela Schattner (eds.), *Sports and Physical Exercise in Early Modern Culture* (Routledge, 2017), 65–85.

[182] McIntosh, *Landmarks*, 60–80.

[183] Ibid.

for six years until he founded a school which evolved into a university. While training the heir, Guarino mixed teaching and lessons on comportment with exercises ranging from riding and hunting to snowball fights.[184] Guarino's inclusion of ball games was inspired by his reading of Roman lawyer and author Pliny the Younger's work *Epistolae*, where the game of *pila* was mentioned.[185] While the emphasis on archery, fighting and swordplay had a clear parallel with military physical culture, the inclusion of swimming, *pila* and dancing were predominately included for bodily development. Guarino's school became renowned across Europe for its educational ethos and enjoyed a great deal of patronage.[186] Da Feltre was one such individual who was inspired by da Verona's holistic model, despite not relying on military training methods. Schattner noted the duo's reputation, and essays extoling their teaching methods across mainland Europe and in England over the fifteenth and sixteenth centuries.[187]

There is another equally important global transition, that being the Mughal Empire's expansion in the sixteenth century. Specifically its conquest of North India. As Faruqui discussed, the Empire held a military power comparable, if not surpassing, that of European powers at its height and was economically wealthy for several centuries before a decline in the eighteenth century.[188] The mixing of societies within the Empire led to cross-cultural exchanges within physical culture practices.[189] From an education standpoint the Muslim *ashraf* class in India which was a sort of administrator class was taught some form of physical culture in wrestling and martial skills.[190] Tied to the Mughal court through religious, racial and clan ties, this education was varied but appears to have been influenced by a mixing of Mughal and Indian training. In O'Hanlon's research they noted that archery and wrestling 'formed part of the education of for the sons of *ashraf* urban elites'.[191]

As a final note in educational discourses surrounding physical culture, it is important to discuss the centrality that European enlightenment (*c.* 1680s–1810s CE) thinkers placed on PE. What I want to end with here is a discussion of French philosopher John Jacque Rousseau (1712–1778 CE) and his texts on education. Rousseau, like a series of other seventeenth- and eighteenth-century philosophers, dedicated a considerable amount of thought

---

[184]Ibid.
[185]McIntosh, *Landmarks*, 60–80.
[186]Ibid.
[187]Schattner, 'Putting ... ', 65–85.
[188]Munis Daniyal Faruqui, *Princes and power in the Mughal Empire, 1569–1657* (Duke University, 2002), 1–15.
[189]M.N. Pearson, 'Recreation in Mughal India', *The International Journal of the History of Sport* 1 (1984): 335–50.
[190]Ibid.
[191]Rosalind O'Hanlon, 'Military sports and the history of the martial body in India', *Journal of the Economic and Social History of the Orient* 50 (2007): 490–523.

to the ideal education for 'natural man'.¹⁹² A thought concept more than anything else, Rousseau, John Locke and others distinguished between pre-socialized and socialized man. In Rousseau's thinking society was often seen as corrupting, and subtly constraining man's natural instincts. This was famously put in Rousseau's opening to *Du Contrat Social* (1762), 'man is born free but everywhere is in chains'.¹⁹³ The question of how to correctly educate man, and to a lesser extent, woman, became a key occupation.

The result of his thinking was 1762 treatise *Emile or On Education,* which became a key educational, and physical educational, text in the eighteenth and nineteenth centuries. It encouraged a great deal of discourse across Europe and eventually the Americas about correct schooling.¹⁹⁴ The treatise, which grappled with questions about raising children in a philosophically sound manner, also devoted a space to PE. In essence, Rousseau favoured a sort of Athenian blending of mind and body training. This was made clear in passages stating that

> The body must needs be vigorous in order to obey the soul a good servant ought to be robust ... The weaker the body, the more it commands; the stronger it is, the better it obeys.¹⁹⁵

Rousseau is a nice touchstone to end on as within his writings we can see a path to the Ancient world and one pointed towards the nineteenth century.¹⁹⁶ That his writings were widely publicized across Europe and cited by multiple European physical educationalists in the late eighteenth and early nineteenth centuries also provides an indication of the transnational currents physical culture was swimming in prior to our own focus.¹⁹⁷ PE has served a variety of purposes in institutional and informal schooling matters from different parts of the world across time. The body within these contexts was often presented as a conduit to health, and a component to overall development. Global practices and pathways prior to the nineteenth century existed and served a platform for later development.

---

¹⁹²Danièle Tosato-Rigo, 'In the shadow of Emile: pedagogues, pediatricians, physical education, 1686–1762', *Studies in Philosophy and Education* 31 (2012): 449–63.
¹⁹³Jean-Jacques Rousseau, *Of the social contract and other political writings* (Penguin, 2012), 1.
¹⁹⁴Tosato-Rigo, 'In ... '.
¹⁹⁵Jean-Jacques Rousseau and William Payne, *Rousseau's Emile or treatise on education* (D. Appleton & Company, 1893), 22.
¹⁹⁶Tosato-Rigo, 'In ... '.
¹⁹⁷Robert Batchelor, 'Thinking about the gym: Greek ideals, newtonian bodies and exercise in early eighteenth-century Britain', *Journal for Eighteenth-Century Studies* 35 (2012): 185–97.

Exercise for fighting

Strong muscles may not win wars, but they certainly don't seem to be a disadvantage. A constant in studies of physical culture, be they ancient or modern, is the primacy and anxiety nations and proto-nations placed on training soldiers' bodies.[198] At times bodies played a symbolic role, acting as proxies for leaders' power.[199] More commonly, they played a practical role, assisting in battles. Military fighting has a very obvious role in the promulgation of physical culture. Troops may 'march on their stomachs' but a less poetic observation is that they march with their muscles. For this reason leaders, and whole societies, have taken an intense interest in how troops trained, and the vigour needed for battle. In this section we will not be detailing each military's systems. Such an exercise would be boring, and futile. Instead I want to focus on three themes within military and combat training – troop training, elite training and the social importance of strength. Focusing on themes, rather than timelines, allows us to play with some of the underlying ways in which physical culture was deployed over millennia.

Training in military cultures has often divided itself between a sense of general physical preparedness and battle-specific practices. Regarding the former, records contain stories of archery, sword fighting and wrestling in several civilizations in Europe, Africa and Asia.[200] Oftentimes paintings or etchings, such records serve as a reminder of the importance that physical practice had in preparing for battle. Conflict-specific training is taken as distinct here from more general physical culture practices and preparations. Likewise many militaries used organized sport as a means of training troops.[201] Harking back to this book's introduction, sport is taken as distinct from physical culture. What do we know about how physical culture was used in ancient, pre-modern and modern warfare? Discounting the observation that marching seems to be a near-ubiquitous form of training across cultures, some variations exist. Crowther's writings on Ancient Egyptian military training found that troops, aside from archery, were encouraged to wrestle and engage in calisthenics.[202] Hübner's work on Ancient Egyptian sources of physical culture (3000–1000 BCE) found a range of exercise practices used by soldiers, and their leader, the Pharaoh – who had to undergo ritualistic fitness tests during the *Sed* festival.[203] At the tomb of Beni Hasan, which dates to the Middle Kingdom (*c.* 2000 BCE),

---

[198] Reed Bonadonna, *Soldiers and civilization: How the profession of arms thought and fought the modern world into existence* (Naval Institute, 2017), 1–12.
[199] Alter, *The ...* , 60–5.
[200] Alfred Bradford, *With arrow, sword, and spear: A history of warfare in the ancient world* (Bloomsbury, 2000), 3–24.
[201] Nigel Crowther, *Sport in ancient times* (Bloomsbury, 2007), 6–10.
[202] Ibid., 12–33.
[203] Donald Kyle, 'Decker on sport in pharaonic Egypt: Recreations and rituals, combats and ceremonies, agonism – and athletics? Sports and games of ancient Egypt', *Sport History Review* 24 (1993): 75–83.

scenes show soldiers and athletes wrestling and stick fighting. Some images also hint at acrobatics and gymnastics (for men and women) and a range of other techniques.[204]

Well known to many readers will be the military systems from Greek city-states. Given the attention given to Athens in previous passages, it is best to focus here on Sparta. Kennell's work on Spartan education and culture is a useful starting point.[205] Dating from the sixth century BCE, Spartan society adopted the *Agoge* system which represented a training programme for all men, excluding the first-born son of the ruling class.[206] Structured across three age groups (aged 7–14, 15–19 and 20–29), the *agoge* system combined education in reading and writing with athletic and military training. Kennell noted that the Spartan *agoge* curriculum was 'heavily weighted toward physical education and military exercises'. Men became eligible for military service aged twenty and, by that point, had a decade of physical and military training. They remained eligible for military service until sixty which meant even those who left the *agoge* system at twenty-nine years old were expected to maintain their fitness. Athenian historian and military leader *Xenophon* (430 BCE– *c.*355 BCE) served under and with Spartan officers during the fourth century BCE. His writings on Spartan military culture noted the requirement all troops had to maintain gymnastic exercise 'so ... they become grander in themselves and appear freer than the others'.[207] Xenophon depicted Sparta as a place which 'transformed boys into soldiers, who were the embodiments of courage, virtue and obedience'.[208] There is also evidence that Spartan women engaged in training, not necessarily for battle, but rather to ensure the birth of strong children. Thus there are stories of men and women competing in foot races and wrestling during formative ages.[209] From the written record, Sparta was undoubtedly one of the most militarized nations we will discuss. Its iconic law-maker, Lycurgus (*c.* seventh century BCE) supposedly claimed that a 'city is well-fortified which has a wall of men instead of brick'.[210] Sparta, at times, centred its training around this ethos.

Ancient Rome displayed a strong military emphasis and militarized society, although not necessarily on the scale of Sparta. Conscious that Rome is something of a misnomer – one could look at the Roman Kingdom (753 BCE–509 BCE), Republic (509 BCE–27 BCE) or Empire (27 BCE–395 CE), we will discuss Allmand's study on Flavius Vegetius Renatus (fourth century

---

[204]Crowther, *Sport* ... , 12–33.
[205]Nigel Kennell, *The gymnasium of virtue* (University of North Carolina, 1995).
[206]Ibid., 10–22.
[207]Gerald Proietti, *Xenophon's Sparta: An introduction* (Brill, 1987), 67.
[208]Kennell, *The* ... , 5.
[209]Spears, 'A ... ' 32–47.
[210]Kenneth Hirth, *The organization of ancient economies: A global perspective* (Cambridge University Press, 2020), 346.

BCE) whose treatise about Roman warfare *De re militari* ('Concerning military matters') proved influential during his own lifetime and well into the Middle-Ages.[211] Utilizing descriptions of Roman armies from the mid-to-late Republic, the treatise sought to detail the periods' military cultures. As is perhaps obvious given the vast nature of the Empire, a great deal of emphasis was given to marching and combat training.[212] It is useful here to turn to Speak's work on Ancient Chinese military training which noted that during the sixth century BCE, soldiers underwent seven years of training. This included running with full armour and carrying heavy weapons. This training was also phased in that winter months were typically to archery, charioteering and wrestling before running, jumping and throwing activities were included.[213] Similar processes were noted in ancient Mesoamerica during the Olmec period (*c.* 1200–400 BCE).[214]

While combat sports, with martial applications arose and were codified in the 'Ancient World', it was European and Asian training schools during the 'Middle-Ages' which held greatest relevancy for the nineteenth century. For European physical culturists, the Crusade centuries (1096–1300) coincided with an intensification of warrior codes and training systems in Asia, South America and Africa.[215] Beginning with Europe, work on 'Middle-Age' chivalry found that the warrior class, in this case knights, were expected to uphold moral practices which could, or could not, be explicitly religious.[216] In all of this, the knight's most 'valued characteristic' was their 'physical prowess'.[217] Across English, French, Spanish and Italian states, knights held high social status. The broad evidence which we have on knights' training points to a mixture of combat training, survival skills and physical conditioning.[218] This began at page hood, sometimes as young as seven, and continued well into manhood.

Culturally comparable traditions existed from the samurai cultures of Japan to the *cuāuhocēlōtl* warrior class within the Aztecs.[219] Another

---

[211] Christopher Allmand, *The De re militari of Vegetius: The reception, transmission and legacy of a Roman text in the Middle Ages* (Cambridge University Press, 2011), 11–80.

[212] Mike Speak, 'Recreation and sport in ancient China: Primitive society to AD 960', in Robin Jones and James Riordan (eds.), *Sport and Physical Education in China* (Routledge, 2002), 40–57.

[213] Ibid.

[214] Karl Taube, Marc Zender, Heather Orr and Rex Koontz, 'American gladiators: Ritual boxing in ancient Mesoamerica', in Heather Orr and Rex Koontz (eds.), *Blood and Beauty* (Cotsen Institute of Archaeology, 2009), 161–220.

[215] John Lynn, *Battle: A history of combat and culture* (Hachette, 2009), 29–110.

[216] Richard Kaeuper, *Holy warriors* (University of Pennsylvania Press, 2012), 94–115.

[217] Stephen Hardy, 'The medieval tournament: a functional sport of the upper class', *Journal of Sport History* 1 (1974): 91–105.

[218] Dennis Showalter, 'Caste, skill, and training: The evolution of cohesion in European armies from the Middle Ages to the sixteenth century', *The Journal of Military History* 57 (1993): 407–30.

[219] Inga Clendinnen, 'The Cost of Courage in Aztec Society', *Past & Present* 107 (1985): 44–89.

interesting example is that of the Mandinka warriors in West Africa whose legacy was captured in fourteenth-century poem, the *Epic of Sundiata*.[220] Sticking, momentarily, with samurai, this system arose in the tenth century and marked a rising military nobility and caste. During the Kamakura period (1185–1333 CE), military ruler Minamoto no Yoritomo chose governors from the *shugo* caste to rule various provinces. Although noted for their brutality, it is worth stressing *shugo* were expected to 'master the bow and the horse as well as the brush and the word'.[221] Like European knights, such warriors were trained in a code of ethics. For us, such observations are important as they stress the importance that discipline of the mind, as well as the body, was presumed to have across cultures. Work on the *cuāuhocēlōtl* warriors in the Aztec empire in South America during the 1300s has likewise cited a distinct warrior culture and training which combined fighting and cultural education. Education was first entrusted to parents for children between the ages of three and fifteen. After this *cuāuhocēlōtl* attended a temple-school where they were trained in the arts and spiritual affairs.[222] Their preparation for warfare was a combination of physical activity, combat training and ball games around religious festivals.

The final related category to consider is training for combat athletes. Such figures, be they gladiators, wrestlers or pugilists, utilized strict and structured methods of training to prepare for competition. Discounting the popular understanding of Roman gladiators, often informed by Hollywood movies, research has made clear just how systemized their training could be.[223] Stemming from 264 BCE and lasting several centuries, gladiators were trained fighters, often, but not always enslaved men, and occasionally women, who fought at exhibitions and festivals.[224] What began as a niche spectacle evolved into a common part of the Roman calendar as leaders became privy to the value in hosting spectacles. It was, as Roman writer Juvenal noted, a 'bread and circus' approach to keeping the populace happy.[225] In terms of training, gladiators were housed and trained in schools (*ludus gladiatorum*) and given exercises and diets to prepare for combat. This training was a combination of callisthenics, sword fighting and specialized combat. Interestingly Juvenal criticized female gladiators for fighting wild boars in games while other writers praised the skill and tenacity of female gladiators against wild animals.[226] While connected to combat, gladiatorial

---

[220]Gordon Innes, *Sunjata: Three Mandinka versions* (Routledge, 2005), 1–22.
[221]Vyjayanthi Selinger, 'The sword trope and the Birth of the Shogunate: Historical metaphors in Muromachi Japan', *Japanese Language and Literature* 43 (2009): 55–81.
[222]Clendinnen, 'The ... '.
[223]Heather Reid, 'Was the Roman gladiator an athlete?' *Journal of the Philosophy of Sport* 33 (2006): 37–49.
[224]Roger Dunkle, *Gladiators: Violence and spectacle in ancient Rome* (Routledge, 2013), 45–78.
[225]Crowther, *Sport in ancient times*, 174–80.
[226]Anna McCullough, 'Female gladiators in imperial Rome: literary context and historical fact', *Classical World* (2008): 197–209.

schools distinguished themselves by the specialized coaching contained within. Gladiator instructors were often former gladiators, and depending on the decade, did, or did not, have an official connection with the military.

It is true that many 'combat gymnasiums' evolved from military fighting. South East Asia provides clear examples. The previously mentioned Indian *akhara* and Persian *zurkhaneh* began as institutions with more formal links to the military before becoming standalone training sites.[227] Sticking with the *akhara*, and Indian wrestling, the publication of the *Manasollasa* in the twelfth century marked a training tract for wrestlers.[228] Phor noted the inclusion of chapters on diet, training and body types, as well as weight-lifting practices (*bharashrama*) for trainees. These weightlifting practices revolved around callisthenics, club-swinging and lifting heavy objects.[229] During the thirteenth century, an allegorical religious text, the *Malla-Purana* was written. Recording a conversation between Krishna and Balarama, it included prescriptions on weight-training, callisthenics and diet. One finds in the *Malla-Purana* an explicit text on training for combat distinct from the battlefield.[230] Accordingly evidence exists of physical culture practices from the *akhara* being distinct from those used to train soldiers. The codification of training manuals and practices for combat sports was not uncommon and, across Europe and Asia instances exist of martial art treatises and fencing manuals being produced from 1200–1600 CE.[231]

One can find a clear and emergent clustering of worldwide training schools around this period. In Europe martial training schools, with a specific focus on fencing, flourished with the German *Fechtschulen* movement and the Italian *Sala d'Arme* school. As Leblanc and Cinato's work on European fencing made clear, fencing masters were respected individuals in pre-modern Europe whose expertise expanded beyond combat into ideas around health and fitness.[232] Likewise in Japanese Koryū Schools martial arts began to grow in importance from the twelfth century.[233] Similar patterns can be found in China and Korea.[234] Such institutions, which intersected with

---

[227] O'Hanlon, 'Military ... ', 490–523.
[228] Alter, *The* ... , 16–19.
[229] Rajesh Kumar Phor, 'Historical analysis of physical activities and sports in ancient India', *Purva Mimaansa* 12 (2021): 132–40.
[230] Patrick McCartney, 'Poles apart? From wrestling and Mallkhāmb to Pole Yoga', *Journal of Yoga Studies* 4 (2023): 215–70.
[231] Alexander Hay, 'The art and politics of fence: Subtexts and ideologies of late 16th century fencing manuals', *Martial Arts Studies* 1 (2015): 60–71.
[232] Hélène Leblanc and Franck Cinato, 'Scholastic clues in two Latin fencing manuals: Bridging the gap between medieval and renaissance cultures', *Acta Periodica Duellatorum* 11 (2023): 39–63.
[233] Wojciech Cynarski, 'Three patterns of group relations in martial arts schools', *Studies in Sport Humanities* 19 (2016): 54–9.
[234] Stanley Henning, 'The Chinese martial arts in historical perspective', *Military Affairs: The Journal of Military History, including Theory and Technology* (1981): 173–9.

military cultures while still remaining outside them, advanced specialized views about how the body moved, and physically improved.

Writing about Indian court wrestlers of the thirteenth century, Alter highlighted the symbolic value that strong bodies had for rulers. Fed and kept comfortable by the rulers, such individuals were a physical expression of the ruler's power and strength. They were a form of 'soft power'.[235] That is, a cultural expression of a region's military strength. This brings us to the last military point to consider, the symbolism of strength. There have been, in many instances, mythological characters and gods revered for their strength. We have already discussed Indian deity Hanuman whose strength was beyond compare. He, of course, had parallels with gods and demi-gods like Thor, Heracles, the Dagda, Gilgamesh, Gilgamesh, Susanoo, Ogun and many other figures. There is, it seems, a keen human association between physical power and divinity. This is to say nothing of the linguistic depiction of armies as strong and powerful, nor the records of extraordinarily strong warriors, many of whom delighted in their strength.[236] Aside from Alter's thirteenth-century warriors, it is interesting to mention fourteenth-century French knight Jean Le Maingre (1366–1421 CE) whose strength included backflips wearing his full body armour, lifting heavy objects and displaying various other gymnastic feats of strength.[237] Such feats were often presented as emblematic of the strength of Maingre's troops. In such instances, individual strength held the potential to be militarily and symbolically important.

Military strength and stories of strong warriors are perhaps the most familiar to readers owing to a multitude of media which features the exploits of real and imagined male and female fighters. Discounting these invented stories, the broader militaristic value of physical culture is paramount. As the next chapters make clear, military physical culture was a core component of the globalization of fitness practices and movements. This was done formally through prescriptions for training, and informally as often happened when schools and social clubs mimicking military physical culture. Indeed there are many instances in which it was militaries who influenced the training of schoolchildren rather than the educational lineages discussed above.

---

[235] Joseph Nye, 'Soft power', *Foreign Policy* 80 (1990): 153–71; Alter, *The* ... , 60–5.
[236] John Carter, 'Muscular Christianity and its makers: Sporting monks and churchmen in Anglo-Norman Society, 1000–1300', *The International Journal of the History of Sport* 1 (1984): 109–24.
[237] David Hoornstra, 'Boucicaut fils and the great Hiatus: Insights from the career of jean II le Meingre, called Boucicaut', in L.J. Andrew Villalon and Donald Kagay (eds.), *The Hundred Years War (Part III)* (Brill, 2013), 105–44.

Making sense of this chapter

Returning to Huizinga, whose treatise on play served as a sort of intellectual companion during this chapter, he depicted play as something outside of ethics or moral judgement.[238] Is there an innate human desire for strength or strengthening activities? An easier question to ask, and answer, is whether strength and strengthening activities played a core role in various civilizations? As this chapter makes clear. This answer is yes, a thousand times yes. While for many centuries the importance of strength was one of practicality, we are about to move into a world wherein strength and fitness were not an expectation of everyday tasks, but rather something requiring cultivation. This separation of 'everyday life' with time for exercise had its roots in the developments discussed here but took on greater precedence in the nineteenth century.

This chapter was not a chronological history of global physical culture. This was something of a buffet of various histories, delineated between health, education, religion and combat. As we moved from one area to the next, the value, meanings and applications of physical culture varied. What remained, however, was the importance of physical culture in multiple histories and the earlier smashing together of global practices in the form of texts, territorial expansions and imperial appropriations. This book is focused on the globalization of nineteenth-century physical culture which, I argue, fundamentally shaped fitness practices of the twentieth century and the present. A pitfall of this argument would be to completely ignore the pre-history, its richness and its own global patterns. This chapter carved out the tramlines and roots that physical culture took. Physical culture became globalized because it deepened a global, and historic, interest in health. It did not create this interest but capitalized on it in new, institutional and commercially successful, ways. With that in mind, let's begin.

---

[238] Anchor, 'History ... '.

2

Globalizing local practices

Swinging, stretching and sweeping are the focus of this chapter. Aside from being a wonderful piece of alliteration, this sentence encompasses three movements which were popularized during the nineteenth century. Swinging refers to the practice of swinging clubs around the body. Stretching refers to the spread of yoga, and sweeping refers to the practice of judo. Swinging, stretching and sweeping are, of course, too simplistic. What unites club-swinging, yoga and judo is the fact that they were local practices which became transformed into global phenomenon in the nineteenth century. This transformation saw them largely emptied of their original meanings and adapted to 'glocal' contexts.[1] Borrowing from cultural transfer scholarship, we could likewise say that these practices were not simply transplanted from one location to another but rather transformed through the process of transfer. It was the transfer itself, and its mechanisms, which smoothed away cultural specificities and reimagined these systems on broader terms.[2]

Chapter 3 examines the globalization of exercise from an institution level. Here we are interested in recreational and medical fields. These were far 'looser' spaces wherein individual action differed greatly. Here we examine how and why trainees were exposed to these practices and for what purpose. Equally important is the fact that these practices originated, or claimed their origins, in Asia, as opposed to Europe or North America. Their histories can be viewed as one of imperialist/Western plundering of foreign practices, of overly romanticized, if not Orientalist views of Eastern health, or as examples of the porous nature of nineteenth-century physical cultures.[3] The reality is that all of these factors were true and fuelled by

---

[1] Joseph Alter, 'Indian clubs and colonialism: Hindu masculinity and muscular Christianity', *Comparative Studies in Society and History* 46, no. 3 (2004): 497–534.
[2] Steen Bille Jørgensen and Hans-Jürgen Lüsebrink, 'Introduction: Reframing the cultural transfer approach', in Steen Bille Jørgensen and Hans-Jürgen Lüsebrink (eds.), *Cultural Transfer Reconsidered* (Brill, 2021), 1–20.
[3] Harald Fischer-Tiné, 'Fitness for modernity? The YMCA and physical-education schemes in late-colonial South Asia (circa 1900–40)', *Modern Asian Studies* 53, no. 2 (2019): 512–59.

broader developments concerning transport and communication. Certainly, Conrad's work on global history made clear the role institutions and structural transformations had in the diffusion of global practices and even beauty standards during this century.[4] This chapter also highlights the role of the 'go-between' in the diffusion of global fitness. The 'go-between' can be simplified as those individuals who operate between two cultures.[5] Go-betweens can be viewed as mediators, arbitrators and figures who introduce or meld different cultural practices.[6] A simple example is of the local man or woman who negotiates peace or trade with imperial invaders, thereby creating a bridge between cultures. As Metcalf's work stresses, this position is not neutral and is often a power brokerage between one culture and another.[7] The 'go-betweens' serve an important role in transforming ideas, building networks and helping translate practices across cultures.[8] While caution is needed in elevating the status of some individuals over others, this chapter contains a number of key 'go-betweens' like Swami Vivekananda who helped popularize yoga, judo instructors deliberately sent abroad and a series of entrepreneurs who shed light on a practice, perhaps for the first time.

Why swinging, stretching and sweeping? These practices were, I contend, some of the most impactful global changes in recreational fitness. Indian club-swinging, as I've argued elsewhere, was one of the first global fitness practices and helped facilitate the later spread of physical culture.[9] Yoga solidified a bridge between physical culture and alternative health practices with some spiritual elements thrown in, likewise Judo got swept up in self-defence pages of physical culture magazines and discourses. Each was promoted in different ways through military, medical, recreational and sporting discourses. Each highlighted the diversity that physical culture practices exhibited and, each practice provided a firm example of how easily modified local practices could be. Regardless of whether it was club-swinging, yoga or judo, each practice changed once it left its point of origin. Here we will explore why this happened and the consequences of this change in the

---

[4]Sebastian Conrad, *What is global history?* (New York: Princeton University Press, 2017); Sebastian Conrad, 'Globalizing the beautiful body: Eugen Sandow, bodybuilding, and the ideal of muscular manliness at the turn of the Twentieth-Century', *Journal of World History* 32, no. 1 (2021): 95–125.
[5]Leyla Rouhi, *Mediation and love: A study of the medieval go-between in key romance and near Eastern texts* (Leiden, 1999).
[6]Natalie Zemon Davis, *Trickster travels: A sixteenth-century Muslim between worlds* (Hill and Wang, 2006).
[7]Alida Metcalf, *Go-betweens and the colonization of Brazil: 1500–1600* (University of Texas, 2006).
[8]Kapil Raj, 'Go-betweens, travelers, and cultural translators', in Bernard Lightman (ed.), *A Companion to the History of Science* (John Wiley, 2016), 39–57.
[9]Conor Heffernan, *Indian club-swinging and the birth of global fitness: Mugdars, Masculinity and Marketing* (Bloomsbury, 2023), 12–46.

nineteenth century. Put simply, this chapter argues that the globalization of club-swinging, yoga and judo transformed these localized practices into a transnational physical culture. They were repurposed through imperial networks and commercial interests to address Western anxieties about health, gender and national fitness.

Given that Indian clubs rose to global prominence in the first half of the nineteenth century, this chapter begins with the clubs' transformation from an Indian and Persian practice into a global one. Particular attention is given to medical and popular discourses on the clubs and, their use in some of the gymnastic practices discussed in Chapter 3. Indian clubs provide the framework for a commercial and informational culture around popular health practices. Next the chapter explores yoga. Singleton's study of yoga made clear that although the practice is centuries old, during the nineteenth century it underwent changes owing to the influx of foreign callisthenic systems into India.[10] Suitably modified, it was popularized within global physical culture environments as a traditionally Indian system. The reality was more complex and represented something of an endless boomerang effect whereby popular yogic practices moved from India to the rest of the world, and back again. Finally this chapter explores judo, the Japanese self-defence system which came to global prominence following Japan's victory in the 1904–5 Russo-Japanese War. Much of this discourse centred on how a smaller nation defeated a stronger adversary. Such conversations were tinged with racial and ethnocentric assumptions but largely fuelled a global judo interest.

As the previous chapter made clear, physical culture served a variety of purposes prior to the nineteenth century and had, already, experienced global transformation. This chapter's purpose is not to set out the nineteenth century as a 'big bang' story wherein what came before bore no resemblance to what came after. Instead this chapter argues for a clear process of *deepening*. Networks grew in importance, it became easier to adapt foreign customs and commercial apparatuses arose to support developments. These developments also centred on a metaphorical global body for men and women. This was a body in need of training but also one capable of reaching perfection through physical culture. Swinging, stretching and sweeping were largely regional practices prior to the nineteenth century. This chapter studies their transformation to global systems. This process standardized certain body ideals and exercise methods across diverse societies, and reflected the power dynamics of colonialism and modernization in this new era of global fitness.

---

[10]Mark Singleton, *Yoga body: The origins of modern posture practice* (Oxford University, 2010).

Club-swinging as origin point

Weighted clubs hold a symbolic and sporting importance in Indian, Persian and Pakistani cultures. They were objects used by deities and mortals in religious texts, as weapons in battle and as implements in training.[11] It is the training element which concerns us, although books on the religious, and artistic, importance of these clubs exist. Likewise for their use in battle.[12] As discussed in the last chapter, training practices in the *akhara* and *zoorkhaneh* saw clubs swung around the body for exercise. Before discussing how these practices came to be popularized globally, we need to discuss the material culture of these clubs. In India these clubs were made of wood, often tall in length and heavy in weight.[13] Those used in Persian cultures were not necessarily as colourful, but were tall and heavy in appearance and weight.[14] The 'Indian clubs' which came to be promoted and used in Great Britain, Europe and the United States were, with few exceptions, smaller in size and blander in appearance. They resembled juggling or bowling pins more so than the original clubs. Nevertheless the name, and at least some of the exercises used with the clubs, linked to their origins.

One of the first European accounts of club-swinging, and Indian physical culture more generally, was British traveller Peter Mundy's 1630 notes which remarked on some wrestlers' athletic feats Mundy witnessed.[15] As Portugal, and later England's, trading and imperial links grew within India, more individuals became familiar with such practices. In 1798 Hugh Boyd, secretary to Lord George Macartney in Madras, wrote about the vast number of muscular bodies and displays he encountered walking the streets. Some years later, William Ouseley, a British orientalist, jotted down a few lines about Indian soldiers serving in the East India Company's military.[16] Outside of their mandated training many Indian soldiers and wrestlers took to displaying their strength using club-swinging and athletic exhibitions. But when did the club move from something which was seen as distinctly Indian or Persian to a global practice? The period 1820 to 1840 was critical in this regard. First, broader geo-political shifts, most notably the Napoleonic wars in Europe, created a new interest in military physical training.[17] This was

---

[11] Heffernan, *Indian Club-swinging*, 27–40.
[12] Alter, 'Indian ... '.
[13] Conor Heffernan, 'What's wrong with a little swinging? Indian clubs as a tool of suppression and rebellion in post-rebellion India', *The International Journal of the History of Sport* 34, no. 7–8 (2017): 554–77.
[14] Michiel Baas, 'Muscles, masculinity and middle classness', in Knut A. Jacobsen (ed.), *Routledge Handbook of Contemporary India* (Routledge, 2016), 444–56.
[15] Heffernan, *Indian Club-swinging*, 31–2.
[16] Ibid., 51.
[17] Dieter Reicher, 'Nationalistic German gymnastic movements and modern sports. Culture between identity and habitus', *Historical Social Research/Historische Sozialforschung* 45, no. 1 (171 (2020): 207–25.

not a phenomenon isolated to England, and the next chapter will explore the connection between the violent beginnings of the nineteenth century and military reforms. In British military thinking, concerns about troop fitness coupled with concerns about troop health.[18] While troop fitness can be taken here to mean mobility and fighting power, troop health referred to the avoidance of disease. Connected to illness and disease, in an Indian context at least, were the poor health outcomes of British men who worked in the East India Company. As more British citizens emigrated to India during the early 1800s, their susceptibility to disease and death created a frenzied search for medical interventions. Harrison's work on colonial medicine and policies has made clear the fear that many British administrators had about working in India.[19] We thus come to an important observation. A need existed for health solutions in two global enterprises – the British military and its colonial service.

Between these groups, the military acted first. In 1824 Henry Torrens, Adjutant-General to the British Forces, oversaw the creation of a training manual entitled *Field Exercise and Evolutions of the Army*. In it Torrens included prescriptions for troops to swing wooden clubs 'in order to supple the recruit, open his chest and give freedom to the muscles'.[20] Torrens had previously served in India so it is likely that he was exposed to these clubs. The only other instance we have of clubs being prescribed for health purposes outside of India or Persia comes from French physician Nicolas Andry whose 1741 work *Orthopédie* recommended club swinging to treat Musculo-skeletal complaints.[21] Torrens likely discovered club-swinging while in India, which we know was a common experience for British troops. What happened next reaffirms this assumption. In 1825, Army and Navy Superintendent of Gymnastic Exercise in Britain, P. H. Clias, advocated club-swinging for troops and the public. Less than a decade later, popular writer, Donald Walker, noted the popularization of club-swinging as practised by the British military. Walker's 1834 manual, *British Manly Exercises*, was one of the century's most important works and enjoyed foreign translations and domestic re-editions.[22] We will return to Walker in a moment's time but it is important to focus on medical concerns and club-swinging.

In 1840 F. H. Brett, a physician in India published *A Practical Essay on Some of the Principal Surgical Diseases of India*. Brett had served over a decade in India, having been appointed to the East India Company's medical corps in the 1820s. Within the book Brett recommended British men coming

---

[18]Kartar Lalvani, *The making of India* (Bloomsbury, 2016), 1–53.
[19]Mark Harrison, *Public health in British India: Anglo-Indian preventive medicine 1859–1914* (Cambridge University Press, 1994).
[20]Heffernan, *Indian Club-swinging*, 27–8.
[21]Jan Todd, *Physical culture and the body beautiful: Purposive exercise in the lives of American women, 1800–1870* (Mercer University, 1998), 29.
[22]Heffernan, *Indian Club-swinging*, 112.

to India should 'practice athletic exercises … and wrestling in imitation of the *Puhlwans* (Indian wrestlers)'.[23] Aside from Brett's work we also have several diaries and letters between administrators and physicians either advocating for, or noting, club-swinging and domestic physical culture practices for those arriving in India.[24] Brett's work did not have as immediate an impact as Torrens but it serves to highlight the two lives of the Indian club. It acted as a physical training tool but also as medical implement. On this latter use, it is telling that outside of the recreational Indian club-swinging soon to be discussed, many physicians in the first half of the nineteenth century used club-swinging as a corrective tool in addressing spinal ailments, muscle weaknesses, nervous disorders and melancholy.[25]

But when did club-swinging become a transnational, even global, practice? We return now to Walker's *British Manly Exercises*. Historians have yet to write an adequate biography of Walker but what we do know

FIGURE 2.1 'Daily Exercise, Mahratta Camp', 1813.[26]

---

[23]F.H. Brett, *A practical essay on some of the principal surgical diseases of India* (Thacker, 1840), 42.
[24]Heffernan, *Indian Club-swinging*, 45–62.
[25]Royal Archives, London, VIC/MAIN/M/5/86.
[26]Thomas Duer Broughton, *Letters written in a Mahratta camp during the year 1809* (London, 1813), 218.

is that he was an author of varied interests. Outside of writing health tracts for men and women, he was also interested in education.[27] *British Manly Exercises* was his most commercially successful text. It was one of the most important sporting texts of the century.[28] It is Walker's book, more than anything else, which helped globalize club-swinging. Its follow-up, *Exercises for Ladies Designed to Preserve and Improve Their Beauty*, was not as successful but proved equally impactful. Aside from informing popular discourses about fitness, both works were cited by physicians seeking using club-swinging in treatments.[29] They also contained illustrations of men and women swinging clubs in various exercises.[30] Much like Mercuriale's *De Arte Gymnastica*, Walker's illustrations helped others visualize the practice and enticed some to try it. This was true of British and foreign audiences. Walker's work for women appeared in the United States as early as 1840, with his comments on the Indian sceptre (a 'female appropriate' club) receiving praise from reviewers.[31] The gendered elements of the club by this point were particularly striking. Men, during the 1830s and 1840s, were typically encouraged to swing clubs weighing anything upwards from 2 lbs. Women were discouraged from swinging anything heavier than 0.5 to 1.5 lbs. The physical clubs were gendered and this was, oftentimes, a global phenomenon. Contemporaries were aware of this. One British physician, Dr. Coulson, recorded in his 1836 book *On Deformities of the Chest* that he distinguished between the clubs bought for male and female clients.[32]

What is often underexamined when discussing this popularization of clubs is the impact it had on users. Returning to Torrens' comment about 'opening' up the chest, the use of small clubs helped remake and shape physiques. There is, a telling, albeit sardonic, review of Walker's book for women which expressed pride that on entering a room the reviewer could easily decipher which women were using Walker's prescriptions.[33] Even Walker was aware of this, choosing exercises for men and women which he believed would open the chest, add power to the trunk and improve comportment.[34] Similar to Gilman's work on posture, the club helped, implicitly, to change body comportment. While it is impossible to know

---

[27]Donald Walker, *British manly exercises: In which rowing and sailing are now first described, and riding and driving are for the first time given in a work of this kind* ... (Hurst, 1835); Donald Walker, *Exercises for ladies; Calculated to preserve and improve beauty, etc* (Hurst, 1836).
[28]Todd, *Physical culture* ... , 96–100.
[29]Ibid.
[30]Walker, *British Manly* ... .
[31]Heffernan, *Indian* ... , 80–1.
[32]William Coulson, *On deformities of the chest* (Hurst, 1836), 35.
[33]Heffernan, *Indian* ... , 80–1.
[34]Walker, *British* ... , 25–30.

figures for who used it in this way, we know the book was popular, global and often a reference point for gymnasts and medics.[35]

The movement of clubs from India to Britain was relatively straightforward and one influenced by Britain's imperial relationship with India. During the 1850s and 1860s the clubs' globalism became more complicated, driven by growing commercial, recreational and military concerns. Beginning with the latter, we return to the British military. Specifically the military of the late 1850s which underwent a decade of profound warfare. European conflict in the Crimean War (1853–6) was complemented by the Anglo-Persian War (1856–7), the Second Opium War (1856–60) and Indian Rebellion (1857–8). Discounting the anger that the Indian Rebellion brought in British newspapers, the Crimean War and its aftermath dominated military conversations, especially among military strategists.[36] Owing to the large number of troop deaths, and the observation that more troops died from illnesses and disease than combat, a series of enquiries were created by the British government to examine sanitary conditions in military camps and how to prepare troops for battle.[37]

Physical training, despite the efforts of Torrens and Clias in the 1820s, was largely a secondary concern in the British military. The logic was that the training for battle, along with sport, was enough to strengthen troops.[38] This set Britain as somewhat unique in mainland Europe and the United States, several militaries had adopted their own form of gymnastics/physical training for troops. Campbell's study of British military cultures found a primacy placed upon sport over gymnastics. This is an important thing to note as it kept British training insular until gymnastic instructor Archibald MacLaren's arrival in the 1850s.[39] Chapter 3 discusses military gymnastics but it is worth noting that the French military created its own standardized training system and school in 1852 with the foundation of the École de Joinville.[40] In Prussia, the Central Gymnastic Institute in Berlin began training officers from 1847.[41] Both French and Prussian systems were,

---

[35]Sander L. Gilman, *Stand up straight!: A history of posture* (Reaktion, 2018), 1–22.
[36]John Shepherd, *The Crimean doctors* (Liverpool University, 1991), 180–195.
[37]*Royal Commission appointed to inquire into the sanitary condition of the army, report of the commissioners appointed to inquire into the regulations affecting the sanitary condition of the army, The organization of military hospitals, and the treatment of the sick and wounded* (London: HMSO, 1858).
[38]Nikolai Bogdanovic, *Fit to fight: A history of the royal army physical training corps 1860–2015* (Bloomsbury, 2017), 13–20.
[39]Ibid., 8–41.
[40]Jean Saint-Martin and Michaël Attali, 'The Joinville school and the institutionalization of a French-style physical education, 1852–1939', *The International Journal of the History of Sport* 32, no. 6 (2015): 740–53.
[41]Roland Naul, 'History of sport and physical education in Germany, 1800–1945', in K. Hardman and R. Naul (eds.), *Sport an Physical Education in Germany* (Routledge, 2002), 15–27.

themselves, global outcomes, as the French system was largely modelled on Spanish trainer Francisco Amorós y Ondeano's system while the Prussian system, despite the region's association with *Turnverein* gymnastics, was modelled on Swedish gymnastics.[42] Incidentally it is worth noting that Amorós y Ondeano's 1847 book *Noveau manuel complet d'éducation physique* claimed that club-swinging had been imported into Paris through an English colonel named Henriot.[43]

Following the Crimean War, the British military resolved to create a new system which would protect and enhance troop's health. In 1858 a Royal Commission *Report on Sanitary Condition of the Army* included recommendations that inquiries be made into the 'French system of gymnastic exercises' and that more investment be made into sporting and gymnastic facilities.[44] In 1859 Secretary of State for War Sidney Herbert dispatched Colonel Frederick officials to France and Prussia to inspect their systems. A report was produced in August 1859 with the recommendation that gymnastics be used in soldiers' preparation for service. By November a private gym instructor, Archibald MacLaren (1820–84), was asked to conduct a gymnastics trial with twelve officers. The 'twelve disciplines' as they were termed, spent several months training under MacLaren and enjoyed changes in strength and bodily measurements. The results were published internally and deemed so successful that the military adopted MacLaren's system.[45] This was combined with the establishment of a Royal Army Physical Training Corps to oversee the delivery of his system and the creation of purpose-built gymnasia.[46] MacLaren spent the 1860s and 1870s treated as an expert on military, and educational, fitness. To that end, he published several books on these subjects. Such was the esteem with which the military treated MacLaren that in 1863 he was asked to oversee the creation of a military gymnasia in India so that the newly revised armies could enjoy his system's benefits.

Of relevance to this chapter was the publication of MacLaren's *A Military System of Gymnastic Exercises* which was printed in the same volume as a training programme by Lieutenant Anderson entitled *A Series of Exercises*

---

[42]Ingrid Brühwiler, 'In-between "Swedish Gymnastics" and "Deutsche Turnkunst: Educating "National" citizens through physical education in Switzerland in the last decades of the nineteenth-century', *Nordic Journal of Educational History* 4, no. 2 (2017): 71–84.
[43]Amoros y Ondeano, *Manuel d'éducation physique, gymnastique et morale* (Roret, 1834), 309.
[44]Bogdanovic, *Fit* ... , 8–41.
[45]James Campbell, 'Training for sport is training for war': Sport and the transformation of the British army, 1860–1914', *The International Journal of the History of Sport* 17, no. 4 (2000): 21–58.
[46]Ibid.

for the Regulation Clubs.[47] These regulation clubs were Indian clubs by another name and proved to be a vital component of British military training cultures. The eventual goal, and somewhat completed outcome, of MacLaren's system was that it be used in every garrison across the Empire.[48] This meant that every soldier was trained using MacLaren's system. Critically many of these individuals went on to teach PE and drill in schools around the world which added a second life for MacLaren's system.[49] Retuning to our point about Walker and the standardization of body ideals, MacLaren's club prescriptions represented an institutional evolution of this point. Soldiers were measured on enlistment and, over twelve weeks, used dumbbells and Indian clubs to build their physique. This was done on very standardized lines – the same exercises *ad nauseum* for countless bodies.[50] The British military, like others around the world, had minimum physique standards. There was a process or measuring and growing body parts. While MacLaren preferred the use of dumbbells, barbells and gymnastic exercises (inspired by his own education in France), he did promote clubs. As per Anderson's 'regulation clubs', these devices were to be used in camps and garrisons where dumbbells and barbells could not be found. This usage evolved over the course of the next two decades but the outcome was clear. Indian clubs became commonly used across British military sites which, in the latter half of the nineteenth century, was in a process of growth in Asia and Africa. This meant that gymnastic equipment, like the clubs, grew in usage and familiarity in a global context.[51] As a final point in this regard it is worth noting that images and medical reports from India in the 1860s and 1870s note the use of 'British' Indian clubs being used among Indian troops.[52] Bharati coined the term 'pizza effect' in 1970 to describe the process by which a nation's cultural touchstones were embraced elsewhere and brought back to their country of origin.[53] In this instance one can see a scenario playing out in which Indian clubs, as created by British thinkers, came to be the dominant form of club-swinging in India, the country which popularized this movement. The power of this change cannot be understated. During the

---

[47]Archibald MacLaren, *A military system of gymnastic exercises for the use of instructors* (Adjutant-General's Office, 1862); Lieutenant Anderson, *A series of exercises for the regulation clubs* (War Office, 1863).
[48]Heffernan, *Indian ...* , 135–8.
[49]J.A. Mangan and Hamad Ndee, 'Military Drill – rather more than "brief and basic": English elementary schools and English militarism', in J.A. Mangan (ed.), *Militarism, Sport, Europe* (Routledge, 2004), 67–99.
[50]Archibald Maclaren, 'Military Gymnasia', *Royal United Services Institution. Journal* 8, no. 31 (1864): 217–30.
[51]Peter Cain and Anthony Hopkins, 'The political economy of British expansion overseas, 1750–1914', *The Economic History Review* 33, no. 4 (1980): 463–90.
[52]Heffernan, 'What's wrong ... ?', 554–60.
[53]Bharati Agehananda, 'The Hindu renaissance and its apologetic patterns', *The Journal of Asian Studies. Association for Asian Studies* 29, no. 2 (1970): 267–87.

1950s Indian physical culturist D. C. Mujumdar produced the *Encyclopaedia of Indian Physical Culture* which sought to protect and encourage domestic physical culture.[54] The club-swinging section focused on the British version.

The club's rising importance from the 1850s was not just about military changes, which predominately impacted men. Equally important was the migration of groups and ideas. We will return briefly to Ondeano's 1847 book *Noveau manuel complet d'éducation physique* which commented on the role British Colonel Henriot had in popularizing club-swinging among French troops.[55] Henriot's grace and athleticism were contrasted with his use of exercises which ran contrary to Ondeano's own system. They nevertheless impacted the military trainer. From Ondeano's *Noveau manuel complet d'éducation physique* one finds a clear growth in French physicians and educators discussing club-swinging as a health practice. One of the most fascinating examples was Napoléon Laisné's 1854 *Gymnastique des demoiselles* or Ladies' Gymnastics.[56] Similar to Walker's *Exercises for Ladies*, Laisné's work demands attention because of the clubs he promoted. In beautiful engravings Laisné supported the use of heavy club-swinging for women.[57] This ran contrary to Walker's more rigid idea of female frailty which had a great deal of support in the Anglophone world. Missing from the French context was a commerce around club-swinging. French manuals from this period typically recommended individuals interested in using clubs should visit a local woodturner who could create some for them. Bespoke or standardized clubs were not yet an item. This does not mean, however, that fitness equipment was uncommon. Perhaps the most famous Parisian gym owner of the nineteenth century, Hippolyte Triat (1813–1881), created a huge site for men to train.[58] Like others, his motivation seemed to stem, in part, from a desire to strengthen men of military-age. Eventually opened to men and women, the gymnasium was stocked with dumbbells, barbells and Indian clubs of various shapes and sizes and said to be of the finest quality.[59]

The period 1840 to 1860 was a critical one in the diffusion of club-swinging around the world and, oftentimes, it was done through informal means such as Henriot in France. In Saxony (modern day Germany), Dr Johann Heinrich Krause wrote about club-swinging, with illustrations similar to Walker's *British Manly Exercises*, as early as 1841.[60] In 1846

---

[54]D.C. Mujumdar, *Encyclopaedia of Indian physical culture* (D.C. Mujumdar, 1950), 614.
[55]Ondeano, *Manuel d'éducation*, 309.
[56]Napoléon Laisné, *Gymnastique des demoiselles. Ouvrage destiné aux mères de famille et contenant la description des exercices avec la construction et le prix des instruments* (Typographie Walder, 1854).
[57]Ibid., 140–5.
[58]Eugen Weber, 'Gymnastics and sports in fin-de-siècle France: Opium of the classes?' *The American Historical Review* 76, no. 1 (1971): 70–98.
[59]Edmond Desbonnet, *The kings of strength: A history of all strong men from ancient times to our own*, translated by David Chapman (McFarland, 2022), 111–31.
[60]Johann Heinrich Krause, *Die Gymnastik und Agonistik der Hellenen* (JA Barth, 1841).

Julius von Kunze published a translation of Walker's text, with explanations of club-swinging included, to a relatively warm reception in Stuttgart.[61] By 1862 Hugo Rothstein, a Prussian military officer and gymnast who travelled to Sweden in 1850 to about their gymnastic system, wrote about *Keulen schwingen* or club-swinging. He used an older periodical which he had edited, *Athenaeum für rationelle Gymnastik,* as a reference.[62] Suitable in his eyes as a tool for boys over the age of 14, club-swinging was connected to the military. Like Ondeano, Rothstein told people to go to a woodturner or construct their own clubs using 'ordinary log wood'.[63] Translated works from other countries exist but it is worth staying with German states, specifically Prussia. Following the wave of revolutions which spread across mainland Europe in 1848 and 1849, Prussia and other states banned the *Turnverein* gymnastic movement. This movement, which originated in Prussia in 1811, was a specialized form of gymnastics created by Friedrich Ludwig Jahn.[64] Before and after, the 1848 uprising against state powers, the *Turnverein* movement had politicized. What began as a health movement with nationalist undertones evolved into a distinct community which served as a meeting space for ideas. As several historians have shown, their banning post-1848 was the result of fears that the *Turnverein* would cause further revolutions.[65] An exodus began among *turners* to other parts of the world, with many migrating to the United States and this process began as early as the 1820s. Hoffman's research on the American *turners* has made clear their impact on sporting and social life.[66] They organized communities, social spaces, changed educational frameworks and helped promote the *Turnverein* system.

This promotion included club-swinging. While it was not the *Turners* who brought Indian clubs to the United States, Walker's book was printed in America in the 1840s, they helped solidify its usage in institutional settings.[67] Turners were helped by those promoting the race science of phrenology who, from the 1850s, began publishing on club-swinging

---

[61]Julius Kunze, *Die Gymnastik. Faßliche Anleitung zu gymnastischen Übungen; enthaltend das Turnen, Schlittschuhlaufen, Schwimmen, Rudern, Reiten, Fahren, Schießen, Jagen; Nach Walker bearbeitet von Julius Kunze* (Verlags Magazin, 1846).
[62]Hugo Rothstein, *Die Geräth-Uebungen und Spiele aus der pädagogischen Gymnastik* (Schroeder, 1862), 6–10. Hugo Rothstein and Per Henrik Ling, *The gymnastic free exercises of PH Ling* (Ticknor, 1853).
[63]Rothstein, *Die Geräth-Uebungen*, 7–8.
[64]Daniel Tröhler, 'Shaping the national body: Physical education and the transformation of German nationalism in the long nineteenth-century', *Nordic Journal of Educational History* 4, no. 2 (2017): 31–45.
[65]Udo Merkel, 'The politics of physical culture and German nationalism: Turnen versus English sports and French olympism, 1871–1914', *German Politics & Society* 21, no. 2 (67 (2003): 69–96.
[66]Annette Hofmann, *Turnen and sport* (Waxmann Verlag, 2004).
[67]Heffernan, *Indian ...* , 177.

and gymnastics as a means of strengthening the next generation against physical weakness.[68] Walsh's study of eugenics and physical culture found that American fitness discourses were intensely linked with questions of class and racial distinctions between white and non-white bodies.[69] The phrenological interest in club-swinging was echoed in American educator Dio Lewis' 1860s work *The New Gymnastics* which enjoyed success in both the United States and Great Britain. Lewis, as Todd found, was a forceful proponent of women's physical culture based, in part, on his phrenological belief that strong women produced strong children.[70] In the same way Walker's books influenced American physical culture, it is possible to find British interest in Lewis' works on women's physical culture. One finds fascinating crosscurrents between European, British and American physical culture. What united them was the practice of club-swinging and a belief that training the body brought physical and moral betterment.

There was, however, money to be made. In 1866 American entrepreneur Sim Kehoe published *The Indian Club Exercise*, a short manual and history on club-swinging. Kehoe's book, one of the most popular of the age, was deeply immersed in the clubs' history. It is worth republishing some of it here.

> As the name implies, the Indian Club is an institution of India. In sketches of Indian life, by missionaries and travelers, we have accounts ... in which mention is made of the swinging of heavy war clubs, of wood, in various graceful and fantastic motions; that the performers of this exercise exhibited great muscular development and herculean strength.[71]

Kehoe also wrote about the role Britain's military played in bringing the clubs to the rest of the world, illustrations found in Walker's book and well-known American proponents. His encounter with Indian clubs came during a tour of England in 1861 when he met British strongman Professor Harrison.[72] Harrison's performances featured the swinging of heavy clubs, similar to those used in India, rather than the sleight clubs Kehoe sold. Kehoe was not the first American to praise Harrison, as the *New York Clipper* published images of Harrison in the 1850s but Kehoe's book illustrated several of the global trends we have discussed.[73] In it we find the pathways across imperial networks and the Anglo-phone pipeline from the United

---

[68]Todd, *Physical Culture ...* , 173–200.
[69]Shannon Walsh, *Eugenics and physical culture performance in the progressive era* (Springer, 2020).
[70]Todd, *Physical Culture ...* , 173–200.
[71]Simon Kehoe, *The Indian club exercise: With explanatory figures and positions: Photographed from life* (Dick & Fitzgerald, 1866), 7.
[72]Ibid., 8.
[73]Heffernan, *Indian ...* , 106–116.

States to Great Britain and vice versa. Kehoe's book coincided with his entrepreneurial effort to mass produce clubs for a general audience. Thus the late 1860s and early 1870s was a time of great commercial output in the realm of club-swinging as 'Kehoe' clubs became a definitive brand.[74]

The period 1860 to 1880, in a global sense, was a high point for club-swinging. One kind finds an increase in books and usage was increasing through recreational and institutional usage. Critically clubs came to be used by those practising Ling, Turner and Sokol gymnastics, the latter being the nationalist gymnastics founded in 1860s Czechoslovakia.[75] Unsurprisingly given a broader sportification of leisure during the nineteenth century, competitions in club-swinging, for men and women, also emerged.[76] Typically done at a national level, club-swinging competitions came in the form of aesthetic competitions or endurance competitions. The most well-known athlete in the late nineteenth and early twentieth centuries was Australian Tom Burrows. Born in Ballarat in the late 1860s, Burrows joined the British military and moved to England in the 1880s where he was an instructor with the Royal Army Physical Training Corps. An all-round athlete, he was proficient in club-swinging, cricket and prize-fighting. His fame as a club swinger stemmed from his ability to swing clubs continuously for hours. From the 1890s to the early 1900s Burrows' engaged in public club-swinging feats for 20 hours without fail, then 40 hours and so on until he reached over 100 hours without stopping.[77]

This feat, which pushed Burrows into a state of delirium, was matched by other endurance club-swingers from New Zealand and Australia. Where Burrows differed was his broader entrepreneurial activities. Attached to the British military, Burrows travelled to Africa and Australasia where he entertained soldiers with his feats. He also made use of these visits to establish business connections, as happened in the late 1890s when he became manager of a Music Hall in Egypt.[78] This ability to leverage imperial connections served Burrows well. In 1898 *Health and Strength* magazine was established in Great Britain (itself being the collaboration between an American and English entrepreneur). *Health and Strength* was not 'just' a magazine but a community. In 1906 the magazine announced the creation of a 'Health and Strength' League for its national and international members. For a small fee, members were given a membership number, and a small brass badge with the slogan 'sacred thy body as thy soul'.[79] It was an idealistic effort but the League helped solidify the magazine's by-then

---

[74]Ibid., 107–115.
[75]Claire Nolte, *The Sokol in the Czech Lands to 1914* (Springer, 2002), 107–115.
[76]Conor Heffernan, 'Born swinging': Tom Burrows and the forgotten art of endurance club-swinging', *Sport in History* 39, no. 1 (2019): 45–73.
[77]Heffernan, *Indian* ... , 195–224.
[78]Ibid.
[79]Alan Radley, *The illustrated history of physical culture* (Radley, 2001), 50.

global audience. Based in London, the magazine welcomed submissions on physical culture from around the world. For obvious reasons, many of the international contributors were based in British colonies. This meant Irish, Indian, Australian and South African contributors were regularly featured, as were imperialist pieces about physical culture in British Africa.

Burrows was a cause célèbre within the magazine and was afforded writing positions. This coincided with his granting of access to *Health and Strength* journalists whenever Burrows attempted a new club-swinging record. Burrows used the magazine to promote his tours of South Africa, South America and the United States wherein he corresponded with League members prior to arrival and offered members the opportunity to speak with him at events. From 1890 to the outbreak of the Great War Burrows travelled to Argentina, South Africa, the United States, Egypt, England and among other locations practising club-swinging.[80] His was an embodied form of the global processes already discussed. What differentiated Burrows from individuals like Professor Harrison was that Burrows never performed with large Indian clubs. The distinction here being that Harrison used a club very similar to those found in India or Persia whereas Burrows' interests were entirely European/Western.[81]

A later chapter on physical culture will explain why club-swinging fell from popularity but here it is sufficient to note that Burrows fame came at a point when club-swinging was beginning to fall in usage. This was in a recreational context where individuals took to physical culture exercises and in an institutional context wherein club-swinging was replaced by gymnastic regimes. Before ending it is useful to discuss the 1904 St. Louis Olympic games which featured club-swinging as part of the gymnastics event. Club-swinging appeared twice at Olympics hosted in the United States, first in 1904 and again in 1932.[82] The clubs used were the European appropriations and the competitors were based in the United States, many of whom were members of *Turnverein* clubs. Its Olympic inclusion serves as an encapsulation of the club's symbolism. They originated in Asia, transformed and were transported across the world. They were even included in the Olympics which was effectively a Western affair.[83] Furthermore, those who competed in it were themselves the product of global fitness behaviours.

The trajectory of club-swinging was different from yoga and judo but the basic premise holds. This was a localized practice which became popularized in recreational practices around the world. Its original meanings were almost entirely absent from the start and, where some did refer to them, it was often in passing tones. The exercise fit a variety of health needs, and seemed to address large questions about men and women's bodies. Furthermore

---

[80]Heffernan, *Indian ...* , 195–224.
[81]'Harrison: One of the strongest men in the world', *The New York Clipper*, 3 May 1856.
[82]Heffernan, *Indian ...* , 178.
[83]Ibid.

it was parallel to, if not part of, a broader sporting movement which was global. This process, an 'emptying' of the clubs as Alter labelled it, was made possible through an intensification of print media, concerns about the body and a growth in exercise commerce.[84] Club-swinging was not just a simple case of transference from India and Persia to the wider world. It was caught up in an exciting and incoherent but powerful conversation between physicians, educators, athletes, coaches, entrepreneurs and journalists about preserving one's health. This same conversation, and the anxieties which fuelled it proved equally powerful in 'emptying' other local practices. For now, it is worth stressing that across territorial borders, the exercises used with the clubs, weights recommended and bodies advertised remained largely static. People learned to move their bodies the same way in different parts of the world, and develop the same muscles. They also, implicitly or explicitly, agreed with the idea that the body now needed to be developed.

Yoga as physical culture?

One of the earliest yoga texts, attributed to Patanjali, who lived sometime between the second century (BCE) and fourth century (CE) distilled yoga as 'the stilling of the fluctuations of the mind'.[85] At the time of writing, it is possible to find thousands of 'yoga' workouts designed to 'boost your butt', 'lose weight', and choose romantic partners.[86] Something has obviously changed following Patanjali. This is an admittedly facetious opening and one which does not adequately describe what yoga is, and is not, within a global context. The first point to note is that many readers will associate yoga with stretching, breathing and perhaps self-actualization but yoga is a broad label for countless variants. Historically yoga, which originated in Asia, was divided into four forms of devotional practice (faith-based acts, meditation, self-enquiry and focusing on the divine).[87] This simplifies a rich and complex history, with innumerable offshoots but it serves as a basic introduction. The paths most familiar to readers are undoubtedly *Raja Yoga* and *Hatha Yoga* with *Raja* yoga being a focus on mental and spiritual practice and *Hatha* being a physical practice.[88] Many modern practices combine the two but here they will be treated, tentatively, as separate phenomenon. The reasons for this lie, in part, in Swami Vivekananda (1863–1902 CE), an

---

[84]Alter, 'Indian clubs … '.
[85]Navtej Singh Johar, 'The contemplative spectator: Seeing as a mode of stilling mind', in Gabriele Brandstetter, Gerko Egert, Holger Hartung (eds.), *Movements of Interweaving* (Routledge, 2018), 321–42.
[86]Sarah Hentges, *Women and fitness in American culture* (McFarland, 2013).
[87]*Karma, Bhakti, Rāja* and *Jñāna* yoga to be exact.
[88]J. Andy Smith, Tammy Greer, Timothy Sheets and Sheree Watson, 'Is there more to yoga than exercise?' *Alternative Therapies in Health & Medicine* 17, no. 3 (2011): 22–9.

Indian nationalist and spiritual leader whose 1896 book *Raja Yoga* has been credited as helping ignite a global interest in yoga. Within *Raja Yoga* Vivekananda made a clean distinction between *Raja Yoga* and *Hatha Yoga*

> We have nothing to do with it here [hatha yoga], because its practices are very difficult, and ... do not lead to much spiritual growth. Many of these practices you will find in Delsarte and other teachers ... but the object in these is physical, not psychological.[89]

We will return to Vivekananda's comments about 'Delsarte and other teachers' in a moment, but for now it is important to stress the complexity of yoga, and global understandings of yoga in fitness during the late nineteenth and early twentieth centuries. While many credit the birth of 'modern' yoga to the interwar period (1919–39) or the 1960s and 1970s, it is possible to find yoga as physical culture and yoga as health practice emerging during our period.[90] Furthermore, and as Singleton and Goldberg noted, postural yoga was influenced itself by a broader global physical culture movement.[91]

With so many caveats, the obvious question is where to begin? The history of yoga is millennia old, although the kind practised from the late nineteenth century onward is of a newer variety.[92] Likewise it is important to note that yoga was not some sort of 'hidden' practice within India and appeared as early as the sixteenth century in European travel logs. It even had an earlier history of migration across Europe.[93] One of the reasons Vivekananda distanced himself from Hatha yoga was because of imperial attitudes to Hatha yoga practitioners who were classed as wandering thieves or dangerous in Western readings.[94] The globalization of yoga has been covered elsewhere, so here we will focus on three distinct but intersecting currents during the nineteenth century.[95] The first is a broader global interest in Indian spirituality and philosophy among Western scholars and spiritual practitioners. The second is the rise of physical culture as a distinct phenomenon and its intersection with local exercise practices within India. The final element is the beginnings of yoga being treated as a fitness practice in European and North American texts. In some cases, this meant using

---

[89] Swami Vivekananda, *The complete works of Swami Vivekananda, volume 1: Addresses at the parliament of religions, Karma-Yoga, Raja-Yoga, lectures and discourses* (Discovery, 2017), 100.
[90] Elliott Goldberg, *The path of modern yoga: The history of an embodied spiritual practice* (Simon and Schuster, 2016); Elizabeth De Michelis, *A history of modern yoga: Patanjali and western esotericism* (A&C Black, 2005).
[91] Singleton, *Yoga body*; Goldberg, *The path* ... .
[92] Ibid., 3–24.
[93] Suzanne Newcombe, 'Yoga in Europe', in Knut Jacobsen and Ferdinando Sardella (eds.), *Handbook of Hinduism in Europe* (Brill, 2020), 555–87.
[94] Singleton, *Yoga*, 74–80.
[95] Goldberg, *The Path* ... , De Michelis, *A History* ... , Singleton *Yoga*.

the language of fitness to describe yoga or the use of yoga within fitness texts. More so than club-swinging, and the soon-to-be-discussed judo, the practice of yoga (and what individuals claimed to be yoga) was changed utterly during this century.

The global interest in yoga and spirituality can be divided into two groups. The first group consists of imperial and academic authors who focused on translating Hindu and Muslim texts. The second group represents a spiritual movement that arose in the late nineteenth century. This movement started in the United States and spread to Europe, representing a different approach to Indian spirituality. This crude distinction helps differentiate some of the ways that Indian culture and spirituality were approached and interpreted by Westerners.[96] One was academic and the other, less so. Brett, the British colonial physician who advocated for the medical use of club-swinging, was one such example.[97] Advantageous health practices, like club-swinging, were explained and rationalized with 'superior' Western medicine. Gelders and Balagangadhara's study of Indian literature and religious texts covers this phenomenon.[98] While knowledge of Indian culture increased among academics and imperial administrators during the nineteenth century, it was often understood through the prism of a Western worldview.[99]

As familiarity with Indian culture grew, through imperial and print expansions into Indian culture, interest in Indian spirituality led to new spiritual movements emerging such as the Theosophical Society led by Russian mystic Helena Blavatsky (1831–91 CE). Founded in New York during the 1870s, the Theosophical Society was influential in spreading material about Hinduism, Islam and Buddhism and held offices around Europe.[100] While it would be incorrect to cite the Theosophical Society as a proponent of Indian culture, its mismatch of European and Asian spiritual ideas was emblematic of a broader appreciation of non-Abrahamic texts.[101] This leads us to a critical moment in the popularization of yoga as a global practice, the 1893 Parliament of the World's Religions. Held in Chicago, the Parliament brought together religious leaders from East and West in the first organized interfaith movement.[102] Present at the Congress was Vivekananda who represented Hindu thought. The ovation he received at the Congress

---

[96]Singleton *Yoga*, 10–20.
[97]Brett, *A practical* ...
[98]Raf Gelders and S.N. Balagangadhara, 'Rethinking orientalism', *History of Religions* 51, no. 2 (2011): 101–28.
[99]Bernard Cohn, *Colonialism and its forms of knowledge: The British in India* (Princeton University Press, 1996).
[100]Peter Washington, *Madame Blavatsky's Baboon* (Schocken,1996).
[101]J.J. Clarke, *Oriental enlightenment* (London: Routledge, 1997).
[102]Alan Neely, 'The parliaments of the world's religions: 1893 and 1993', *International Bulletin of Missionary Research* 18, no. 2 (1994): 60–4.

helped establish him as the 'first Hindu missionary' in the United States.[103] He argued that Hindu thought, and especially Krishna's teachings, synthesized the messages of the Buddha, Jesus and Muhammad. Born into an aristocratic family in Calcutta in 1863, Vivekananda became a monk under the tutelage of his guru Ramakrishna (1836–86) whose religious practice was a mixing of Hinduism and other beliefs. After Ramakrishna's death Vivekananda toured India, preaching his guru's message and deepening his sense of Hindu nationalism.[104]

While Vivekananda's book on *Raja Yoga* largely eschewed Hatha yoga, it is important to contextualize his settings, and relationship with his body. Vivekananda came to spirituality, and to Indian culture, at a time of nationalist revival. In 1867 the Tagore Family sponsored a Hindu Mela, the goal of which was to celebrate and promote Hindu cultures, including sporting culture.[105] This latter point was not a trivial one. From the Indian Rebellion of 1857, if not earlier, British administrators often mocked the supposed effeminacy of Indian men from Bengal, contrasting their 'effeminate' physiques with the 'martial' races thought to reside in northern provinces.[106] Part of the Hindu revival was to challenge Imperial claims about Indian men. From 1857 until the outbreak of the Great War, wrestling and to a lesser extent football, became arenas for Indian men to prove their nation's strength.[107] This began in India, when Indian men wrestled Europeans and in the early 1900s, patrons paid for Indian wrestlers to travel to Europe to compete. One fascinating example of how politically important wrestling became was Indian wrestler Ghulam's trip to Paris in 1899. Accompanying him was Motilal Nehru, a political activist and father of the first Indian Prime Minister Jawaharlal Nehru.[108] The most famous Indian wrestling tour came during the early 1900s when Muslim wrestler Gama the Great (1878–1960) led a troupe of Indian wrestlers across Britain. Defeating several high-profile wrestlers, Gama returned to a hero's welcome in India.[109] There was, then, a significant grouping of Indian nationalists who saw the physical body as a means of liberation. Returning to Vivekananda, his philosophy on earthly matters has been summarized, somewhat unfairly, by later writers as the

---

[103]Torkel Brekke, *Makers of modern Indian religion in the late nineteenth-century* (Oxford University, 2002), 46.
[104]David Miller, 'Modernity in Hindu monasticism: Swami Vivekananda and the Ramakrishna movement', *Journal of Asian and African studies* 34, no. 1 (1999): 111–26.
[105]John Rosselli, 'The self-image of effeteness: Physical education and nationalism in nineteenth-century Bengal', *Past & Present* 86, no. 1 (1980): 121–48.
[106]Heather Streets, *Martial races: The military, race and masculinity in British imperial culture, 1857–1914* (Manchester University, 2004), 18–51.
[107]Ajay Jacob Thomas, 'Reconfiguring colonial hierarchies: Examining the "European native wrestling" debate in the late nineteenth-century India', *The Indian Economic & Social History Review* 59, no. 2 (2022): 171–98.
[108]Ronojoy Sen, *Nation at play: A history of sport in India* (Columbia University Press, 2015), 168.
[109]Alter, *The Wrestler's*, 74–80.

three Bs: biceps, beef and the *Bhagavad Gita*. This linking of physical and spiritual strength was made clear in Vivekananda's message to a group of young Indian men to 'you will understand the Gita better with your biceps, your muscles, a little stronger'.[110]

Vivekananda's appearance at the 1893 Congress was, in Banerjee's estimation, a redefining of Indian manhood that was situated in spiritual masculinity.[111] Accordingly his prayers to the goddess Kali included a plea to make him a man. Likewise Chatterjee and Naha have likened Vivekananda's moral messaging as a sort of muscular Hinduism, which borrowed from the Victorian muscular Christian movement in Britain.[112] Vivekananda's book on yoga has been credited as the first influential text for Anglophone practitioners. Works by M. N. Dvivedi and Ram Prasad, were published by the Theosophical Society in the previous decade but none had the impact of Vivekananda's text.[113] Written as an interpretation of Patanjali, the book emerged after Vivekananda toured Europe, thanks to the sponsorship of American backers. Vivekananda's book stressed that yoga was a scientific practice, one which was part of a broader 'world' religion and accessible to all. Next he claimed that his yoga was not based in physical practices.[114] Concerning the former, Goldberg noted Vivekananda's comparison between the science of yoga with chemistry and laboratory-based science.[115] While the book, written for an American audience, did recommend taking 'certain physical helps' so that the body would be 'sufficiently controlled', Vivekananda's system disavowed postural-focused yoga forms and practices.[116] Hatha yoga, the most physically involved form, was defined as the 'science of controlling body and mind, but with no spiritual end in view'.[117] It offered few benefits for spiritual seekers and was treated as distinct, and lesser, than Vivekananda's system. For keeping the body strong, Vivekananda recommended 'to take care of what we eat and drink, and what we do; always use a mental effort, what is usually called "Christian Science," to keep the body strong'.[118]

While religious differences may well have existed, Foxen has stressed Vivekananda's genius in separating Raja and Hatha yoga.[119] Throughout the

---

[110] Swami Vivekananda, *The indispensable Vivekananda: An anthology for our times* (Orient Blackswan, 2006), 189.
[111] Sikata Banerjee, *Make me a man!: Masculinity, Hinduism, and nationalism in India* (State University of New York Press, 2012), 68.
[112] Amitava Chatterjee and Souvik Naha, 'The muscular monk', *Economic and Political Weekly* 49, no. 11 (2014): 25–9.
[113] Singleton, *Yoga*, 5.
[114] Ibid., 130–40.
[115] Goldberg, *The Path* ... , 100–25.
[116] Singleton, *Yoga*, 15–25.
[117] Govinda Chandra Dev, *The philosophy of Vivekananda and the future of man* (Ramakrishna Mission, 1963), 96.
[118] Swami Vivekananda, *Complete works of Swami Vivekananda* (Partha Sinha, 2019), 76.
[119] Anya Foxen, *Inhaling spirit* (Oxford University, 2020), 220–45.

fifteenth and eighteenth centuries, wandering bands of ascetics disrupted trade routes across India. Under British administration, little distinction was made between ascetic warriors, those who practised yoga and Muslim *fakirs*.[120] Oftentimes these terms were inter-changeable to class a wandering religious man. As the East India Company, and the British government, began to crack down on these wandering groups in India, many resorted to begging and performances, oftentimes incorporating seemingly incredulous postures.[121]

FIGURE 2.2 Note the three men mimicking 'fakir' body manipulation akin to modern yoga practices. Painting by Thomas Loggon, *c.* 1740.[122]

---

[120]Rachel Parikh, 'Yoga under the Mughals: From practice to paintings', *South Asian Studies* 31, no. 2 (2015): 215–36.
[121]Rianne Siebenga, 'Colonial India's "Fanatical Fakirs" and their popular representations', *History and Anthropology* 23, no. 4 (2012): 445–66.
[122]*Wiki Commons*. Available at https://en.wikipedia.org/wiki/Isaac_Fawkes#/media/File:Coloured-Isaac-Fawkes.jpg.

In the popular Western mind, yogis, or those labelled as such, were viewed at best as curios and at worst as criminals around the time of Vivekananda's book.[123] His focus on the science of Raja yoga and its distinctiveness protected his works from suspicion. One review in *The Arena*, a Boston magazine, praised Vivekananda's book for building on the European interest in Indian spirituality and summarizing a system which promised to help readers transcend their mental limitations.[124] Noting that while Vivekananda's methods may not 'seem so rational to us', its labelling as a science gave it some credibility. It made 'no foolish mysteries' and 'put forth its system in a plain and simple manner'.[125] This was the birth of the European and American interest in yoga as practice as opposed to an academic subject. From its publication, the work was published into dozens of languages and enjoyed a large following.[126]

We have already noted Vivekananda's inclusion about 'Delsarte and other teachers'. His knowledge of the Delsarte system was not unusual, as Delsarte's practices had become popular during the nineteenth century, especially among performers.[127] What was unusual was that practitioners of Delsarte's practice explicitly included yogic breathing, thereby bridging physical and mental forms of practice.[128] Named after French singer and orator François Delsarte (1811–78 CE), Delsarte's practices were focused on helping those in the arts connect with their bodily emotions.[129] Delsarte discovered 'scientific laws' about the body and emotional expression after he lost his voice through poor training. Eventually his observations were formalized into a system which was combined movement, emotional expression and a spiritual system.[130] Thomas' work on dance described Delsarte's system as a 'quasi-mystical science of aesthetics' wherein individual gestures held spiritual significance.[131] While we are interested in America's embracing, and ultimately changing, of Delsarte's system, it should be noted that his popularity among dance instructors meant his influence can likewise be found in European contexts. Indeed, several scholars have made clear

---

[123]Singleton, *Yoga*, 70–80.
[124]Gopal Stavig, *Western admirers of Ramakrishna and his disciples* (Advaita Ashrama, 2010), 252.
[125]Ibid.
[126]Singleton, *Yoga*, 70–85.
[127]Walsh, *Eugenics and ...* , 19–55.
[128]Nancy Ruyter, *The cultivation of body and mind in nineteenth-century American Delsartism* (Bloomsbury Publishing USA, 1999), 106–15.
[129]Ibid., 80–95.
[130]Ibid.
[131]Helen Thomas, *Dance, modernity and culture* (Routledge, 2003), 46.

that Delsarte system shaped German and British dance practices during this time.[132]

It was in America that Delsarte's system morphed into a broader practice.[133] In 1877 actor Steele Mackaye (1842–94) established a school of expression where he taught Delsarte's system. Mackaye was well placed, having studied with the Frenchmen in 1869 and 1870, before the outbreak of the Franco-Prussian War forced his return to America.[134] In New York, Mackaye delivered lectures and a system of movement termed 'Harmonic Gymnastics'.[135] While Mackaye was influential in bringing the system to America, his successor, Genevieve Stebbins (1857–1943) transformed it. Originally an actor, Stebbins became an influential teacher of Delsarte's system and produced several books on Delsarte practices. She also introduced her own, and others, ideas into the practice.[136] In the preface to one of her 1890s works, Stebbins credited Delsarte, physical educationalist Dudley Allen-Sargent, an anthropologist and a physician.[137] Later works, like the 1899 *Genevieve Stebbins System of Physical Training* noted her introduction to breathing exercises many associate with yoga. These she learned at a class in London wherein 'the patients were tired brain workers, some of them Oxford professors; the teacher was a Hindu pundit'.[138] She asked for information and soon discovered the 'dynamic breathing' which became a pillar of her method.[139]

American Delsartism introduced physical practice into Delsarte's system. By the early 1900s, Stebbins stated that Ling gymnastics, a system discussed in Chapter 3, was a component of body-work.[140] While Vivekananda dismissed the Delsarte system as similar to Hatha yoga, the blending of breathwork, spirituality and movement was, as Singleton made clear, an earlier indicator of 'modern yoga' practices.[141] The Delsarte system, which mentioned yoga practices and breathing before Vivekanada's *Raja Yoga* was released, was arguably the first global instance of yoga mixing with physical

---

[132]Patricia Vertinsky, 'Transatlantic traffic in expressive movement: From delsarte and dalcroze to margaret H'Doubler and Rudolf Laban', *The International Journal of the History of Sport* 26, no. 13 (2009): 2031–51.
[133]Ibid.
[134]Ashton Kohl Arnoldy, 'Genevieve Stebbins and the philosophical roots of somatics', *Journal of Dance & Somatic Practices* 14, no. 1 (2022): 23–33.
[135]Nancy Lee Chalfa Ruyter, 'American Delsartism: Precursor of an American dance art', *The International Journal of the History of Sport* 26, no. 13 (2009): 2015–30.
[136]Suzanne Bordelon, 'Embodied ethos and rhetorical accretion: Genevieve Stebbins and the delsarte system of expression', *Rhetoric Society Quarterly* 46, no. 2 (2016): 105–30.
[137]Genevieve Stebbins, *Dynamic breathing and harmonic gymnastics* (Werner, 1893), vi.
[138]Genevieve Stebbins, *The Genevieve Stebbins system of physical training* (Werner, 1899), 21.
[139]Foxen, *Inhaling* … , 137–52.
[140]Kelly Jean Lynch, 'Aesthetic dance as woman's culture in America at the turn of the twentieth-century', *Feminist Modernist Studies* 5, no. 3 (2022): 247–60.
[141]Singleton, *Yoga*, 10–22.

culture.[142] But what about those yogic practices which adopted American and European physical culture?

Singleton's claim that 'modern' yoga was influenced by European physical culture systems becomes our focus here.[143] Chapter 4 focuses exclusively on physical culture and global fitness cultures. Here some introductory comments are needed. Originating in the early 1880s, individual practitioners and performers began to use the term 'physical culture' to describe their health interest. While there were no obvious behavioural or philosophical differences between physical culture and earlier terms such as gymnastics or callisthenics, the term gained a powerful social capital from the 1880s to the outbreak of the Great War in 1914.[144] What differentiated physical culture from previous health movements was the celebrity attached to it. Whereas previously it was individual health systems, and the people who created them, which gained notoriety, the physical culture movement saw a shift towards celebrating individuals for their aesthetic appearance or strength.[145] Their body, rather than their knowledge, was often taken as 'proof' of their expertise. This was certainly true of Prussian strongman Eugan Sandow (1867–1925) who came to international attention during the 1880s in England. Sandow has been treated by academics as the world's first physique star.[146] He labelled himself, and was celebrated as, the world's most perfectly developed physique.[147] Based in England, Sandow embarked on several world tours during the 1890s and early 1900s in the United States, and Australasia, including India. The most definitive account of Sandow's Indian tour, written by Watt, made clear the impact Sandow had.[148] Though reaffirming the idea that Indian men were physically lesser than British counterparts, Sandow promised individual and national salvation through physical culture. Focusing on 'dialogue and cultural exchange', Watt outlined Sandow's influence in helping inform contemporary and later health regimes in India.[149] Indeed it is telling that many Indian yogis and bodybuilders who grew to fame in the interwar period (1918–39), were inspired or at the very least tried, Sandow's system following his tour.

It appears that many interwar Indian health experts, be they physical culturists or yogis, used Sandow's commercial apparatus as a template for

---

[142]Ibid., 144–7.
[143]Singleton, *Yoga*, 10–22.
[144]Jan Todd, 'Reflections on physical culture', *Iron Game History* 13, no. 2 (2015): 2–8.
[145]Benjamin Pollack and Janice Todd, 'Before Charles Atlas: Earle Liederman, the 1920s king of mail-order muscle', *Journal of Sport History* 44, no. 3 (2017): 399–420.
[146]David Chapman, *Sandow the magnificent: Eugen Sandow and the beginnings of bodybuilding* (University of Illinois Press, 1994), 1–22.
[147]Ibid., 119–25.
[148]Carey Watt, 'Cultural exchange, appropriation and physical culture: Strongman Eugen Sandow in colonial India, 1904–1905', *The International Journal of the History of Sport* 33, no. 16 (2016): 1921–42.
[149]Ibid.

their own enterprises. This meant mimicking his use of correspondence courses, writing monographs or using bombastic statements to describe themselves. Singleton noted Yogi Rishi Singh Gherwals' 1920s courses wherein the California-based Yogi used postal courses similar to Sandow.[150] Far more important, for us, is the inspiration later figures drew from Sandow's system. During Sandow's tour of India, one Bengal newspaper described his system as an effort 'to concentrate the mind upon the physical effort, so that mind and body may both work together to produce muscular development ... '.[151]

Taken out of context, such a passage would not seem foreign to a modern yoga class. Neither, of course, is the *sūryanamaskār* ('sun salutation') pattern which has become a staple in global yoga classes. The person responsible for its creation, or at least its modernization, was Pratinidhi Pant (1868–1951), Rajah of Aund, and a devoted exerciser. In 1938 Pant published *The Ten Point Way to Health* which has largely been taken as a starting point for the popularization of *sūryanamaskār* within yoga practices.[152] Within it Pant recorded a decade of practice using Sandow's exercises which began in 1897 when 'we purchased all his [Sandow's] apparatus and books'. Another early figure in the popularization of the *sūryanamaskār* was Indian physical culturist K. V. Iyer (1897–1980), who we will be returning to in later chapters. Iyer's physical culture system included the *sūryanamaskār* and he claimed that his exercise systems were an amalgamation of yoga practices and those adopted from European physical culturists.[153] Iyer and Pant were just two of several interwar Indian health experts who cited Sandow, and his tour, as transformational for their exercise preferences. It was for this reason Alter credited Sandow with greater influence over modern yoga than Swami Vivekananda or his contemporaries.[154]

It was not just Sandow, of course, who influenced health practices within India. Equally important were physical culturists like Bernarr MacFadden. MacFadden's American *Physical Culture* magazine often commented on, and featured Indian physical culturists such as K. V. Iyer. Indeed a young Iyer appeared in MacFadden's magazine during the 1920s.[155] Likewise German

---

[150]Singleton, *Yoga* ... , 136.
[151]David Waller, *The perfect man: The muscular life and times of Eugen Sandow, victorian strongman* (Victorian Secrets, 2011), 90–102.
[152]Singleton, *Yoga* ... , 124–30.
[153]Mark Singleton, 'Yoga and physical culture: Transnational history and blurred discursive contexts', in Knut Jacobsen (ed.), *Routledge handbook of contemporary India* (Taylor & Francis, 2015), 172–84.
[154]J.S. Alter, *Yoga in modern India: The body between science and philosophy* (Princeton University, 2005), 28.
[155]Aishwarya Ramachandran and Conor Heffernan, 'Building the transnational "Body Beautiful" KV Iyer and the circulation of bodybuilding practices between India and the United States', *Sport History Review* 52, no. 2 (2021): 279–97.

strongman Max Sick (1882–1961) served as an influence for Bishnu Charan Ghosh's (1903–70) system of muscle control which was redeveloped by Bikram Choudhury (1944–) to create the hot yoga phenomenon, Bikram Yoga.[156] Ghosh's writings have been taken by many to be foundational in the development of basic yoga asanas.[157] Sick's system, which featured acts of tensing and withdrawing muscle groups, was replicated in Ghosh's 1930 work *Muscle Control*.[158] That Sick, an individual strongman who never toured India, encouraged local physical culturists was likely down to the reach of physical culture magazines (like *Health and Strength* magazine), and the British military, as many troops based in Asia wrote to Sick thanking him for his system.[159] This is to say nothing of the impact that formalized exercise systems like the Ling Gymnastic and Bukh Gymnastic systems had in India.

Sticking specifically with Ling Gymnastics, founded by P. H. Ling in Sweden in 1814, Singleton and others have noted its relationship with later yoga forms. While books on the *Swedish Movement Cure* discussed the therapeutic effects of Indian 'bodily exercises' as early as 1860, there was a clear cross-pollination between Ling and domestic physical culture.[160] Indian scholar, and translator of several important yoga texts, S. C. Vasu (1861–1918) likened the yoga asanas within his 1895 translation of *Gheraṇda Saṃhita,* as 'gymnastic exercises, good for general health and peace of mind'.[161] Basu's understanding of gymnastics was likely informed by the gymnastic exercises used by the British military and the role the Young Men's Christian Association (whose first Indian branch was established in 1854) had in promoting Ling movements.[162] Many of the original touchstones for yoga interpretations were informed by a broader and global physical culture movement during the nineteenth century. While Vivekananda was influential in raising global awareness of yoga, the systems which emerged during the twentieth century were an odd combination of traditional and historic yoga terms, practices that were often inspired by European physical culturists.

It is worth examining the few, but illustrative, moments in which Western physical culturists promoted yoga as fitness. We will end with American author William Walker Atkinson (1862–1932) and his books on yoga under

---

[156]Singleton, *Yoga* ... , 132–5.
[157]Jerome Armstrong, 'Uncovering Vyāyāma in Yoga', *Journal of Yoga Studies* 4 (2023): 271–302.
[158]Maxick, *Muscle control, or body development by will-power* (Ewart, Seymour & Co, 1913).
[159]Carey Watt, 'Physical culture and the body in colonial India, c. 1800–1947', in Harald Fischer-Tiné and Maria Framke (eds.), *Routledge Handbook of the History of Colonialism in South Asia* (Routledge, 2021), 345–58.
[160]Singleton, *Yoga*, 80–90; Joseph Alter, 'Yoga and physical education: Swami Kuvalayananda's Nationalist project', *Asian Medicine* 3, no. 1 (2007): 20–36.
[161]S.C. Vasu, *The Gheranda Sanhita: A treatise on Hatha Yoga* (Tatva-Vivechaka, 1895), xxii.
[162]Vertinsky and Ramachandran, 'The "Y" ... '.

the pseudonym Yogi Ramacharaka.[163] Atkinson was illustrative of late nineteenth- and early twentieth-century figures with an interest in the occult and eastern religions. Writing on 'mental science', magnetism and 'new thought', Atkinson's interests were varied. During the 1890s he developed an interest of Hinduism. Vivekananda's influence over Atkinson's writings can be found in the multiple passages which Atkinson plagiarized from the Swami's own work.[164] Nevertheless his 1904 monograph *Hatha yoga; or, The yogi philosophy of physical well-being, with numerous exercises, etc* is still of interest. Written by 'Yogi Ramacharaka' (a fictious name and one open to critiques of orientalism), the book blended Hatha and Raja yoga with gymnastic exercises to recentre reader's mental states and satisfy the desire to 'get back to Nature'.[165] Atkinson should be read in conjunction with Stebbins who appropriated elements from yoga to market, or develop, their training systems. In either instance, the authors adapted what they wanted out of yogic practices, and mashed it together with more generalized physical culture literature to sell products.[166] Unlike the previously studied Indian club, which was used primarily with health, and institutional health in mind, it is difficult not to be cynical about how yoga was globalized by Western entrepreneurs.

Critiquing physical culture 'which has for its object the enlargement of certain muscles and the performances of the feats of 'strongmen', Atkinson promoted exercises intended to be 'fun', playful and 'natural'.[167] Showing his debt to, or plagiarism of, Vivekananda, he compared yogic exercises 'to the calisthenic exercises and Delsarte movements, in favour in the West'.[168] Despite his protestations against physical culture, Atkinson used physical culture movements and terminology under the guise of Hatha yoga. To increase energy and strength into the arms, trainees were encouraged to fasten 'the gaze or attention' upon the arm while making some 'muscular motion'.[169] Such advice was indistinguishable from modern culturists such as Sandow, Sick, Edwin Checkley and others.[170] Atkinson's lamentations that exercise used to be part of everyday life but, due to American industrialization, individuals were disconnected from their bodies was similar to physical culture tracts. In effect, this was a physical culture book, with an orientalist understanding of yoga, written under a questionable pseudonym which presented itself as at odds with physical culture. Atkinson was not unique

---

[163]Singleton, *Yoga Body*, 130–6.
[164]Anya Foxen, *Biography of a Yogi* (Oxford University, 2017), 39–45.
[165]Yogi Ramacharaka, *Hatha yoga; or, The yogi philosophy of physical well-being, with numerous exercises, etc* (Yoga Publication Society, 1904), 9.
[166]Conor Heffernan, 'All muscle and no brains?: Contextualizing the fitness entrepreneur in sport history', *Sporting Traditions* 39, no. 2 (2022): 13–32.
[167]Ramacharaka, *Hatha yoga*, 170.
[168]Ibid., 170–2.
[169]Ibid., 6–8.
[170]Edwin Checkley, *A natural method of physical training* (Bryant, 1892).

as it is possible to find a blending of yoga and physical culture or yoga as physical culture classes throughout the United States, Germany, Spain and England among other nations during the early 1900s.[171]

Yoga, unlike Indian clubs, retained a deeper connection to its place of origin. Whereas the origins of Indian clubs were distorted when they entered the global marketplace, even questionable invocations of yoga, such as Atkinson, rooted it as a distinctly Indian (and non-Western practice). It still retained the trappings of an original culture. Below the surface, however, the same process of transformation occurred. Print cultures, global tours and fitness courses changed understandings of what yoga was. During our period, it is possible to trace the mixing of Western and Asian exercise practices with little regard for what was old or new. This was the case for 'traditional' yogis and enterprising physical culturists or writers. Similarities accounted for, it is worth noting the differences between club-swinging and yoga. The British military was central to the popularization of club-swinging. Once transported to Europe, it became a looser and recreational practice. The connections and bonds behind the spread of yoga were not formalized. Even the Theosophical Society lacked the same institutional might as the military.[172] Yoga was, from an early practice, diffused recreationally, while relying on individuals and groups. Both club-swinging and yoga succeeded in helping standardize body movements, offer seeming solutions to dissatisfaction with modern life and, importantly, promise something more. Differences existed, but once yoga became adjacent to, if not part of the physical culture context, it adopted some of its trappings. Likewise the yogis' focus on spirituality helped certain systems gain a vocabulary and philosophy for its understandings. If one takes Vivekananda's 1896 *Raja Yoga* as a starting point for popular culture as so often happens, it is telling that despite his derisory view of movement yoga, it was this latter form which became the most dominant. Part of the reason, it seems, was that movement yoga already fit pre-existing discourses about the body as a means of individual and national salvation. In time, movement yoga incorporated many of the movements familiar to those with experience of Western physical culture. Was yoga invented during this time? Of course not but, as Singleton noted, 'modern' or 'global' yoga certainly was.[173]

---

[171]Newcombe, 'Yoga in ... ', 555–87.
[172]Mriganka Mukhopadhyay, 'The occult and the orient', *Presidency Historical Review* 1, no. 2 (2015): 9–37.
[173]Singleton, *Yoga*, 1–35.

Judo as global practice

'Modern yoga' was the product of transnational practices but this was largely an organic process. There was no one institution or person who leads the popularization of these practices but rather multiple groups and institutions chaotically adopting the practice for their own means. Judo, jujutsu or jiujitsu (the terms were problematically used interchangeably in the late nineteenth and early twentieth centuries) did not follow this pattern. The practice of jujutsu is centuries old – written records date to the Nara period (*c.* 710–*c.* 794) – but judo is a much more recent phenomenon.[174] We will begin in the late nineteenth century when modern judo was created. Before getting into that however, a basic question to ask is why judo? The answer lies in the depth of judo's popularity. Taking 'modern' judo's starting point as 1882, when Jigoro Kano founded the Kodokan dojo in Tokyo, this sport/physical culture practice spread to North and South America, Europe, Africa and other parts of Asia at an impressive speed.[175] The idea of using an opponent's strength against them proved popular for women's suffragist groups in England, Indian nationalists, American imperialists and many more.[176] Judo instructors, similar to the Hindu and Muslim wrestlers previously discussed, travelled to other countries to show the supremacy of their system. Importantly, many judo instructors positioned themselves as physical culture experts, and judo as a physical culture practice. In 1907, Sada Kazu Uyenishi published *The Text Book of Ju Jutsu as Practised in Japan* with Health and Strength publishing. Uyenishi cited judo as 'not only the finest system of self-defence extant, but that it is also second to none as a system of Physical Culture', and one that produced muscular tone and rapidity of movement.[177] An interesting parallel was William Bankier, a strongman with the stage name 'Apollo', who published *Ju-jitsu: What It Really Is* in 1904. Like Uyenishi, Apollo presented judo as self-defence **and** physical culture.[178]

Judo's global popularity was predicated on its ability to protect the 'weak'. Unlike club-swinging or yoga, its spread was deliberate. The other element of judo's globalization were seismic shifts in *Meiji*-era Japan (1868–1912). The Meiji era was defined by a clear effort by Japan's emperor and

---

[174]Shohei Sato, 'The sportification of judo: Global convergence and evolution', *Journal of Global History* 8, no. 2 (2013): 299–317.
[175]John Stevens, *The way of Judo: A portrait of Jigoro Kano and his students* (Shambhala, 2013), 93–111.
[176]W. Rouse and B. Slutsky, 'Empowering the physical and political self: Women and the practice of self-defense, 1890–1920', *The Journal of the Gilded Age and Progressive Era*, 13 (2014): 470–99.
[177]Sada Kazu Uyenishi, *The text-book of Ju-jutsu: As practised in Japan: Being a simple treatise on the Japanese method of self defense* (Athletic Publications, 1921).
[178]William Bankier, *Ju-jitsu: what it really is* (Health Promotion, 1905).

politicians to 'Westernize' Japan.[179] While initially this Westernization meant a shift of Japanese educational, medical and martial institutions towards Western practices, an eventual middle-ground was met between preserving and changing Japanese culture.[180] One of the larger motivations to this Westernization was to quell domestic tensions and protect Japan from increasing Western colonization.[181] Concerning the latter, the idea was, in essence, to prove to Western nations that Japan was a contemporary. Judo acted as a form of soft power, especially after Japan's victory over Russia in the Russo-Japanese War of 1904–5. Given the multitude of studies on judo in different national histories, we will focus on Great Britain, the United States and South America.[182] In each instance, judo was adopted for a variety of health, physical culture, political and martial purposes. What united this uses was the sense that modernity was troubling bodies, and societies. The solution lies in the disciplining and standardizing of the body and its movement.

Judo is steeped in mid- to late-nineteenth-century Japanese politics. In 1867 Emperor Mutsuhito (1852–1912) succeeded Emperor Osahito (1831–67) and his reign was fixated on Japanese modernity.[183] Osahito's reign was defined by internal turmoil and isolationism from the West. This latter effort was largely futile as, during the 1850s, the 'Perry Exhibition', led by American explorer Matthew Calbraith Perry established diplomatic relations between Japan and the United States. This marked the end of Japanese isolationism.[184] The 'forced opening' of Japan combined with the rise of Mutsuhito brought opposing tensions in Japanese society. There was, in the first instance, a desire for a 'Westernizing' within the country. This was evident in the importation of Western arts, political and legal structures, and sports.[185] There was a flurry of Western literature translations from the 1870s to 1890s in Japan as the domestic market attempted to satisfy an insatiable hunger for texts.[186] It was not just print, however, which migrated. Guttman and Thompson's survey on Japanese sport noted the volume of Western experts invited to Japan to help 'uplift' the nation.[187] For its part, over eleven thousand Japanese students went abroad between 1868 to 1902. They were followed by thousands more labourers, the majority of

---

[179]Daikichi Irokawa, *The culture of the Meiji period* (Princeton University, 1985).
[180]Michio Nagai, 'Westernization and Japanization: The early Meiji transformation of education', *Tradition and Modernization in Japanese Culture* (1971): 35–76.
[181]Ibid., 9–32.
[182]Sato, 'The sportification of judo'.
[183]Marius Jansen, *The making of modern Japan* (Harvard University Press, 2002), 500–35.
[184]Mark Peattie, 'Japanese attitudes toward colonialism, 1895–1945', in Ramon Myers and Mark Peattie (eds.), *The Japanese Colonial Empire 1895–1945* (Princeton University Press, 1984), 80–127.
[185]J. Miller, *Adaptions of Western literature in Meiji Japan* (Springer, 2001), 22–76.
[186]Guttmann and Thompson, *Japanese sports*.
[187]Ibid., 69.

whom went to Great Britain or the United States.[188] There was a clear effort on the part of Meiji and his ruling Cabinet, to emulate the Western-style nation-state. This became evident in the 1880s when efforts were made to establish a new constitution for Japan, and comparisons were made between Prussian, American, French and Spanish examples.[189] A clear privileging of Western gymnastics and sports over domestic practices can be found during this period.[190] Missionaries and invited experts were two of the main transmitters of Western practices. So, on the one hand, the 'forced opening' of Japan meant an openness to globalization.

This was met, however, with an equally strong xenophobic and nationalist undertone in Japanese social and political life. There was, as Doak made clear, a militaristic-nationalistic current that existed in Japan during this period.[191] Nagai explained this as a reaction against the importation of Western 'best practice'.[192] An impulse existed to counter Westernization by creating Japanese analogues to Western rituals and institutions. Parallels of Western culture were needed, rather than outright copies. These give-and-take tensions belied an issue which many Meiji politicians and representatives glossed over when touring Western nations – Japan's transformation was largely driven by self-preservation.[193] Internally, conflicts among military rulers (*shogunate*) created pressure to 'modernize'. This coincided with external pressures from Western powers to establish diplomatic relations.[194] The efforts to Westernize Japan were, to an extent, efforts to avoid the fate of China in becoming an imperial conquest. Ravina's work on Meiji diplomacy stressed the anxiety among politicians and representatives to present Japan as an equal nation-state with the West.[195] This also informed some, but not all, of Japan's expansions into Taiwan and Korea during the 1890s and 1900s as well as the signing of treaties with Britain, France and Russia. This is to say nothing of the Russo-Japanese War of 1904–5 which was, in effect, a moment Japanese rulers had feared, and prepared for, since the 1860s. The war centred on Japan and Russia's rival imperial ambitions. Despite Japan's modernizing processes, a great deal of imperial and racial

---

[188]Michael Weiner, *Race and migration in imperial Japan* (Routledge, 2013), 39–80.
[189]Carol Gluck, 'Japan's constitution across time and space', *Colum. J. Asian L* 33 (2019): 41.
[190]Guttmann and Thompson, *Japanese sports*, 80–97.
[191]Kevin Doak, National identity and nationalism', in William M. Tsutsui (ed.), *A Companion to Japanese History* (Wiley, 2007), 528–44.
[192]Michio Nagai, 'Westernization and Japanization: The early Meiji transformation of education', in Donald Shively (ed.), *Tradition and Modernization in Japanese Culture* (Princeton University Press, 1971), 35–76.
[193]Mark Ravina, *To stand with the nations of the world: Japan's Meiji restoration in world history* (Oxford University Press, 2017), 17–55.
[194]Ibid., 56–82.
[195]Ibid.

ideas about the supposed inferiority of Japanese men existed in the West.[196] That a physically 'inferior' power defeated a Western one in battle, and one with a great military lineage, seemed to prove Japan's status as a world power.

A great deal of discourse around Japan's victory over Russia centred on the use of judo by Japanese soldiers.[197] The idea that Japanese soldiers defeated Russians in unarmed combat misunderstood the realities of modern warfare. Likewise the discourse that Japanese military generals 'used their opponent's strength against them' was driven by orientalist discourses.[198] Nevertheless judo seemed to explain Russia's defeat in popular culture and intensified the West's interest in it. Judo was a product of the Meiji period. It was an offshoot of a much older jiu-jitsu lineage but was clearly informed by Western sporting practices. Judo (meaning 'the way of pliancy') was designed as a modernizing and educational sporting form. Its creator, Kano Jigoro (1860–1938), trained in jujutsu while a student and, in 1882, founded the Kokodan dojo.[199] His system sought to distance itself from jujutsu and create a new form of fighting which could be used to create patriotic and strong Japanese men.[200] This anxiety was one replicated in European and American contexts during the first half of the nineteenth century.[201] Rather than judo, it was military gymnastics which was deemed to be the cure-all. In either case, disciplining and standardizing men's bodies, and how they moved, was implemented at a mass scale.[202] Writing on jujutsu, Kano described it as a dying form during the 1880s and one unfit to uplift his nation.[203] When he established Kododan, Kano's first task was to overcome the government's resistance to martial arts within educational and martial settings. Perhaps unsurprisingly given what we have already discussed, Western physical practices, specifically military gymnastics, was often presented as superior to domestic physical cultures.

The Meiji government routinely 'struck down proposals to allow judo and kendo' into school settings. Kano adopted a two-step method for gaining

---

[196] Rotem Kowner, '"Lighter than yellow, but not enough": Western discourse on the Japanese "Race," 1854–1904', *The Historical Journal* 43, no. 1 (2000): 103–31.

[197] Kotaro Yabu, 'Diffusion of Judo in the United States during the Russo-Japanese War: Aiming to overcome the' match-based historical view', *Martial Arts Studies* 6 (2018): 41–51.

[198] Alexander Nordlund, 'A war of others: British war correspondents, orientalist discourse, and the Russo-Japanese War, 1904–1905', *War in History* 22, no. 1 (2015): 28–46.

[199] Mike Callan, Charlotte Bird, Slavisa Bradic, María del Carmen Campos Mesa, Oscar del Castillo Andrés, Maja Sori Doval, Jean-Pierre Dziergwa et al., 'Global consensus statement; How can judo contribute to reducing the problem of injurious falls in older adults? *The Arts and Sciences of Judo (ASJ)* 4, no. 1 (2024): 14–27.

[200] Yabu, 'Diffusion'.

[201] Roberta Park, 'Muscles, symmetry and action:' do you measure up?' *The International Journal of the History of Sport* 24, no. 12 (2007): 1604–36.

[202] George Mosse, *The image of man: The creation of modern masculinity* (Oxford University Press, 1998), 5–45.

[203] Yabu, 'Diffusion … '. 45.

legitimacy.[204] He co-opted existing martial artists and physical education instructors by awarding them high ranks in the judo network. Second, and in a move replicated when instructors travelled abroad, Kano pitted judo against established fighting systems to show its value.[205] In a historically unverifiable but symbolically important story, judokas competed against jujitsu wrestlers from the Tokyo Metropolitan Police Department. The *judokas* won all but a few matches. Soon after, the superintendent general, Michitsune Mishima, adopted judo as a mandatory course for all officers.[206] What is undeniable is judo's rising popularity. In 1886, Kano's dojo had 98 enrolments. By 1889, 605 new students registered.[207] Kano's reputation was rising as evidenced by a paper he delivered with Reverend Thomas Lindsay in 1888 on 'Jujutsu' to the Asiatic Society of Japan.[208] The audience was a hodgepodge of English-speaking diplomats, businessmen and professors. Kano's paper serves as a nice starting point for our globalization interest.[209]

Great Britain and the United States experienced a surge of Japanese immigration, as well as diplomatic visits, during the late nineteenth century. Such transnational links allowed judo to travel. Whereas judo was brought to the United States by judoka, Yamashita Yoshitsugu (1865–1935), it was Englishman, Edward Barton-Wright (1860–1951), who popularized judo in England as Bartitsu.[210] Working in Japan from 1895 to 1898, Barton-Wright studied judo, at Kano's Kodokan and a rival dojo. Returning to England in 1898 he established his own self-defence system, 'Bartitsu', which combined elements from judo, boxing (English and French methods) and stick-fighting.[211] This mixing of judo with other sporting and self-defence methods was, as we have already encountered, a common occurrence once physical culture systems left their point of origin. What was notable about Bartitsu was how blatant its transformation was compared to say yoga. An apt comparison is the introduction of club-swinging into Britain and the United States which saw a different form of club-swinging emerge under a new name.

Barton-Wright did not bring judo or jiujitsu to England, but popularized it. It was Japanese banker Tetsujiro Shidachi (1867–1946), who published papers on jiu-jitsu and gave a demonstration in 1892 at a time when English poet Rudyard Kipling (1865–1936) was writing about Japanese 'wrestling

---

[204]C. Hurst, 'Kendo', in T. Green (ed.), *Martial Arts of the World* (ABC Clio, 2001), 249–254.
[205]Yabu, 'Diffusion ... '.
[206]John Stevens, *The way of Judo: A portrait of Jigoro Kano and his students* (Shambhala Publications, 2013), 27.
[207]Ibid., 32.
[208]Ibid., 32–5.
[209]Ibid.
[210]David Brough, 'Self-defence with a walking-stick: Revisited', *Martial Arts Studies* 11 (2021): 101–9.
[211]Ibid.

tricks'.[212] It was not until Barton-Wright that the practice gained a popular audience in Britain.[213] In 1899, Barton-Wright began publishing a series of articles in *Pearson's Magazine* concerning self-defence and the role Bartitsu in protecting men.[214] Godfrey's work on self-defence has stressed British fears that the urbanization had made cities, for the middle-class, seemingly dangerous.[215] Take Barton-Wright's article on the 'new art of self-defence', which detailed how to get 'a troublesome man out of the room' and included illustrations of Barton-Wright dressed in his suit disarming assailants.[216] Barton-Wright's claims to have been under constant knife attacks during a residence in Portugal were fanciful but echoed fears that cities were unsafe.[217]

While Barton-Wright held an appreciation for judo, his writings were steeped in racial and imperial logic. Contrasting England and the United States with 'foreign countries', he noted the foreigners' 'quickness to fight'.[218] Barton-Wright's writings held sway in England and Europe. Dutch physical culturist Pieter Toepoel wrote in his 1910 book on jujutsu *Het origineele Ju Jutsu* that he was introduced to Japanese arts after he read an 'English Magazine about an international system of self-defence'.[219] Though short-lived, Bartitsu became globally known thanks to Arthur Conan-Doyle's Sherlock Holmes series. Resurrecting the famous detective from his death in 'The Final Problem', Doyle explained that Bartitsu or the 'Japanese system of wrestling', saved him from death after Sherlock plunged to his seeming death while wrestling archnemesis James Moriarty.[220]

Barton-Wright was clearly appreciative of Japanese judo and jiujitsu. To that end he invited two jiu-jitsu instructors, Yukio Tani (1881–1950) and Sadakazu Uyenishi (1880–c. 1930s), to teach at his Bartitsu School in London.[221] When Barton-Wright's school closed, the duo built careers as Music Hall wrestlers, physical culture writers and instructors. Both taught jiujitsu rather than judo but contemporary discussions typically confused the two.[222] After his relationship with Barton-Wright ended, Tani joined

---

[212]Yorimitsu Hashimoto, 'Soft power of the soft art: Jiu-jitsu in the British empire of the early 20th century', *Questioning Oriental Aesthetics and Thinking: Conflicting Visions of 'Asia' under the Colonial Empires* 38 (2011): 69–80.
[213]Brough, 'Self-defence ... '.
[214]E.W. Barton-Wright, 'The new art of self-defence', *Pearson's Magazine* 7 (1899): 402.
[215]Emelyne Godfrey, *Masculinity, crime and self-defence in Victorian literature: Duelling with danger* (Springer, 2010), 59–110.
[216]Barton-Wright, 'The ... '.
[217]Ibid.
[218]Ibid.
[219]Pieter Toepoel, *Het origineele Ju Jutsu (Dzjoe Dzjutsj)* (Baarn, 1919), 1–6.
[220]Emelyne Godfrey, 'Urban heroes versus folk devils: Civilian self-defence in London (1880–1914)', *Crime, Histoire & Sociétés/Crime, History & Societies* 14, no. 2 (2010): 5–30.
[221]Paul Bowman, *The invention of martial arts: Popular culture between Asia and America* (Oxford University Press, 2021), 49–53.
[222]David Brough, 'The golden square Dojo and its place in British Jujutsu history', *Martial Arts Studies* 10 (2020): 66–72.

the Music Hall scene with William 'Apollo' Bankier. Two years into their partnership, Apollo wrote a book on jiujitsu detailing it as a physical culture perspective. Tani, to his credit, borrowed a great deal from Apollo's theatrical playbook as evidenced by the boisterous public challenges he made to European and Indian wrestlers touring England.[223] Uyenishi wrote a text on ju-jutsu for *Health & Strength*'s publishing house furthering the martial art's connection with physical culture.[224] Highlighting the growing confusion around ju-jutsu and judo, Uyenishi distinguished between the way of judo versus the art of ju-jutsu.[225]

Judo and jujutsu evolved in their uses within England, especially as those brought over by Barton-Wright, and those who arrived independently, tapped into the burgeoning physical culture model. In 1903 Uyenishi established his own dojo in London and, from there, began to instruct men and women. This was not the first instance of women being trained in judo or jujutsu.[226] Kano's instructors in Japan had begun teaching women in the 1890s. Returning to Uyenishi, his Golden Square dojo ran classes for men and women. Some women to train under Uyenishi were Edith Garrud (1872–1971), Emily Diana Watts (1867–1968) and Phoebe Roberts (1887–1937).[227] Garrud, and her husband William, took over the running of Uyenishi's dojo in 1908. William trained men while Edith trained women. Edith became a figure of national and international fame when she became involved in the Women's Freedom League in 1907.[228] As Edith's commitment grew, she utilized her jujutsu skills for the cause. This initially meant music hall exhibitions wherein Edith played a suffragette campaigner who tossed a police officer over her shoulder. When Edith joined the Women's Social and Political Union, she taught other women jujutsu.[229]

Seeking to distance herself, at least publicly, from accusations about planned violence, Garrud echoed Barton-Wright in stressing self-defence.[230] The difference between male and female self-defence within urban spaces was the implicit but significant threat of sexual assault for women. Garrud's writings were found in suffragette materials but she also gained attention in *Health & Strength* magazine.[231]

Equally notable was Emily Diana Watts who published *The Fine Art of Jujitsu* (1906), generally accepted to be the first jujitsu book written by a

---

[223] Simon Keegan, *Bushido: The complete history of British Jujutsu* (New Haven, 2019).
[224] Uyenishi, *The Text-Book*.
[225] Ibid., 1–32.
[226] Amanda Callen-Spenn, 'A history of women in judo', in Mike Callan (ed.), *Women in Judo* (Routledge, 2021), 5–16.
[227] Mike Callan, Conor Heffernan and Amanda Spenn, 'Women's Jūjutsu and Judo in the early twentieth-century', *The International Journal of the History of Sport* 35, no. 6 (2018): 530–53.
[228] Ibid.
[229] Ibid.
[230] Ibid.
[231] Ibid.

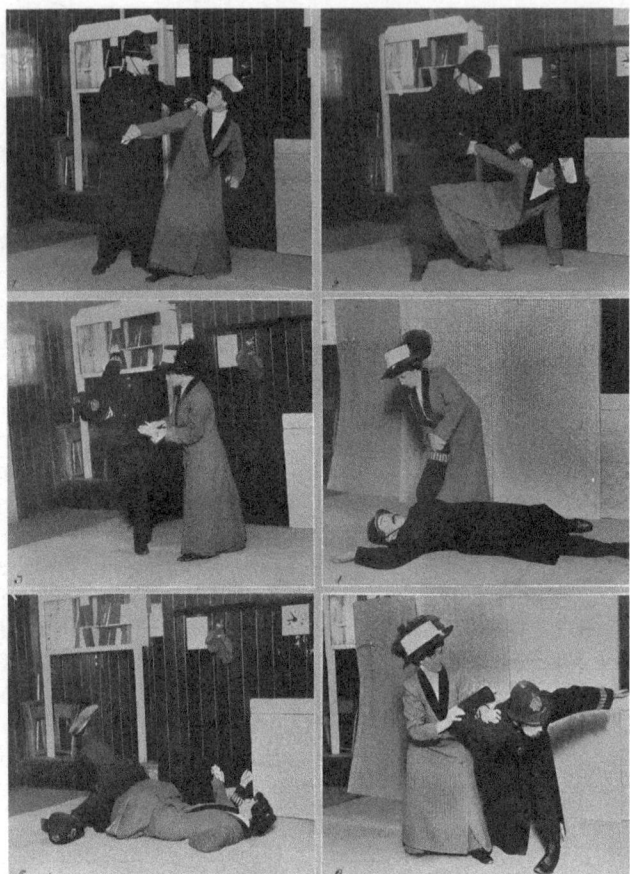

FIGURE 2.3 Edith Garrud jujutsu demonstration, c. 1910.[232]

woman.[233] The book's preface opens with British physician Thomas Lauder Brunton's gambit that *mens sana in corpore sano* before detailing a variety of moves to immobilize opponents.[234] Watts returned to publication several years later in 1914 with a more generalized physical culture book.[235] Phoebe Roberts married a fellow instructor and toured Spain and Portugal with a series of martial artists thereby becoming one of the first women to instruct jujitsu in Europe.[236] While Japanese martial artists were central to the diffusion of judo and jujutsu in Britain, it is telling how much of the sport's

---

[232] *Wiki Commons.* https://en.wikipedia.org/wiki/Edith_Garrud#/media/File:Edith_Garrud_and_a_Policeman.jpg.
[233] Emelyne Godfrey, *Femininity, crime and self-defence in victorian literature and society: From Dagger-Fans to Suffragettes* (London: Springer, 2012), 86–106.
[234] Emily Watts, *Fine art of Jujutsu* (Heinemann, 1906), v.
[235] Diana Watts, *The renaissance of the Greek ideal* (Stoke, 1914).
[236] Amanda Callen Spenn, 'A History … '.

popularization relied on distinctly British fears about self-defence and race concerns.

The timing of the Russo-Japanese War (1904–5) coincided with a high point of British racial anxieties.[237] During the height of the Second South African War (1899–1902) fears abounded British society about the rejection rates among incoming enlisted soldiers due to their physical conditioning. When a governmental committee investigated the matter, they cited issues concerning access to food, living conditions and medical care, but popular discourse claimed modernity and industrialization had physically weakened Britain's populace.[238] Initial losses by British troops to South African forces were explained in battlefield reports noting the South African fighters, hardened by manual labour. Compounding racialized fears were the sporting tours of colonial teams during the early 1900s which resulted in several instances of British teams losing.[239] The Russo-Japanese War, which seemed to showcase how physically smaller nations could defeat their opponents, offered promise for Britain's ailing groups and a warning concerning future conflict.

Similar motivations existed elsewhere. In the United States, American businessman Samuel Hill (1857–1931) invited judoka Yamashita Yoshitsugu (1865–1935) to train his son, thereby marking one of the first judo moments in American history. Hill visited Japan as part of his travels and was interested in imbuing his son with 'the ideals of the Samurai class'.[240] Hill's enthusiastic, though orientalist, view of judo aside, he funded Yoshitsugu's trip to the United States in 1903. His first event was a judo exhibition, by invite only, to politicians and sportswriters before moving on to meet Japanese groups in America.[241] In March 1904, Yoshitsugu and Japanese naval attaché Commander Takeshita Isamu (1870–1949) met President Theodore Roosevelt (1858–1919). Their visit came a month after the first shots in the Russo-Japanese War and marked a piece of 'sporting diplomacy'.[242] Roosevelt became briefly interested in the practice undertook lessons from Yoshitsugu. In one letter, Roosevelt thanked Yoshitsugu for their lesson and praised him for not injuring him as he could not have done his work with Congress 'interrupted by anything unnecessary'.[243]

---

[237]Vanessa Heggie, 'Lies, damn lies, and Manchester's recruiting statistics: Degeneration as an "urban legend" in Victorian and Edwardian Britain', *Journal of the History of Medicine and Allied Sciences* 63, no. 2 (2008): 178–216.
[238]Ibid.
[239]Geoffrey Levett, 'Degenerate days: Colonial sports tours and British manliness 1900–1910', *Sport in History* 38, no. 1 (2018): 46–74.
[240]Yabu, 'Diffusion … ', 45–6.
[241]Ibid.
[242]Stuart Murray, *Sports diplomacy* (Routledge, 2018), 1–14.
[243]*Letter from Theodore Roosevelt to Yoshiaki Yamashita*. Theodore Roosevelt Papers. Library of Congress Manuscript Division. https://www.theodorerooseveltcenter.org/Research/Digital-Library/Record?libID=o290769.

In 1905 Yoshitsugu was given a position at the US Naval Academy to teach judo.[244] This continued into 1906 before Yoshitsugu returned to Japan. Roosevelt was worried that American troops were being surpassed by powers like Japan, hence the Americans needed to learn their rival's fighting style.[245] There is no denying that Yoshitsugu acted as a cultural ambassador for Japan and judo. Judo's founder, Kano, wrote to Yoshitsugu during his trip and implored him to 'do all you can to create a permanent foundation' for judo.[246] The diffusion of judo, in this regard, was more organized and systemized than in Great Britain although the fears about racial degeneracy and global power remained.[247]

Equally similar was the adoption of judo among women in the United States. Rouse's work on judo and jiujutsu highlighted the same concerns about self-defence for women.[248] It also echoed the 'music hall-ification' of judo and jiujitsu wherein Japanese and American judokas began to offer judo wrestling matches as entertainment.[249] What distinguished the United States, and furthered judo's globalization was the publication of *The Complete Kano Jiu-Jitsu (Judo)* in 1905 by Higashi Katsukuma (1881–?) and Harrie Irving Hancock (1868–1922). Katsukuma made his fame as a judoka.[250] He regularly fought against American wrestlers (not always successfully) and was adept at promoting himself. In a 1905 article, Katsukuma praised American wrestlers but claimed judo and jujitsu were the best means of fighting.[251] Importantly Katsukuma's losses against American wrestlers were influential in turning many Americans, and journalists against judo.[252] Hancock is better remembered as a spy novelist author than as a martial artist but it is his judo book with Katsukuma which remains in print to this day.

The duo's co-authored work was a success. It gained national success within the United States and was translated into several languages in Europe and South America.[253] While Kano's empire relied on instructors as proselytisers, Hancock and Katsukuma's work spread rapidly across borders.[254] It was advertised in traditional and outdated terms by the authors.

---

[244]Yabu, 'Diffusion ... ', 45–8.
[245]Weny Rouse, 'Jiu-Jitsuing Uncle Sam: The Unmanly art of Jiu-Jitsu and the yellow peril threat in the progressive era United States', *Pacific Historical Review* 84 (2015): 448–77.
[246]Yabu, 'Diffusion ... ', 45–8.
[247]Estelle Freedman, 'Crimes which startle and horrify': Gender, age, and the racialization of sexual violence in white American newspapers, 1870–1900', *Journal of the History of Sexuality* 20, no. 3 (2011): 465–97.
[248]Wendy Rouse, *Her own hero* (New York University, 2017).
[249]Matt Hlinak, 'Judo comes to California: Judo vs. Wrestling in the American West, 1900–1920', *Journal of Asian Martial Arts* 18, no. 2 (2009): 8–20.
[250]Hancock Irving and Katsukuma Higashi, *The complete Kano Jiu-Jitsu* (Putnam, 1905).
[251]Hugh Leonard and Katsukuma Higashi, 'American Wrestling vs. juJitsu', *The Cosmopolitan* 39, no. 1 (1905): 33–42.
[252]Robert Edgren, 'The Fearful Art of Jiu Jitsu', *Journal of Combative Sport*, March (2000). Available at https://ejmas.com/jcs/jcsart_edgren1_0300.htm.
[253]Stevens, *The way* ... , 14–15.
[254]Kei Okada, 'Jiu-Jitsu beats bodybuilders: British experience of Fad for Jiu-Jitsu and "Physical Culture" from late 19th to the early 20th century', *Japan Journal of Sport Anthropology* 2004, no. 6 (2005): 27–43.

Judo was the 'art of the gentleman' practised by the 'samurai' and warrior classes.[255] Kano was credited not with creating judo, but depicted as one of many instructors. The book opened with Colonel Oliver Wood of the US Military and a praiseworthy report of Kano's judo.[256] Moves were labelled as defensive manoeuvres suitable for men and women. Hancock critiqued those who labelled the judoka's ability to use their opponent's strength against them as 'foul' play, instead marketing the system as scientific.[257] Finally Kano's judo was celebrated for its adoption by the Japanese army, navy and police departments. So successful was it that 'the older and greatly inferior systems have begun to drop into disuse'.[258]

In Brazil naval officers translated the book into Portuguese, attaching their own foreword which warned elites about the nation's future should they continue to neglect physical culture.[259] In Germany, Dr Erwin Bälz translated Hancock's book and, in the forward, noted his own conversion to judo and jiujitsu during his time in Japan.[260] In Bälz's estimation it was 'the ideal form of gymnastics'. Similar to his Brazilian counterparts, Bälz included claims about its national value for the German state. An incomplete but illustrative search of Katsukuma and Hancock's book finds translations in France (1905), Germany (1905), Finland (1905), Russia (1908), Poland (1906), Brazil (1905) and Sweden (1905).[261] This is to say nothing of the reprints and re-editions in several of these countries.

There was one problem. Katsukuma and Hancock's book had no link to Kano. In 1928 Kano visited Berlin where he found the book, adorned with his image. Kano wrote the following message:

> This books says *The Complete Kano Jujitsu* but I should say this book teaches nothing of my Judo.[262]

While Sato credited Kano and instructors as the primary transporter of judo culture, there is little denying the influence of Katsukuma and Hancock's fabricated book.[263] The book reflected a border pattern within global fitness cultures, and one found in club-swinging and yoga. That is the near complete emptying of the form's original meanings and re-interpretation

---

[255]Yabu, 'Diffusion ... ', 45–8.
[256]Carl Brown and Todd Henschell, *American law and the trained fighter* (Ohara, 1983), 67.
[257]Irving, and Higashi. *The Complete* ... , 1–33.
[258]Ibid., v.
[259]José Cairus, 'Modernization, nationalism and the elite: The genesis of Brazilian jiu-jitsu, 1905–1920', *Revista tempo e argumento* 3, no. 2 (2011): 100–21.
[260]Sabine Frühstück and Wolfram Manzenreiter, 'Neverland lost: Judo cultures in Austria, Japan, and elsewhere', in Harumi Befu, Sylvie Guichard-Anguis (eds.), *Globalizing Japan* (Routledge, 2003), 91–115.
[261]Jonesy, 'The Early ... '.
[262]Stevens, *The way* ... , 14–15.
[263]Sato, 'The ... '.

by new groups. This book is perhaps the most fascinating example as what began as a bastardized version of Kano's style was re-interpreted in multiple nations and plugged into each nation's national anxieties and aspirations.

It is worth highlighting the limits of jiujitsu and judo. In this regard, Brazil provides a fascinating study. Cairu's work on jiu-jitsu focused on a 1909 fight between Francisco Cyríaco, an Afro-Brazilian capoeira fighter with judoka Sada Miako.[264] Miako was, at that time, overseeing the training of the Navy's elite corps. Capoeira was an idiosyncratic fighting style unique to Brazil. When Cyríaco defeated Miako it was framed as a battle between the elite and Brazil's working-class. One newspaper contrasted the 'foreign martial art adopted by the Navy, against another, which despite being genuinely Brazilian, remained marginalized'.[265] There were also racial undertones with the 'victory of a mulatto' which was contrasted with the foreign fighter.[266] Racial structures in Brazil were often mapped onto its class system with those of Afro-Caribbean descent viewed as lesser in political frameworks.[267] Jiujitsu, and judo, was associated with the elite, and lighter-skinned Brazilians. Capoeira's superiority was a political victory as much as a sporting one. Public losses set back popular perceptions of Japanese martial arts and it was for this reason that Kano was strict on his judokas avoiding such events. One of the most successful 'judo tours' was that of Mitsuyo Maeda who having travelled to France and Spain embarked on a tour of South America.[268] Trained by Kano, Maeda established himself as the Principal Theater in Mexico where he offered 100 pesos to anyone he could not throw. Following several high-profile matches he travelled to Cuba where he challenged celebrity American fighters Frank Gotch (wrestling) and Jack Johnson (boxing).[269] From 1912 to 1914 Maeda travelled across South America visiting El Salvador, Costa Rica, Honduras, Panama, Colombia, Ecuador and Peru. In Peru, Maeda worked alongside those tasked with training naval or police officers. Maeda settled in Brazil where he became a pivotal early figure in the development of what is now known as Brazilian jiu-jitsu.

Maeda, despite being in contact with Kano, was emblematic of the wandering expert diffusion found in the globalization of club-swinging and yoga. What differentiated Kano's judo from club-swinging and yoga was the formalized approach Kano took in exporting judokas to various parts of the world. Kano encouraged instructors to act as judo diplomats. Despite this, Kano was unable to control judo diffusion around the globe. Judo

---

[264] Cairus, 'Modernization … ', 100–121.
[265] Ibid.
[266] Ibid.
[267] Tiago Fernandes Maranhao, 'Molding the Body, Forging the Nation: Race, Physical Culture, and the Shaping of Brazil (1822–1930)', PhD diss., 2020.
[268] Cairus, 'Modernization … '.
[269] Ibid.

was part of a broader geo-political desire to place Japan as an equal with European and American powers. There is a temptation then to view judo in geo-political terms. The reality is that once it entered the 'global market' of fitness, it was brought into general fears about gender, self-defence, physical culture and racial fitness. This points to a commonality in nineteenth- and early twentieth-century global worldviews. Domestic processes were emptied, and refilled with transnational anxieties.

Conclusion

I have spent the past decade researching club-swinging. What interested me was its ability to explore global fitness practices during the nineteenth century. At face value, it appeared to be unique. A domestic process was popularized and in that popularization bore little resemblance to its origin. I often returned to the importation of 'new' club-swinging into India as a symbol of this power.[270] Club-swinging was not unique. The diffusion of yoga and judo/jujutsu/jiujitsu followed similar purposes. While club-swinging was popularized because of health concerns, yoga was promoted on largely spiritual lines and judo concerning self-defence. Once popularized, they became means for exploring, and solving concerns across borders. What is important to stress about this is how organic this process seemed to be. While institutions are part of this story, it was driven by popular cultures and conversations. This transformation was predicated on the success of commercial and entertainment practices, underpinned by structured approaches.

What can be learned from these cases? First that these practices underwent a consistent pattern of 'emptying and refilling', whereby their original cultural meanings were stripped away and replaced with new significance that addressed anxieties about modernity, health and national fitness.[271] These anxieties were not confined to the West and could be found in Asia and South America. While institutions like militaries and schools were important in establishing practices, their adoption was driven by commercial and popular cultural forces, with entrepreneurs, performers and writers serving as key agents. The globalization of fitness was predicated on the movement of people and products. Free from institutional boundaries it was possible to find a chaotic merging of ideas and contexts. These cases demonstrate the emergence of a global body ideal, as these diverse practices became instruments for addressing shared transnational anxieties about modernity's impact on bodies, revealing how the late nineteenth century witnessed the emergence of a globalized discourse about the body that

---

[270]Heffernan, 'Indian club-swinging in ... ', 95–120.
[271]Alter, 'Indian clubs ... '.

transcended national boundaries while still being adapted to local contexts. This discourse can be centred standardizing how the body looked and moved would solve anxieties about race, health, geopolitics and more. What is clear, from these practices, is that there was, in a sense, a global body. This body, if healthy, provided salvation for individual and national health. This was a body which demanded training and marshalling and was a body which could not be physically frail. The individualization of these concerns, set against national backdrops, allowed individuals to gain celebrity and status based on their prowess. The next chapter examines a more rigid institutionalization of physical culture during the same century.

3

Institutional and international gymnastics

In 1762, John-Jacques Rousseau (1712–78) summarized his philosophy in one line, 'man is born free and everywhere he is in chains'.¹ In 1793, Johann GutsMuths (1759–1839) provided a similar cry for physical education, 'we are weak because it does not occur to us to be strong'.² It is an observation that is simplistic and challenging. Born in Saxony-Anhalt, GutsMuths wanted to motivate future generations to be physically strong. Physical weakness, in his diatribe, was reflective of individual failings but threatened the sovereignty of the state.³ GutsMuths is typically treated as a founding figure in European gymnastics.⁴ His rallying cry for strength reflected a growing institutional interest in physical training. Writing within the context of physical education (PE), GutsMuths believed it was the role of schools to train students. During the same period, European militaries began to take the need to train soldiers seriously. This went beyond marching and extended into gymnastic systems.⁵ Institutional physical culture was one of the most significant shifts in the role of the state during the nineteenth and twentieth century. This is a large claim to make but one born out of new realities. Over the period studied here, physical training in schools and militaries exposed millions of individuals to specified bodily training. Some may have enjoyed it, more may have loathed it but regardless, individuals were trained in these

---

¹David Williams, *Rousseau's platonic enlightenment* (New York: Penn State, 2010), 147.
²Jonathan Black, *Making the American body* (University of Nebraska Press, 2013), 3.
³Heikki Lempa, 'The body in motion: The image of man in physical education in late eighteenth-century Schnepfenthal', in Axel Fliethmann and Christiane Weller (eds.), *Anatomy of the Medical Image* (Brill, 2021), 95–111.
⁴Michael Krüger, 'German sport history as reflected in "Sporting Art"', *The International Journal of the History of Sport* 35, no. 17–18 (2018): 1748–76.
⁵Henning Eichberg, 'Body culture and democratic nationalism: "Popular Gymnastics" in nineteenth-century Denmark', *The International Journal of the History of Sport* 12 (1995): 108–24.

exercises. Aside from sheer numbers, military training can be taken as a precursor to state involvement in healthcare, as the primary motive given for physical training was often to restore the citizenry's health.[6] Modern life and industrialization were thought to be damaging and devitalizing, hence the need for intervention.

A key assertion of this book is that a 'global body' emerged during this period. As a reminder, the argument is that new, and popular, forms of physical culture inculcated in individuals the idea of how an ideal body looked and moved. The globalization of exercise meant that people were globally trained using the same movements. This meant that the physical development of individuals had a sort of homogenizing effect.[7] Physiques and perceptions about physiques, changed. In this chapter, we will see how concerns about gender, race and religion crossed borders, and were often presented as national and international salves. This chapter opened with Rousseau's quote not for its emotional gravitas but because of its impact. Rousseau was not a gymnastics instructor but his writings on education encouraged a new generation of physical educators to bring the practice into schools.[8] One can draw a line between Rousseau and GutsMuths despite their geographical and geopolitical distances. That gymnastics were globalized in the nineteenth century is beyond doubt. Studies have traced the migration of such systems across Europe, North America and the colonized world in Africa and Asia.[9]

This chapter does not focus exclusively on a single training system but on several systems which simultaneously globalized. Whereas recreational practices were often globalized chaotically, institutional fitness were deliberately diffused. Peoples travelled to other countries to inspect systems. Medical books and tracts were written following the encouragement from politicians, governments and militaries. A global consensus, forced and voluntary, built around a simple but pervasive idea. Global histories are replete with observations about transmissions, flows and circulations.[10] Gänger has challenged global historians to avoid vaguely alluding to somewhat magical 'processes' and tease out what it means for something to become a global phenomenon. The problem with vagueness is that it presents globalization as a sort of smooth and unimpeded process.[11] Resistance, false starts and failures plague every global process and the

---

[6]Howard Markel, 'Worldly approaches to global health', *Public Health* 128 (2014): 124–8.
[7]Richard Winett and Ralph Carpinelli, 'Potential health-related benefits of resistance training', *Preventive Medicine* 33 (2001): 503–13.
[8]Eugen Weber, 'Gymnastics and sports in Fin-De-Siècle France: Opium of the classes?' *The American Historical Review* 71 (1971): 70–98.
[9]Danièle Tosato-Rigo, 'In the shadow of Emile: Pedagogues, pediatricians, physical education, 1686–1762', *Studies in Philosophy and Education* 31 (2012): 449–63.
[10]Stefanie Gänger, 'Circulation: Reflections on circularity, entity, and liquidity in the language of global history', *Journal of Global History* 12 (2017): 303–18.
[11]Ibid.

history here is no different. What I do want to introduce, however, is the idea of a global script used to inform gymnastic practices. I am struck, in this regard, by Secord's work on knowledge. In it, Secord asked a pertinent question – how and why does knowledge cease to be the 'exclusive property of a single individual or group and become part of the taken-for-granted understandings?'[12] The previous chapter placed a great deal of importance on cultural go-betweens as transmitters and translators of physical culture practices. Here we will focus on institutions, and imperial institutions as agents in the transformation of physical culture as well as our cultural go-betweeners.

This chapter begins with the philosophical and classical origins of the late eighteenth and early nineteenth-century gymnastic interest with reference to Rousseau, thinkers like Johann Basedow (1724–90), Christian Salzmann (1744–1811) and GutsMuth, among others. As will become clear, the French Revolution and Napoleonic Wars played a critical role in the first 'wave' of gymnastic globalization in the 1810s and 1820s. From there, the chapter focuses on the militarization of gymnastics which intensified in the mid-nineteenth century. Although gymnastics was revived as an educational endeavour, military gymnastics dominated and, generally speaking, military gymnastics routinely influenced the teaching of physical education in schools more broadly. With that in mind, the chapter finishes with a discussion of physical education (PE) and the spread of a narrow grouping of PE systems around the world. Globally, the world looked to GutsMuth and decided to 'be strong'. For some, this was a time of enthusiasm. Individuals were encouraged to be healthier, and bonded over exercise. For others these systems were imposed, often through callous methods. In the enthusiasm to transform bodies, few questioned the utility and outcomes.

The 'modernizing' of gymnastics

To understand how and why gymnastics globalized we have to examine the motivations underpinning it. Here we begin with an examination of Rousseau and other philosophers before discussing the 'first generation' of physical educationalists who put this philosophy to action. The names cited here came to dominate systems discussed in military and schooling contexts. Lest anyone worry that this is solely about philosophy, attention will be drawn also to the wars of the early nineteenth century as a key driver in applying philosophy to practice.

Gymnastics and gymnasium-based practices were not born in the eighteenth century. As many nineteenth-century instructors loved to observe, European gymnastics dated to at least the Greco-Roman period

---

[12]James Secord, 'Knowledge in transit', *Isis* 95 (2004): 654–72.

in the cultures outlined in Chapter 1. Outside of European histories, it is easy to find Asian and African examples of physical training for soldiers and students in the 'pre-modern' age. So no, gymnastics was not born in eighteenth-century Europe but it was popularized and systematized to an unprecedented degree at this time. This continued well into the nineteenth century. To explain how and why this was the case, it is useful to begin with Rousseau. Born in Geneva in 1712, Rousseau's philosophies came at a time when political philosophy sought to question the role of the social contract between a citizenry and its ruler.[13] It is worth contrasting Rousseau's writings with English philosopher, Thomas Hobbes (1588–1679). In 1651, Hobbes published *Leviathan*, in which he argued for a strong ruler who could curb men's passions and maintain order.[14] Pre-modern life was defined as 'nasty, brutish and short'. Unrestricted living would bring *bellum omnium contra omnes* or the 'war of all against all'.[15] Rousseau, in his *The Social Contract* (1762), instead conceived 'natural man' as good. It was society, rather than man's nature, which corrupted.[16] Rousseau's 'appeal to nature' can be crudely surmised as natural methods are inherently more wholesome.[17] The 'appeal to nature' was a through-line in Rousseau's works, including his educational tract *Émile*. *Émile, ou De l'éducation* was published in 1762 and sought to conceive of an educational system to accentuate 'natural' man's inherent goodness and protect them from modernity.

Physical education was part of this process.[18] Rousseau saw the strong body as virtuous and the weak body as weighed down by material affairs. Boys needed to run, jump, 'move about and … shout'.[19] If society wanted to accentuate a man's true nature they needed to let him 'be a man in vigor'.[20] Continuing his attack against a Hobbesian view of the world, Rousseau extended his commentary to women. Inspired by John Locke, and his 1693 *Some Thoughts Concerning Education*, Rousseau saw exercise as a key component in education.[21] What differentiated exercise for boys and girls was the intensity. Writing on Sophie, Émile's future wife, Rousseau stressed the importance of naturalness in education. While Émile's physical

---

[13] Bronislaw Baczko, 'The social contract of the French: Sieyès and Rousseau', *The Journal of Modern History* 60 (1988): S98–S125.
[14] Jean Hampton, *Hobbes and the social contract tradition* (Cambridge University Press, 1986).
[15] Corbera Castellanos, Roger and Josep Monserrat-Molas. 'Potentia eximia & excellentia facultatum: The relation between liberty and power from the Leviathan to De Homine', *British Journal for the History of Philosophy* 32 (2024): 65–78.
[16] Jean-Jacques Rousseau, *Rousseau: The social contract and other later political writings* (Cambridge University Press, 2018), 38–58.
[17] Tosato-Rigo, 'In … '.
[18] Jan Todd, *physical culture and the body beautiful: Purposive exercise in the lives of american women, 1800–1870* (Mercer University, 1998), 1–22.
[19] Jean-Jacques Rousseau, *Rousseau's Émile: Or, treatise on education* (Appleton, 1892), 84–5.
[20] Ibid.
[21] John Locke, *Some thoughts on education* (Bod–Books, 2024), 312–15.

education cultivated strength and force of mind, Sophie was encouraged to be physically active to enhance her beauty and ensure she gave birth to healthy children.[22]

Rousseau was not unique in his interest in strengthening future generations.[23] Where the Frenchman differed was in his connection between PE and birthing healthy offspring. Todd explained that although repressive, Rousseau's writings resulted in a 'new consciousness regarding the need for women's exercise'.[24] Many cited his claim that women 'should not be strong like men, but for them, so that their sons may be strong'.[25] As a final note on Émile, Tosato-Rigo highlighted Rousseau's ambivalent relationship with medical professionals. Despite reading medical literature, physicians play no role in Rousseau's work and, where mentioned, it was derogatory.[26] The bifurcation between physicians and PE was critical during the first half of the nineteenth century, as gymnastic instructors often found themselves educating physicians on exercise.[27]

Rousseau's name became a common one in educational, and gymnastic texts, during the eighteenth and nineteenth century. Part of his fame was fuelled by a growing print economy, which saw *The Social Contrast and Émile*, published widely across Europe.[28] One such individual was Johann Bernhard Basedow (1724–90), a Hamburg reformer who saw in Rousseau a model for educating children. Basedow's first book on education, published in the late 1760s, supported Rousseau's call to nature.[29] His more important work was his 1774 monograph *Das Ekmentarwerk*, a four-volume tome detailing his thoughts on bringing students back to the natural life promoted by Rousseau.[30] Sponsored by the Duke of Anhalt, Basedow put his educational philosophies into practice when he opened a school, the *Philanthropium*, the same year. In its inaugural year, the school devoted five hours a day to study three to recreation and two to manual labour.[31] It was a school open to all students regardless of their sex or religion. Basedow's school attracted a great deal of domestic and foreign interest. Its backers

---

[22]Chloe Louise Underwood, Exercising Virtue (Phd Diss., University of Warwick, 2001), 78–90.
[23]Jenny Davidson, *Breeding: A partial history of the eighteenth century* (Columbia University Press, 2008).
[24]Todd, *Physical Culture*, 12.
[25]Ibid.
[26]Tosato-Rigo, 'In ... '.
[27]Conor Heffernan, *Indian club-swinging and the birth of global fitness: Mugdars, masculinity and marketing* (Bloomsbury, 2023), 63–94.
[28]Robert Wokler, *Rousseau: A very short introduction* (Oxford University Press, 2001), 44–70.
[29]Robert Louden, *Johann Bernhard basedow and the transformation of modern education* (Bloomsbury, 2020), 89–100.
[30]Jan Todd, 'The classical ideal and its impact on the search for suitable exercise: 1774–1830', *Iron Game History* 2, no. 4 (1992): 7.
[31]Ibid., 7–8.

included the Duke of Anhalt, philosopher Immanuel Kant and Russian monarch Catherine the Great. Furthering its appeal was the translation of Basedow's texts into French and other languages during the 1780s.[32]

One of the *Philanthropium*'s instructors, Christian Gotthilf Salzmann (1744–1811), founded his own school in Gotha in 1784. Called the *Salzmannschule Schnepfenthal*, the school borrowed from Basedow's *Philanthropium*, and shared its Rousseau philosophy. PE and manual labour were a core part of the curriculum and to that end we return to GutsMuths. Salzmann appointed the relatively inexperienced GutsMuths to teach PE. GutsMuths held his position for over fifty years.[33] Beginning with similar exercises to Basedow, GutsMuths introduced rope climbing, discus and a variety of other movements. GutsMuth's contribution to physical education was not confined to teaching. It was his writings which garnered international attention. This was seen with his 1793 work, *Gymnastik für die Jugend* ('Gymnastics for Youth').[34] Mosse credited GutsMuths with re-invigorating classical masculinities through the prism of exercise.[35] Lamenting the dangers of modern society, GutsMuth's cited increasing effeminacy among men.[36] This was not the fault of nature, but of society. In gymnastics, GutsMuths wrote:

> We wish gymnastics to act as preservatives against effeminate sensuality, and to steel both the physical and moral man therefore they must be connected with labour.[37]

GutsMuth's text was the 'sound mind, sound body' thesis that had already become somewhat *cliché*. There was something else formulating in GutsMuths' work which was the idea of rigid and rough masculinities created through work. The education system, and society, was making children 'effeminate' and 'hypochondriacal' about health. Worse still were the 'men of fashion' who would eventually 'be converted into women of fashion' if they did not extend their physical labours beyond dance.[38] GutsMuths' system was presented as a 'grand means of educating a whole nation'.[39] The connection between masculinity, nationalism and physical body was woven

---

[32]Ibid.
[33]Johann GutsMuths and Christian Salzmann, *Gymnastics for youth: Or a practical guide to healthful and amusing exercises for the use of schools* (Byrne, 1803).
[34]Johann Christoph Friedrich Guts Muths, *Gymnastik Für Die Jugend: Enthaltend Eine Praktische Anweisung Zu Leibesübungen: Ein Beytrag Zur Nöthigsten Verbesserung Der Körperlichen Erziehung* (1793).
[35]George Mosse, 'Racism and Nationalism', *Nations and Nationalism* 1 (1995): 163–73.
[36]Peter Uwe Hohendahl, 'The new man: Theories of masculinity around 1800', *Goethe Yearbook* 15 (2008): 187–215.
[37]GutsMuths and Salzmann, *Gymnastics*, 185–7.
[38]Ibid., 14–15.
[39]Ibid., 115.

FIGURE 3.1 GutsMuths' depiction of rope climbing and gymnastics, 1793.[40]

throughout his work.[41] 'Gymnastics for Youth' was translated into several languages. Copies appeared in London in 1800, the United States by 1802 and Paris by 1803.[42] It became one of the canonical PE texts of the century.[43]

GutsMuths became more fixated on the strengthening of nationalism through physical exercises. Nor was he the only one to do so. This was

---

[40]Wellcome images. Available from https://wellcomecollection.org/works/wxnc8jhk

[41]Fred Eugene Leonard, 'The beginnings of modern physical training in Europe', *American Physical Education Review* 9, no. 2 (1904): 96.

[42]Ibid.

[43]Lempa, *Beyond* ... , 76–100.

influenced by the tumultuous geo-political climate of late eighteenth and early nineteenth-century Europe. In 1789, revolution erupted across France. The French Revolution (1789–99) was a disjointed and terrifying period in history wherein old structures and regimes fell, replaced by ideological charged but at times optimistic efforts to reshape the world.[44] Here, the Revolution, overthrow of King Louis XVI and the reign of Maximilien Robespierre matter little. It is the immediate aftermath of the revolution and the rise of Napoleon Bonaparte (1769–1821) that nudged the course of fitness history.[45]

Elected as First Consul of the French Republic in 1799, and fighting against a series of European coalitions, Napoleon's successes continued until 1813 when he was beaten at the Battle of Leipzig.[46] The years until his death in 1821 were spent attempting to reclaim his former glories. Napoleon and his generals' successes were down to a series of factors but a critical issue, and one raised by rivals, was his army's physical hardiness.[47] A common but successful tactic was *la manoeuvre sur les derrieres* wherein one fraction of Napoleon's army were placed in front of forces who had to confront them or retreat. As this was occurring, a larger army advanced from behind.[48] Napoleon was not the first general to conceive of this but he, and his generals, used it to great success. The ability to move troops around the field was predicated on some form of physical training. It is here we turn to Guillaume Philibert (1766–1815), a commander, writer and politician under Napoleon. In 1814, Philibert wrote *Essai sur l'infanterie légère* or 'Essay on Light Infantry'.[49] Within it, Philibert devoted a chapter to the typical *éducation physique du soldat* which included running, forced marching, jumping and performing manoeuvres. Physical education, which pertained to the 'body, its strength and its flexibility' was a core component and a link was drawn from physical strength to France's military success.[50] *Essai sur l'infanterie légère* provided a second philosophical impetus for training. Rousseau and GutsMuth linked it to freedom from societal constraints. The French military linked it to battle.

It was not just Napoleon's military who took heed of physical training. GutsMuths and other instructors, humiliated by their state's losses to France, turned to gymnastics. It is at this point we discuss Friedrich Ludwig Jahn (1778–1852). Jahn was a Prussian educator who joined the Prussian

---

[44]Gail Bossenga, 'Origins of the French revolution', *History Compass* 5 (2007): 1294–337.
[45]Robert Asprey, *The rise of Napoleon Bonaparte* (Hachette, 2008).
[46]Peter Hofschröer, *Leipzig 1813* (Bloomsbury, 2012).
[47]Alan Forrest, *Napoleon's Men: The soldiers of the revolution and empire* (A&C Black, 2002), 154.
[48]David Chandler, *The campaigns of Napoleon* (Simon & Schuster, 2009), 67–100.
[49]Guillaume Philibert Duhesme, *Essai Sur L'infanterie Légère, Ou Traité Des Petites Opérations De La Guerre, À L'usage Des Jeunes Officiers: Avec Cartes Et Plans* (Michaud, 1814).
[50]Ibid., 202–6.

army after Napoleon's forces overrun a joint Prussian-Saxon army.[51] In 1807, Prussia and Russia signed the Treaty of Tilsit with Napoleon in which Prussia ceded land and the French created a series of client states.[52] Defined as a nation with a great military lineage, Prussia's defeat sparked a new wave of nationalism.[53] Efforts to reform military and education system following 1807 were centred on restoring national pride and sparking nationalist fervour.[54] Jahn was swept up in this sentiment.[55] In 1810, Jahn published *Deutsches Volkstum* ('The German Nation'). A rallying cry against French occupation, *Deutsches Volkstum* was consumed by a fascination with the *Volk* ('the people'), an unidentifiable force of individuals with the potential to act towards a collective good.[56] Quoting fitness writers from GutsMuths to Mercurialis, Jahn's book was a polemical call for Prussian nationalism which, crucially, connected gymnastics to the nation-state.[57] Where GutsMuths focused on education and gender, Jahn connected gymnastics to national pride and identity. Like GutsMuths, he attacked the vices of the aristocracy and looked towards as education system which would renew Prussia.[58] Eisenberg saw within *Deutsches Volkstum* a near singular goal to spread the 'idea of an army recruited from the people' and an eventual revolt against French influence.[59]

In 1811, Jahn sequestered several acres of land from the Prussian army to create a dedicated training space known as the *Turnplatz* (an open-air gymnasium).[60] The *Turnplatz* provided a space for Jahn to refine his system, give demonstrations and train mass groups of people. It is estimated that in 1813, 10,000 spectators watched a demonstration of 500 Turners.[61] By 1817, between 1,400 and 1,600 Turners trained at the *Turnplatz* and there is evidence of Turner societies in other German states.[62] Jahn connected gymnastics to national salvation. So too, incidentally did GutsMuths who, as we have covered, was initially more concerned with masculinity. Writing two years after the Congress of Vienna (1814–15), a post-Napoleonic treaty designed to reshape Europe, GutsMuths wrote that

---

[51]Christopher Thomas Goodwin, 'Surviving crisis: The Napoleonic upheavals and the "Time of the French" as cultural Trauma in Prussia, 1806–1812', *War & Society* 41 (2022): 1–20.
[52]Ibid, 1–2.
[53]Ibid., 1–20.
[54]Christiane Eisenberg, 'Charismatic nationalist leader: Turnvater Jahn', in Pierre Lanfranchi, Richard Holt and J.A. Mangan (eds.), *European Heroes* (Routledge, 2013), 14–27.
[55]Ibid.
[56]Ibid.
[57]Friedrich Ludwig Jahn, *Deutsches Volksthum* (Comp., 1810), 250–2.
[58]Rolland Ray Lutz, 'Father jahn and his teacher-revolutionaries from the German student movement', *The Journal of Modern History* 48 (1976): 1–34.
[59]Eisenberg, 'Charismatic ... '.
[60]Ibid.
[61]Ibid., 19.
[62]Ibid., 23.

The defence of freedom and independence of a people is founded on God but also on the *physical and intellectual power* [emphasis added] of a true national character.[63]

Jahn's Turner system found later parallels in Czechoslovakia where the Sokol system of gymnastics emerged in the 1860s on a nationalist and cultural revivalist ethos.[64]

Translation of Jahn's books was accompanied by foreign media reporting on the Turners very early into the 1810s.[65] This raised awareness of Jahn's system and it was further popularized by the spread of physical educationalists across Europe who paid homage to him. Interestingly, when discussing Jahn's system outside of Prussia, European authors often ignored, or downplayed, its nationalist ethos, similar to the 'emptying' processes of physical culture practices discussed previously. Individuals focused on movements and mechanisms but, when brought overseas, the initial messages were lost. Equally important in the diffusion of Jahn's systems was the migration of turners. In the late 1810s, Jahn was imprisoned by Prussian authorities for his political beliefs. This led to an exodus of Turners across Europe and North America seeking to escape persecution.[66] This pattern arose again in the 1840s when, in the wake of the 1848 European uprisings, turners faced persecution following the involvement of many turners in rebellion. Migration processes accelerated the spread of Turner systems and philosophies and resulted in the creation of Turner expat communities in other countries.[67]

Jahn's system was one of two popular gymnastic protocols in the nineteenth century. The other was the Ling model. Named after Per-Henrik Ling (1776–1839), Ling's model had four components with different groups in mind: students, medical patients, soldiers and general trainees.[68] Born in Sweden, Ling undertook theology at Lund University in 1793 and travelled Europe for several years, beginning in Denmark where he served in the military and continued his studies.[69] It was here where Ling trained under Franz Nachtegall (1777–1847). Nachtegall opened his gymnasium in Copenhagen in 1799. He subsequently taught gymnastics to the German military and was appointed as a professor of gymnastics

---

[63]Johann GutsMuths, *Turnbuch Für Die Söhne Des Vaterlandes* (Wilmans, 1817), xvi.
[64]Claire Nolte, *The Sokol in the Czech Lands to 1914* (Palgrave Macmillan, 2002).
[65]Fred Eugene Leonard, 'Friedrich Ludwig Jahn, and the development of popular Gymnastics (Vereins-Turnen) in Germany', *American Physical Education Review* 10 (1905): 1–19.
[66]Annette Hoffmann and Gertrud Pfister, 'Tunen – a forgotten movement culture', in Annette Hoffmann (ed.), *Turnen And Sport* (Verlag, 2004), 11–24.
[67]Annette Hoffmann and Gerald Gems, eds., *Turnen around the world* (Lexington, 2023).
[68]Oswald Holmberg, 'Per Henrik Ling: His life and gymnastic principles', *Physical Educator* 1 (1940): 77–80.
[69]Jens Ljunggren, *A political history of sport in Sweden* (Springer, 2024), 39–60.

at Copenhagen University.[70] For our purposes, Nachtegall is significant in spreading GutsMuths system in Denmark and introducing Ling to it. Under Nachtegall, Ling developed interest in GutsMuths' system and took a personal appreciation in gymnastics. Ling grew doubly interested in gymnastics when he used gymnastics to cure a gout problem.[71]

In 1804, Ling returned to Sweden as a fencing master. Over time, his profile grew and, in 1813 Ling was granted permission by the Swedish government to create a Royal Gymnastic Central Institute (GCI).[72] The following year, a degree from the institute became a prerequisite for anyone seeking to teach in a public school. By 1820, gymnastics was an obligatory subject in Swedish Grammar schools, and for all schools by 1842.[73] Ling impressed on the Swedish government the idea of the body as a machine, which moved 'according to certain mechanical laws'.[74] Such an idea was common in appeals to 'modern' methods during the nineteenth century and the idea of a body controllable by rational laws.[75] Additionally, Ling's institute came at a time when geo-political concerns prompted the Swedish government to physically strengthen the populace for fear of conflict. The Institute's charter promised to 'educate skilled teachers for the diffusion of gymnastics ... for citizens in general and for the state of war'.[76] Ljunggren contrasted Ling with Jahn in two fundamental ways. Ling was sponsored by the State, whereas Jahn was a voluntary zealot. Second, Ling conceptualized the body in far more scientific and rational ways. Or at least used language to intimate as much.[77]

In 1836, Ling published *Reglemente* för *Gymnastik* which argued for the need to see the body as one entity. 'Real power' was found in the 'uniformity among all parts of the body' and the purpose of gymnastics was to bring equal strength to all body parts.[78] Books on bayonet fencing as well as a book on training soldiers were released.[79] Similar to Jahn, Ling's system spread through the movement of texts and trainers. During the 1830s, the GCI sent instructors abroad as quasi-missionaries for Ling's system. This evolved into formal exchanges with other countries wherein individuals from Europe

---

[70]Ibid.
[71]Ibid.
[72]Suzanne Lundvall, 'From ling gymnastics to sport science', *The International Journal of the History of Sport* 32, no. 6 (2015): 789–99.
[73]Johannes Westberg, "Girls' Gymnastics in the service of the nation', *Nordic Journal of Educational History* 4 (2017): 47–69.
[74]Ljunggren, *A Political History*, 39–60.
[75]Vanessa Heggie, 'Bodies, sport and science in the nineteenth-century', *Past & Present* 231 (2016): 169–200.
[76]Ljunggren, *A Political History*, 39–45.
[77]Lundvall, 'From ... '.
[78]P.H. Ling, *Reglemente För Gymnastik* (Trycker, 1836).
[79]Fred Eugene Leonard, 'Per Henrik Ling, and his successors at the stockholm normal school of gymnastics', *American Physical Education Review* 9, no. 4 (1904): 227–43.

or the Americas came and trained in the Ling system while simultaneously demonstrating other gymnastic systems.[80] This created an institutionalized form of knowledge exchange. What aided Ling's system as a global entity was its multifaceted nature and what many saw as its relatively apolitical nature. In particular, Ling gymnastics was the preferred training system for women among many instructors during the 1840s and 1850s as it was perceived to be a gentler system.[81] To that end, the GCI created pathways for female instructors in the 1860s.[82] It would be ridiculous to say Turner and Ling were the only systems of importance during the nineteenth century. Scholars of Sokol and Danish gymnastics, in particular, would take me to task for suggesting it.[83] Turner and Ling did, however, have the greatest global influence and it is for that reason that we examine their diffusion.

The growth of military gymnastics

A defining feature of militaries across the nineteenth century was their adoption of gymnastic programmes. Given the number of men who served in European, North American and Asian forces, it is difficult to underplay the importance of this shift from a physical culture perspective. Here we will examine the early experiments in military gymnastics in the first half of the nineteenth century before examining its formalization from the mid-century in Europe. From there, British military gymnastics are studied as a portal into discussions of colonial and non-Western experiences. This strain of physical culture began with a simple premise, how to measure and improve troop health. From there, it evolved into a global form of exercise, physical development and panics about troop health.

French, British and other European armies began to measure and institute height measurements for soldiers during the eighteenth century with the French first studying soldiers' heights wholesale in 1716.[84] Obviously, physical requirements varied on necessity. Curtis' study of the British military during the American Revolutionary War (1775–83) noted a significant relaxation in height requirements for British soldiers to meet

---

[80]Pia Lundquist Wanneberg, 'Gymnastics as remedy: A study of nineteenth-century Swedish Medical Gymnastics', *Athens Journal of Sports* 5 (2018): 33–52.
[81]Johannes Westberg, 'Adjusting Swedish Gymnastics to the female nature: Discrepancies in the gendering of girls' physical education in the mid-nineteenth-century', *Espacio, Tiempo Y Educación* 5 (2018): 261–79.
[82]Westberg, 'Girls' ... '.
[83]Henning Eichberg, 'Body culture and democratic nationalism: "Popular Gymnastics" in nineteenth-century Denmark', *The International Journal of the History of Sport* 12 (1995): 108–24.
[84]John Komlos and Francesco Cinnirella, 'European heights in the early 18th century', *Vswg: Vierteljahrschrift Für Sozial-Und Wirtschaftsgeschichte* (2007): 271–84.

demands for bodies.⁸⁵ From the mid-nineteenth century, soldiers' physical measurements began to include chest sizes.⁸⁶ The nineteenth century was a period when attention shifted away from the length of one's physique to rather its bulk. This coincided with, and was encouraged by, the gymnastic revolution of the nineteenth century.⁸⁷ One of the first military studies of chest size was published in 1817. The 'Statement of the sizes of men' was taken from local militias and promised to reveal the influence climate, food and occupation had on bodies.⁸⁸ The study was revisited by Belgian statistician Adolphe Quetelet (1796–1874) to aid in the creation of 'normal' averages for physique sizes.⁸⁹ Critically, many military gymnasts used soldiers' physical improvements as proof of their system's value. While militaries around Europe and North America did not formally introduce physical culture programmes until the mid-century, there were some early efforts worth discussing, such as P. H. Clias in Britain.

In 1820, Swiss instructor Phokion Heinrich Clias (1782–1854 CE) met Britain's ambassador. The ambassador, concerned about his son's condition, asked Clias to restore the boy's health. Four years previously, in 1816, Clias published his first gymnastics book, *Anfangsgrnde der Gymnasik oder Turnkunst*.⁹⁰ Clias' book presented gymnastics as a necessary platonic to the corrupting vices resident in Switzerland noting, 'strength and agility of the body, courage, and presence of mind, are the most precious qualities of a people ... '.⁹¹

References were made to ancient Athens and Rome and to GutsMuth's 1793 work on gymnastics.⁹² It mixed military, health and educational concerns and presented his system as the cure for weak and unpatriotic bodies. Had Clias remained in Bern, this book would have been an acutely nationalist but uninteresting one. A follow-up text, published in French in 1819 (*Principes de gymnastique*), proved less politically charged but unremarkable.⁹³ Clias' encounter with the ambassador forces us to view his first text in another light. Once the ambassador's son recovered, Clias was

---

⁸⁵Edward Ely Curtis, *The organization of the British army in the American revolution* (Mich., 1926), 59–70.
⁸⁶Heinrich Hartmann, *The body populace: Military statistics and demography in Europe before the First World War* (MIT Press, 2019), 70–99.
⁸⁷Park, 'Muscles ... '.
⁸⁸Adolphe Quetelet, 'Statement of the sizes of men in different counties of Scotland, taken from the local Militia', *Edinburgh Medical and Surgical Journal* 13 (1817): 260–4.
⁸⁹Elise Smith, '"Why do we measure mankind?" Marketing anthropometry in late-Victorian Britain', *History of Science* 58 (2020): 142–65.
⁹⁰Jan Todd, *Physical culture and the body beautiful: Purposive exercise in the lives of American women, 1800–1870* (Mercer University Press, 1998), 63–81.
⁹¹P.H. Clias, *Anfangsgründe Der Gymnastik Oder Turnkunst* (Jj Burgdorfer Kunst-Und Buchhändler, 1816), 3.
⁹²Ibid., 10–12.
⁹³P.H. Clias, *Gymnastique Élémentaire Ou Cours Analytique Et Gradué ...* (L. Colas, 1819).

appointed Superintendent of Physical Training for the Royal Military and Naval Academies for the British army in 1822.[94] Alongside his military duties, Clias published another book, opened a school and trained instructors, including England's first female gymnastic instructor, Marian Mason.[95] Clias book enjoyed several re-editions while his public demonstrations were, in one historian's estimation, positively electrifying.[96] Contrasting his English book from *Anfangsgrnde der Gymnasik* highlights a shift in Clias' approach. Gone were invocations to the fatherland. Instead, Clias' system promised to strengthen British physiques which, although unsurpassed in intellect, were physically lacking.[97] Removed from his homelands, Clias resorted to generic concerns about health.

In terms of impacting the broader trajectory of military gymnastics, Clias' influence was muted as he returned to mainland Europe after three (possibly four) years in England.[98] A more impactful starting point for military gymnastics, which evolved into an institutional system, can be found in Spanish-French instructor Francisco Amorós y Ondeano. Amorós (1770–1848), who was a critical figure in the formalization of gymnastics. Born in Valencia, Amorós served under Spanish king, Charles IV where he was director of the *Real Instituto Militar Pestalozziano de Madrid*, a Spanish military institute created in 1805 to train students in callisthenics.[99] In 1808, Napoleon's forces defeated Spain, dethroned Charles and replaced him as monarch.[100] Amorós transitioned into a new role under French rule and enjoyed a series of political titles.[101] In 1813, Amorós moved to Paris as a political refugee where he wrote political tracts, established educational institutes and wrote gymnastic texts.

Amorós opened a gymnasium in 1817, which raised the interest of the French minister involved in public education. Next, in 1819, Amorós published *Gymnase civil français*, a pamphlet concerning civilian and military gymnastics which enjoyed several re-editions.[102] Like Jahn, Amorós' pamphlet linked gymnastics to national salvation. Despite being about educational gymnastics, Amorós's work was more concerned with the

---

[94]Todd, *Building* ... , 63–81.
[95]Conor Heffernan, '"An elegant and able practitioner." Marian Mason and the rise of women's calisthenics in nineteenth-century Britain', *Sport in History* (2024): 1–17.
[96]Todd, *Building* ... , 63–81.
[97]P.H. Clias, *An elementary course of gymnastic exercises: Intended to develope and improve the physical powers of man; with the report made to the medical faculty of Paris on the subject; and a new and complete treatise on the art of swimming* (London, 1825).
[98]Todd, *Building* ... , 63–81.
[99]Rafael Fernández Sirvent, *Francisco Amorós Y Los Inicios De La Educación Física Moderna: Biografía De Un Funcionario Al Servicio De España Y Francia* (Universidad De Alicante, 2005), 60–76.
[100]Sirvent, *Francisco* ... , 106–10.
[101]Ibid., 106–45.
[102]Ibid., 217–26.

nation-state and military.[103] Later editions, found in the 1820s and 1830s, included transcripts from Amorós's speeches which included statements like 'gymnastics adds to the courage of soldiers'.[104] Also in 1819, Amorós established a gym for firefighters and, in 1820 a *Gymnase Normal Militaire* was created with Amorós as its director.[105] Amorós remained in this capacity for the rest of his working life and in 1830 created his training opus, *Manuel d'éducation physique, gymnastique et moral*.[106] *Nouveau Manuel* was clear that *des résultats de ce genre sont d'une utilité incalculable à l'armée* ('results produced by gymnastics were invaluable for the military)'.[107] Clias and Amorós, despite their differing biographies, both proved successful as cultural transmitters of a broader gymnastics revolution. They were widely read, appropriated systems from different countries and created lineages for their systems.

It was Amoros' 'disciples', Napoléon Laisné (1810–96) and Commander d'Argy (1805–70), who furthered his vision. In 1852, the *Ecole de Joinville* military school was established with Amoros' system as its guide.[108] Acknowledging that Amoros' system was guided and influenced by Swiss gymnast Johann Heinrich Pestalozzi, they noted a desire to distinguish the 'French method' of gymnastics from other European systems. Like Ling's Institute, it became the critical hub for knowledge and, it was the gymnastics systems at the *Ecole* which came to be used for the later institutionalization of PE in French schools.[109] Few critics of Amorós' existed. The same could not be said for Prussia. From the 1820s to 1840s, *turner* gymnastics were effectively banned in Prussia owing to their political nature. Hope that it would be embraced fully in its homeland returned in 1842 when Prussian King Frederick William IV (1795–1861) paved the way for the reinstitution of gymnastics in institutional settings.

This, itself, was the consequence of reports in the late 1830s that Prussian children were weak.[110] While it seemed an obvious decision to turn back to the *turner* system, vocal opponents existed. This was on both ideological

---

[103]Francisco Amorós, *Gymnase Normal, Militaire Et Civil, Idée Et État De Cette Institution Au Commencement De L'année 1821* (Imprimerie, 1821).
[104]Francisco Amoros, *Manuel D'éducation Physique, Gymnastique Et Morale* (Roret, 1830), 145.
[105]Sirvent, *Francisco ...* , 254–60.
[106]Amoros, *Manuel ...* .
[107]Ibid., 9.
[108]Grégory Quin, 'A professor of Gymnastics in hospital. Napoléon Laisné (1810–1896) introduce Gymnastics at the «Hôpital Des Enfants Malades»', *Staps* 4 (2009): 79–91.
[109]Jean Saint-Martin and Michaël Attali, 'The joinville school and the institutionalization of a French-style physical education, 1852–1939', *The International Journal of the History of Sport* 32 (2015): 740–53.
[110]Roland Naul, 'History of sport and physical education in Germany, 1800–1945', in Ken Hardman and Roland Naul (eds.), *Sport and Physical Education in Germany* (Routledge, 2005), 15–27.

and pedagogical grounds and while other gymnastic systems existed, a decision was taken by the Prussian military to look abroad for inspiration.[111] Prussia was not unique. Its geopolitical rival, Russia adopted Prussian and Swedish gymnastics in the first half of the century before eventually adopting the Sokol gymnastics system at the end of the century.[112] What made Prussia case so interesting was that it was home to one of the most global gymnastics systems in the turners. In 1845, the General Hermann von Boyen (1771–1848) sent two men, Hugo Rothstein (1810–65) and Gustav Techow (1813–90), to Sweden to investigate Ling's system. They subsequently spent three months at the Danish Royal Central Institute (established 1806) where they underwent further training.[113] Rothstein was passionate about the Ling system and, to that end, wrote a 300-page manual advocating its usage in 1847.[114] This coincided with the first gymnastic course held for Prussian military personnel as overseen by a newly created Central Gymnastic Institute.[115] Rothstein and Techow's reports were vital in gaining support for the creation of a new gymnastic institute for Prussia's military. As the Institute's director, Rothstein oversaw the purging of *turner* 'relics' from Prussia.[116] A key distinction between the Ling system favoured by Rothstein and the *turner* system was that the latter required apparatus. It is difficult to overstate Rothstein's enthusiasm for Ling. Not only did he advocate for its usage with troops, his writings were published in Germany and beyond.[117] One of the first important English texts on Ling was a translation of Rothstein's.[118] The exclusion, or institutional forgetting of Jahn's system in Prussia, led to a 'clash of gymnastic systems' which was to replay itself again in late nineteenth-century America, albeit in a muted tone.[119] In 1860, Carl Euler (1828–1901) was hired as an instructor at Rothstein's institute and began to question the supremacy of Ling's system.[120] Where, he demanded, were the parallel and horizontal bars used by *turners*? Tensions arose

---

[111]Ibid.
[112]Irina Sirotkina, 'National models of physical education and the Sokol Gymnastics in Russia', *Sociologiceskoe Obozrenie* 16 (2017): 320–39.
[113]Julia Helene Schöler, *Über Die Anfänge Der Schwedischen Heilgymnastik In Deutschland: Ein Beitrag Zur Geschichte Der Krankengymnastik Im 19. Jahrhundert* (Münster (Westfalen), Univ., Diss., 2005), 30–5.
[114]P.H. Ling and H.G. Rothstein, *Die Gymnastik, Nach Dem Systeme Des Schwedischen Gumnasiarchen* (Schroeder, 1847).
[115]Berit Elisabeth Dencker, 'Popular Gymnastics and the military spirit in Germany, 1848–1871', *Central European History* 34, no. 4 (2001): 503–30.
[116]Naul, 'History ... ', 15–22.
[117]Ibid.
[118]Mathias Roth and P.H. Ling, *The gymnastic free exercises of PH Ling* (London, 1853).
[119]Park, *Sharing, Arguing, and Seeking Recognition: International Congresses, Meetings, and Physical Education, 1867–1915*, 519–48.
[120]Michael Krüger, 'Body Culture and Nation Building: The History of Gymnastics in Germany in the Period of Its Foundation as a Nation-State' (1996): 409–17.

between those who supported Ling and those who supported Jahn in a dispute known as the *Barrenstreit* ('parallel bar dispute').[121]

So contentious was this dispute that the Prussian government intervened in 1863, three years after Euler's enquiries began.[122] A parliamentary enquiry was called and, before parliament stood medical doctors, gymnasts and military officers. Krüger's *Barrenstreit* study noted the referee adopted by physicians.[123] They were there to discuss the health merits of each system and quell nationalist tensions around a 'foreign' system. Eventually, a scientific board was gathered who asserted that parallel bars were justifiable.[124] The dispute, however, was about more than health. Schöler's work cited several submissions to the board about the incompatibility between a foreign system and Prussian concerns. In contrast, the *turner* system was treated by Prussian critics as overly physical, lacking nuance and concerned with exhibition power.[125] The 'gymnastic trial' marked an explicit conversation about the globalization of gymnastics and its impact on trainee's bodies.

The failure of Ling gymnastics was never definitive and a telling attribute of this period was how often systems were reintroduced in different contexts. The *turner*'s victory was a pyrrhic one as criticisms levelled against it opened its utility to scrutiny. Naul traced a steep decline in the use of Ling gymnastics following the *Barrenstreit*.[126] Between 1870 and 1914, however, a Swiss-German mixture between the *turner* system and the system of Adolf Spiess (1810–58) was introduced. Spiess shared Rothstein's disapproval of *turner* gymnastics but a melding of systems proved acceptable to military and educational leaders.[127]

One country which did strike out on its own was Great Britain. Despite Clias and club-swinging, it was during the 1850s that attention was dedicated to military gymnastics.[128] While developments on the continent did play a role, this shift was driven by internal concerns about troop health. The Crimean War (1853–6) was influential here as a galling statistic for many in Britain was that the military camp and hospital were more deadly than the battlefield.[129] The Crimean War's larger scale (which demanded over 100,000 British troops over three years) was complemented by a series of smaller, but at times equally scaring, wars around the Empire. This was

---

[121] Michael Krüger, 'History of Sports Medicine in Germany', 338–45.
[122] Ibid.
[123] Ibid.
[124] Fred Eugene Leonard, *A guide to the history of physical education* (Lea & Febiger, 1927), 124–40.
[125] Schöler, *Über* ... .
[126] Naul, 'History ... ', 15–27.
[127] Rebekka Horlacher, 'The emergence of physical education as a subject for compulsory schooling in the first half of the nineteenth-century', *Nordic Journal of Educational History* 4 (2017): 13–30.
[128] Heffernan, *Indian Club-swinging*, 127–45.
[129] Andrew Lambert, *The Crimean War* (Ashgate, 2011), 147.

the decade when the Indian Rebellion (1857) and Second Anglo-Chinese War (1856–60) occurred. There was a considerable strain on the military in terms of manpower. Manpower and mortality, two of the primary concerns of any State, prompted action.

In 1858, a Royal Commission on the army's sanitary condition was published which noted the laboured routines in British camps.[130] This was contrasted with the French military where soldiers engaged in daily gymnastics. While the report was more concerned with sanitation, venereal diseases and medical checks, it did recommend enquiries into the French gymnastic system and the establishment of sporting and gymnastic facilities.[131] In 1859, Secretary of State for War Sidney Herbert (1810–61) pressed the army's General Commanding-in-Chief to send officers to Paris and Berlin to examine their geo-political rivals' systems. Of the two, it was the French method which impressed.[132] Britain was not unique in taking an interest in mainland European practices. In the mid-to-late 1850s, Superintendent of the United States Military Academy Richard Delafield (1798–1873) spent several years touring Europe examining various military programmes. One of his fellow travellers George McClellan (1826–85 CE) reported the French gymnastic system to be particularly impressive and, following Delafield's return, efforts were made to institutionalize training into the Military.[133] The idea, however, that one could learn or be inspired by others' systems was telling about the porous nature of gymnastics. There was a clear and deliberate effort to learn from other nations.

In Britain, efforts were advanced to find an instructor who could reform Britain's training. That individual was Scotsman Archibald MacLaren (1819–84). MacLaren studied fencing and gymnastics in Paris as a student and was a studious thinker. When he was given twelve non-commissioned officers to train in his Oxford gymnasium, he took meticulous notes of their physical improvements and took photographs.[134] Despite trainees' inexperience, many of whom MacLaren declared had not 'the most robust stamp', his system was successful.[135] A plan was set in place to establish a Royal Army Physical Training Corps to oversee troop training and a series of gymnasiums were built across the Empire, the first being found in Aldershot in 1860.[136]

---

[130] HMSO, *Royal commission appointed to inquire into the sanitary condition of the army, Report of the commissioners appointed to inquire into the regulations affecting the sanitary condition of the army, the organization of military hospitals, and the treatment of the sick and wounded* (HMSO, 1858).
[131] Ibid., Xiv–Xxxiii.
[132] Ibid.
[133] Richard Delafield, *Report on the art of war in Europe in 1854, 1855, 1856* (Bowerman, 1860).
[134] HMSO, *Army medical report: Statistical, sanitary and medical reports for the year 1860* (Harrison, 1862), 197.
[135] Heffernan, *Indian Club-swinging*, 132–40.
[136] Nikolai Bogdanovic, *Fit to fight: A history of the royal army physical training corps 1860–2015* (Bloomsbury, 2017), 244.

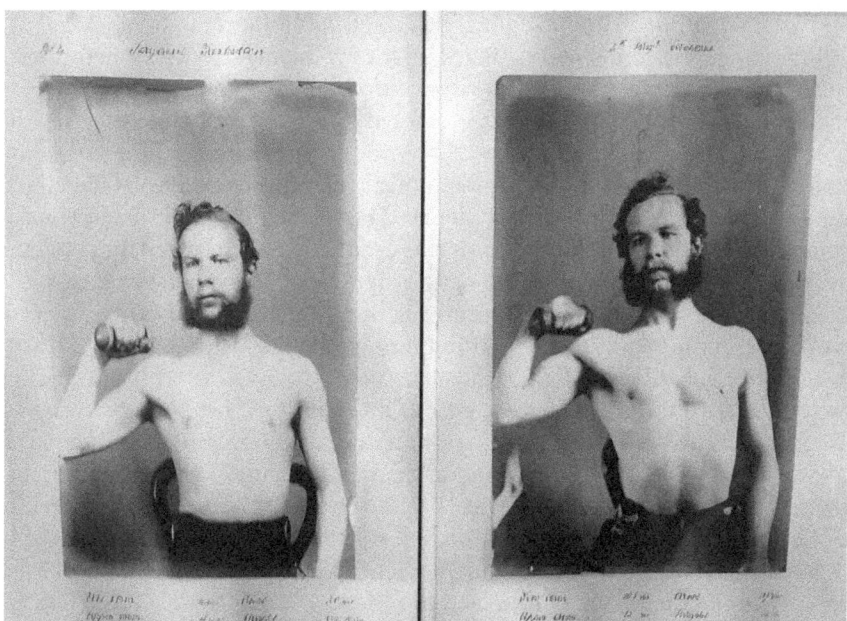

FIGURE 3.2 Before and after images of MacLaren's initial student, c. 1860.[137]

While MacLaren's was initially relatively silent on the broader European interest in gymnastics, his *Physical Education* evaluated French and Prussian systems and contrasted them with the British system.[138] The former was deemed too complicated while the latter focused on a few exercises done with passionately. MacLaren expressed a greater admiration for the French although critiqued it for being 'based on, in many respects, erroneous principles of physical culture, yet productive of great benefit'.[139] Its rationale did not match MacLaren's system which could be described as a combination piece of light-weight exercises, equipment-based gymnastics and Ling-esque movements, although on Ling's system, MacLaren deemed it suitable for 'invalids'.[140] Accompanying his system was a promotion of club-swinging and fencing. What elevated MacLaren's system was its place in the British military. In sheer numbers, this meant MacLaren's system, whether adhered to diligently or not, was among the most popular in the world.[141] It was not just soldiers trained in these systems, as the military system was adopted within schools across Empire and by institutions like the YMCA.[142]

[137] Author's Collection.
[138] Maclaren, *Physical Education*, Lxxxiii-Lxxiv.
[139] Ibid., Xci.
[140] Ibid., Lxxxiii.
[141] Ashley Jackson, *The British Empire: A very short introduction* (Oxford University Press, 2013), 13–25.
[142] J.A. Mangan and F. Galligan. 'Militarism, drill and elementary education', *International Journal of the History of Sport* 28, no. 3–4 (2011): 568–603.

Nationalism, at an implicit or explicit level, was important in the spread of military gymnastics as was a eugenic zeal for producing stronger generations. Industrialization was cited as a force in enfeebling and devitalizing men and the ability to quantify health was presented as a means of improving health outcomes.[143] This rationalization of the body stood in contrast to systems like club-swinging which used a more holistic view of the body. Nevertheless, the systems discussed, as well as other modalities (Sokol, Spiess, Danish, etc.) were those exported globally. It is at this point, we return to Britain's system as it provides an exemplar of how and why European gymnastics spread to other parts of the world. As Britain was the largest colonial power, it was worth beginning with its colonial military gymnastics. In 1863, the British War Office asked MacLaren to help to spread his system to India.[144] The answer, according to MacLaren, was to invest in facilities and instructors. To that end the first British gymnasium in India was constructed in the late 1860s and one of MacLaren's initial trainees became Chief Instructor of the Lucknow Gymnasium.[145] Thus began the introduction of MacLaren's system, although the reality was complex. Studying *Medical and Sanitary* reports published in the 1870s and 1880s from Bombay, Bengal and Madras reveals an ongoing issue with a lack of funding.[146] As early as 1863, letters were addressed from India to the Quartermaster General demanding more investment. The general tone of such letters was disbelief – how could the 'perfect' solider be fostered without a gymnasium? What better system existed for moulding the body with perfect rigidity, deepening the chest and staving off illness?[147] The letter, unauthored, chimed with broader discourses in India about the climate and positive impact gymnastics had on the 'natives'.[148]

Military gymnastics in British India was divided in application. For British men military gymnastics was a means of protecting them against the climate or, should illness befall them, recuperation.[149] For 'natives', gymnastics would bring physiques up to European standards and instil in them a sense of Britishness. A great deal of research has centred on the role sport played as a socializing agent in the British Empire.[150] Sport was credited with inculcating men in a sense of discipline, godliness and work ethics. The 'muscular Christian' movement, discussed later, encouraged the idea of using

---

[143]Hans Bonde, 'The time and speed ideology: 19th century industrialisation and sport', *The International Journal of the History of Sport* 26, no. 10 (2009): 1315–34.
[144]Bogdanovic, *Fit to Fight*, 19–25.
[145]Ibid.
[146]Heffernan, *Indian Club-swinging*, 135–8.
[147]Deputy Inspector General Inglis, 'Extract from the general sanitary report of the Madras Presidency for 1863', in *Parliamentary Papers 1863* (Hmso, 1863), 374–80.
[148]Ibid.
[149]Heffernan, *Indian Club-swinging*, 55–80.
[150]John Macdonald Mackenzie, *A cultural history of the British Empire* (Yale University, 2022), 109–38.

sport as a means of increasing men and boys' allegiances to Britain.[151] Sport was the primary mover of this ethos, but gymnastics played a role, albeit on a more disciplinarian basis. The British categorization of Indian bodies from effeminate to martial is known but even martial races were deemed to be physically inferior and in need of gymnastic intervention.[152] Britain was not unique in exporting its system across the Empire, and nor was it solely India where gymnasiums and MacLaren's system were brought into usage. British gymnastics were brought to South Africa, New Zealand, Australia and other parts of Africa.[153]

Looking at France and Germany (which was unified into a single state in 1871), a similar pattern of gymnastic exportation existed. Ndee's research on German East Africa (1885–1914) positioned gymnastics as a means of socializing soldiers and students into a shared sense of German identity.[154] This was similar to the 'muscular Christian' ethos circulating British society and experiments with physical activity. Whereas the globalization of Western gymnastics was often prompted with reference to health and discipline, the idea of 'civilizing' groups often underpinned colonial gymnastics. It is for this reason this book focuses on the cultivation of a 'global body', rather than a global system. A global system of gymnastics did not exist, but a chaotic hodgepodge of varying motives. On the other hand, the movements and their physique implications often remained untouched. Ndee cited the Mpwapwa military school in modern Tanzania which used German gymnastics (a mixture of Jahn, Spiess and Rothstein's systems) to 'mould Africans into useful soldiers capable of defending the German empire'.[155] It also served as a means of disciplining men and reinforcing divisions between colonizer and colonized.

Akin to the British categorization of martial and non-martial bodies, the German use of drill was a sort of symbolic violence, designed to undermine and critique non-white bodies. Was Germany unique? Nope. Gymnastics was used to 'civilize' and discipline men in the Congo Free State, whose previous leader King Leopold II (1835–1909) was a staunch supporter of Swedish gymnastics and competitive sport.[156] One 1897 article in *La Belgique Maritime et Coloniale* by 'Steenbeke' praised the 'natural' physicality of Congolese

---

[151] John Macaloon, 'Introduction: Muscular Christianity after 150 years', in John J. Macaloon (ed.), *Muscular Christianity and the Colonial and Post-Colonial World* (Routledge, 2013), Xi–Xxiv.
[152] John Rosselli, 'The self-image of effeteness: Physical education and nationalism in nineteenth-century Bengal', *Past & Present* 86, no. 1 (1980): 121–48.
[153] Francois Johannes Cleophas, *Physical education and physical culture in South Africa, 1837–1966* (Springer, 2024), 1–26.
[154] Hamad Ndee, 'Germany and Eastern Africa: Gymnastics in Germany in the nineteenth-century and the diffusion of German Gymnastics into German East Africa', *The International Journal of the History of Sport* 27 (2010): 820–44.
[155] Ibid.
[156] Pascal Delheye, Thomas Ameye and And Stijn Knuts, 'Expansionism, physical education and olympism: Common interests of King Leopold II of Belgium, Cyrille van overbergh and Pierre De Coubertin (1894–1914)', *The International Journal of the History of Sport* 31 (2014): 1158–77.

men and women, arguing that while physical activity was at the foundation of their lives, 'an appropriate physical training will later be introduced to improve the intellectual development of the indigenous people'.[157] This was the civilizing mission made manifest through physical culture. One of the early forerunners in this regard were the French who implemented gymnastics in its Indonesian colony as early as the 1860s.[158] While it took until the 1930s for the French military school to publish specific guidelines for colonial training, Bloom's work made clear the 'civilizing' role gymnastics was thought to play in France's colonies during this age.[159] While Germany was somewhat of a minnow when it came to colonialism and Belgium attempted to isolate itself from the broader European colonial project, Britain and France occupied large land masses. The depth of gymnastics, and indeed sport, varied but its existence is beyond doubt. While the record does not allow us to make wholesale observations about the impact this had, a banal point is that this exposed millions of soldiers to European gymnastics. Yes resistance occurred and teaching was underfunded but these systems existed. Furthermore, they were amplified in their rhetoric.

Colonialism does not fully account for the spread of military gymnastics globally. This is especially the case in parts of the world untouched by colonialism, at least officially. Here it is useful to contrast Brazil with Japan. European gymnastics were brought to Japan during this period as a means of solidifying its geo-political position. Brazil came to gymnastics through a different, and ironically far more 'European' trajectory. Having achieved independence from Portugal in 1822, Brazil was an ethnically diverse country which effectively held a caste system between different racial groups with those with the fairest skin typically having access and control over resources.[160]

Like Argentina, Brazil experienced an influx of German and French immigrants from the mid-nineteenth century.[161] This included a steady stream of *turners* versed in Jahn's system. While Swedish gymnasts arrived in South America during the nineteenth century, it was *turners* who exhibited the greatest influence.[162] Why I suggested Brazil followed a 'European trajectory' towards gymnastics can be found in a series of conflicts (Uruguayan War of 1864–5 and the Paraguayan War 1864–70) which brought anxieties in Brazil

---

[157]Steenbeke, 'District De L'équateur', *La Belgique Maritime Et Coloniale* 19 (1897): 221–4.
[158]Evelyne Combeau-Mari, 'Sport in the French colonies (1880–1962): A case study', *Journal of Sport History* 33 (2006): 27–57.
[159]Peter Bloom, *French colonial documentary* (University of Minnesota Press, 2008), 19–24.
[160]Sidney Chalhoub, 'The politics of silence: Race and citizenship in nineteenth-century Brazil', *Slavery and Abolition* 27 (2006): 73–87.
[161]Giralda Seyferth, 'The diverse understandings of foreign migration to the South of Brazil (1818–1950)', *Vibrant: Virtual Brazilian Anthropology* 10 (2013): 118–62.
[162]Evelise Amgarten Quitzau, 'Between Gymnastics and sport: Education of the body and preservation of identity in German-Brazilian Gymnastics societies', *Educação Em Revista* 35 (2019): E217174.

about troop health and readiness.¹⁶³ The debates, which included a great deal of racial anxiety, were not dissimilar from those found in Britain during the 1850s. Da Costa and colleagues cited multiple revisions to Brazilian military training during this period as illustrative of this concern.¹⁶⁴ During the 1850s and the Paraguayan War (1864–70), the Brazilian military contracted Prussian officers. This, combined with organic migration from Prussia to Brazil, meant that the *turner* system was the most easily accessible.¹⁶⁵ A Prussian second Lieutenant (Pedro Guilhermino Meyer), already working in Brazil, was appointed Gymnastics Quartermaster at the military school.¹⁶⁶ Maranhão's work on physical culture and eugenics in Brazil was clear that the military discourses surrounding this adoption differed little from those found elsewhere.¹⁶⁷ Gymnastics would reform and discipline the citizen's body, allow for physical development, and increase one's attachment to the nation. It also adopted a sort of colonial role for darker-skinned men as it was used to 'civilize' them.¹⁶⁸

European gymnastics seemed to promise rationality, order and hygiene. In Japan, the same motivations existed albeit the caveat that Meiji diplomacy was attempting to court Western favour and respect through hard and soft politics.¹⁶⁹ Focused on school physical education, Manzenreiter detailed the reverence with which *heishiki taisō* (military gymnastics) was treated by Japanese intellectuals as a core component of statehood.¹⁷⁰ Mori Arinori (1847–89), Minister of Education from 1885 until his assassination in 1889, placed military training as a core component in economic development, educational policy, health reforms and national security.¹⁷¹ The adoption of Prussian gymnastics had its routes in a Japanese military mission to Europe in 1884. Ostensibly a fact-finding mission of Austrian, Russian and German military systems, the tour resulted in Prussian General Jakob Meckel (1842–1906) moving to Japan as a government advisor.¹⁷² Meckel's arrival caused

---

¹⁶³Lothar Wieser and Michael Krüger, 'Physical education, gymnastics, games and sports in Brazil-The German impact', *Educação Em Revista* 35 (2019): 1–20.
¹⁶⁴Mg Da Costa et al., 'História Da Ginástica No Brasil: Da Concepção E Influência Militar Aos Nossos Dias', *Navigator: Subsídios Para A História Marítima Do Brasil. Rio De Janeiro* 12 (2016): 63–75.
¹⁶⁵Ibid.
¹⁶⁶Tiago Fernandes de Albuquerque Maranhão, *Molding the Body, Forging the Nation: Race, Physical Culture, and the Shaping of Brazil (1822–1930)* (PhD diss., Vanderbilt University, 2020).
¹⁶⁷Ibid., 114–64.
¹⁶⁸Silvana Vilodre Goellner et al., '"Strong mothers make strong children": Sports, eugenics and nationalism in Brazil at the beginning of the twentieth-century', *Sport, Education and Society* 17 (2012): 555–70.
¹⁶⁹Wolfram Manzenreiter, *Sport and body politics in Japan* (Routledge, 2013).
¹⁷⁰Ibid., 34–8.
¹⁷¹Ibid., 84–90.
¹⁷²Bernd Martin and Peter Wetzler, 'The German role in the modernization of Japan – the pitfall of blind acculturation', *Oriens Extremus* (1990): 77–88.

tension with a pre-existing French mission in Japan which had already begun to train soldiers using French gymnastics.[173] This had ramifications in China which following the Sino-Japanese War of 1894–5 likewise adopted German gymnastics. The Japanese military continued to use the German system until 1900 when they switched to Swedish gymnastics.[174]

How then, to close a history which begins with the French revolution and ends with an aspirational world power wantonly switching between systems? The institutionalization of gymnastics around the globe meant millions experienced some form of physical culture whether they enjoyed it or not. This raised baseline understandings of training and familiarity with what impact training could have on the body. Next we need to consider what that physical impact actually was. One of the most ambitious, and joyful, reads we can turn to is Gilman's history of posture. Examining more than just gymnastics, Gilman pondered what impact regimented training had on the body.[175] Global systems, be they Swedish, German, French or English, transformed trainees' physiques if given the right attention and nutrition. There was, in theory and in many instances practice, a global body constructed across these systems. Weight was shed, shoulders pulled back, chests expanded and limbs made mobile. There was an embodied consequence of this transformation we cannot ignore. Enlisted men were put through a routinized system. Many may have had 'extracurricular' exercise preferences or not fully committed themselves to military gymnastics but their bodies underwent a baseline of movements. Finally, and accepting that as systems crossed borders they were emptied of their original meanings, it is true that a set of global discourses emerged around the need for military training: men's bodies were weak, industrialization was devitalizing, science could reform this process and training could increase fealty to the nation-state. This focus was entirely on the adult body but it set a template for discussions around children.

Training schoolchildren

Thus far this chapter has focused on male bodies for good reason. Military gymnastics was a dominant driver of physical culture during the nineteenth century. Indeed, a large debate within the global physical education community was whether competitive sport or military drill should be used

---

[173] Allen Guttmann and Lee Thompson, 'Educators, imitators, modernizers: The arrival and spread of modern sport in Japan', in J.A. Mangan (ed.), *Europe, Sport, World* (Routledge, 2013), 23–48.
[174] Toshiyuki Ichiba, 'Traces of German Turnen in Japan', in Annette Hoffman and G.P. Fister (eds.), *Turnen Around the World* (Lexington, 2023), 275–80.
[175] Sander L. Gilman, *Stand up straight!: A history of posture* (Reaktion, 2018), 1–20.

to train children's bodies.¹⁷⁶ PE, that is to say, the mandatory training of schoolchildren, was institutionalized in the nineteenth century in Europe, Australasia, parts of Africa and the Americas. Where PE differed from military gymnastics, it included an emphasis on boys' *and* girls' bodies. Likewise, it was driven by actions within schools but also extra-curricular institutions like the YMCA, Boy Scouts and other charitable bodies. On the one hand, it is possible to tell a neat history of PE beginning with Denmark's introduction of PE in schools in 1814 and continuing to list subsequent countries.¹⁷⁷ The more difficult pathway is to examine three revolving philosophies around PE concerning the differences between sexes, PE's presumed benefits and which system was superior. These debates began in the early nineteenth century and continued throughout the century.

What differences, if any, exist between boys' and girls' bodies? As gymnastics became a force in the late eighteenth and early nineteenth century, this question was asked with regularity by physicians, educators and philosophers the world over.¹⁷⁸ The nineteenth century was not the first time women were encouraged to partake in physical culture, but it was a period when the facilities and discourses around women's exercise were unprecedented. As a starting point, we return to Rousseau's *Emile*, which distinguished between exercise for boys and girls. The former needed to be pushed physically to become a whole person. Sophie, Emile's female counterpart, needed exercise, but only in moderate doses.¹⁷⁹ Women's bodies were not as physically robust as men's or, that, at least, was the idea in a great deal of medical literature.¹⁸⁰ Todd playfully cited two schools of thought in early nineteenth-century physical education – one which treated girls like baby-faced dolls, and the other which sought to cultivate 'vibrant' womanhood.¹⁸¹ Nuance existed, but this split serves as a useful framework for distinguishing between boys' and girls' physical education across the century. As early as the 1820s instructors like P. H. Clias and Monsieur Beaujeu presented the idea that women needed some form of vigorous training. Beaujeu, a Frenchman who taught gymnastics in Ireland, was particularly vocal. Citing Clias, Salzmann, Gutsmuths and other individuals in his 1824 book, Beaujeu encouraged 'violent' exercise for girls designed to improve strength.¹⁸² Beaujeu's physical education experiments extended

---

[176]David Kirk, 'Physical education and regimes of the body', *The Australian and New Zealand Journal of Sociology* 30 (1994): 165–77.
[177]Rachel Bryant, 'World trends in physical education', *Journal of the American Association for Health, Physical Education, and Recreation* 21 (1950): 32–3.
[178]David Kirk, 'Physical education: A gendered history', in Dawn Penney (ed.), *Gender and Physical Education* (Routledge, 2002), 36–50.
[179]Jean Bloch, 'Rousseau's reputation as an authority on childcare and physical education in France before the revolution', *Paedagogica Historica* 14 (1974): 5–33.
[180]Ibid.
[181]Todd, *Physical Culture*, 11–25.
[182]Conor Heffernan and Conor Curran, 'Much ado about nothing?: The problems of Irish physical education, 1820–1920', *Sporting Traditions* 37 (2020): 65–86.

into observational medical trials as evidenced by one medical monograph which concluded that Beaujeu's exercises resulted in less illness in his female student.[183] On the one hand, there existed those who believed physical boundaries between the sexes were not large enough to necessitate different training.[184] The other side of the debate believed that women should engage in exercise with a caveat. Because women's bodies were presumed to be frailer, they required gentler exercises.[185] Critically, within the Anglophone world there were innumerable physicians, surgeons, philosophers and politicians who endorsed this idea.

Some of this was grounded in misunderstandings about female menses and reproduction but a great deal reflected a broader gendered society in which women occupied a secondary role.[186] A similar situation arose in the formalization of sport during the same period wherein women were excluded from more physical sports for fear they would be too harmful or masculine for their physiques.[187] In British physical culture, this took on perhaps its most influential shape in Donald Walker's 1830s books on fitness. Todd cited Walker's 1834 book *British Manly Exercises* as one of the nineteenth century's most popular fitness books. It popularized club-swinging, enjoyed several reprints, informed ideas in the United States, was routinely referenced by physicians and was translated into other texts. Its messaging and rationale for physical activity were simple. Modern society was devitalizing men and making them ill, or worse, effeminate.[188]

Buoyed by his success, Walker returned three years later with *Exercises for Women Designed to Improve and Preserve Their Beauty*. Within it, Walker discouraged vigorous activity as overly taxing for women's bodies and stressed the damage that exercise could bring to women's bodies.[189] Walker's book encouraged gentler exercise, lighter-weights and less variety for women, and it was warmly received. Walker was not a minority within British society. Marian Mason, Britain's first female fitness instructor, echoed similar views in her callisthenics book.[190] Those promoting vigorous training for women were in the minority within fitness circles.[191] Within the Anglophone world, this even created a split in training nomenclature where gymnastics referred to boys and men's fitness and callisthenics for girls and women's fitness.[192] In the United States, Todd found a similar pattern

---

[183]Heffernan, *The history of physical culture*, 91–126.
[184]Ibid.
[185]Todd, *Physical culture*, 11–25.
[186]Patricia Vertinsky, *The eternally wounded woman* (Manchester University, 1990), 41–50.
[187]Jaime Schultz, *Qualifying times: Points of change in US women's sport* (University of Illinois, 2014), 50–60.
[188]Park, 'Muscles ... ', 1604–1636.
[189]Donald Walker, *Exercises for ladies; Calculated to preserve and improve beauty, etc* (Hurst, 1836).
[190]Heffernan, 'An elegant ... ', 1–17.
[191]Todd, *Physical culture*, 211–30.
[192]Heffernan, 'An elegant ... ', 1–8.

arising in the 1830s when independent schools, such as that run by author Catherine Beecher, adopted gymnastics.[193] At the core of this division were the anticipated outcomes instructors and patrons hoped to create. Training for boys was linked to the defence of the nation-state, competition, godliness and marriage. Trained bodies were indicative of malleable and patriotic ones. Training for women was situated within discourses about race science, healthy children, beauty and avoiding or correcting deformities.

What of the non-Anglophone world? British books, such as those written by Walker and Mason, were translated into European languages but other cultures had their own debates and anxieties.[194] Trangbaek's work on Danish physical culture is useful as Denmark was the first country to introduce gymnastics as a mandatory subject within primary schools, for both sexes, in 1814.[195] The actual spread of institutional physical education in schools, across the global fitness community, tended to come in the latter half of the century. From 1814 to 1828, gymnastics was a school subject in Denmark before it was restricted for boys on the basis that boys needed to be trained in the military model.[196] Nevertheless, the first decade of experimentation left an indelible mark on Danish physical culture as found in the establishment of extra-curricular PE institutions for girls in the 1830s.[197] What of Sweden? Ling's gymnastic system was one of the most progressive of its era and contained different gradients for soldiers, exercisers, patients and children. It was also, arguably, the most important form of PE during the nineteenth century, finding proponents in Europe, Russia, Asia, the United States and colonial Africa.[198] Studying Anton Santesson (1825–92 CE), one of the main authors on girls' gymnastics in the Ling tradition, Westberg discussed the educationalization of Ling gymnastics in a global setting.[199] Westberg distinguished between gymnastics for boys, envisioned within a nation-state context, and that for girls, which focused on grace and delicacy.[200] This is not to cast this discourse as inherently conservative. After all, the very idea of women exercising was antithetical to many people's views in Sweden and Europe.[201] Any sort of physical activity was preferable over none at

---

[193]Todd, *Physical Culture*, 137–45.
[194]Heffernan, 'An elegant … ', 1–17.
[195]Else Trangbaek, 'Discipline and emancipation through sport', *Scandinavian journal of history* 21 (1996): 121–34.
[196]Ibid.
[197]Ibid.
[198]Angela Wichmann, 'Diversity versus unity: A comparative analysis of the complex roots of the World Gymnaestrada', in Annette Hofmann, Gerald Gems and Maureen Smith (eds.), *Global Perspectives on Sport and Physical Cultures* (Routledge, 2018), 113–28.
[199]Johannes Westberg, 'Girls' Gymnastics in the service of the Nation: Educationalisation, gender and Swedish Gymnastics in the mid-nineteenth-century', *Nordic Journal of Educational History* 4 (2017): 47–69.
[200]Ibid.
[201]Vertinsky, *The eternally* … .

all and, indeed, the barring of women entirely from many sports during the same period shows that 'none at all' was an option. Likewise, Park's research on the period between 1675 and 1800 in England, France and Spain has discussed the progressiveness, despite the gendered worldview, of PE.[202] Nevertheless, Santesson's writings, which were widely translated in Scandinavia and further beyond, continued the myth of female delicacy.[203] In effect, two systems existed. One for boys and the other for girls.

Male and female instructors were critical in spreading Ling's system and in the normalization of PE.[204] Scandinavia, in particular, became a hub for female gymnastic instructors be they trained in Ling's institute or Paul Petersen's institute in Denmark (founded 1886).[205] Some who trained there, such as Madame Österberg (1849–1915), founded their own teacher training colleges in the Ling method. Österberg founded a training college in England in 1885 and certified a new generation of female instructors. Österberg's institution has often been celebrated as a revolutionary hotbed, striking new professions for women but, at its core, Österberg's teachings centred on a simple premise – women's highest calling was birthing and raising healthy children.[206] Therein lies the great contradiction in the globalization of PE. Work on Germany, France, Spain, Brazil and Argentina found a distinction in discourses between boys and girls.[207] The former were trained for the military, as a means of counteracting the effeminizing nature of industrialization. Girls were almost unanimously trained for motherhood or for beauty and marriage. These discourses were rooted in national cultures but were aided by the mass movement of books and individuals.[208] Boys' PE tended to be imparted by a military instructor of some descript. They were thus exposed to drill sergeants of various kinds and, on this note, it is telling just how much the historiography of drill in Europe and South

---

[202] Roberta Park, 'Concern for the physical education of the female sex from 1675 to 1800', *Research Quarterly. American Alliance for Health, Physical Education and Recreation* 45 (1974): 104–19.

[203] Westberg, 'Girls' Gymnastics … '.

[204] Wichmann, 'Diversity … '.

[205] Hans Bonde, 'Farmers' gymnastics in Denmark in the late nineteenth and early twentieth centuries', *The International Journal of the History of Sport* 10 (1993): 193–214.

[206] Anne Bloomfield, 'Martina Bergman-Osterberg (1849–1915): Creating a professional role for women in physical training', *History of Education* 34 (2005): 517–34.

[207] Gertrud Pfister, 'The medical discourse on female physical culture in Germany in the 19th and early 20th centuries', *Journal of Sport History* 17 (1990): 183–98; Grégory Quin and Anaïs Bohuon, 'Muscles, nerves, and sex: The contradictions of the medical approach to female bodies in movement in France, 1847–1914', *Gender & History* 24 (2012): 172–86; Raúl Sánchez García and Antonio Rivero Herraiz. '"Governmentality" in the origins of European female PE and sport: The Spanish case study (1883–1936)', *Sport, Education and Society* 18 (2013): 494–510.

[208] Vasilis Kaimakamis et al., 'The spread of gymnastics in Europe and America by pedagogue-gymnasts during the first half of the 19th century', *Science of Gymnastics Journal* 3 (2011): 49–60.

America utilizes Foucauldian theories on power and discipline.[209] Indeed, a large debate in the British Empire from the 1850s onwards was whether drill was appropriate for schoolboys.[210] Girls were often given more delicate styles of exercise. Oftentimes combined with dance, as was the case in North America and South East Asia, girls' PE was more cautious owing to the presumed inferiority of women's physiques.[211]

Women were given the freedom to exercise, but only to a certain extent, and rarely pushing to their physicality. Returning to Todd's distinction between baby-face dolls and vibrant womanhood, the nineteenth century was largely one concerned with baby-face dolls.[212] It is worth stressing similarities in Asia and the colonial world between physical education and

FIGURE 3.3 Girls exercising on bars. Charlestown High School USA, c. 1899.[213]

---

[209]Chisholm, 'The disciplinary ... '.
[210]Mangan, and Galligan. 'Militarism, ... '.
[211]Chisholm, 'Gymnastics and ... ', Elena Valdameri, 'Training Female Bodies for New India: Women's Physical Education between Global Trends and Local Politics in Colonial South Asia, c. 1900–1939', *The International Journal of the History of Sport* 39 (2022): 1240–64.
[212]Todd, *Physical Culture*, 11–25.
[213]Digital Commonwealth, https://ark.digitalcommonwealth.org/ark:/50959/cf95jp86c (accessed 4 December 2024).

military gymnastics. In both instances, Western ideas were deliberately imported into the nation. Take Japan, during the 1870s, which saw works on French, German and American PE circulated zealously by schoolmasters and politicians. During this period, the head of the Japanese Ministry of Education Tanaka Fujimaro (1845–1909) visited Amherst College to learn from their PE programmes.[214] This evolved into a contract for Amherst College graduate Dr George Leland (1870–1924) to visit Japan and oversee the implementation of American PE.[215] Leland was versed in the Jahn mode of gymnastics and brought a German/American hybrid to the country. His system, outlined in *New Physical Education,* and subsequently translated into Japanese, was a two-tiered model separating the genders. Vigorous or hard gymnastics were offered to boys, and light callisthenics for girls.[216] Speak's work on Chinese PE reveals a similar pattern, albeit an initially informal one. Brownell cited the tensions which arose during this period between those promoting Western PE and those steadfast in preserving Chinese physical cultures.[217] Proponents in China for Western PE explicitly cited Western women's ability to birth healthier offspring as a benefit of these systems.[218] Ignored in this context were those contemporary Western concerns about Western women not birthing healthy children.[219]

A similar situation existed in colonial parts of Asia and Africa wherein gendered ideas around PE reiterated differences between white and non-white bodies. A formative article by Roselli on Hindu nationalism and physical culture during the nineteenth century proves useful here. Studying colonial claims that Indian men were weaker than their British counterparts, Roselli tracked efforts of Hindu nationalists to use PE to strengthen boys to prove colonizers wrong.[220] At the same point, British administrators used PE to reify colonial distinctions between British rationality and Indian people. Both groups, colonist and colonized, agreed on the centrality of the trained body for political purposes. Valdameri likewise discussed how Indian girls were trained in callisthenics in the hope of protecting them against modernity while simultaneously ensuring the birth of healthy children.[221] This situation can also be found in German and French colonies in Africa.[222]

---

[214]Benjamin Duke, *The history of modern Japanese education* (Rutgers, 2009), 245–60.
[215]Ibid., 245–70.
[216]Ikuo Abe, Yasuharu Kiyohara and Ken Nakajima, 'Sport and physical education under fascistization in Japan', *InYo: Journal of Alternative Perspectives* 9 (2000): 1–25.
[217]Susan Brownell, *Training the body for China: Sports in the moral order of the People's Republic* (University of Chicago, 1995), 46–60.
[218]Ibid.
[219]Walker *Exercises* ... .
[220]Rosselli, 'The ... '.
[221]Valdameri, 'Training ... '.
[222]Gertrud Pfister, 'Colonialism and the enactment of German identity – "Turnen" in South West Africa', *Journal of Sport History* 33 (2006): 59–83; Evelyne Combeau-Mari, 'Colonial sport in Madagascar 1896–1960', *The International Journal of the History of Sport* 28 (2011): 1557–65.

It would be wrong to solely attribute the rise and spread of global PE to gender. The focus on gender was, itself, a vessel for social and geopolitical concerns. Grander debates were couched into debates about race science and breeding.[223] Poskett's work on phrenology and global science provides a useful framework. Phrenology, a now-defunct science which studied skull size and shape in the hope of uncovering mental and personality traits, was an influential race science during this century.[224] Used in multiple disciplines, it seemed to promise rationality in studying people. The reality was a prejudiced science which served to protect existing power structures of men over women and white over non-white.[225] Regardless, Poskett highlighted a global network of phrenologists whose conversations were shaped by the translation of books, posting of skulls and attendance of lectures.[226] Beginning in Western Europe and America, Poskett traced the spread of these ideas around the globe and, in the same way examined here, how these further ports in turn influenced Western society.[227]

Many phrenologists believed in hereditary traits as 'exposed' by the body but, critically, many original proponents ascribed to the pre-Darwinian theories proposed by French zoologist Jean-Baptiste Lamarck (1744–1829).[228] Ascribing to the idea of 'natural laws', Lamarck's 1809 *Philosophie Zoologique* was something of a damp squib on publication but was arguably one of the century's most important books in race and science.[229] Widely translated from its original French, the book's core arguments were that use or disuse would cause a body to grow or shrink over generations and that such changes were inheritable. An example given by Lamarck was that of the blacksmith. Beholden to physical work, the blacksmith developed muscular arms. This trait would be inherited by the Blacksmith's son. It was the blacksmith analogy which seemed to resonate most with individuals interested in physical culture.[230] A topic thus discussed in this chapter but not fully expounded on until now is the importance of race science and racial fitness. The reason for this is simple. Such discourses were at their most pervasive when centred on children.

---

[223]Wendy Kline, *Building a better race: Gender, sexuality, and eugenics from the turn of the century to the baby boom* (University of California Press, 2001).
[224]James Poskett, *Materials of the mind: Phrenology, race, and the global history of science, 1815–1920* (University of Chicago, 2019).
[225]Ibid., 1–25.
[226]Ibid.
[227]Ibid.
[228]Jürgen Martschukat, *The age of fitness: How the body came to symbolize success and achievement* (Wiley, 2021), 43.
[229]Ernst Mayr, 'Lamarck revisited', *Journal of the History of Biology* (1972): 55–94.
[230]Todd, *Physical culture*, 176.

Work on the ancient world has shown similar concerns about generational health and fitness.[231] We have already discussed Rousseau's concern about breeding in the eighteenth century and how commonplace such fears were. What differentiated the nineteenth century was the global reach of these concerns and the age's wider technological changes. Industrialization, first in Europe and the United States, followed in varying degrees in other parts of the world, and seismically changed human life.[232] Some changes were minor but others, like the advent of electricity, were revolutionary. This brought with it a space for wonder but also anxiety. Peña's work on electricity and magnetism during this period stressed the fear electricity brought in the public consciousness.[233] Could it be used for medical research? Was the body an electrical object? How could it be harnessed? Technology and science were no longer the preserve of the laboratory but something public. Also public facing were concerns about hygiene and sanitation during this period. Gilbert's work on the 'body politic' in Britain traced the linking of clean and healthy spaces, to clean and healthy bodies, to ideas of statehood.[234] Interest in the body and efforts to control, clean and change it, existed simultaneously with new advances in consumer and institutional technologies.

Race science, be it phrenology or Lamarckism, existed within this space, playing on fears about technology and modernity while offering solutions and promised improvements. Phrenology and Lamarckism slowly ebbed in social popularity in the latter half of the century, to be replaced by British scientist Francis Galton's (1822–1911 CE) theory on eugenics.[235] First coined as a term by Galton in 1883, eugenics differed from Lamarckism in following a form of evolution derived from Charles Darwin's (1809–82 CE) works. Darwin's observations focused on gradual adaptions in species over generations through a process of natural selection. Random genetic mutations existed and acquired traits were not guaranteed to be inherited.[236] While it is more nuanced than this, Darwin's theory became readily understood in fitness and sporting circles as 'survival of the fittest'.[237] This idea also fit neatly into a growing capitalist system defined by individual work ethic. One of the first books on Victorian sport and health, written by Bruce Haley,

---

[231]D.J. Galton, 'Eugenics: Some lessons from the past', *Reproductive BioMedicine Online* 10 (2005): 133–6.
[232]Poskett, *Materials*, 1–24.
[233]Carolyn Thomas De La Peña, *The body electric: How strange machines built the modern American* (NYU Press, 2003), 12–45.
[234]Gilbert, *Citizen's body*, 1–23.
[235]Debbie Challis, *The archaeology of race: The eugenic ideas of Francis Galton and Flinders Petrie* (A&C Black, 2013).
[236]Denis Noble, 'Charles Darwin, Jean-Baptiste Lamarck, and 21st century arguments on the fundamentals of biology', *Progress in Biophysics and Molecular Biology* 153 (2020): 1–4.
[237]Martschukat, *The age*, 10–34.

pinpointed the idea of improvement as synonymous with Darwinism.[238] While phrenology and Lamarckism built the pathway for racial science in the nineteenth century to become globalized, Darwin's theory of evolution, first published in 1859, was immediately translated into other languages, and crystallized debates about health, sport and colonialism.[239] Eugenics became a catch-all for racial science debates and to justify the colonization of peoples by 'stronger' European races.

For those attempting to persuade politicians and educators of the need for PE, race science was an easy argument. Work on the North and South America, Europe and Asia has pinpointed the late nineteenth century as a time when educators used such ideas to legitimize the subject.[240] From a global perspective, race science, be it eugenics or phrenology, intensified in social importance at the exact moment that PE became a mandatory subject around the world. While Denmark was unique in pioneering the subject in 1814, the majority of European states began to introduce it seriously in the 1860s and 1870s. This continued into colonial Africa and Australasia. A similar pattern was found in North and South America. At the core of such decisions, and indeed, substantiating the gendered debates previously discussed, were concerns over race science.

European, South American and North American PE discourses were drawn primarily from educational and race science debates, but they, and the colonial world, were also shaped by the 'muscular Christian' ideal of civilizing bodies and souls through exercise. An evolution of the previously discussed *mens sana in corpe sano*, the movement first emerged in Great Britain during the nineteenth century.[241] Many cite author Thomas Hughes' (1822–96 CE) 1857 novel *Tom Brown's School Days* as a sort of foundational text for this ideal.[242] Focused on the fictitious Brown and his time at Rugby School, the story revolves around the transformative power of sport. The story crystallized a growing Victorian belief that sport taught boys patriotism, discipline and sacrifice.[243] In extremes, the muscular Christian movement was taken as a near direct pathway to devotional spirit, hence its appeal to Catholic and Protestant groups in the West. It even had parallels in other spiritual traditions. We have already noted the Hindu melas of the 1860s which employed a similar framework, as a sort of muscular Hinduism. Likewise Zionist leader Max Nordau (1849–1923) pushed for the idea of a muscular Judaism in the late nineteenth and early

---

[238]Bruce Haley, *The healthy body and Victorian culture* (Harvard University Press, 1978), 10–16.
[239]Piotr Badyna, 'Were the natural sciences global in the 19th century? The case of Charles Darwin', in L. Koczanowicz (ed.), *Interpreting Globalization* (Brill, 2021), 80–90.
[240]Park, 'Physiologists ... '.
[241]Watson et al., 'The development of muscular Christianity'.
[242]Ibid., 1–4.
[243]Neil Carter, *Medicine, sport and the body* (Bloomsbury, 2012), 19–25.

twentieth century.[244] What distinguished the Muscular Christian movement from other traditions was its institutionalization.[245]

It was through sport that the British colonial office believed foreign peoples could be education in the tenets of Empire. It served to 'civilize' and bring them closer to a British ideal. This was not just a colonial manoeuvre either. The popularization of nineteenth-century sport was propelled by a sporting-religious zeal encapsulated by the phrase muscular Christian.[246] This ideal found proponents in the United States where it served a similar purpose and work has likewise traced its influence in mainland Europe.[247] So what could be viewed as a peculiarly Anglophone phenomenon had global resonance. Research has typically situated the muscular Christian movement within the globalization of sport.[248] It provided support for sport but also provided a 'higher purpose' to PE and gymnastics.

The muscular Christian movement also spurred on an institutionalization of PE and children's gymnastics in the form of the Young Men's Christian Association (YMCA). Founded by Victorian businessman George Williams (1821–1905) and several associates in London in 1844, the YMCA was established to improve young men's 'spiritual condition'. What began as a civic group tasked with publishing pamphlets evolved into a global movement.[249] Cantor cited the 1851 Great Exhibition as a pivotal moment for the YMCA as, following its involvement, sister branches emerged in Europe, Hong Kong and the United States. By 1855, a YMCA World Conference was held in Paris and the organization continued to grow.[250] Its initial focus, of protecting men from the vices of modernity, extended into education and physical betterment. In other words, the YMCA contributed to, and was supported, by the Muscular Christian ethos. Initially, the YMCA was reluctant to engage with 'mere' leisure.[251] While it was not until the 1870s and 1880s that formal YMCA gymnasiums began to open, many branches offered gymnastics classes to boys from the late 1850s. Pioneering branches, in this regard, were the American ones, specifically the New York YMCA which specified the need for physical self-improvement as a core

---

[244]Todd Samuel Presner, *Muscular Judaism* (Routledge, 2007), 1–23.
[245]J.A. Mangan, 'Christ and the imperial games fields: Evangelical athletes of the Empire', *The International Journal of the History of Sport* 1 (1984): 184–201.
[246]Richard Holt, *Sport and the British: A modern history* (Oxford University Press, 1990), 76–95.
[247]Clifford Putney, *Muscular Christianity: Manhood and sports in protestant America, 1880–1920* (Harvard University Press, 2009).
[248]Mangan, 'Christ ... '.
[249]William Baker, 'To pray or to play? The YMCA question in the United Kingdom and the United States, 1850–1900', *The International Journal of the History of Sport* 11 (1994): 42–62.
[250]Geoffrey Cantor, *Religion and the great exhibition of 1851* (Oxford University Press, 2011), 78–90.
[251]Baker, 'To pray ... '.

YMCA goal.[252] By 1890, roughly 400 YMCA gyms existed in the United States.[253]

As elsewhere, the YMCA contributed to, and challenged, racial and gendered distinctions. Moore's work on African-American gymnasium instructors noted that as early as the 1860s, some YMCA gyms *did not* enforce a colour line.[254] Elsewhere, however, YMCAs were part of a colonial and Christian zeal to 'civilize'. By the late nineteenth century, the American YMCA movement expanded its reach into Asia.[255] Such missionary visits were accompanied by sport and PE. Zhang's research on China noted the YMCA's work with missionary schools and the centrality of sport and PE. Zhang presented a contrast between the German gymnastics taught in national schools with the American gymnastics taught by YMCA instructors.[256] A similar situation was noted in Brazil during the 1860s and 1870s wherein American YMCA instructors offered gymnastics outside the school curriculum.[257] Returning to Asia, Fisher-Tiné's research on India in the late nineteenth and early twentieth centuries featured recordings from American YMCA instructors aware that their PE systems were in direct competition with other physical cultures.[258] Depending on the country, the YMCA and its sister organization the Young Women's Christian Association (founded in 1855) offered PE classes to boys and girls. Variations existed in the provision of gymnastics, but instructors usually used a system derived from Swedish or German gymnastics.

While other voluntary organizations with a global reach utilized PE to train boys and girls, the YMCA was critical in providing another form. It provided facilities, instructors and, critically, indoctrination. Many 'Y' missionaries, especially those from American branches, went to Asia and Africa with the explicit purpose of using education and recreation to convert locals to Catholicism. Supported by the muscular Christian ideal, such work put the Christian ethos into action, sprinkled with colonizing rhetoric. One YMCA historian recalled the American Y's enthusiasm for gymnastics and the 'era of gymnasium building' it spurred in domestic and foreign hubs.[259]

---

[252]Ibid., 44.
[253]Ibid., 46.
[254]Louis Moore, 'Fit for citizenship: Black sparring masters, gymnasium owners, and the white body, 1825–1886'. *The Journal of African American History* 96, no. 4 (2011): 448–73.
[255]Harald Fischer-Tiné, 'Fitness for Modernity? The YMCA and physical-education schemes in late-colonial South Asia (circa 1900–40)', *Modern Asian Studies* 53, no. 2 (2019): 512–59.
[256]Huijie Zhang, *Missionary schools, the YMCA and the transformation of physical education and sport in modern China (1840–1937)* (Ph.D. thesis, 2015, University of Western Australia).
[257]Claudia Guedes, '"Changing the cultural landscape": English engineers, American missionaries, and the YMCA bring sports to Brazil–the 1870s to the 1930s', *The International Journal of the History of Sport* 28 (2011): 2594–608.
[258]Fischer-Tiné, 'Fitness ... ?'
[259]Tomáš Tlustý, 'The American YMCA and its physical education program–first steps to world expansion', *Studies in Sport Humanities* 20 (2016): 39–47.

In 1889, the American Alliance for Health and Physical Education, (AAHPE), hosted a conference which brought together those preaching dance, Ling gymnastics, German Gymnastics, French approaches, British sport and other approaches. There was, at heart, a desire to agree on a single 'American system' which could be used across all PE curricula.[260] This goal proved unachievable but the desire to 'hash out' an agreed-upon method amid so many differing approaches was replicated in Europe during the nineteenth and early twentieth centuries.[261] As a closing observation on PE, it highlighted just how normalized the idea of PE had become within the century. From having to justify the need for PE with reference to political philosophers and Athenian culture, instructors moved onto the more developed stage of consolidating, rather than advocating for, their subject. Critically, it showed just how clustered global PE systems had become that disciplinary boundaries between Swedish and German gymnastics were fought not in Europe, but across the Atlantic. While it lagged somewhat behind military gymnastics, the expanse of PE mirrored the same trends. It pushed more people, willing or unwilling, into gymnastics and increased global knowledge surrounding physical culture.

Conclusion

The most subtle, but important, takeaway from this chapter is the magnitude of institutional physical culture. Imagine, for a moment, travelling to London in 1800 and asking one hundred people to demonstrate an exercise for their legs. Repeat that experiment in 1850 and again in 1900. Replicate it in the United States, Brazil, Russia, Japan, etc., and parts of the colonial world. It is my conviction that rudimentary exercise knowledge was more common in 1850 or 1900 than 1800. Why does this matter? Institutionalized gymnastics and physical culture exposed millions to rigid forms of bodily movement still used today. It developed their physiques along pre-scripted lines, developing their musculature and posture to reach idealized goals. The physical body, or 'global body', became linked to nationalism and race science with physical culture seen as not leisure, but necessity. Institutional exercise physically changed individuals but symbolically imprinted strict ideas about 'fit' and 'unfit' bodies, about masculine and feminine bodies and about the future of races. The movements and discourses people became familiar with laid a fertile ground for the eventual rise of the physical culture movement discussed shortly. For now, it is enough to reiterate the importance

---

[260]Ibid.
[261]Gertrud Pfister, 'Cultural confrontations: German Turnen, Swedish gymnastics and English sport–European diversity in physical activities from a historical perspective', *Culture, Sport, Society* 6 (2003): 61–91.

of political and medical support for physical culture in the military and in schools, the rolling out of physical culture programmes in both Western and non-Western states, albeit the latter being primarily done by force and the cultural normalization of focusing on these bodies. As occurred in other chapters, a certain amount of 'emptying' took place once systems left their origins and were transported into global fitness spaces. A trite but important observation to make is that the schoolchildren who undertook PE grew into adults with a knowledge of physical culture. Soldiers were decommissioned and many remained in fitness spaces, often as instructors. Others turned to different professions but retained their training knowledge. The movements, and the messages attached to them, lasted past classes and sessions. The global knowledge of exercise in 1900 versus 1800 was beyond compare. So too was the value placed on physical culture by teachers, physicians, politicians, philosophers and colonial administrators.

4

Physical culture and selling fitness

In 1889, Prussian strongman Eugen Sandow tore his clothes off in a London auditorium, thereby changing the fitness world as we know it.[1] There is more backstory to this, but it is good to open with something catching. Why Sandow tore off his clothes, and why it mattered, has taken up a great deal of my academic career. It is a starting point for what would be termed the 'physical culture' movement and is, fittingly, an act of showmanship, two traits which defined said movement.[2] Born in 1867, Sandow was the first major physique star. He toured the world, appeared in one of the first-ever films, hosted bodybuilding competitions, created a fitness magazine and sold everything from cigars to cocoa powder. Conrad's history of beauty situates Sandow as one of the key emblems of masculine beauty in the early 1900s.[3] At the time of his stripping, Sandow was less impressive. Still a young man, he spent his teens and early twenties as an athletic vagabond. Trying his hand at wrestling and posing, Sandow met older strongman Professor Louis Atilla (Ludwig Durlacher). Atilla had performed feats of strength for Queen Victoria in 1887 and toured over Europe. He trained under the world's first strongman of note, Felice Napoli, and was, at the time, running a gym in Belgium.[4] We have not, thus far, focused too much on strongmen and women, these being professional performers. The reason is simple. Up until the late nineteenth century, such individuals did little to advance the popularity or spread of physical culture. They were largely curios in a field

---

[1] David Chapman, *Sandow the magnificent: Eugen Sandow and the beginnings of bodybuilding* (Chicago: University of Illinois, 1994), 24–34.
[2] Broderick Chow, *Muscle works: Physical culture and the performance of masculinity* (Northwestern University Press, 2024).
[3] Sebastian Conrad, 'Globalizing the beautiful body: Eugen sandow, bodybuilding, and the ideal of muscular manliness at the turn of the Twentieth-century', *Journal of World History* 32 (2021): 95–125.
[4] Kim Beckwith and Jan Todd, 'Requiem for a strongman: Reassessing the career of Louis Attila', *Iron Game History* 7 (2002): 42–55.

driven by politicians, physicians and instructors. The advent of physical culture placed these individuals, 'fitness celebrities', into the limelight.

Back to Sandow and his pant-less escapade. Under Atilla's tutelage, Sandow developed a flair for drama. During a trip to Holland, press stories claimed Sandow destroyed the floor of an apartment he was letting because he had so many heavy weights in his room. He also caused a brief stir when he destroyed novelty strength machines around the city, leading to reports of a mysterious strongman who had destroyed the machines not once, but thrice.[5] Eventually, the duo set their eyes on a London strongman, named Samson, whose shows included a challenge to the audience. If anyone could match Samson's feats of strength they would win £500. At the time, such contests were commonplace, and laden with trickery. Competitors used specialized equipment which only they could lift or, in some cases, secretly added weight before an audience member lifted it. Samson issued his challenge, only to be met by Sandow dressed in an oversized suit. The optics of the visibly powerful Samson being challenged by a smaller man in an oversized suit caused confusion. Sandow climbed on the stage and ripped his clothes off to reveal a body both muscular and lean. Not yet at his peak, it was a physique that would soon be called the most perfectly developed in the world. Sensing a ruse was taking place, Samson foisted his assistant on Sandow, who Sandow duly defeated. Buying for time, Samson refused to face Sandow, instead agreeing to face him in three days' time.[6]

In the intervening period, Sandow's name echoed throughout the press. Such was the seriousness with which the contest was treated, the judges on that second night included the marquis of Queensberry and Lord de Clifford. Sandow won the contest, won a contract for his own show and began his ascent into mainstream cultures.[7] We will return to Sandow shortly but this brief anecdote is illustrative of what's to come. Sandow and his generation of strongmen and strongwomen were core figures in the physical culture movement. Their expertise did not come from education, experience or professions but from their physiques. Understanding the age of physical culture as roughly the 1880s to the outbreak of the Great War in 1914, it is no exaggeration to say the mantle of expertise in fitness shifted to strength athletes. This is a bold claim but one which will bear fruit as the chapter progresses. It was strength athletes who began to inform transnational health behaviours, they who delivered lectures and they who sold products. Braudy characterized the nineteenth century as a time when individuals could become celebrities and rise above their station.[8] Sport and physical culture offered a pathway. This was not done in a vacuum. The success of physical culture was predicated on the fitness practices discussed

---

[5]Chapman, *Sandow*, 12.
[6]Ibid., 24–35.
[7]Ibid., 35–60.
[8]Leo Braudy, *The frenzy of renown: Fame & its history* (Oxford University, 1986).

in the last two chapters. The physical culture era can be viewed then, as a sort of palimpsest, an idea inscribed upon a pre-existing model. What differed was its unregulated and uneven development.

How did physical culture differ from gymnastics, club-swinging or yoga? They certainly intersected but physical culture differed in its commercial reach. It was a private phenomenon fuelled by business interests conveying, sincere or not, a solution to individual and global health problems. Sandow was a figurehead, and one of the most successful entrepreneurs, but he was joined by dozens of global names. Studying physical culture as a commercially global culture, this chapter begins with an examination of what physical culture was and who could be viewed as global physical culturists as opposed to regional ones. It also answers a critical question of why the 1880s and not, say the 1850s or 1860s as a starting point? From there, the chapter explores the 'empire of things' which accompanied physical culture's popularity in the form of globally sold products.[9] The chapter ends by examining the print networks found within magazines which tightened bonds between physical culturists around the world. The rise of physical culture between 1880 and 1914 exemplifies the intersection of commercial interests and cultural norms, illustrating how globalized ideals of health were shaped through market mechanisms and embodied performances. Figures like Sandow transformed fitness from a localized, often class-bound activity into a commercial empire driven by print media, mail-order equipment, and public spectacles. This commodification did more than spread fitness; it codified ideals of the 'perfect body' tied to race, class and gender hierarchies. By globalizing these ideals, physical culture not only reinforced Eurocentric and patriarchal norms but also opened contested spaces where local adaptations challenged and reinterpreted these narratives.

What is physical culture?

How does a term originate? When did 'jogging' become the description for a new kind of running? Or working out come to denote a training program? Furthermore, when did body-building first come into popular parlance? What happens within modern fitness spaces when one confuses bodybuilding with weightlifting or powerlifting? These are pedantic questions, and ones we have answers to, but it is critical to explore when a phrase takes a cultural meaning. Physical culture was presented as something different from the previous gymnastic and exercise trends studied. It was presented as modern, scientific and, for want of a better phrase, trendy. Writer P. G. Wodehouse

---

[9]Frank Trentmann, *Empire of things: How we became a world of consumers, from the fifteenth century to the twenty-first* (Penguin, 2016).

warned *Vanity Fair* readers in 1914 of the 'physical culture peril' which afflicted men. Whereas once they sprang from bed to bath to breakfast, they now delayed their ritual to partake in boorish exercises.[10] Wodehouse himself, despite objections, trialled Sandow's exercises.[11] In that sense, he was no different to Leopold Bloom, the protagonist of James Joyce's *Ulysses*. Unhappy with his life, and physique, Bloom committed to resuming his Sandow exercises.[12] These were not gymnastic, club-swinging or yogic practices. No, these were physical culture exercises.

Writing in 1908, physical culturist Alexander Wallace Jones claimed that twenty years ago 'physical culture was scarcely known. Nowadays everyone understands its meaning'.[13] For contemporaries, there was a time one could distinguish before the physical culture movement and after it became popular. Todd's study of physical culture traced its Anglophone origins to Adolphus Vongnieur's *Treatise on the Bane of Vice*, published in 1787. There, physical culture meant growth and maturation.[14] In the 1860s, American instructor Dio Lewis attached its meaning to health and fitness in a monthly magazine.[15] Lewis included physical culture as a subtitle, rather than a focus. From Lewis, it is possible to see how physical culture crept from subtitles to titles in health tracts. In Britain, it followed a largely similar trajectory, emerging within educational settings as a label for PE before pushing into more mainstream discussions. It soon came to be used as a catch-all phrase for exercise in pursuit of physical perfection and became new ubiquitous with the publication of magazines such as *Physical Culture* in the United States (established 1899), Sandow's *Magazine of Physical Culture in Great Britain* (established 1898) or *La Culture Physique* in France (established 1904).[16]

It was from the mid-1880s that institutional gymnastics, race science discourses, the muscular Christian movement and codification of sport grew in prominence. Physical culture was not immune to the century's broader sporting movement. In Central Europe, Germany and Austro-Hungary led the way. Stemming, in part from the *turnverein* movement, weightlifting gymnasiums and competitions can be traced to the 1870s and 1880s. The creation of weightlifting contests, often in beer halls, had a significant impact on the possibilities and understandings of what a strong body was.[17] Thus

---

[10]P.G. Wodehouse, 'The physical culture peril and how the Nation may be easily saved from it', *Vanity Fair* May (1914): 31–4.
[11]David Waller, *The perfect man: The muscular life and times of Eugen Sandow, Victorian strongman* (Victorian Secrets, 2011), 137.
[12]Austin Briggs, 'The mismeasure of bloom: Sandow, folklore, scientific racism, eugenics', *James Joyce Quarterly* 59 (2022): 597–615.
[13]A.Wallace Jones, *Fifty exercises for health & strength* (Gale and Polden, 1908), 9.
[14]Jan Todd, 'Reflections on Physical Culture', *Iron Game History*, no. 2–3 (2015): 2–8.
[15]Ibid.
[16]Jan Todd, Joe Roark and Terry Todd, 'A briefly annotated bibliography of English language serial publications in the field of physical culture', *Iron Game History* 1 (1991): 25–40.
[17]Gottfried Schödl, *The lost past* (IWF, 1992), 10–44.

far, the systems we have examined, club-swinging withstanding, centred on bodyweight exercises. Yes you needed pommel horses and bars for gymnastic movements but the use of heavy weights was minimal. Indeed, for a great deal of the nineteenth century, individuals often distinguished between 'safe' (meaning light-weight or bodyweight movements) and 'dangerous' exercises (meaning heavy weights). This concern was echoed in the sporting world where European and American physicians spent a great deal of time warning about the dangers of excessive exercise.[18]

An illustrative example can be found in American physician George Barker Windship (1834–76) who took to physical culture in the 1850s. He did this first by using gymnastics but eventually using a self-created device known as a health lift. Using this machine, Windship lifted hundreds of pounds. Windship's 'health lift', and its imitations, spurred a brief health craze during the 1860s open to men and women. Deriding physicians who criticized heavy weightlifting as dangerous, Windship's early death from a stroke was taken as 'proof' that one should not lift heavy weights. It is true, of course, that strongmen performers existed before and after this time, but they were curios as opposed to role models.[19] In Central Europe, however, a series of innovations in the production of dumbbells and barbells facilitated the growth of weightlifting clubs, and competitions. These competitions were less theatrical and more grounded in sport than Sandow's theatrical contest with Samson.[20]

Weightlifting contests emerged in Austria and Germany in the 1870s, oftentimes in *turner* clubs and, in scenes immortalized in print and paintings, in beer halls. That Vienna was the site of weightlifting's first national governing body in 1890 lends some credence to Austria's importance.[21] Webster's work on weightlifting found that, by 1885, two distinct weightlifting styles emerged in Europe in 'clean' versus 'continental' weightlifting.[22] The distinction between these two was simple enough. Continental lifting allowed athletes to be more lax when lifting a barbell overhead from the ground. Clean lifting was focused on strict form with minimal contact between body and the barbell. The first world weightlifting championship was held in London in 1891. Weightlifting was subsequently included in the inaugural 1896 Athens Olympics.[23] Without belabouring the point, sporting competitions had two consequences. Competition brought innovation, especially with regards

---

[18]James Whorton, '"Athlete's heart": The medical debate over athleticism, 1870–1920', *Journal of Sport History* 91 (1982): 30–52.
[19]Joan Paul, 'The health reformers: George Barker windship and Boston's strength seekers', *Journal of Sport History* 10 (1983): 41–57.
[20]Jan Todd, 'The strength builders: A history of barbells, dumbbells and Indian clubs', *The International Journal of the History of Sport* 20 (2003): 65–90.
[21]Schödl, *The lost* … .
[22]David Webster, *The iron game* (John Geddes, 1976), 12–24.
[23]Gherardo Bonini, 'London: The cradle of modern weightlifting', *Sports Historian* 21 (2001): 56–70.

equipment. Koyda's dissertation on weightlifting stressed the changes barbells underwent during the period 1880–1914.[24] Barbells and dumbbells became commonplace, athletes could vary their weights and barbells became more efficient in terms of weight distribution.[25] Variability was a key factor. Fixed barbells have an unchangeable weight, that is, a 50-kilogram barbell will only ever be a 50-kilogram barbell. Variable barbells have weights which can be raised or lowered.[26]

The ability to lift heavier weights meant individuals could get stronger and build more muscle. The Todds and Jason Shurley once cited the introduction of strength coaching in American sports as a seismic shift. Athletes got bigger, faster and stronger thanks to strength coaching.[27] The slow but evident popularization of weightlifting as a sport, and its accompanying technological changes were one of the, if not the, most important shifts in nineteenth-century fitness. Athletes were no longer limited in the amount of weight they could lift. Bodies became larger, stronger and more muscular.[28] Yet it is true that the vast majority of individuals engaging in physical culture did not lift heavy weights. In fact, many physical culturists dissuaded individuals from lifting heavy weights, a point we will discuss. But oftentimes leading physical culture figures, the experts of their time, trained with heavy weights.

Professional strongmen and women broke into the zeitgeist across Europe and North America at the same moment weightlifting emerged as a sport. Many of these individuals trained in weightlifting gyms and built their bodies through weightlifting regimes. Body images and perceptions changed, thanks to leaner physiques built through heavy weightlifting. This was combined with a new leisure culture across Europe and North America which privileged music hall or vaudeville acts.[29] Whereas strength performers prior to this were largely confined to the circus or village fair, music halls provided regular employment, provided one was entertaining. They offered variety shows wherein singing might be combined with plays, satirical acts, feats of strength and poetry.[30] For the strength performer, this represented a boon and, in time, many pivoted from the stage to other elements of social life. From his victory over Samson, Sandow slowly but successfully parlayed his stage successes into a public profile. By the mid-1890s, he was regarded

---

[24]Mark Kodya, *An exploration of the history of weightlifting as a reflection of the major socio-political events and trends of the 20th century* (Master's thesis, Empire State College, 2005), 30–55.
[25]Ibid; Todd, 'The strength ... '.
[26]Kimberly Ayn Beckwith, *Building strength: Alan Calvert, the Milo Bar-bell company, and the modernization of American weight-training* (The University of Texas at Austin, 2006).
[27]Jason Shurley, Jan Todd and Terry Todd, *Strength coaching in America: A history of the innovation that transformed sports* (University of Texas, 2019), 1–23.
[28]Ibid.
[29]Christopher Balme, *The globalization of theatre 1870–1930* (Cambridge University Press, 2020).
[30]Keith Gregson and Mike Huggins, 'Sport, music-hall culture and popular song in nineteenth-century England', *Culture, Sport Society* 2 (1999): 82–102.

as a health expert and routinely interviewed for his thoughts on longevity. In the mid-1900s, he spoke to government commissions and opened a 'Curative Institute'. Sandow's education on medicine, or even PE, was null. His expertise stemmed from his physique. Although unique, his leap from the stage to the mainstream was mimicked by others.

Physical culture was a global phenomenon from Europe to Africa, America and Australasia.[31] In the remainder of this section we will discuss the 'main characters', physical culture's global culture and the mechanics

FIGURE 4.1 Sandow in pose, *c.* 1902.[32]

---

[31]Conor Heffernan, 'State of the field', *History* 107 (2022): 143–62.
[32]*Wiki Commons*. Available at https://commons.wikimedia.org/wiki/File:%22A_New_Sandow_Pose_%28VII%29%22,_Eugen_Sandow_Wellcome_L0035269_%28cropped%29.jpg

of physical culture as a commercial enterprise. Before getting there, it is useful to locate a hub for our discussions.[33] That mantle, undoubtedly, goes to Great Britain. While the United States was a hotbed of physical culture, it was Britain where innumerable foreign physical culturists came to work in the late nineteenth and early twentieth centuries. With its vast network of music halls, public appetite for physical culture and links across Empire, Britain represented a fertile ground for aspiring strongmen and women to build business empires.[34] Physical culture centred around the Anglophone world prior to the outbreak of the Great War. London hosted the first international weightlifting competition in 1891, Sandow hosted his business interests in London and it was British physical culture magazines which had large, global, audiences.[35]

Sandow established the world's first dedicated fitness magazine, *Sandow's Magazine of Physical Culture* in 1898, and its contemporary British magazine *Health & Strength* founded in 1898 was distributed around the Empire.[36] On *Health & Strength*, its issues in the early 1900s featured readers across Australasia, Africa and North America.[37] In 1906, the magazine, driven by concerns about the 'national physique', established a *Health and Strength League* whose membership totalled 13,000 members in 1911 and nearly double that by 1914. In 1910, its annual was estimated to have 90,000 readers.[38] While Bourke was correct in citing the magazine as working-class one, a great deal of physical culture was directed towards the middle-class gentleman.[39]

Britain acted as a middle-ground between Europe, the United States and Australasia, as well as Africa. It is telling that many of the 'great' physical culture celebrities cut their teeth in Britain. Such celebrities varied, however, in the extent of their fame. Physical culture marked a new endeavour for these individuals, some of whom considered themselves to be athletes more so than performers.[40] Others clearly positioned themselves as entrepreneurs. Using Vamplew's understanding of sporting entrepreneurs as 'change agents in the supply of sports products', we will focus on those who attempted, and

---

[33]Bárbara Polo-Martín and César Ducruet, 'Coupled connectivity in the global complex network: The case of United Kingdom (1880–1925)', *Applied Network Science* 9 (2024): 15.
[34]Graeme Kent, *The strongest men on earth* (Biteback, 2012), 1–45.
[35]Lucy Boucher and Conor Heffernan, 'A great weight lifted: the history of the British Amateur Weight-lifting Association', *Sport in History* 44 (2024): 369–80.
[36]Laurel Brake and Marysa Demoor, eds., *Dictionary of nineteenth-century journalism in Great Britain and Ireland* (Academia Press, 2009), 277.
[37]Joanna Bourke, *Working class cultures in Britain, 1890–1960* (Routledge, 2008), 35–8.
[38]George Mosse, *The image of man: The creation of modern masculinity* (Oxford University Press, 1998), 137.
[39]Michael Anton Budd, *The sculpture machine: Physical culture and body politics in the age of empire* (New York University Press, 1997), 11–30.
[40]Kent, *The Strongest ...* , 11–56.

often succeeded, in developing markets and products.[41] There are a litany of individuals to choose from in this regard but there are two of global importance to consider: Sandow and Bernarr MacFadden. From his victory over Samson in 1889, Sandow became the age's most globally significant physical culturist. The next physique athlete to make a similar impact did not come until Arnold Schwarzenegger in the 1970s.[42] Following several years touring in England, Sandow set out for the United States in 1893. There he truly became an entrepreneur. Under the guidance of Flo Zeigfeld (1867–1932), Sandow performed across America.[43] More importantly, he hosted private posing sessions, produced his first monograph, appeared in a Thomas Edison film and innumerable newspapers. When Sandow returned from America in 1896, he embarked on a health empire. In 1898, he produced the first explicit fitness magazine in *Sandow's Magazine of Physical Culture*, which was accompanied by his globally popular book, *Strength and How to Obtain It*. From 1897 to 1916, when he went bankrupt, Sandow opened gymnasiums, sold equipment, supplements, cigars and multiple other products.[44] Additionally, he embarked on tours of Africa and Australasia, hosted a physique competition, trained troops and gained a ceremonial position of physical culture instructor to the British monarch.

As two Sandow biographers made clear, Sandow was a man desperate for status. As a fitness figure, he gave lectures to physicians, offered to train troops for the British military (and did so), he wore the garb of the gentleman and, audaciously, opened a Curative Institute.[45] Sandow was regarded not as a curio, but as a sort of scholar-in-arms of human perfection by individuals like Francis Galton (1822–1911) and was, at one point, treated as infallible by many journalists, physicians and politicians. He was, in reality, a strongman of dubious education and cut-throat capitalism but more on that later. His veneer was one of respectability. The same could not be said of Bernarr MacFadden (1868–1955). Born Bernard McFadden in 1868, Macfadden was one of physical culture's enigmatic figures. Changing his name in the 1880s to Bernarr, believed to be more powerful-sounding, MacFadden was America's answer to, and antithesis of, Sandow.[46] Like Sandow, he produced a fitness magazine, *Physical Culture*, first published in 1899. He hosted physique competitions, wrote extensively on health, opened his own restaurant and founded several spas. He also courted

---

[41]Wray Vamplew, 'Products, promotion, and (possibly) profits: Sports entrepreneurship revisited', *Journal of Sport History* 45 (2018): 183–201.
[42]Dominic Morais, 'Branding iron: Eugen Sandow's "modern" marketing strategies, 1887–1925', *Journal of Sport History* 40 (2013): 193–214.
[43]Chapman, *Sandow*, 84–90.
[44]Morais, 'Branding … '.
[45]Conor Heffernan, 'Desirable bodies and Eugen Sandow's curative institute in edwardian England', *Social History of Medicine* 35, no. 1 (2022): 195–216.
[46]William Hunt, *Body love* (Popular Press, 1989).

the favour of political elites, notably during the interwar period when he trained troops in Italy and Portugal under two separate dictators.[47] There was even a short-lived, but unsuccessful, presidential run during the 1930s. Furthermore, MacFadden went on global tours and left a legacy in some of these countries. In Britain during the late 1890s, MacFadden joined forces with bicycle entrepreneur, Hopton Hadley, to market a muscle developer. With Hadley's support, he created fitness magazine *Physical Development* in 1898. MacFadden sold his shares in *Physical Development* to Hadley in 1899, who subsequently changed the title to *Health and Strength*.[48]

That was the 'Sandow' side of MacFadden, which engaged in global tours, created businesses and forged relationships with individuals ranging from Bernard Shaw to Upon Sinclair. MacFadden was, however, a firebrand with strange ideas. During his trips to England, MacFadden briefly gave a lecture in Ireland on disease. He fled the stage when the boos from Irish doctors became too voluminous.[49] MacFadden lived by the natural fallacy.[50] He pushed for raw diets, held open views towards sex and positioned himself as superior to, but engaged in battle with, the medical profession. MacFadden's works included ideas like pulling one's hair to prevent hair loss, raw milk diets and fasting to cure illnesses.[51] In the aftermath of his second physique competition, hosted in New York, MacFadden fled the United States under allegations of peddling solicitous images of female competitors.[52] When he returned in the mid-1900s, he was a regular target for the medical profession.[53] And yet, he built a magazine empire which counted millions of readers by 1914. Many of his readers were not based in the United States but further abroad. While MacFadden and Sandow never crossed paths, the two reached the greatest heights as global figures. One courted respectability, the other controversy, but their reach was domestic and, critically, international.

What constituted the 'second rung' of physical culture? There were several figures within the Anglophone, Saxophone and Francophone world. In France, Edmond Desbonnet (1867–1953) was the foremost recreational voice on health. Establishing a series of successful franchises, Desbonnet's

---

[47]Ryan Murtha, Conor Heffernan and Thomas Hunt, 'Building American Supermen? Bernarr MacFadden, Benito Mussolini and American fascism in the 1930s', *Sport in Society* 24 (2021): 1941-55.
[48]James Woycke, *Esprit de Corps: A history of North American bodybuilding* (Self-Published, 2016), 8-10.
[49]Conor Heffernan, *The history of physical culture in Ireland* (Palgrave, 2020), 30.
[50]Olaf Stieglitz, '"Mentally superior children are born of physically superior people": Bernarr Macfadden's "physical culture" world and the influence of Eugenic thought in American fitness culture, 1900s-1930s', *Amerikastudien/American Studies* (2019): 241-64.
[51]Hunt, *Body*, 1-40.
[52]Jan Todd, 'Bernarr Macfadden: Reformer of feminine form', *Journal of Sport History* 14 (1987): 61-75.
[53]Ronald Deutsch, *The nuts among the berries* (Ballantine, 1967).

greatest contribution to physical culture was the establishment of *La Culture Physique*, a fitness magazine which ran from 1904 to 1967.[54] While other mainland European magazines were influential, such as *Kraft und Schönheit* (Strength and Beauty, est. 1901) in Germany, *La Culture Physique* was the most highly regarded.[55] The titles of such magazines were, themselves, rather derivative. Indeed, it is funny to see just how often 'Strength and Health' emerged elsewhere. See, for example, contemporary Spanish magazine *Salud y Fuerza* (Health & Strength) or *Strength* magazine in America, as well as later *Strength and Health*. Returning to *La Culture Physique*, part of its esteem came from Desbonnet's standing. Desbonnet as entrepreneur sold magazines, gym memberships and raised awareness of performers like Louis 'Apollon' Uni (1862–1928).[56] *La Culture Physique* published not only on French physical culture but on global physical culture matters and often featured snippets from around the world.

On our artificial second wrung must also sit individuals like American entrepreneur Alan Calvert (1875–1944), and British athletes/entrepreneurs W. A. Pullum (1887–1960) and Thomas Inch (1881–1963). Each helped advance weightlifting technologies in improved dumbbell and barbell equipment.[57] Critically, such equipment was sold to the masses in Britain and the United States. Calvert also founded *Strength* magazine in 1914, which can be credited as America's first weightlifting magazine.[58] He was matched by Pullum and Inch, the latter of whom is credited with creating plate-loaded barbells (the technology still used today). For obvious reasons, those selling heavy-duty training equipment tended to be confined to their own countries due to transport cost. One exception was Swedish physician Gustav Zander (1835–1920), who created a series of therapeutic exercise machines based on Ling's gymnastics. Zander was not a physical culturist like Sandow or MacFadden but his machines came to popularity during the same time. Establishing a Therapeutical Institute in Stockholm, Zander's fortunes changed at the 1876 Centennial Exhibition where his machines were awarded a gold medal for innovation.[59] De la Peña traced the evolution of health spas in late nineteenth-century America and Europe with Zander's successes.[60] Targeted at elite men and women, seeking reprieve from the stresses of modern life, such spas used Zander's machines. Zander's machines

---

[54]David Chapman and Edmond Desbonnet, *The kings of strength* (McFarland, 2022), 1–22.
[55]Bernd Wedemeyer-Kolwe, '*Der neue Mensch*': *Körperkultur im Kaiserreich und in der Weimarer Republik* (Königshausen & Neumann, 2004), 212.
[56]Ibid., 382–400.
[57]Randy Roach, *Muscle, smoke & mirrors* (Openhouse, 2008), 111–40.
[58]Kim Beckwith and Jan Todd, 'Strength: America's first muscle magazine, 1914–1935', *Iron Game History* 9 (2005): 11–28.
[59]Roberta Park, 'Health, exercise, and the biomedical impulse, 1870–1914', *Research Quarterly for Exercise and Sport* 61 (1990): 126–40.
[60]Carolyn Thomas De La Peña, *The body electric: How strange machines built the modern American* (NYU Press, 2003), 72–88.

seemed to promise scientific solutions to many of the same issues physical culturists purported to solve. By 1906, he lay claim to 146 cities with Zander health institutes in Europe, North and South America.[61]

The bottom rung was the travelling performer. Writing a popular history of this time Kent referred to this new era of strength performers as 'adaptable ... prepared to take almost any risks ... to attain their coveted top-of-the-bill status'.[62] These individuals managed to sustain several decades of careers and produce ancillary goods and services. Four of the biggest names to consider are George Hackenschmidt (1878–1968), Arthur Saxon (1878–1921), Louis Cyr (1863–1912) and Katie Sandwina (1884–1952).[63] All four of these performers toured North America, Africa and Europe. Three of them, Saxon, Cyr and Hackenschmidt, could be considered legitimate athletes. Saxon and Cyr took part in weightlifting competitions while Hackenschmidt is better known as a wrestler. All four parlayed their strength into transnational tours with lead billing, and in more than one instance, books and sponsorships. Their names were known throughout the physical culture world and they represented the ceiling for what a certain kind of physical culturist could achieve. Even Sandwina, whose arrival in the United States was heralded as a sort of new dawn for the female form (women could be strong AND feminine ... imagine!), never escaped her stage origins.[64] For every MacFadden, Sandow or Desbonnet, there existed several dozen well-known physical culturists whose entrepreneurial efforts never broke out of being a performer.

While the above categorization may seem insulting, it is anything but. The ability to achieve transnational fame and a several-decade career as a performer was revolutionary. Stage shows offered a true means of fame, provided one was entertaining. To that end, individuals used a variety of feats, be it lifting cannons, horses or audience members. They gave posing demonstrations and tapped into the national anxieties of their times by appearing in nationalist garb if required. Some became famed for 'optimizing' basic human functions. Danish physical culture Jørgen Peter Müller (1866–1938) sold millions of copies of *Mit System* (My System) in the early 1900s which included prescriptions on breathing. His works were translated across Scandinavia and the Anglophone world as Müller opened a health studio in London in 1912. Others like Austria-Hungarian Max Sick (1882–1961) taught individuals muscle control techniques to build their bodies without dumbbells or barbells.[65]

---

[61]Ibid., 73.
[62]Kent, *The Strongest Men*, 14.
[63]I have chosen their stage names as I wish to avoid detailed biographies.
[64]Jan Todd, 'Center ring: Katie Sandwina and the construction of celebrity', *Iron Game History* 10 (2007): 29–33.
[65]Hans Bonde, 'From hygiene to salvation: JP Muller, international advocate of gymnastics', *The International Journal of the History of Sport* 26 (2009): 1357–75.

Physical culture, as a term, and as a commercial practice was a global phenomenon. The very phrase became 'a thing' in and of itself. Prior to 1940, the phrase 'jogging' was meaningless. Fast forward two decades and the phrase had a definitive meaning. In 1870, 'physical culturist' may have had a vague familiarity with some. By 1914, critics like the acerbic but always entertaining Wodehouse understood its meaning. A term was born and its broadness term meant that new pathways existed. If you wanted to be a vegetarian physical culturist you could follow MacFadden. For raw strength, Inch, Saxon or Cyr was useful. If it was a respectability born out from 'muscledom', look no further than Sandow. This was a global phrase with significant value and its genius lay in the ability to be simultaneously specific and vague. This allowed a broad swathe of individuals to come to its use. These individuals were, however, something of a monolith in terms of race and gender. Those who embarked on world tours, sat atop playbills and marketed goods were nearly exclusively white, European or American.

While non-white entrepreneurs existed in local markets their influence often paled in comparison to the 'celebrities'. While this may seem to be an offshoot of broader power relations globally, it held a symbolic importance. Many individuals wrote passionately about eugenics, improving racial stock and racial differences. Some, like Sandow, reiterated these comments when touring Asia and Africa. There were exceptions. When Richard Fox (1846–1922), editor of the *Police Gazette*, an American sporting magazin, held a bodybuilding contest in the early 1900s, he published images of muscled African-American men with captions like 'black Hercules'.[66] More common were depictions and conversations couched in racialized terms and soft imperial ideas about races. Walsh's study of physical culture in America depicted it as an embodied practice for re-affirming whiteness.[67] The same certainly held true on the global stage as physical culture magazines continually returned to artificial lineages to Greco-Rome, endorsements of built physiques using 'modern' equipment and a tired but powerful trope about civilized versus non-civilized bodies.[68] A fine example of this power of Greco-Roman ideals can be found in the scores and scores of Asian and African contributors to British and American physical culture magazines posing like Sandow and modelling their bodies on his. One such individual, K. V. Iyer from India, came to physical culture in the pre-war period and, writing for Indian audiences in the 1920s and 1930s, explicitly cited Sandow and Greco-Roman conceptions of beauty as the ideal for Indian men.[69] Resistance existed in India, and indeed during Sandow's tour several

---

[66] "A Black Hercules," *The National Police Gazette*, June 13, (1903), 82.
[67] Shannon Walsh, *Eugenics and physical culture performance in the progressive era: Watch whiteness workout* (Springer, 2020), 1–45.
[68] Peter Miller, 'The imaginary antiquity of physical culture', *The Classical Outlook* 93 (2018): 21–31.
[69] Ramachandran, and Heffernan, 'Building the Transnational ... '.

Indian wrestlers explicitly challenged ideas of Sandow's perfection, but a globalizing streamline existed.[70]

What of women? Physical culture allowed *some* muscular women to gain celebrity and acclaim. Research to this very day stresses the pressure strong and muscular women face societally. Conditioned to expect a narrow view of what a woman's body should look like, individuals have long questioned the femininity of powerful women.[71] While current moods are shifting, I raise this issue to stress how unique a strongwoman's body was in 1901 but also to re-iterate the gendered structures which often kept them in secondary positions. A number of strongwomen, with fascinating stage names, appeared like Minerva, Athleta, Charmion or Vulcana.[72] I want to end by discussing the previously mentioned Sandwina. Sandwina, whose name was taken to mimic Sandow, toured the United States in the early 1990s. When Sandwina came to New York, she garnered a great deal of media attention.[73] The discourse around her was that she was beautiful, and an attentive wife with curious strength. She passed as acceptable, admittedly within the over-the-top world of physical culture, but the focus on her femininity, as Todd explained, was done to normalize her.[74]

Sandwina was, arguably, the biggest name among strongwomen but her economic opportunities were hampered. Whereas Sandow, and other strongmen could, and did, produce books, Sandwina was not afforded the chance. She could perform feats of strength on stage, but the average woman was encouraged to build slender and svelte, but not strong bodies. Nor did Sandwina market supplements, or give lectures on strength. She enjoyed a multi-decade career as a strongwoman which was a remarkable feat. Yet the monolithic global physical culture market was decidedly male when it came to money. And, as the next sections make clear, physical culture was about health and money.

Empire of things

In 1903, Sandow sued Hungarian gymnasium owner Josef Szalay over copyright infringement. The issue at hand was a spring-grip dumbbell.[75] Szalay had, in Sandow's mind, copied his patented equipment. The court agreed, and Szalay was forced to cease operations. This was not the first, nor the last time, Sandow sued a rival. A few years prior, Sandow had sued

---

[70]Watt, 'Cultural exchange'.
[71]David Chapman and Patricia Vertinsky, *Venus with biceps: A pictorial history of muscular women* (arsenal pulp, 2010).
[72]Ibid.
[73]Todd, 'Center ring', 7.
[74]Ibid.
[75]Boucher and Heffernan, 'A great … '.

Arthur Saxon after Saxon claimed to have beaten Sandow in competition. That Saxon **had** beaten Sandow in a weightlifting competition was beside the point.[76] In the early 1890s, Sandow sued a printing house for publishing posters of Sandow in signature pose. This image had been used to promote a variety of ales and beers without Sandow's permission. On this last issue, Sandow was justified. One instance from Irish stout manufacturer Murphy's Stout used this image and even included a fake testimonial from Sandow stating that 'from experience I can strongly recommend J.J. Murphy's stout'.[77]

Sandow was something of a paradox. His belief in physical culture may well have been genuine and there was a social good inherent in many of his messages. He was, at heart, also a capitalist who understood that physical culture was lived through commerce.[78] Here, we will look at the trade of fitness equipment, supplements and photographs, the three most popular items of fitness commerce before discussing less successful, and savoury products. Physical culture, as well as the desire to shape one's body, was regulated by a complex and commercialized system proffering equipment, books and supplements. We have already discussed club-swinging and its commercial undertones although it is worth stating here that physical culture largely brought about the decline of club-swinging as a practice. While it continued to be used, it lost its desirability in the face of other physical culture equipment. This is not conjecture but was a common complaint among Indian club swingers who positioned themselves as under threat from the 'new' fitness environment.

What constituted physical culture equipment and why does it matter? Here we return to Sandow, the man who globalized spring-grip dumbbells and pulleys. In 1897, Sandow became the Whiteley Exerciser Company's European agent. Founded by Alexander Whiteley, the company sold pulleys which could be attached to a doorframe, similar to suspension training equipment sold today.[79] Initially targeting swimmers, they pivoted in the early 1890s to physical culture. Beckwith notes that MacFadden exhibited the Whiteley pulley at the 1893 Chicago World Fair. Sandow marketed the Developer and mentioned it in his 1897 work, *Strength and How to Obtain It*. He claimed to have discovered Whiteley's device in America and impressed the inventor with his own comparable equipment. As per Chapman, Sandow cut ties with Whiteley in 1898 and set up a manufacturing plant in France to produce his patented 'Sandow Developer'. Nominally the same, it included a few modifications distinguishable from Whiteley. It was, in Chapman's

---

[76]Chapman, *Sandow*, 106–110.
[77]Conor Heffernan, 'Sandow and Stout: An Irish Story', *Physical Culture Study*, 19 September 2016. https://physicalculturestudy.com/2016/09/19/sandow-and-stout-an-irish-story/
[78]Webster, *The Iron Game*, 23–45.
[79]Chapman, *Sandow*, 114–15.

estimation, one of the century's most popular pieces of workout equipment and was produced long after Sandow's death in the 1920s.[80]

Next Sandow marketed a spring-grip dumbbell. This dumbbell encapsulated Sandow, and his partner's, genius. Lightweight, the dumbbell can be described as two metal plates with springs between them. Trainees pressed the two plates together, thereby compressing the springs. First marketed in Sandow's magazine, the dumbbell, combined with the Developer/pulley, became a popular device for adults and children. Eschewing the heavy weights which built his physique, Sandow claimed the key to muscle and health was concentration. There existed in this, a knowledge asymmetry between Sandow and clients. Sandow was aware that his products would not produce physiques comparable to his but knew his audience would be reticent to lift heavy weights. While beneficial, Sandow's dumbbells were sold with half-truths.[81] Sandow marketed a product with promising results using concentration and a loosely defined idea of science. The rhetoric was simple – squeezing the grips ensured trainees were concentrating on the muscle and would build the physique of their dreams.[82] With each purchase, Sandow's customers were given measurement charts to track progress. For men, they could compare their measurements to Sandow.

Sandow sold other products, but the dumbbell and developer were his most popular. They were sold throughout the world through three means. First, they accompanied Sandow on world tours. Daley previously noted the frequency with which Sandow's shows and lectures were accompanied by the opportunity to buy his equipment.[83] Depending on one's geography, one could purchase them from Sandow's base in London. Unfazed by his own experience with Whiteley, Sandow also established agents within countries to sell his equipment. These agents advertised themselves as Sandow retailers and kept his influence alive in numerous countries.[84] While Sandow's booklets boasted his equipment had been supplied to 'nearly all the Crowned Heads of Europe', it was regular consumers who took to them.[85] Users of Sandow's dumbbell have been noted in Europe, the United States, Australia, New Zealand, India, South Africa and other ports of Sandow's tours.[86] What is more interesting is the fact that Sandow's equipment was sold in South America, where he never toured. Fernández's research on Sandow's commerce in Chile found Anglo-Argentine businessmen responsible for

---

[80]Ibid., 114–17.
[81]Conor Heffernan, 'All muscle and no brains?: Contextualizing the fitness entrepreneur in sport history', *Sporting Traditions* 39, no. 2 (2022): 13–32.
[82]Ibid.
[83]Caroline Daley, *Leisure and pleasure: Reshaping and revealing the New Zealand body 1900–1960* (Auckland University, 2013), 49–67.
[84]Ibid.
[85]'Sandow Grip Dumbbell Pamphlet', *Eugen Sandow Patent Spring Grip Dumbbells* (1910), 1.
[86]Heffernan, 'All muscle … ? … '.

selling Sandow's equipment.[87] A similar occurrence was found in a study of Sandow in Meiji Japan during the same period.[88]

The study of exercise equipment pales in comparison to the study of medical devices. Concerning the latter, research has made clear the impact personal and professional devices have on individual's relationship with their own bodies. Moving closer to physical culture, electric devices during the same period were linked to the rise of new, and oftentimes poorly constructed ideas about modernity, and self-hood.[89] Purchasing a Sandow device, or any physical culture good, represented a shift in fitness patterns. Purchasing exercise equipment marked an implicit acknowledgement that one was dissatisfied with their body and that the only solution was a combination of self-work and consumption.[90] For this reason, some of Sandow's clients expressed, vocally, their anxiety and anger about their physiques and lives. Improving one would, it was assumed, improve the other. Critically Sandow offered mail-order courses for his products. This came to be a new line for physical culturists the world over. Clients subscribed to monthly courses and, typically, messages, especially for men, were heavily gendered. They promised to perfect individuals' masculinity, improve their sexual prowess and/or make them better partners.[91]

Was Sandow the sole physical culture entrepreneur? Of course not. The United States had MacFadden and Calvert, among others, Britain had Inch, Pullum, and so on. France had Desbonnet, etc., but none matched Sandow's reach which was built on Sandow's marketability. During Sandow's tour of America physical educationalist Dudley Allen Sargent measured his body and declared it to be the most perfect specimen ever seen. Some years later, a bust of Sandow's body was commissioned in London's Natural History Museum to serve as an example of white male perfection.[92] On tours, Sandow was routinely examined by the medical professionals, who praised his physique. His body, and the fascination with it, transcended borders, reaching those places, like Chile, that Sandow never visited.

---

[87]Felipe Martínez Fernández, 'Fuerza, vigor y consumo: El caso de Eugene Sandow en Santiago de Chile, 1900–1930'. in *11° Congreso Argentino de Educación Física y Ciencias 28 de septiembre-2 de octubre de 2015 Ensenada, Argentina*. (Universidad Nacional de La Plata. Facultad de Humanidades y Ciencias de la Educación. Departamento de Educación Física, 2015.)

[88]藪耕太郎 and ヤブコウタロウ. 'Did the Japanese dream of a muscular body?: Western style of physical training in the Meiji era', 仙台大学紀要 50 (2018): 1–9.

[89]Herbert Sussman, *Victorian technology: Invention, innovation, and the rise of the machine* (Bloomsbury, 2009).

[90]Conor Heffernan, 'Body projects as a historical phenomenon', *Rethinking History* 24 (2020): 417–41.

[91]Aaron Wood, 'Eugen sandow: Performing new masculinities', *Eidos. A Journal for Philosophy of Culture* 5, no. 4 (2021): 21–38.

[92]Chapman, *Sandow*, 119–24.

Perhaps the most ambitious supplement from this period was Plasmon, a forerunner to modern protein powders. Originally created as a Prussian medical aid, Plasmon was sold to a group of businessmen to be marketed in England as a health supplement. Specifically, it promised to increase the 'pro-teid' content of all foods.[93] To that end, agents created a Plasmon cookbook in 1906 to teach mothers, in particular, how to add Plasmon to foods. It was not just, however, a domestic product. Plasmon was, as advertising made clear, suitable for muscle-building. Its advertising, and company logo, included a strongman inspired by Greek antiquity. Plasmon was not unique in this context, Scottish firm Iron-Bru did something similar, but it was unique in courting physical culturists as ambassadors.[94]

During the early 1900s, Plasmon used three individuals to market its athletic and strength-building properties. They were C. B. Fry, Eugen Sandow and Eustace Miles. Given Fry's fame came from competitive sport, although he did class himself at various points as a physical culturist, Sandow and Miles will get our attention. Miles, a vegetarian, presented Plasmon as an effective

FIGURE 4.2 Plasmon advertisement from 1903.[95]

---

[93]Conor Heffernan, 'Superfood or superficial? Plasmon and the birth of the supplement industry', *Journal of Sport History* 47, no. 3 (2020): 243–62.
[94]Ibid.
[95]Author's collection.

substitute for meat. Sandow's endorsements were far more concerned with physical power and perfection.[96] In *Plasmon, What is It?* Sandow claimed to have spent several weeks consuming nothing but Plasmon. Rather than wilt, his strength increased![97] The transformation of Plasmon from medicine to marketplace, even though its time in England was short-lived, highlighted the fuzzy boundaries of health during this period. What could be used to cure was also used to commercialize. Similarly, the shift from Prussia to England showed how easily products could be transmuted.

The photograph was an equally valuable product during this period. Physical culturists engaged in photo manipulation as early as the 1890s.[98] Photographs were, in a sense, physical culture's lifeblood. Correctly staged, images could immortalize individuals and provide 'scientific' proof of their perfection.[99] We have already discussed the surge of physical culture magazines from this period. It is worth noting that many of them circulated the same images of Sandow, Sandwina, Saxon etc. while opening space for lay physical culturists to submit images. A common tactic among entrepreneurs was to allow readers submit images of themselves for competitions, appraisals or updates.[100] There was thus a 'two-way' trade in photography. At the upper echelon, there existed images of celebrity physical culturists shared around the world. For the average physical culturist, male or female (although it was predominantly male), they travelled to photography studios and purchased images of themselves.

There are two areas of physical culture commerce worth exploring in detail before discussing the rise of, and impact of, physical culture's print community. The first being the shift in gymnasium spaces and the second the movement of peoples. One of the few histories of the gymnasium traced its lineage from ancient Athens to the modern fitness centre.[101] Dedicated training spaces have long existed, but there is an argument to be made for a shift between the gymnastic and physical culture of gymnasium in the nineteenth century. The rise of gymnastics in the nineteenth century ushered in a change in fitness geographies and architectures. Obviously an overlap existed, as older gymnasiums simply added new equipment or renovated their training spaces, **but** new bespoke physical culture training spaces emerged from the 1890s.

---

[96]Heffernan, 'Superfood or superficial? Plasmon and the birth of the supplement industry'.
[97]Ibid.
[98]Rachel Ozerkevich, 'Retouched and remarkable: Female athletes in La culture physique (1904) as historical and visual documentation', *Sport History Review* 1 (2023): 1–20.
[99]Fae Brauer, 'Virilizing and valorizing homoeroticism: Eugen sandow's queering of body cultures before and after the wilde trials'. *Visual Culture in Britain* 1 (2017): 35–67.
[100]Rachel Ozerkevich and Conor Heffernan, 'Physical culture, posing, and the medium of fitness magazines', *Early Popular Visual Culture* (2024): 1–22.
[101]Eric Chaline, *The temple of perfection: A history of the gym* (Reaktion, 2015).

What constituted a physical culture gym? How different was, say, Desbonnet's gymnasium in France to those of Professor Louis Atilla in New York? Or what about German gym owner Theodor Siebert's (1866–1961) Gymnastics and Athletic Club of Alsleben-on-the-Saale? Speaking broadly on research concerning North American and European gymnasiums, one can distinguish between strength and lifestyle gymnasiums. While there was a class dimension to this split, and some research does consider strength gyms to have been a more working-class pastime, it is better here to focus on the motivations of such places.[102] It is clear that Sandow's gymnasiums in England, Desbonnet's gyms in France and Attila's gymnasium in New York were destination places.[103] They were fashionable and marketed to men and women of means. In Sandow's case, plush furniture and expensive fittings made his London gymnasium more akin to a luxury hotel. In Desbonnet's case, some have noted a catering to the bourgeoise male and female.[104] The multimodal use of the gym by Sandow and Desbonnet was something of a pastiche of the Athenian gymnasium which served as a place for meeting and training. In New York, Atilla's gymnasium, opened in 1893, was adorned with signed images of celebrities. Atilla's site became something of a hub for travelling strength athletes but it also catered towards average men and women seeking to improve their bodies. Such gyms were, in a sense, indistinguishable from MacFadden's health resorts, older water cure spas in Europe or John Harvey Kellogg's contemporary Battle Creek enterprise.[105] They were part of a broader conspicuous consumption in physical culture.

The irony of such spaces is that many were run by individuals who had built their physiques in basic weightlifting gymnasiums. The inverse of plusher gymnasiums was those dedicated to strength. Some German and Austrian clubs are one example. Another interesting example is Szalay's (1861–c.1915) London gym. Szalay was, in many ways, the 'father' of British weightlifting and his gym became a hub for British and foreign athletes to train.[106] Szalay was not the only coach with an international reputation. Russian Vladislav Krajewski likewise attracted men from Central European to his St. Petersburg gymnasium.[107] Szalay concerns us here. In the first instance, he was a product of globalization. Born in Austro-Hungary, he moved to Frankfurt in the early 1880s, where he joined a weightlifting club. From there, Szalay moved to London and opened a hairdressing salon and barbershop with accompanying gymnasium. Szalay's gym became the first port of call for many incoming strength athletes from Europe and America.[108]

---

[102]Schödl, *The lost past*, 12–45.
[103]Heffernan, 'Desirable Bodies'.
[104]Chapman and Desbonnet, *The Kings*, 20–44.
[105]James Whorton, *Crusaders for fitness* (Princeton, 1982).
[106]Boucher, and Heffernan, 'A great … '.
[107]George Hackenschmidt, 'European corner: How I met Dr. Krajewsky', *Iron Game History* 1 (1990): 13.
[108]Boucher, and Heffernan, 'A great … '.

Through *Health & Strength* magazine, Szalay gained a reputation as a strength authority. Weightlifting records at his gym were verified prior to a lift, and many of weightlifting judges trained there. Thus Szalay welcomed dozens of international strength athletes because such individuals knew they could use his gym as a launching pad for strength performances.[109] This was not the first time that gyms became pilgrimage sites for others. As early as the 1860s, American journalists travelled to England to visit strongman Professor James Harrison's gymnasium for the *New York Clipper*.[110] What differentiated then and the early 1900s was the number of well-known gyms around the world and their clientele. The gym's reputation was both internationalized and written about extensively in physical culture press, but so too were the clientele.

The movement of people is critical in the globalization of physical culture. This is a point returned to repeatedly in this book. What has not been considered is the commercialization of individuals. This came in two distinct forms. First the precarity of the strength performer and second the strength client. More work is needed on the material realities facing strongmen and women despite the volume of research conducted elsewhere on professional performers.[111] While strength athletes differed from these individuals in their performances, they did not in their salaries, or precarity. The globalization of physical culture meant the globalization of strength performers as commodity. This created a sort of uniformity across performers. In some instances, this was deliberate and outrageous. Sandow encountered many 'copy-cat' performers including Irving Montgomery, an American strongman who toured as Sandowe.[112] Less egregious acts included Katie Brumbach adopting the name Katie Sandwina to benefit from Sandow's brand. These, admittedly fun, anecdotes pointed to strict hierarchies within the strength world. For every Sandow, Saxon, Sandwina or Cyr, there were a litany of 'lesser' strongmen and women seeking to earn a living. Two British examples highlight the difficulties many faced.

Julia Veidlere is not a name typically found in histories of physical culture but does hold the distinction of being one of the first female strength performers to earn celebrity in the music hall. Debuting in 1884, Veidlere, or Victorine to her audience, was a top billing in the mid-to-late 1880s.[113] Endorsing muscle balms and regularly interviewed in the press, Victorine's performances included holding back 'wild horses' and carrying heavy safes. Victorine was a sponsored athlete, earned a living as a performer

---

[109] Alan Stuart Radley, *The illustrated history of physical culture* (Radley, 2001).
[110] Heffernan, *Indian Club-swinging*, 111–14.
[111] Deborah Rohr, *The careers of British musicians, 1750–1850* (Cambridge University Press, 2001).
[112] Chapman, *Sandow*, 80.
[113] Conor Heffernan, '"A strong woman's troubles": Victorina and the strong woman in Victorian Britain', *Women's History Review* 30 (2021): 354–74.

and sold a now untraceable book about her life.[114] In 1892, the London Pavilion Company hired Victorine with an instruction to emulate Sandow's performance. At that time, Sandow's shows included a sleight-of-hand piece, wherein he carried a pony overhead on stage. Victorine paid £30 a week to copy him. On Victorine's debut, the pony refused to cooperate. When raised to a height, it protested to the extent that an animal tamer rushed across stage to calm it. Victorine struggled to perform the feat, for obvious reasons, but did complete it.[115] The audience applauded but the Company weren't pleased and cancelled her contract. For her part, Victorine and her husband Gustav sued the company but were unsuccessful. As word reached others about Victorine's 'failure' and litigiousness, bookings dried up. In 1893, the duo fled Britain in the wake of mounting debts.

That Victorine fled Britain after several months without bookings highlighted the difficulty of this lifestyle. William Murray (1873–1949) is another example. Winner of Sandow's 1901 Great Competition, an early physique contest, Murray struggled to establish himself as a performer. This was surprising given the competition's publicity, and his connection to Sandow. Acting as a judge for Sandow's competition, Arthur Conan Doyle recalled Murray wandering around London with a trophy, confused by his surroundings.[116] The scene was apt for Murray's career. Following his victory, Murray spent the next decade touring England as a professional athlete. He adorned many of the trappings others did, appearing in Greco-Roman clothing, adopting artistic poses and using his own 'wondrous' feats but his bookings were in regional theatres and his position on the play bill was more likely to be in the middle, rather than the top.[117] Why was this the case?

The answer lies in marketing. Murray was a strong man but one at odds with his industry.[118] At various points, Murray eschewed the idea that he was a 'mere' performer and promoted the idea that he was, instead, an athlete. Murray did not profess to have achieved an otherworldly physique through a patented program, nor did he profess to holding the 'secret' to perfection. In fact, the few interviews he gave revealed an honest man naive to the salesmanship needed to thrive. Had Murray followed Sandow, he would have said that he was sick as a child but, following Sandow's course, or better yet, his own course, he perfected his body.[119] The trope of the 'sickly childhood' or the 'turning point' in one's health was well-worn. Strongman Arthur Saxon, who matched Murray in his honesty, once wrote that he was

---

[114]Ibid.
[115]Ibid., 365–74.
[116]Conor Heffernan, 'Uncovering the history of William Murray', *Iron Game History* 16 (2022): 13–24.
[117]Ibid., 18–22.
[118]Ibid., 10–18.
[119]Sandow claimed to have been cured by physical culture in *Strength and how to obtain it* (Gale & Polden, 1897).

born strong while simultaneously criticizing those who pretended to be weak.[120] Some performers undoubtedly gained wealth but many struggled on precarious contracts. This is to say nothing of those used as curios within the physical culture industry.

Sandow provides a final example. At three points in his career, Sandow used individuals as exemplars and props. In 1889, Sandow's shows featured 'Goliath' (Karl Westphal) who Sandow 'discovered' in Germany. For a three-month period, Sandow and Goliath mocked wrestled on stage, lifted heavy objects and provided contrasting spectrums of strength and beauty. Ultimately Sandow found him too 'idle' and cast him aside.[121] A different tactic was taken during the 1890s and early 1900s when Sandow gave medical lectures during tours. Here he was often accompanied by a 'student' who had achieved success using Sandow's system. Other times they would be covered in lines to denote the muscle groups and prodded by physicians. Such individuals followed Sandow to Australia and New Zealand as curios for medical and lay audiences.[122] In the photographs left behind, Sandow wore the professional attire of a gentleman while his student played the living model.

FIGURE 4.3 Sandow and pupil.[123] A memorable meeting of the medical profession to study the medicineless cure of illness.

---

[120] Arthur Saxon, *The development of physical power* (Health&Strength, 1906), 3.
[121] Chapman, *Sandow*, 36–9.
[122] Daley, *Leisure*, 49–67.
[123] 'The Romantic Career of Eugen Sandow', *Tatler*, 3 August 1910, 4.

The most unpalatable example of human curios came on Sandow's return from his 1904–05 Asian tour. To a heroes return Sandow told journalists that

> I have chosen and brought back with me a native of every country I have visited ... thirty-two in all, including Chinese, Hindus, Kaffirs, and natives of the Punjaub ....[124]

His use of racialized language was echoed by his daughter who asked if Sandow brought 'any little n****r boys for her to play with'. Of the group, a small troupe of Indian wrestlers was included but the general message was that Sandow would uplift lesser races physically.[125] Bodies, white and non-white, were part of the physical culture trade.

Global print communities in physical culture

During the interwar period (1919–39), K. V. Iyer submitted images of himself to an American fitness magazine. Iyer noted his physical culture, his inspiration in Sandow and his Vedantic beliefs. Editor, Mark Berry, responded by praising Iyer's body and proclaiming disinterest in his beliefs.[126] The exchange is one I often return to when discussing the power, and limitations of physical culture media. During our period, there was an incredible expansion of physical culture magazines which served domestic and global audiences. The two most influential were British-based magazines *Health & Strength* and *Sandow's Magazine of Physical Culture*. Before explaining why this was the case, it is useful to discuss what a physical culture magazine actually did. Physical culture was an embodied practice but was informed by books, magazines and images. Physical culture magazines were, for many, the only site for information on muscle growth, weight-loss, sleep and exercise. Many physical culture exercises were adopted from older gymnastic movements but entirely new movements, using physical culture equipment were promoted. For those interested in strength training, this included an array of pushing and pulling movements using dumbbells and barbells, while for those using light-weight equipment, it meant instructions on how to hold and move their bodies. Books and magazines, with text and image, taught people these movements, especially if individuals trained at home. Images and texts thus played a fundamental role in helping to shape individual's physiques.[127] There is a rather banal observation here ... it is possible to enlarge muscle groups through weight-training. This changes how one looks, moves and feels. Thus if magazines encouraged overhead pressing, this would, within reason, build and shape the shoulders.[128]

---

[124]Chapman, *Sandow*, 161.
[125]Ibid.
[126]Ramachandran, and Heffernan, 'Building ... '.
[127]Heffernan, 'Body ... '.
[128]Ibid.

The workouts and explanations found within magazines fundamentally influenced people's bodies in implicit and explicit ways. They also solidified strength and beauty standards through images. Budd previously discussed the primacy of images within these magazines in Europe and the United States.[129] With cover images, full-page spreads and illustrations, magazines bombarded readers with photographic evidence of health. While images of women tended to be more modest, it was common to include half-naked images of men flexing.[130] Printed on cheap paper, magazines were accessible and presented as a respectable pastime (although one with appeal to same-sex desires). Magazines tended to publish images of the same strength celebrities be it a Sandow, Saxon, Cyr, Sandwina, etc. There existed a global currency of photographs solidifying who the physical culture stars were and ideal body standards. It is not, however, the publication of 'celebrity' physical culturists which is interesting but rather the publication of reader submissions.

Two features were common to magazines around the world: some form of reader responses where they could ask questions, submit testimonials or, images of themselves.[131] A fascinating example of this can be found in the submissions of Irishman W. N. Kerr in the early 1900s. Kerr submitted images of himself to British periodicals *Health & Strength* and *Vitality*. He also submitted images of himself to the American periodical *Physical Culture*.[132] The images showed his physical development as noted by his increases in muscularity over time. They also raised questions about his interests. Kerr had access to British and American physical culture magazines from his base in Ireland. This was not uncommon, nor was his decision to submit images. For the individual, magazines offered opportunities to display their bodies in ways impossible two decades before.[133] Limitations existed, women were rarely featured in provocative pose and white bodies were given privilege, but magazines offered a transformative way of displaying one's physique.[134] Magazines, for many, gave them a new vocabulary for the world and their bodies. It was no longer their chest but their pectoral muscles, their arms were divided into biceps and triceps, etc. The commodification of physical culture followed what Polanyi terms the 'double movement', while it represented the expansion of market logic into bodily practices, it simultaneously generated communities organized around these practices.[135] This tension

---

[129]Michael Anton Budd, *The sculpture machine: Physical culture and body politics in the age of empire* (New York University Press, 1997), 31–57.
[130]Ibid.
[131]Heffernan, 'Body ... '.
[132]Conor Heffernan, 'Truly muscular Gaels? W.N. Kerr, physical culture and Irish masculinity in the early twentieth-century', *Sport in History* 41 (2021): 1–24.
[133]Budd, *The Sculpture Machine*, 31–57.
[134]Heffernan, 'Body ... '.
[135]Eppo Maertens, 'Polanyi's double movement: A critical reappraisal', *Social Thought & Research* (2008): 129–53.

between commercial and communal aspects of physical culture can be seen in initiatives like the *Health and Strength League*, which combined subscription models with community.

A cursory glance through *Health & Strength* or *La Culture Physique* reveals reader submissions about finding training partners, gymnasiums, clothing.[136] In some instances, individuals sought models to pose for paintings or photographs while others sold objects. In later decades, such personal advertisements became spaces for seeking partners – be it a heterosexual or same-sex relationship.[137] This 'imagined community' had real implications for individuals and the firmest example of this is the *Health and Strength League* founded in 1906.[138] The *League* served as a marketing tool to connect readers.[139] Just as Anderson argues that capitalism enabled readers to imagine themselves as part of a community through shared reading experiences, magazines like *Health & Strength* and *Physical Culture* allowed readers to envision themselves as members of a global movement. On joining the League, readers were given a badge, magazine subscription and league number.[140] *Health & Strength* was produced in London but, echoing Britain's imperial empire, was sold in Asia, Africa and North America.[141] It was commonplace for the magazine to count members, and reader submissions, from India, Australia, South Africa and elsewhere.

Its transnational reach can be illustrated in a short anecdote about club swinger Tom Burrows (c. 1860–1944).[142] Prior to the Great War, Burrows set a number of world records in club swinging. In 1912, Burrows embarked on a tour of South Africa to compete and to complete a number of public engagements.[143] Before and after tours, Burrows used *Health & Strength*, and its League to inform readers about his trips. When visiting Durban, South Africa, Burrows corresponded with Leaguer No. 8245 (Mr. MacDonald) who expressed an interest in visiting with, and meeting Burrows in person.[144] The League had a membership of 13,000 subscribers

---

[136] Ozerkevich and Heffernan, 'Physical culture … '.
[137] David Johnson, *Buying gay: How physique entrepreneurs sparked a movement* (Columbia University Press, 2019).
[138] Benedict Anderson, *Imagined communities: Reflections on the origin and spread of nationalism* (London: Verso, 1983), 1–24.
[139] Mark Singleton, *Yoga body: The origins of modern posture practice* (Oxford University Press, 2010), 153.
[140] Ina Zweiniger-Bargielowska, *Managing the body: Beauty, health, and fitness in Britain 1880–1939* (Oxford University Press, 2010), 92.
[141] Heffernan, 'Born … ', 45–73.
[142] Ibid.
[143] Ibid.
[144] Tom Burrows, 'Leaguer Tom Burrows sends a message', Health and Strength, 7 July 1912. Coutley Collection (University of Texas Stark Archives). https://archives.starkcenter.org/handle/11048/2895. Accessed 7 December 2016.

by 1911. That was 13,000 readers from around the Empire who identified, in some way, as a 'leaguer'.[145] The League was, undoubtedly, the clearest and keenest manifestation of a global physical culture. Yes it was primarily British in nature, and the British branches were the most popular, but it retained a global element through the magazine. It was not uncommon for individuals to find communality at home and abroad thanks to the League. Roy and Saha's work notes Russian strongman Owana Kramer's tour to Lucknow prior to the Great War.[146] Indian writer and bodybuilder, Sachindra Majumdar, gained Kramer's respect by lifting the strongman's barbells and by wearing a *Health and Strength* badge.[147] Concurrent with the role leagues and societies played in other parts of globalizing life, the League brought individuals together across borders.[148]

What is largely lost to historians is the emotive aspect to joining the League. What motivated individuals to spend money on an invisible club with few very obvious benefits outside of a badge? What did it mean when the badge arrived at long last at someone's residence? Were their envelopes torn open excitedly? There was a material, emotive pattern to League membership hinted at in some of remaining correspondences. Irishman Michael Stokes once wrote to *Health and Strength* excitedly about what it meant to be a League member.[149] The League connected him to like-minded individuals and provided him with a marker to represent his physical culture passions. Others took their league membership as a sort of passage from their previous slovenly life to one defined by health. The previously mentioned Kerr professed to be a proud vegetarian and one who cited his League membership as a sign of his commitment to fitness.[150]

Elsewhere I have used reader questions and submissions to explore the global emotional worlds of physical culture magazines.[151] Within these magazines young men, and it was predominantly men, wrote about their bodies in new ways, expressing feelings of disgust, anxiety and pride. Returning to Kerr, he wrote about his physical culture commitment and physical development. He wrote about finding friends through physical culture, leaving physical culture magazines in the Dublin mountains and finding a sense of purpose in his life.[152] In Kerr's case, we know that he had

---

[145]Mosse, *The image of man*, 137.
[146]Tirthankar Roy and Prasenjit Saha, *Wondrous wrestlers* (Boibishwa, 2024), 105–7.
[147]Ibid.
[148]Gary Magee and Andrew Thompson, *Empire and globalisation: Networks of people, goods and capital in the British world, c. 1850–1914* (Cambridge University Press, 2010), 45–63.
[149]Heffernan, *The history of physical culture*, 46–9.
[150]Heffernan, 'Truly muscular ... ?'
[151]Conor Heffernan, 'Hearts and muscles: Emotional communities and physical culture magazines in 1900s Ireland', *Gender & History* 33 (2021): 129–48.
[152]Heffernan, 'Truly muscular ... ?'

FIGURE 4.4 Indian strongman, Professor Rama Murti Naidu, c. 1915. Here Naidu uses *The Strand* to mimic European strongmen and gain foreign interest in his feats.[153]

a vibrant life in Ireland. He was a member of a local gymnasium and won Ireland's inaugural physique contest in 1908.[154] Yet he felt the desire to join a broader physical culture community in Britain and America.

He was not unique. F. A. Hornibrook, who gained fame in interwar Britain, regularly appeared in Sandow's magazine, from his New Zealand base.[155] Running a physical culture school, Hornibrook submitted images of students to Sandow. In an image which encapsulates this entire book, Hornibrook included an image of his Fijian trainees in his interwar book, *The Culture of the Abdomen*. Here we see Irishman Hornibrook, who moved to New Zealand, training Fijian men using Prussian strongman Sandow's system. It is, quite frankly, an incredible image.

It is worth noting that *La Culture Physique* in France, Sandow's *Magazine of Physical Culture* in Britain and *Physical Culture* in the United States all commented on global events, from warfare and health to politics and dietary practices. They also commented on and enforced ideas about, racial differences. In Sandow's magazine in 1900, readers were treated to an article on 'Hindoo' physical culture which contrasted the 'primitive practices' with

---

[153]'Professor Rama Murti Naidu', *The Strand* 18 (1915): 696.
[154]Ibid.
[155]Ina Zweiniger-Bargielowska, 'The culture of the abdomen: Obesity and reducing in Britain, circa 1900–1939', *Journal of British Studies* 44 (2005): 239–73.

FIGURE 4.5 Hornibrook and his Fijian Sandow trainees, c. 1900s.[156]

modern physical culture.[157] MacFadden's magazines were far more explicit, using phrenological theories to contrast the white man's intelligence with 'lesser', non-white, races.[158]

Physical culture entrepreneurs were consistent in asking global readers to submit images, questions and queries. They also, occasionally, offered competitive outlets. Sandow's *Magazine of Physical Culture* offered an 'Empire' competition.[159] This was done in 1902, one year after Sandow hosted a physique show in London. Sandow's empire magazine appears to have been driven, partly, by a desire to extend his global readership.[160] In 1902, Bernarr MacFadden embarked on a tour of Great Britain and Ireland. Readers of *Physical Culture* were told that MacFadden enjoyed sold-out lecture tours and that *Physical Culture's* English readership was over 10,000

---

[156]F.A. Hornibrook, The culture of the abdomen (Wood, 1924), 16.
[157]C. Lord, 'Physical culture among the natives in India', *Sandow's Magazine of Physical Culture* 4 (1900): 103–108.
[158]R. Marie Griffith, *Born again bodies: Flesh and spirit in American Christianity* (University of California, 2004), 128–35.
[159]'Our Empire and Muscle Competition', *Sandow's magazine of physical culture*, Vol. X, *January to June (1903)* (Harrison & Sons, 1903), 219–20.
[160]'Our Empire and Muscle Competition', *Sandow's Magazine*.

subscriptions.[161] When MacFadden announced his own physical culture competition to discover the 'Most Perfectly Developed Man and Woman', it was reported that centres could be found around the United States but also in Great Britain and Ireland.[162] The following weeks saw a range of submissions from these countries but also those from Geo. Dupain in Sydney Australia. Geo. Smith in Canada and M. S. Pullum from India.[163] A semi-final was scheduled to be held in London before the 'European' winner would join their American counterparts for the final. There is no evidence of anyone making this voyage.[164] In MacFadden's case, the cash prize of $1000 was undoubtedly useful, but useless, in tempting foreign contestants.[165] Nevertheless, individuals were afforded the opportunity to submit images of themselves into these forums. To belabour the point, magazines were a forum for men, and occasionally women, to set parameters for the 'perfect' male body. This was revolutionary. Prior to the advent of physical culture magazines, it was impossible for an 'ordinary' individual to submit half-naked images of themselves for print and publication.

Individuals, from around the world, had an outlet to showcase their bodies, in a meaningful way. They also learned how to showcase their bodies. Ozerkevich has examined the tricks, including photographic manipulation, people used to appear as muscular as possible.[166] Some of these methods, such as propping hands underneath the biceps, were straightforward. Others were more nuanced. It was common for magazines to include posing advice, either through articles or critiques. There was also, of course, implicit learning which came from seeing images of professional and lay physical culturists posing in issues. A cursory look at some of the larger physique competitions during this period shows dozens of men largely adopting the same poses to showcase their muscles. Contrast this image of Martin Willis from Sandow's magazine in 1903 with the previously shown Fijian men. Separated by thousands of miles, they both used the same front double-bicep pose.

Physical culture had a twofold effect on the body. Workouts trained and moulded the flesh while magazines and books, taught individuals to hold their musculature to maximum effect. In the case of women, and MacFadden's magazine was the greatest proponent of women's physical culture, poses were used to showcase their delicacy and leanness.[167] Some may point to film as a teaching tool, and it is true that Sandow and the victors of Bernarr MacFadden's 1904 physical culture competition appeared in films, but the

---

[161]'Editorial department', *Physical culture* VI (1902): 290.
[162]'No contest ... ', *Physical culture* 9 (1903): 537.
[163]'Contest images', *Physical culture* 10 (1903): 470.
[164]'No contest ... ', *Physical culture*.
[165]'No contest ... ', *Physical culture* 9 (1903): 537.
[166]Ozerkevich, 'Retouched ... '.
[167]Todd, 'Bernarr ... '.

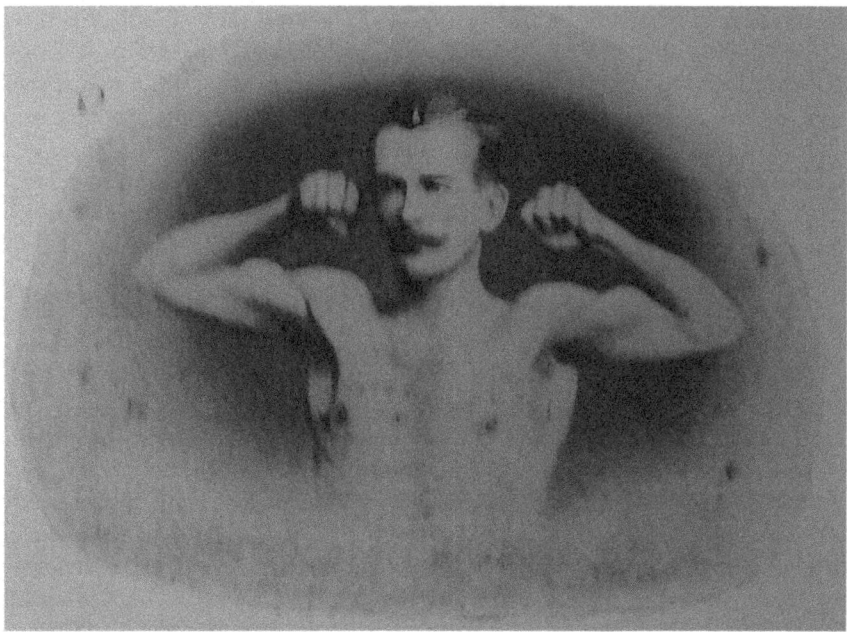

FIGURE 4.6 Martin Willis front double bicep pose.[168]

printed page held greater sway. Self-selection by editors existed but a critical mass grew whereby submissions from Indian men displayed the same postures as those from South Africa, New Zealand, Canada, etc.[169] Greco-Roman statues often informed this practice but a whole new generation of poses to showcase muscularity grew.

Physical culture was a print empire divided between magazines, monographs and mail-order courses. Each served a function. Magazines and mail-order courses provided a regular and point of contact for physical culturists while monographs existed as reference and motivational scripts. Before digging into the richness of such texts, it is worth exploring their titles. Titles serve to promise new worlds and realities in the health space.[170] Physical culture books promised to teach readers how to eat, breathe and live. Sandow's 1897 *Strength and How to Obtain It*, discussed his fabricated background before expounding on the 'tenets' of health.[171] Hackenschmidt's 1908 *The Way to Live* discussed training and philosophy.[172] For those

---

[168]'Reader's Responses', *Sandow's magazine of physical culture, Vol. X, January to June (1903)* (London, 1903), 240.
[169]Ozerkevich, and Heffernan, 'Physical culture ... '.
[170]John Tholen, 'The title page: Creating commercial credibility', in John Tholen (ed.), *Producing Ovid's' Metamorphoses' in the Early Modern Low Countries* (Brill, 2021), 30–70.
[171]Sandow, *Strength and How ...* .
[172]George Hackenschmidt, *The way to live: Health & physical fitness* (Health&Strength, 1908).

interested in raw power, Saxon's 1906 *The Development of Physical Power* was complemented by Inch's 1905 *Scientific Weight Lifting*.[173] We have already discussed the proliferation of jiu-jitsu and judo books under the guise of physical culture and likewise with yoga but some physical culture books did lean on esoteric and Eastern ideas of the body.

These included Alois Swodaba's 1914 *Swoboda System of Conscious Evolution of Mind and Body*, Edwin Checkley's 1913 *A Natural Method of Physical Training* and Max Sick's 1913 *Great Strength by Muscle Control*.[174] There also existed a litany of books on physical culture for busy individuals, and physical culture for children. For women, J. P. Mueller's 1913 *My System for Ladies; Fifteen Minutes' Exercise a Day for Health's Sake* promised results with minimal effort while his 1914 work *My Breathing System* promised to teach humans how to ... breath.[175] While many works were targeted at men, with promises of musculature, those for women promised *harmonic gymnastics* a la Genieve Stebbins or Eustace Miles' 1907 *System of Physical Culture, Health & Strength* which included a 'Women's chart on Ten Rules of Health'.[176] This is to say nothing of Marguerite MacFadden's 1904 *Physical Culture for Babies* or Bernarr MacFadden's 1904 *Health-Beauty-Sexuality: From Girlhood to Womanhood*.[177]

In such works, individuals were treated to life histories, workout information, advertisements, dietary aids and philosophies. This is to say nothing of the images and illustrations contained therein or, anthropomorphic charts accompanying them. It was a common approach for books to include anthropomorphic charts, or guidelines for the perfect measurements. Individuals were encouraged to build, or slim, their bodies to meet these ideals and use them as a measuring stick for others. The overlaps with eugenic and racial ideals are obvious. Sandow's books were notable for their inclusion of anthropomorphic charts and promises that within a short period readers could, too, become a Sandow. Monographs held aspirational methods and had a sort of evangelical zeal. Sandow's 1902 *Gospel of Strength* spoke of universal forces and praising nature with a quasi-religious bent.[178]

---

[173] Saxon, *Development of* ... ; Thomas Inch *Scientific weight lifting* (Health&Strength, 1905).
[174] A.P. Swoboda, *Swoboda system of conscious evolution of mind and body* (Swoboda, 1914); Edwin Checkley, *A natural method of physical training* (Scholar's Choice, 1895); Maxick, *Great strength by muscle-control* (Health&Strength, 1913).
[175] J.P. Muller, *My system for ladies-15 minutes' exercise a day for health's sake* (Read Books, 2011); J.P. Müller, *My breathing system* (McKay, 1914).
[176] Genevieve Stebbins, *Dynamic breathing and harmonic gymnastics: A complete system of psychical, aesthetic and physical culture* (Werner, 1893); Eustace Miles, *The eustace miles system of physical culture: With hints as to diet* (Health&Strength, 1907).
[177] Marguerite Macfadden, *Physical culture for babies* (Physical Culture, 1904); Bernarr Macfadden and Marion Malcolm, *Health–beauty–sexuality, from girlhood to womanhood: Plain advice to girls that will be found invaluable as they grow from girlhood into womanhood* (Physical Culture, 1904).
[178] Eugen Sandow, *The gospel of strength according to sandow* (Sandow, 1902).

While institutional gymnastics exposed countless men, women and children to physical culture, physical culture books became teachers in proselytizing the spread of physical cultures. Just how popular, and importantly, how global, were these texts?

With the proviso that individual physical culture books were published specific to local contexts, it is undeniable that a global market existed for books. This, itself, can be divided between Anglophone and non-Anglophone copies. Gymnastic texts had been in circulation since the early nineteenth century and were global products. It was commonplace, if not expected, for gymnasts across Europe and beyond to be familiar with Jahn, Ling, etc. What differentiated gymnastic texts from physical culture ones was the scale of sales. Sandow's monographs accompanied him throughout his tours. Thus we have evidence of Sandow's books circulated in the United States, South Africa, South East Asia and Australasia.[179] Occasionally, and in conjunction with local entrepreneurs, Sandow produced bespoke books such as *Sandow on Physical Training*, published during his American tour or *The Gospel of Strength*, published in New Zealand. Sandow took pride in noting 'foreign' readers of his books, often highlighting his readership's diversity.[180] There were also, of course, translations to consider. Sandow's *Strength and How to Obtain It* was translated into German, Chinese and Spanish among other languages. The appearance of Sandow's books in Chile and China is a remarkable testament to the global appeal and commercial weight of his messages.[181] Books, more so than magazines, seemed to have an enduring appeal.

Whereas magazines were consumable, books represented a more durable product. In Sandow's case, it is possible to find inter-war writings from the 1920s to early 1930s reusing images and writings from his books. Books, more than magazines, could be shared and reshared. Pages developed dog ears and may have gone missing but the semi-permanency of the book gave a lasting taste of physical culture for countless individuals. We know that certain physical culture books sold prolifically and in many cases, it is possible to trace reprints and second-hand copies sold in future decades. Iser has stressed the interactivity of the book.[182] Whereas magazines could solicit reader submissions, books could be written on, pages torn or earmarked. They provided a material and sensual engagement with physical culture for adults and children. Critically, many books followed the same messages and tropes, thereby solidifying truisms about health. Here it is useful to consider

---

[179] Joseph Alter, *Gandhi's body: sex, diet, and the politics of nationalism* (University of Pennsylvania, 2011), 95.
[180] 'Hints from Sandow and Editorial Chat', *Sandow's magazine of physical culture, vol. XI, July to December (1903)* (Harrison&Sons, 1903), 443–4.
[181] Fernández, 'Fuerza, ... '; Conrad, 'Globalizing ... ', 96.
[182] Wolfgang Iser, 'Interaction between text and reader', in Andrew Bennett (ed.), *Readers and Reading* (Routledge, 2014), 20–31.

three messages often found in texts. The first, and one still found today, was the 'weakling' story. Sandow's *Strength and How to Obtain It* detailed his illnesses as a child. It was not until Sandow took to physical culture that he transformed his physique.[183] This message, that hard work could transform one's life, was repeated in a multitude of texts. Equally alluring was the idea of curing illnesses through physical culture, this being a core message in many of MacFadden's books.[184]

The transformation myth was often complimented by messages that physical culture was scientific and that natural practices worked best. Yes these messages seem contradictory but logic rarely got in the way. Fyfe and Lightman have explained the allure of 'science' as a sales mechanism.[185] The basic premise is that in the age of industrialization and a presumed modernity on the part of contemporaries, labelling products as scientific and/or modern was a sign they were worthy of purchasing. In physical culture books, such as those by Hancock, Macfadden and Sandow, physical culture was described with the science of the calorie, and Taylorist ideas about time-management.[186] Crude understandings of biology and racial fitness, as found in William Grant Hague's book, were likewise used to contextualize practices.[187] Science sold well but so too did the 'naturalist fallacy'. Physical culture books often contained passages about the need for clean air, natural foods and natural movement. Some of this was a reaction to urbanization, but there was also a harking back to the philosophies of Rousseau which held man in his natural state was served best. Thus books emerged on how to eat, breath and move. Sandow's books often contained all three, advising readers to build themselves physically, follow his scientific methods and follow natural processes.[188]

Danish physical culturist J. P. Mueller sold millions of copies of *My System* during the same era. First published in Mueller's native tongue, *My System* was sold in Europe, England and the United States.[189] Mueller from Sandow differed in promoting a system more broadly in tune with natural methods. Bonde credited the German translations of Mueller's novels with providing inspiration for the fresh air, hiking and air bath

---

[183]See footnote 138.
[184]Stieglitz, 'Mentally superior ... '.
[185]Aileen Fyfe and Bernard Lightman, 'Science in the marketplace', in Aileen Fyfe and Bernard Lightman (eds.), *Science in the marketplace: Nineteenth-century sites and experiences* (University of Chicago, 2019), 1–22.
[186]H. Irving Hancock, *The physical culture life* (Putnam, 1905); Bernarr Macfadden, *Macfadden's encyclopedia of physical culture* (Physical Culture, 1912); Sandow, *Sandow on Physical*.
[187]William Grant Hague, *The eugenic mother and baby: A complete home guide* (Hauge, 1913), 35.
[188]Sandow, *Strength and How* ... .
[189]Muller's 1935 *My System* claimed the book had been translated into 24 languages.

movement.¹⁹⁰ Wedemeyer's study of German bodybuilding likewise credited Hackenschmidt and Lionel Strongfort (1878–1973), with publishing highly popular books, first in English and subsequently in several languages.¹⁹¹ American mogul MacFadden's books were read in Britain and Ireland and held some sway in continental Europe.¹⁹² Such individuals were published by a raft of new physical culture publishing houses. MacFadden oversaw *Physical Culture* publications and produced an incredible amount of works prior to 1914. A more important publishing house was undoubtedly *Health & Strength* based in London and attached to the magazine. Not only were the publishing house's books sold throughout the British Empire, they published on alternative forms of physical culture like as jiu-jitsu. If one were to query the difference between the mid-century publication of health books, the answer lies in the emergence of publishing houses and the volumes sold. Such factors deepened the appeal and power of recreational physical cultures for domestic and global audiences.

Conclusion

An easy pitfall many historians can fall into is describing physical culture as a schism from previous generations. In such retellings, physical culture is the 'big bang' of modern fitness and something which emerged from the ether.¹⁹³ The reality is more complex. Physical culture movement was more connected to the world of nineteenth-century health than the twentieth. What was physical culture if not a deepening of the institutional practices discussed in previous chapters? It was a commercial and ideological democratization of fitness which had primarily focused on soldiers and schoolchildren. Many physical culturists used the same rhetoric as those decades before them. They discussed the influence the Greeks and Romans held over physical culture, the connection between the individual and the state and the devitalizing nature of modernity. Couple this with allusions to race science or phrenology. The primary difference between the gymnastics boom and physical culture movement, undoubtedly, was the commercial scale of recreational fitness. Physical culture meant the production of equipment, supplements and literature at a remarkable pace, and one with a global spread. Observing a trend is, of course, not the same as appreciating it. The core, and somewhat cruel, question to ask is: what impact did physical culture have? How was it substantially different from previous trends? It increased an individual's knowledge but, more importantly, their

---

¹⁹⁰Bonde, 'From Hygiene ... ', 1357–63.
¹⁹¹Bernd Wedemeyer and Anthony Haywood, 'Bodybuilding in Germany in the late nineteenth and early twentieth centuries', *Iron Game History* 3á (1994): 4–7.
¹⁹²Singleton, *Yoga*, 89.
¹⁹³Heffernan, 'State of ... '.

enthusiasm in physical exercise. Prior to Sandow's popularity, it was rare to find substantive discussions about perfecting the body in public discourses. Likewise, it was relatively impossible for individuals to engage in bodily practices in such public forums. Photography and cheap postage opened up new worlds for individuals. The physical culture movement effectively set the template, the very structure, with which fitness evolved across the twentieth century and in our age. What was Eugen Sandow if not an early fitness 'influencer'?

Through the circulation of standardized photographs, measurement charts, and training methods, physical culturists from London to Lahore evaluated and modified their bodies against universal metrics. Sandow's proportions became a template reproduced in photographs and anatomical charts worldwide, while magazines like *Health & Strength* created what we might call a global anatomical vocabulary, teaching readers to view bodies through the same lens of muscular development and proportional harmony. This wasn't simply about aesthetics. It represented a shift in how bodies were understood and valued in public parlance. Physical culture created what we might term a global bodily imagination, a shared understanding of how the ideal body should look, move and be built. While this standardization had problematic implications, particularly in its promotion of white ideals, it established patterns of bodily commodification. What was Plasmon or Iron Jelloids if not dubious nutritional supplements of their time? And what was MacFadden if not an early adopter of anti-establishment and natural rhetoric in the fitness space? Strength competitions, physique shows and gyms grew in importance and existence. Furthermore, the rhetoric of fitness, the idea of perfecting the body and the tropes about escaping illness or unhappiness through fitness were borne from this era. The difficulty in studying physical culture is holding the balance between the 'old' world of the nineteenth century and the 'new' world of the twentieth century and beyond. Physical culture belonged to both worlds and, in essence, shaped both.

It is, however, the individual level that matters. In 1897, Sandow toured Dublin as part of a short performance run. F. A. Hornibrook, then a young man, attended Sandow's performances and later wrote about the visceral excitement he felt seeing the Prussian.[194] That moment changed Hornibrook's life. He took to Sandow's exercises and, in time, opened a Sandow school in New Zealand before becoming a fitness writer in his own right. What is remarkable about Hornibrook is that he was *unremarkable*. Calvert in the United States saw Sandow and too was turned to a life of physical culture and fitness, this time inventing and selling strength equipment.[195] In India, we have countless writers, including Iyer, crediting Sandow with helping

---

[194]Heffernan, *The history of physical culture* ... , 35.
[195]Chapman, *Sandow*, 79.

popularize physical culture. At an individual level, men and women became inspired to change their bodies.[196] This was a shared global desire expressed in local contexts. That was the power and allure of physical culture. It was not an invisible force of globalization like banking networks or governing philosophies, it was a living and malleable object. One could point to its global leaders and next, to their bulging biceps. Finally you could point to the masses of trainees around the world seeking to emulate them.

---

[196]Ibid., 160.

5

Protected practices

Fitness became globalized during the 'long' nineteenth century and this had a profound impact on how millions of people interacted with, and thought about their bodies. It was, as this book made clear, transformative. And yet, we know that fitness was not a nineteenth-century ideal nor one confined to a certain state or culture. Multiple forms of physical culture existed and were practised around the globe prior to our period. What differentiated 'pre' and 'post' globalization was that during the nineteenth century many of these practices joined across borders. Globalization was not, of course, a pantomime villain, destroying local practices and forcing everyone to join a monolithic physical culture. The previous chapters have highlighted how diverse physical culture could be. Local experiences existed. Some vehemently protested against foreign practices and ideas. Others, perhaps the majority who didn't engage in practices, simply ignored newer practices in favour of what they always did.

This chapter is a discussion of failure and conflict. The failure of certain practices to globalize and the conflict between 'new' and 'traditional'. That, however, is too restricted a view. To examine why some practices 'failed' to globalize is to moralize. What this chapter is interested in is contradiction. Why did some practices globalize and others didn't? One of my favourite books, *Born Losers*, scrutinized the concept of failure in America. In it, Sandage explained how modern understandings of failure originated in the nineteenth-century economic chaos of American markets and that failure, was a relative term. What for some was the making of their own origin myth, that is, the entrepreneur who 'bounced' back, was for others a mark of shame.[1] We need to be careful then about using the 'f' word.

So what do we mean when we say 'failure' to globalize? We could turn to Bayly and note that the partial globalization of physical practices mirrors Bayly's 'birth' of the modern world which was a process marked *not* by

---

[1] Scott Sandage, *Born losers: A history of failure in America* (Harvard University, 2005).

smooth integration but by 'archaic globalizations' and local autonomies.[2] Just as global trade networks of the nineteenth century connected some regions while bypassing others, physical culture practices spread unevenly. This created 'strange parallels' in a different context.[3] Such ideas may, however, seem too pre-determined and create the assumption that globalization meant progress or inevitability. We could instead, bastardize Scott's anarchist history and talk about the art of 'not being governed' by neighbouring ideas.[4] Or turning what about the art of creolization, the picking and choosing of outside practices?[5] This would certainly be the case in our discussion about weightlifting. Or indeed Robertson's 'particularization of universalism' which examines the negotiation between local and global forces?[6] Although we are interested in the 'failure' of globalization, this chapter is more interested in the *persistence of local behaviours*.[7]

I have deliberately chosen practices which **were globalized** after 1914, some as recently as the 1980s or the 2000s. Doing helps us understand the commercial and institutional realities of physical culture during the long nineteenth century. The focus here is on those practises which remained relatively localized. We will ease into this process, beginning with weightlifting before moving into more national and localized forms of physical culture like stone-lifting and swinging heavy clubs.[8] In weightlifting, national identities and disputes impeded the foundation of a singular set of rules. From 1891 to 1900, several global competitions were held, including one at the inaugural modern Olympics. The problem was that none of these competitions used the same rules, judging standards or equipment. Efforts to standardize weightlifting on a global scale, largely led in mainland Europe, were fraught with conflict during this period about which nation's rules should be used.

The chapter next moves to stone-lifting. Stone-lifting, as discussed in Chapter 1, was often seen as a rite of passage from boyhood to manhood or one with a religious connotation. Stone-lifting, as a practice, largely became globalized during the 1980s when the World's Strongest Man competition

---

[2]C.A. Bayly, *The birth of the modern world, 1780–1914: Global connections and comparisons* (Blackwell, 2004), 1–19.
[3]Victor Lieberman, *Strange parallels: Southeast Asia in global context, c. 800–1830* (Cambridge, 2003–2004), 1–18.
[4]James Scott, *The art of not being governed: An anarchist history of upland Southeast Asia* (Yale University Press, 2009).
[5]K. Brathwaite, *Contradictory omens: Cultural diversity and integration in the Caribbean* (Savacou Publications, 1974).
[6]Roland Robertson, 'Social theory, cultural relativity, and the problem of globality', in Keri E. Iyall Smith (ed.), *Sociology of Globalization* (Routledge, 2018), 61–7.
[7]Jürgen Osterhammel, *The transformation of the world: A global history of the nineteenth-century* (Princeton University Press, 2014), 322–74.
[8]Which can be distinguished from the previously studied lightweight Indian clubs.

included it.⁹ Since then the practice has grown in popularity. Given stone-lifting's later global appeal, it is important to understand why this practice remained a localized one in the nineteenth century. Here we will focus primarily on Scottish and Basque cultures, examining sporting and folkloric studies.

Finally the chapter studies heavy club-swinging in the form of Indian *joris*. That Indian clubs became a global practise by the mid-nineteenth century but heavier club-swinging did not, is a fascinating contradiction within this global history. This is to say nothing of those soldiers who used heavy club-swinging to impress/ intimidate European soldiers in military camps.¹⁰ Yes, some strongmen in Europe and America used heavy clubs, but the practice was a niche one. The reasons why, and the tensions in India between lightweight Indian clubs and the heavy *joris* will be explored. It is only by exploring the limits and boundaries of global physical culture that we can appreciate the transformative nature of nineteenth- and early twentieth-century fitness. The persistence of regional strength practices during the nineteenth century's 'global body' movement demonstrates that physical culture's globalization was not inevitable but selective, with some practices deliberately maintaining their local character despite pressures to standardize and commercialize.

Cleaning up weightlifting

Weightlifting should be one of the easiest sports to judge. Weights and athletes can be weighed, leaving no confusion about fairness. An athlete either lifted a weight, or didn't. Weightlifting is often used as a 'catch-all' term for gym activities. Here, weightlifting is used in a purest sense to describe practices that eventually came to be included in Olympic games.¹¹ For readers, that means a sport centred on two exercises: the clean and jerk, and the snatch. Despite its simplicity, weightlifting is one of the most politically fraught sports hosted in the modern-Olympics.¹² Within the sport, subjectivities about whether or not a weight was lifted to a full range of motion remain contentious. During the 1970s, a third lift, the military press, was removed from the sport owing to complaints about athlete's

---

⁹Conor Heffernan, 'The lift seen around the world: Hafþór Björnsson and legitimacy in strongman', in Jüörg Krieger, April Henning, Lindsay Parks Pieper and Paul Dimeo (eds.), '*Time Out': Sport and the Corona Lockdown* (Common Ground, 2021), 1–20.
¹⁰Kate Imy, 'Fascist yogis: Martial bodies and imperial impotence', *Journal of British Studies* 55, no. 2 (2016): 320–43.
¹¹Gherardo Bonini, 'Weightlifting', in John Nauright and Sarah Zipp (eds.), *Routledge Handbook of Global Sport* (Routledge, 2020), 392–3.
¹²Olympic weightlifting has been criticized for drug violations, administrative mismanagement and judging standards.

bending the rules, and their backs, to lift weights.[13] Some may object to the inclusion of weightlifting given the introduction's distinction between sport and physical culture. Foregoing the temptation to say that rules are meant to be broken, a more accurate case is to plead for nuance. It is necessary to study weightlifting because weightlifting was physical culture 'sportified'. Furthermore, weightlifting clubs were attended by athletes and recreational gym-goers. The exercises used in the sport of weightlifting had a direct impact on athletes and the non-competitive physical culture community.

The modern governing weightlifting body, the International Weightlifting Federation (IWF), traces the first world weightlifting championship to London in 1891 and its own origins to 1905. At face value, this counters the claim that weightlifting was not globalized during the nineteenth century. Such a retelling ignores a simple observation, few people agreed on the rules of weightlifting prior to 1920. As Fair noted, 'twelve world championships from 1898 to 1920 were unofficial and ... there was *no prewar governing structure* (emphasis added) for weightlifting ... '[14] While weightlifting appeared at the 1896 Olympic games, it was absent in 1900, 1908 and 1912. Its inclusion in the 1904 St. Louis Games was due to the host's interest, and its inclusion in the 1906 intercalated Olympics met with little fanfare.[15] It was after 1920 that the sport became a regular Olympic feature, and not until 1928 that a global consensus was reached concerning what exercises should be used.[16] Even the IWF's claim that it originated in 1905 seems dubious as efforts to create a global governing body, as occurred in 1905, 1912 and 1913, were short-lived. A true origin point can be found in 1920.[17] This is not to criticize the IWF for misusing history but to argue that a linear history for Olympic weightlifting can only begin in 1920 or, to be pedantic, 1928 when the sport agreed on which movements to use.

It cannot be overstated how disparate weightlifting was in the pre-war period.[18] Some competitions used dumbbells and single-arm presses, others focused on pulling weights from the floor or pressing weights overhead. Complicating matters was the confusion the sport faced thanks to the significantly greater popularity of professional strongmen and women.[19] This marks our first starting point. The physical culture movement was, in

---

[13]John Fair, 'The tragic history of the military press in Olympic and world championship competition, 1928–1972', *Journal of Sport History* 28 (2001): 345–74.
[14]Ibid., 346.
[15]John Fair, 'The iron game and capitalist culture: A century of American weightlifting in the Olympics, 1896–1996', *The International Journal of the History of Sport* 15 (1998): 18–19.
[16]Bonini, 'Weightlifting', 397–8.
[17]Ibid.
[18]Fair, 'The iron ... ', 18–19.
[19]Lucy Boucher and Conor Heffernan, 'A great weight lifted: The history of the British Amateur Weight-lifting Association', *Sport in History* 44 (2024): 369–93.

an entertainment setting, sustained by professional athletes. Many used the language and techniques of weightlifting during performances. They pressed objects overhead and challenged audience members to compete. There was, however, a great deal of chicanery involved in performances.[20] An apt comparison to make is the difference between amateur and professional wrestling. Both use the same movements but the latter is pre-scripted and concerned with entertainment. In weightlifting, professional shows were, in some instances, rigged, with athletes claiming to have lifted inconceivable weights.[21] Further complicating matters was the fact that many performers also competed in 'legitimate' contests. Eugen Sandow, though he disputed the result, competed against Arthur Saxon in 1893 and lost. Saxon regularly broke weightlifting records in Josef Szalay's London weightlifting gym.[22] Quebecois strongman Louis Cyr took part in weightlifting competitions funded by the *National Police Gazette* in North America. Cyr also engaged in strongmen feats with wild horses.[23] Sadly Cyr never challenged a horse to a strength contest. Weightlifting's struggle for recognition in the pre-war period was to disentangle itself from the professionals. This was achieved with varying levels of success.

A more pressing matter was ... the press. A dividing line in weightlifting centred on how to push a barbell overhead. Specifically, should one use the 'French' or 'German'/continental method? The French method used a stricter form wherein barbells were lifted from the floor to the breastbone before being pressed overhead with a straight back.[24] The 'German'/continental method allowed athletes to rest the barbell on their stomach, before dragging it to the breastbone and pressing it overhead using an arched back. Simplified, the German method allowed athletes to lift heavier weights. Aesthetically, the French method was more graceful. Differences extended to one-arm pressing.[25] The pre-war period was largely one of infighting within weightlifting about which method to use. Critically both camps refused kowtowing to the other and preferred to persist with their own practices.

Now we turn towards efforts to standardize weightlifting. The nineteenth century was, after all, one of codification. Sports like football, rugby, cricket, boxing, etc., all created national, and in some cases, international rules

---

[20]Broderick Chow, *Muscle Works* (Northwestern University Press, 2024), 126–32.
[21]Jan Todd, "Reflections on physical culture: Defining our field and protecting its integrity', *Iron Game History* 13 (2015): 5.
[22]David Chapman, *Sandow the magnificent: Eugen Sandow and the beginnings of bodybuilding* (University of Illinois Press, 1994), 107–8.
[23]Guy Reel, *National police gazette and the making of the modern American man, 1879–1906* (Springer, 2006), 132.
[24]Gottfried Schödl, *The lost past* (IWF, 1992), 10–44.
[25]Ibid.

FIGURE 5.1 German weightlifter showcasing the array of equipment found in the Germania club, Kaiserslautern, c. 1895.[26]

during this time.[27] In 1890, the *Österreichischer Athleten-Bund* was founded in Vienna, thereby becoming the world's first national weightlifting body. The following year, the *Deutscher Athleten-Verband* was founded, nominally governing Germany and counting 1,000 members.[28] These bodies covered more than just weightlifting. In the case of the *Deutscher Athleten-Verband*, member M. Josef Bader noted that while weightlifting competitions were held, they were married with other endeavours to avoid the over-production of 'knobbly' muscled athletes.[29] There were also clubs who refused to join

---

[26] "Franz Kelley, Kaiserslautern," *Internationale Illustrierte Athleten Zeitung*, May 26, (1895), 13.
[27] Stefan Szymanski, 'A theory of the evolution of modern sport', *Journal of Sport History* (2008): 1–32.
[28] Schödl, *The lost*, 21.
[29] Ibid., 21–30.

these associations in their respective regions.[30] Some historians have cited this as a critical starting point, as is also the case with a 'World' weightlifting championship held in London in 1891.[31] The origins of this competition lay not in a mobilizing effort to unite weightlifting but rather as an expression of sporting entrepreneurialism on the part of British man John Astley Cooper (1858–1930). At a time when international weightlifting contests were non-existent, Astley hosted a series of competitions in London. Initially hosting an English qualifier among twelve athletes, Astley sponsored an international show in March pitting English champion, E. Lawrence-Levy, against competitors from Belgium France, Poland and Italy.[32] Reports in *The Sporting Life* commended the men's strength but depicted the affair as a dreary one, noting that 'the weightlifting in the evening was rather slow'.[33] Likewise, many struggled to understand the rules utilized. The German system of continental lifting was employed and athletes were scored across single and two-handed events. Bonini celebrated the hosting of the event, but noted it was a lacklustre affair, receiving little attention and made little impact on weightlifting.[34] Illustrative of its lack of influence was the fact that the eventual world governing body, the IWF, failed to recognize it for several decades. It was not until 1898 that another world championship was hosted.[35]

The next 'global' weightlifting event was the inaugural 1896 Olympic games. The brainchild of Frenchman Pierre de Coubertin (1863–1937), the Olympics, were a result of nineteenth-century globalization.[36] Coubertin was impressed with the strength of sport in British culture and his brief time in England in the 1880s converted him to the power of sport.[37] Hosted at the home of the ancient Olympics, Coubertin's iteration was not, initially, successful. Many of the games had difficulties attracting athletes, and attention, prior to 1914.[38] Yes, these games existed, but it was not until the interwar period that one could count them as a global force. While weightlifting's inclusion was significant, rules remained an issue. In the absence of a governing body, the hosts decided the rules. Welcoming seven athletes from Denmark, Germany, Britain, Hungary and Greece, the event was, controversially, split between two lifts. Despite travelling from England

---

[30]Ibid.
[31]Gherardo Bonini, 'London: the cradle of modern weightlifting', *Sports Historian* 21 (2001): 56–70.
[32]'Sir John Astley's Weight Lifting Competition', *The Sporting Life*, 27 February 1891, 1; 'Weight lifting Competition', *The Morning Post*, 7 March 1891, 3.
[33]'Amateur Weight Lifting', *The Sporting Life*, 31 March 1891, 4.
[34]Bonini, 'London ... '.
[35]Ibid.
[36]Barbara Keys, *Globalizing sport* (Harvard University Press, 2013), 27–35.
[37]Ibid.
[38]Allen Guttmann, *The Olympics: A history of the modern games* (University of Illinois Press, 2002), 21–36.

to compete, Lawrence Levy refused to compete when he realized that the two-handed lift would be done with a barbell, rather than dumbbells.[39] Levy remained as a judge, along with Prince George of Greece and Denmark. When Danish weightlifter Viggo Jensen and British weightlifter Launceston Elliot lifted the same amount in the two-handed press, Prince George attempted to award Jensen the points based on his aesthetic style. Levy intervened, pointing out that the winner should be chosen upon the greatest weight lifted.[40]

The *Birmingham Mail* called it a 'trying and tedious' event.[41] Jensen won the two-handed event but lost out on a gold medal to Elliot in the single-arm press. Despite returning a winner, Elliot was shocked at the event's organization. His father, Gilbert, wrote to the *Pall Mall Gazette* complaining about the event's disjointed nature. He also accused the judges of being unaware of different pressing styles, including the 'Sandow' style used by Elliot.[42] Weightlifting was absent from the 1900 Olympics and it is worth noting that the 1904 Olympic Games in St. Louis, which welcomed five athletes from Greece, Germany and the United States, had a different set of rules.[43] Weightlifting at the Olympics did not reappear until 1920, and that again under a different set of rules. It is important to add that the inability of 'Olympic' weightlifting to maintain stability was not unique. While annual weightlifting competitions were hosted from 1898 to 1914, they varied in the rules employed. They typically welcomed a small pool of athletes, the most being fifty-seven in the 1910 games.[44] To finish the Olympic story, it is difficult to disagree with Schödl's assertion that the Olympics had little impact on weightlifting's trajectory.[45]

A more important trend was the ongoing efforts of Italian weightlifter Marquis Luigi Monticelli Obizzi (1863–1946) to create a weightlifting federation and framework for what exercises should be included, what style to use and whether competitors should be divided based on weight, height or experience. Fabrizio labelled Obizzi as one of the 'extraordinary personalities in the history of Milanese sports'. He established weightlifting clubs while simultaneously advocating for greater efforts globally.[46] Obizzi was joined by like-minded figures in other countries like Theodor Sibert (1866–1961) who was attempting to create commonalities between German, French and Russian weightlifting. Studying the formalization of Seibert's

---

[39]Richard Mandell, *The first modern Olympics* (Blacktoad, 1976), 130–3.
[40]Ibid.
[41]'Crown Prince', *Birmingham Mail*, 16 April 1896, 2.
[42]'The Weightlifting Contest', *Pall Mall Gazette*, 15 April 1896, 9.
[43]George Matthews and Sandra Marshall. *St. Louis Olympics 1904* (Arcadia, 2003), 89–94.
[44]Gottfried Schödl, *World championships seniors 1997–2007* (IWF, c., 2007), 1–2.
[45]Schödl, *The lost …* , 21–30.
[46]Felice Fabrizio, *Storia e leggenda dello sport milanese: le attività fisico-sportive a Milano dal 1735 al 1915* (Infinito, 2016), 114–17.

system, Wedemeyer explained that various strength disciplines existed, and, owing to this, 'there was no regulated training ... or an athlete-appropriate daily routine'.[47] Confusion concerning which rules to use meant that each nation, and even club, had their own cultures. Furthermore, in Austria and Germany, Wedemeyer distinguished between the popular act of lifting weights and the rarer practice of organizing competitions.[48] There were also disagreements as to whether weightlifting should be a 'healthy' pursuit.[49] This was a big sticking point between French physical culturist Edmond Desbonnet (1867–1953) and his German counterparts.

That Sibert befriended Desbonnet during the early 1900s, and prior to that the 'father' of Russian weightlifting, Wladislaw von Krajewski (1841–1901), helped to smooth over some conflicts in weightlifting.[50] Progress was made, for example, during the 1905 World Weightlifting Championships when it was decided to institute bodyweight categories to divide competitors.[51] Prior to this point some championships were based on 'experience'. A truism in strength circles is that the heavier one is the more weight they are likely to lift.[52] That weight categories were decided on was no small feat. During the early 1900s German weightlifting magazine *Kraft und Gewandtheit* published multiple articles concerning what lifts should be used competitively.[53] When Franz Kraus, vice-president of the Austrian federation, suggested a combination of French, German and British lifts, to be done as a 'dodecathlon', he was criticized for daring to mix different styles.[54] Likewise ignored was Obizzi's suggestions that a two-arm snatch, two-arm clean and jerk and two-arm press be used, this being the exact order used in the sport from 1928.[55] For every friendly letter and half-step towards unity, disputes erupted. Take, for example, the 1905 World Weightlifting Championship, held in Germany. While the contest was remarkable for using bodyweight categories, it was infamous for the French's rejection of German exercises as vulgar. Desbonnet's explanation that 'people of lower descent' used German movements did little for relations.[56]

Nevertheless, during the summer of 1905, it seemed weightlifting had reached an agreement. That year, August Köttgen, of the German Athletic Federation, sent letters to counterparts in Belgium, Denmark, England,

---

[47]Bernd Wedemeyer, *Der Athletenvater Theodor Siebert (1866–1961)* (Klatt, 1999), 124.
[48]Ibid., 60–88.
[49]Ibid.
[50]Ibid., 51–75.
[51]Schödl, *The lost*, 21–30.
[52]Harry Selkow, 'Yes, Mass Moves Mass," *elitefts*, 6 June 2018. See https://www.elitefts.com/coaching-logs/yes-mass-moves-mass/?srsltid=AfmBOoqA_Qp8ALFeL2oTPCMZ6Hzv9CTQ3aUQ0xtJqpFcXI0VQiDqwEuE.
[53]Boucher and Heffernan, 'A Great Weight ... ', 376.
[54]Schödl, *The lost*, 25.
[55]Ibid., 27.
[56]Ibid., 29–32.

France, Italy, Holland, Austria-Hungary, Russia, Sweden, Switzerland and the United States. His letter talked about a brotherhood of weightlifters before discussing the current state of the sport

> For several years, the various Associations have been organising so-called international competitions, the terms of which invariably suited the rules customary in the host country.[57]

An *Amateur-Athleten-Weltunion* (Amateur Athletic World Union) was founded with Denmark, Germany, Holland and Italy as original members. It was entrusted with organizing competitions, soliciting applications from other nations, and expanding the sport's popularity.[58] That seven athletes, from two nations, competed soon after in a world championship made clear how small its influence was.[59] The *Weltunion* became largely irrelevant by 1907, for reasons we shall discuss, and disbanded in 1912. Yet, the IWF traces its history to 1905. In much the same way that William Webb Ellis did not 'invent' rugby by handling a ball during a soccer match, it is fanciful to link the IWF to 1905.[60] Especially given the sport was not formalized and did not enjoy global 'buy-in' until the IWF's foundation in 1920.

The spectre at the *Weltunion*'s feast was the absence of France and Austria-Hungary. Britain's absence was felt, but not as keenly as France or Austria-Hungary which boasted over a hundred national clubs.[61] Some, in France, did favour joining the *Weltunion*, and indeed Parisian periodical *Les Sports* published endorsements in 1905 for the *Weltunion*.[62] The same periodical announced, just a short time later that the *Haltérophile Club de France* was hosting a World Championships in Paris. This marked the third World Championship, held by a different governing body, that year.[63] It was a farcical situation that only one nation – France – competed.[64] The *Weltunion* carried on and organized a European Championship in Holland the following year. This was a presumptuous move as the *Weltunion* had yet, at that point, to agree a constitution. This was achieved that year and, critically, included a list of approved lifts using the German method.[65]

The Constitution and high point of the *Weltunion* came at the same period of the 1906 Intercalated Olympics. A largely forgotten event, the games were part of a proposed cycle of events to be held in-between the

---

[57]Bonini, 'Weightlifting', 395.
[58]Ibid.
[59]Schödl, *World championships* … , 1–2.
[60]William Baker, 'William Webb Ellis and the origins of Rugby Football', *Albion* 13, no. 2 (1981): 117–30.
[61]Schödl, *The lost*, 42–6.
[62]Ibid., 49–52.
[63]Ibid., 52–6.
[64]Schödl, *World championships* … , 1–2.
[65]Schödl, *The lost*, 51–5.

regular four-year Olympic cycle.⁶⁶ The Games were created to appease the Greek delegation, which had wanted every Olympics to be held in Greece, and second, to celebrate the ten-year anniversary of the first Olympics. It also marked a desperate, but successful, attempt to revive the Game's mystique following 1900 and 1904.⁶⁷ Athletes from five nations took part in the weightlifting event, making it one of the most 'international' weightlifting events of the pre-war period.⁶⁸ The hosts did not, however, consult with the *Weltunion* and chose to test two different events.⁶⁹ Returning to Schödl, his history was brimming with disbelief that this happened

> Why, for heaven's sake ... in this environment plagued by mounting disagreement and distrust, this once-in-a-lifetime chance of a convergence ... remained unexploited?⁷⁰

In 1906, the World Championships moved from Italy to Switzerland due to internal hosting difficulties. Much to the dismay of the *Weltunion*, the Swiss hosts disregarded agreed-upon lifts in favour of its preferred movements.⁷¹ German weightlifter, and author of 1912 book *Mannesschönheit*, Albert Stolz penned a series of complaints deriding the Swiss competitions and questioning the *Weltunion*'s value.⁷² Stolz furthered his discontent in an article in *Illustrierte Athletik-Sportzeitung* in 1907 wherein he rejected efforts to revise the *Weltunion* and petitioned for German withdrawal.⁷³ Germany withdrew from the *Weltunion*, as did other members, thereby killing the attempted global federation.

The *Weltunion* was an important first step in attempting to globalize weightlifting but it failed to convince nations to disregard their own rules. If I was a German/continental lifter, I knew that switching to the French method would make me weaker. Why vote for something that made me a worse athlete? Conversely, if I was a French lifter, I knew switching to the German/continental method would make me stronger, but I would likely be at a disadvantage compared to those accustomed to the system. Why vote for something that makes me a worse athlete? Now add in geo-political tensions and a degree of jingoism.⁷⁴ What about equipment? Should a global manufacturer be used? Who gets to decide? It was a mess. Furthering the

---

⁶⁶Karl Lennartz, 'The 2nd International Olympic Games in Athens 1906', *Journal of Olympic history* 10 (2002): 3–24.
⁶⁷Ibid.
⁶⁸Schödl, *World Championships ...* , 1–2.
⁶⁹Schödl, *The lost*, 58–61.
⁷⁰Ibid., 58–61.
⁷¹Ibid.
⁷²Ibid., 61–4. Albert Stolz, *Mannesschönheit durch gesunde körperliche Ausbildung* (Taschenbuch, 1912).
⁷³Schödl, *The lost past*, 61–4.
⁷⁴Desbonnet and Chapman, *The kings of strength*, 2–40.

problem was that when the public thought of weightlifting, they thought about professional strongmen and women who used a variety of methods.[75] What makes weightlifting's failure to globalize interesting is that many weightlifting clubs also hosted wrestling. Wrestling, despite a multiplicity of styles, enjoyed far greater governance during this period. This was the case for wrestling featured at the Olympics, and popular expressions of the sport.[76]

The *Weltunion* dissolved in 1907 but world championships continued to be hosted in Germany and Austria until 1914.[77] When the 1908 London Olympics did not feature weightlifting, it caused a stir within the sport, and precipitated the re-emergence of a British amateur weightlifting association.[78] Equally damning was the fact that the 1912 Stockholm Olympics did not include weightlifting. This marked two Olympic cycles without the sport at a time when the legitimacy of the Olympic project had grown. Richard Nielsen, one of the founding members of the *Dansk Atlet-Union*, and a *Weltunion* member, approached the Olympic Committee in charge of wrestling at the 1912 games about the possibility of hosting a convention aimed at the *Weltunion* re-establishment.[79] Invitations were sent to weightlifting federations in Europe and a date was set for 15th July. Of those invited, only the Swedish delegation refused owing to what they perceived to be poor judging decisions in wrestling events held earlier. Germany and France sent delegates and the calamities of the previous few years seemed to have shocked them into cooperation.[80] A decision was made to resurrect the *Weltunion*, and to host a constitutive assembly for the end of 1913. Symbolically, it was Péter Tatics, from Hungary, who was made chairman of the newly titled *Internationaler Weltverband für Schwerathletik* (International World Federation for Strength Athletics).[81] Unlike the *Weltunion*, the federation explicitly organized itself around the Olympics, a point which furthered the need for consensus.[82] After a 'lively' conversation, a decision was centred around a combination of one-hand and two-handed lifts. The following year, in 1914, weightlifting was accepted into the Olympic fold and scheduled for the next games.[83]

Obviously, the outbreak of war (1914–18) delayed weightlifting's Olympic re-entry. The Great War resulted in the cancellation of the 1916 Berlin Games and, by the time of the 1920 games in Antwerp, weightlifting's

---

[75]Boucher and Heffernan, 'A Great … '.
[76]Schödl, *The lost*, 61–4.
[77]Ibid., 64–75.
[78]Boucher and Heffernan, 'A Great … '.
[79]Schödl, *The lost*, 64–72.
[80]Ibid.
[81]Ibid., 72–7.
[82]Ibid.
[83]Ibid.

governance changed. The perception that Germany and Austria-Hungary were responsible for the War made these nations pariahs. This was evident in the 1920 Olympics which denied entry to these nations.[84] Weightlifting did appear in the 1920 Olympics but was now governed by the *Fédération Internationale Haltérophilie (FIH)*.[85] Austria and Germany were excluded from the FIH and did not join until the mid–1920s. That Germany was not re-admitted to the Olympics until 1928 shifted power to the *Fédération*, which favoured French standards.[86] Bonini noted that Austria continued to favour continental lifting styles as late as 1927, three years after it joined the FIH.[87] They even hosted what Bonini described as a 'pirate' contest in 1923 but this was poorly attended.[88] Such incidents do, however, suggest that the previously formed *Internationaler Weltverband* would have experienced problems had War not intervened. The celebrated cooperation which underpinned the *Internationaler Weltverband's* formation in 1914 was never tested and, by the interwar period, geopolitical shifts pushed French standards in three Olympic cycles (1920, 1924 and 1928).[89] Whether by quirk or circumstance, the sport globalized around a solid set of practices by 1928. As a sporting practice, weightlifting was beset by national tensions and preferences prior to 1914. It held all the trappings of a 'modern' sport but split on regional lines.[90] The 'battle' between French and continental styles, which began in the early 1890s, took three decades to resolve and showed how complicated, and contradictory, physical culture could be. Local traditions sometimes over-powered the global.

Raising stones

In 1977, American television channel CBS hosted the World's Strongest Man (WSM) contest. The premise was simple. Bring together athletes from different sports and test them in a range of exercises to determine who was strongest. Because it was a televised spectacle, entertainment was at a premium.[91] Hence, early years of the competition tasked strongmen with races carrying refrigerators and squatting Playboy bunnies.[92] It was part-television and part-sport and critically, the WSM inadvertently gave birth

---

[84]Bonini, 'Weightlifting', 395–400.
[85]Ibid.
[86]David Webster, *The Iron Game* (Webster, 1976), 24–6.
[87]Bonini, 'Weightlifting', 396–7.
[88]Ibid.
[89]Schödl, *The lost*, 72–80.
[90]Allen Guttmann, *From ritual to record* (Columbia University Press, 1978).
[91]David Webster, *Sons of Samson II* (Ironmind, 1998), 50–70.
[92]Ibid., 50–88.

to the rise of strongman, and later, strongwoman, events.[93] These strength events are modern equivalents to the popular strength shows of the late nineteenth and early twentieth century. They play on the variety which underpinned these shows and often pay homage to this era by re-creating historic lifts or using nineteenth-century implements.[94] This historical bent explains why, in 1986, 'McGlashen' stones featured at the WSM. Modelled on the Braemar Scottish lifting stones, the McGlashens marked the first time stone-lifting featured at the WSM and can be viewed as an origin point for the globalization of lifting-stones.[95] We have already discussed lifting stones in Chapter 1 but, as a refresher, they are culturally significant stones found in multiple countries. While the technique needed to lift stones differs, the premise is the same in that lifting stones denotes one's strength and, often, masculinity.[96] On this latter point, it is important to add that while stories of women's lifting-stones exist, stones have, historically, been a test of masculinity.[97]

The 'McGlashen Stones' were smooth, round stones now known as Atlas stones.[98] Historic lifting-stones did not come become a mainstream strength practice until the 2010s when American equipment manufacturer Rogue Fitness published a series of documentaries on lifting-stones in Iceland, Scotland and the Basque region.[99] From that period to the present day, historic stone-lifting has become a globally popular practice.

Why would anyone do this? And what are the implications of this later globalization? A third, perhaps crueller question is what any of this has to do with the nineteenth century. We will grasp the nettle and begin with the last question. In the modern period, a great deal of stone-lifting's mystique is their longer history, and many will use documents or figures from our period to justify a stone's uniqueness.[100] Concerning the implications of individuals moving around the world to lift stones, there is a clear 'emptying process at play'. Recall the traditional Indian club stripped of its cultural resonance and repurposed as an exercise club. Stone-lifting was, and is, a localized practice within communities. Strength tourism, even discussed from the perspective of an observer, disrupts local narratives and replaces them, at some level, with a global equivalent. Whereas local cultures may be linked to a village's history and hierarchies, at least traditionally, global strength cultures often focus on the act of strength itself.[101]

---

[93]Ellen Staurowsky, 'ABC sports: The rise and fall of network sports television', *International Journal of Sport Communication* 13, no. 2 (2020): 275–8.
[94]Heffernan, 'The Lift … '.
[95]Mike Bonner, *The composite guide to strongman competition* (Chelsea House, 2000), 46.
[96]Martin Jancsics and Bill Crawford, *STONELIFTING* (Self-Published, 2018), 5–10.
[97]Ibid.
[98]See the 1998 World Strongest Man contest in Morocco.
[99]https://www.roguefitness.com/theindex.
[100]Jancsics and Crawford, *STONELIFTING*, 1–6.
[101]Ibid., 7–18.

Motivations, especially in a modern age, have yet to be explored but it is worth noting the appeal that these 'tests of manhood', as they are commonly understood, have for contemporary athletes.[102] Lifting heavy stones was, and is, a practice far removed from a physical culture gym. Its culture combines strength feats, local stories and gendered rites into an often isolated practice. Critically, some of the most popular lifting stones of the present day, such as the Scottish Dinnie Stones, were first recorded in the nineteenth century. There is then, a linking between past and present and, more importantly for us, an invitation to stop and consider why stone-lifting globalized in the latter half of the twentieth century. For historians, stone-lifting is a difficult practice to capture given that it was often discussed in oral traditions and done in rural regions.[103] Nevertheless, there is a solid base of research from the nineteenth century which we can call upon.

Indeed, the first point to mention, and one that connects stone-lifting to the above history of weightlifting, is that stone-lifting contests existed during the nineteenth century, and were connected to weightlifting. Schödl noted that Swiss weightlifting officials advocated for the inclusion of stone-lifting competitions during the 1900s but that this was largely, and quickly, disregarded by German, Austrian and French officials.[104] The first official Swiss strength competition involving stones was the *Unspunnenfest* in 1805 wherein the *Unspunnenstein,* an 83-kilogram stone, was thrown as far a distance as possible.[105] Contrast this with Bavarian stone-lifting wherein a large stone was simply lifted up from the ground. This was done in beer halls rather than in open fields as part of a cultural event. The most famous German stone-lifter was Hans Steyrer (1849–1906). Known as the 'Bavarian Hercules', Steyrer gained international acclaim for his ability to lift a 508 lbs stone with one finger. Steyrer was so popular that he became the most featured strongman on *International Illustrierte Athleten Zeitung*, Germany's primary strength magazine.[106]

In Britain, stone-lifting was a known and celebrated occurrence. Scottish all-round athlete Donald Dinnie (1837–1916) was recorded lifting two heavy stones, over 770 lbs combined, and walking with them across the length of the Potarch Bridge in Scotland.[107] Now called the 'Dinnie Stones', the stones were 'rediscovered' by David Webster in the 1950s and are a

---

[102]Alyssa Ages, 'The quest to pick up the lost lifting stones of Ireland', *GQ Magazine*, 28 August 2023. Available at https://www.gq.com/story/the-quest-to-pick-up-the-lost-lifting-stones-of-ireland, accessed 17 June 2024.
[103]Peter Martin, *Twixt the stone and the turf* (Peter Martin, *c.* 2014).
[104]Schödl, *The lost*, 55–65.
[105]Gil Mayencourt, 'The Gymnast and the Shepherd: The invention of a national games' tradition in Switzerland', *The International Journal of Sport and Society* 13, no. 2 (2022): 1–21.
[106]Desbonnet and Chapman, *The kings of strength*, 258–60. Jurgen Giessing and Jan Todd, 'The origins of German bodybuilding: 1790–1970', *Iron Game History* 9, no. 2 (2005): 14.
[107]Frank Zarnowski, 'The amazing Donald Dinnie', *Iron Game History* 5, no. 1 (1998): 3–11.

mainstay in modern strength sports.[108] The stone's mythology serves as a starting point for half-truths and failed starting points in the globalization of stone-lifting. During the 1920s, American physical culturist George Jowett (1891–1969) published *The Strongest Man on Earth*, a celebratory biography of Quebecois strongman Louis Cyr (1863–1912). In Jowett's retelling, Cyr travelled to Scotland to lift the Dinnie Stones and showcase his strength.[109] There is no verifiable evidence that Cyr, who did travel to Great Britain in 1892, interacted with Dinnie.[110] Jowett's *Strongest Man on Earth* took Dinnie's stones as an opportunity to embellish Cyr's reputation and hinted at some form of global stone-lifting culture. Whereas Cyr did not travel to lift Dinnie's stone, we have evidence that Steyrer welcomed Estonian wrestler George Hackenschmidt to his 'strength museum'. Then in his sixties, Steyrer kept his former implements next to his tavern as an entertainment piece. According to Hackenschmidt's biography, he met with

FIGURE 5.2 German stone-lifting, *c.* 1898.[111]

---

[108]David Webster, *Donald Dinnie: The first sporting superstar* (Ardo Pub., 1999), 1–5.
[109]George Jowett, *The strongest man that ever lived* (Physique Publishing,1949), 47.
[110]Josh Buck, 'Louis Cyr and Charles Sampson', *Iron Game History* 5, no. 3 (1998): 18–28.
[111]Franz Defregger, Die Kraftprobe. 1898. Wiki Commons. Available at https://commons.wikimedia.org/wiki/File:Franz_von_Defregger_-_Die_Kraftprobe_-_2901_-_Kunsthistorisches_Museum.jpg.

Steyrer following a wrestling tournament. Hackenschmidt enjoyed Steyrer's repertoire of strength tricks and then

> Merely for the joke of the thing, I lifted with one hand a stone to which some weights were attached, the whole weighing 660 lb.[112]

There is, perhaps, a kind retelling of this event as an early iteration of stone-lifting practices becoming globalized or, indeed, an inkling of strength tourism. I would argue that this appears to have been more of a case of serendipity. Nevertheless, I began with these stories, one real and one imagined, because they serve the grander narrative of stone-lifting.

The first, and substantive, sense of a global stone-lifting practice came during the 1900 Paris Olympics. A forgotten fact is that stone-lifting was included as a gymnastics event.[113] Like weightlifting, gymnastics events wavered between the 1896 and 1900 Olympics. During the 1896 games, gymnastics was split between 'traditional' gymnastic exercises including pommel horses and rope climbing. Many of these events were retained for the 1900 games, but events were added, including weightlifting.[114] Specifically, a 50-kilogram stone-lifting event.[115] Athletes were tasked with lifting a stone from the ground to overhead. The movement was done with both arms and each lift needed to be performed with perfect form.[116] Concerning the archival record, outside of the 1900 Olympic Report and writings in *Les Gymnast*, a French gymnastics periodical, there is little evidence for how stone-lifting appeared.[117] What is clear is that the event occurred and was reasonably well received although not to the extent that it was repeated.

The Olympic inclusion of stone-lifting was no different to the inclusion of the horse high jump which also appeared at the Paris games. The Olympic project was experimenting with its identity and structure. Stone-lifting was one of many efforts to test athletes. It wasn't repeated in subsequent games but it was a clear effort to include stone-lifting within a global event. Taking part in that Olympic event were 135 competitors from eight nations.[118] It was an indication that stone-lifting, a highly localized practice, could appear on a global stage. Why was it not repeated and why, given the general chaos in weightlifting, did stone-lifting not appear in weightlifting?

There are broader observations one can make about why stone-lifting did not progress to being a global pastime, or a broader part of the physical

---

[112]George Hackenschmidt, *The way to live* (Athletic Publications, 1908), 132.
[113]Concours Internationaux D'exercices Physiques Et De Sports, *Rapports Publiés Sous La Direction De M. D. Mérillon Délégué Général* (Paris: IOC, 1901), 92.
[114]Ibid., 90–2.
[115]Ibid.
[116]Ibid.
[117]'Manifestations et incidents', *Le Petit Journal*, 26 November 1900, 1.
[118]Ibid.

culture movement. The first is that stones are not very useful commercial products. They are difficult to standardize, cumbersome to transport and awkward to lift.[119] One of the primary focuses of this book has been the commercialization of fitness with the emergence of physical culture books, magazines and equipment. Lifting-stones did not fall into this category, and, even if one did have the ability to transport stones, there were usability issues.[120] Physical culture equipment was designed to be as straightforward as possible to use. Sandow and others marketed spring-grip dumbbells that could be used by adults and children alike.[121] Others, like Calvert, or Pullum in Britain, sold barbells alongside instructions on how to use them. Stones were awkward in shape, and tricky to lift. They could not be stored safely away and for those living in cities, could not be easily hidden in one's home or apartment. Stone-lifting was also a heavy-lifting practice at a time when the general public was generally fearful of lifting heavy weights.[122] Finally, stones are not easily adjustable. A spring-grip dumbbell could be made 'heavier' by adding additional springs. A barbell could be made heavier by loading more shot or, in time, by adding additional plates. Stones were difficult to make heavier or lighter. One could, of course, stack stone on top of the other but that would have been a health hazard.

Stones, like Indian clubs, did not fit into the aesthetic of the physical culture industry. They were difficult to sell, market and use. They could not be easily adapted, or scaled, and they did not fit into ideas of modernity or science. And yet, the 1900 Olympics hinted at a potential inroad for this practice. We also know that some physical culture performers did use stone-lifting in their shows. Edmond Desbonnet's *Rois de la Force*, published in 1911, is useful here. Desbonnet noted a series of strength performers who lifted stones with one finger, or with teeth, as part of their shows.[123] Likewise, even Eugen Sandow credited himself with stone-lifting feats. In Sandow's case, his 1894 book, *Sandow on Physical Training*, credited Sandow with a '1,500 pounds' stone lift using a harness lift.

Thus people were familiar with the practice in the physical culture community. We also have evidence, in the British Empire and beyond, that stone-lifting was exhibited in military settings. Informally, there is evidence that Indian soldiers engaged in stone-lifting in military camps as a means of diversion and exhibition. A short piece in *The Royal Magazine* in 1914 celebrated an 'Indian Hercules' who lifted heavy stones.[124] Stone-lifting was

---

[119] Jancsics and Crawford, STONELIFTING, 1–4.
[120] Kimberly Ayn Beckwith, *Building strength: Alan Calvert, the Milo Bar-bell Company, and the modernization of American weight-training* (The University of Texas at Austin, 2006), 12–76.
[121] Conor Heffernan, 'All muscle and no brains?: Contextualizing the fitness entrepreneur in sport history,' *Sporting Traditions* 39, no. 2 (2022): 13–32.
[122] Joan Paul, 'The health reformers: George Barker Windship and Boston's strength seekers', *Journal of Sport History* 10, no. 3 (1983): 41–57.
[123] David Chapman and Edmond Desbonnet, *The kings of strength* (McFarland, 2022), 72–84.
[124] 'An Indian Hercules', *The Royal Magazine* 32 (1914): 252.

an institutionalized practice elsewhere. There are a number of reports from the late nineteenth century that, in China, a soldier's training included stone-lifting.[125] For those who failed in stone-lifting or sword practice, they were required to try to enlist again in several years' time.[126] The *Tokio Times* explained this process with the introductory lines that 'the Chinese army is as backward in its tactics as in its armament'.[127] The instruction in physical training was 'a mere burlesque of infantry drill' and successful Chinese officer described as ignorant.[128] With the proviso that such comments cannot be divorced from a broader imperialist framework, the institutionalization of stone-lifting in a martial setting could have been, in another world, a starting part for a broader globalization.[129] The use of stone-lifting in physical culture performances and in some military settings could have built a critical mass for stone-lifting to be globalized but of course, it did not.

Instead, it is possible to identify a *deepening* of local practices in stone-lifting in some parts of the world, rather than globalization. It is difficult, if not outright impossible, to record the history of stone-lifting and it would be foolish to attempt it. What differentiated the nineteenth century from the eighteenth or seventeenth century was not, necessarily, that more people took to stone-lifting but rather that more records were written. The explosion of interest in the study of languages, geography, religion and culture created a complex and nuanced record around stone-lifting. Beginning Scotland, perhaps the most enduring and varied European stone-lifting culture, Martin previously used Scottish placenames, mythologies and government reports from this era to identify the practice.[130] The Scottish context is also interesting given the revival of the Highland Games during the nineteenth century. An act of cultural heritage and celebration, the Highland Games are multi-sporting events and cultural festivals celebrating Scottish culture.[131] Banned for several centuries under British law, the Games were revived in the early 1800s following the repeal of laws banning Highland dress, festivals and music.[132] Donaldson's work on the games is useful here as it stresses the early globalization of the Highland Games.[133] There is evidence of Games being hosted by Scottish migrants in Canada and the United States during the 1810s. What exactly did these games entail? Depending on the event, the Games included throwing events, athletic events such as racing

---

[125]Alfred Cunningham, *The Chinese soldier and other sketches* (Daily Press, 1902), 77.
[126]'Strength of the Chinese Military', *Tokyo Times* 5 (1879): 91–3.
[127]Ibid.
[128]Ibid.
[129]Heffernan, 'State of the field', 143–62.
[130]Martin, *Twixt the Stone and the Turf*.
[131]Sarah Solberg, 'International: The highland games', *Journal of Health, Physical Education, Recreation* 45 (1974): 19–21.
[132]Grant Jarvie, 'Highland gatherings, Balmorality, and the glamour of backwardness', *Sociology of Sport Journal* 9 (1992): 167–78.
[133]Emily Ann Donaldson, *The Scottish highland games in America* (Pelican, 1999).

and strength events such as tug-of-war or stone-lifting.[134] The selection of events was dependent on local cultures and Games were held throughout the Highlands. They were a decentralized practice which, during the nineteenth century, was loosely connected. Such was the cultural force of the Games that, by the mid-nineteenth century, they received the official patronage of British monarch Queen Victoria (1819–1901).[135] There is also some evidence of the Highland Games influencing, or at least impressing, Olympic founder Pierre de Coubertin after he saw them at the 1889 Paris Exhibition.[136] While stones were often thrown in the air, heavy stone-lifting was included early in such events.[137] Take, for example, the *New Times* in from 1818 which noted a Glengary event which included 'lifting the stone'.[138] The same festival was described, in more detail, four years later in the *Belfast Commercial Chronicle*, wherein an unnamed journalist sympathized with those athletes who 'failed in lifting the stone, a Garry pebble of some eighteen stones weight'.[139] The same event, reported in the Scottish *Caledonian Mercury*, praised the 'mere stone mason' who completed the event.[140] Recorded newspaper accounts of stone-lifting are more sporadic in later decades, although there is evidence that lifting-stones existed as part of various region's Highland celebrations. What is less clear, and there is little evidence for, is whether stone-lifting was included in Highland events in North America and Oceania. Given the longer oral histories preserving historic lifting stones (some of which date back to the seventeenth century), it is likely that the practice remained a Scottish one. What is important is that competitions of note, with clear global connections, be they Highland Games or the Olympics, did hold space for lifting-stones.

It is useful to turn to Guttman's understanding of sporting modernization. Guttman previously cast structural characteristics like the creation of rules, record-keeping, sporting officials and competition as modernization features.[141] At Highland events, there is evidence that many of these characteristics were at play. What did not exist was a formal federation to homogenize different forms of stone-lifting. While some Highland events focused on lifting and carrying a stone, others focused on lifting stones from the ground. Scottish stone-lifting has deep cultural ties to Scottish cultural nationalism. This is aided, in no small part, by the volume of lifting-stones.[142] Thus it is unsurprising that concurrent with the 'revival', of the Highland

---

[134]Jancsics and Crawford, STONELIFTING, 5–10.
[135]Jarvie, 'Highland gatherings … '.
[136]James MacKillop, *Highlanders: Unlocking identity through history* (McFarland, 2024), 184.
[137]Jancsics and Crawford, STONELIFTING, 5–10.
[138]'Sporting Extraordinary', *New Times*, 17 October 1818, 3.
[139]'Savage Sports', *Belfast Commercial Chronicle*, 28 October 1818, 1.
[140]'Sporting Extraordinary', *Caledonian Mercury*, 17 October 1818, 2.
[141]Guttmann, *From Ritual to Record*.
[142]Jancsics and Crawford, STONELIFTING, 5–10.

games in the nineteenth century, it is possible to work on the Scottish language, geography, histories of Scottish tribes and sporting heroes giving text to stone-lifting.[143] One such example is James Logan's 1830s work *The Scottish Gael*, which celebrated the manhood rites of historic Scottish tribes engaged in lifting stones to prove their strength.[144] Scottish stone-lifting did experience a level of formalization and 'sportification' during the nineteenth century but one that intimately linked to Scottish identity. At a time when other sporting and strength cultures were being emptied on the global stage, Scottish stone-lifting was being imbued with more significance.

Scotland was not the only country to experience some form of 'modernization' in terms of stone-lifting. In the Basque Region of Spain and France, the practice of *Harri-Jasotze/Harri jasotzea* was formalized during the late nineteenth century. Unlike Scottish stone-lifting, *Harri-Jasotze* is a far more recent phenomenon. A combination of round, cylindrical, rectangular and cube stones is lifted to the shoulder.[145] While *Harri-Jasotze* today focuses on distinct stone objects, that practised in the late nineteenth and early twentieth centuries was more varied and disorganized. Stone-lifting events and competitions existed in Japan during this period, for example, but the proximity of stone-lifting in Scotland, the Basque Region and Switzerland to France and Germany raises fascinating questions about how and why the practice did not become globally sportified. Recas cited rural and agrarian labour as the starting point for *Harri-Jasotze*.[146] While this is not remarkable, the more interesting facet was the marriage between this style of stone-lifting and gambling in Basque culture.[147] Without a gambling culture, Basque stone-lifting would not have arisen, nor survived. This reflected a broader wave of sport gambling which arose during this period in Basque sports. There is evidence of stone-lifting existing before this point and, to that end, evidence exists of a Francisco Arizmendi (or Arratola) who 'earned great respect in the town-square' thanks to his strength.[148]

Basque stone-lifting occurred in a similar fashion to the Highland Games in that it was often done in conjunction with some other activities. There are stories of stone-lifting being coupled with events centred on dragging a stone along the ground or, occasionally, mainstream strength activities concerning dumbbells and barbells.[149] The first recorded competition of stone lifting came in 1885 when two men met in Ermua (in Biscay/northern Spain).

---

[143]Martin, *Twixt the Stone*.
[144]James Logan, *The Scotish gaël, or, celtic manners* (Marsh, Capen & Lyon, 1833).
[145]Lucio Doncel Recas, *Harri-Jasotze: Levantamiento de piedras en Euskadi y Navarra* (Vision Libros: Madrid, 2021).
[146]Ibid., 30–6.
[147]Ibid.
[148]Ibid., 36.
[149]Bartosz Prabucki, *Traditional sports and games in the contemporary world: The new face of sport?* (Cambridge Scholars Publishing, 2022), 88–94.

Attracting a great deal of attention, not least among gamblers, the event focused on the lifting stones to shoulder height.[150] Bets were laid between lifts and, in front of 1,200 people, the weights increased until one man failed.

Newspapers proved to be critical in the spread of stone-lifting. It was here challenges were publicized for stone-lifting and other feats of strength. The implements used were those easily accessible to working-men, and it was exclusively men mentioned. In this context, it is clear that stones were 'just' another object to test one's strength. They did not come with the same lineage of manhood rites as happened in Scotland. Two things, however, changed during this period. The first was the formalization of lifts. At a time when many strength competitions were being crafted and created, the practice of lifting stones to the shoulder, as opposed to just raising it from the ground, became the most accepted form.[151] This change created a distinct form of Basque stone-lifting. The second, far more important change, was the increasing frequency with which stone-lifting events were held.

In other contexts, it would be silly to cite a 'foundational' figure for a stone-lifting culture. For Basque stone-lifting, historians are clear that Bittor Zabala ('Arteondo') standardized stone-lifting practices.[152] From 1910 to 1945, Arteondo popularized four distinct lifting objects (a ball, a cylinder, a cube or a cuboid). For this reason, he has been credited as being a great 'reformer' of the sport.[153] He even created a 'regulation' stone in 1917. What is clear is that the formalization placed a structure around a disorganized but ultimately popular sport. How popular does popular mean? Walton's study of Basque sports classified it as a golden age for these sports of rural and sporting backgrounds.[154] There were even stone-lifting celebrities as promoted within these newspapers. Arteondo is a fine example of this and his fifteen-year undefeated run in stone-lifting competitions solidified him as the sport's first celebrity.

Unlike the Highland games, there is little evidence that *Harri-Jasotze* was practised outside the Basque Region. While the Basque diaspora existed, especially in North America, they did not bring this practice with them.[155] Part of the reasoning behind this is practical – stone-lifting was a geography and work-dependent practice. And part of this lack of movement spoke to its initial disconnect from Basque cultural identity. During the twentieth century, and especially the latter half, stone-lifting became enmeshed with

---

[150]Recas, *Harri-Jasotze*, 38.
[151]Ibid., 36–45.
[152]Arana, Andoni. 'HARRIJASOKETA'. *Auñamendi Eusko Entziklopedia*, aunamendi.euskoikaskuntza.eus/artikuluak/artikulua.php?id=eu&ar=76816&ep=118566
[153]Aperribai, JC. 'ARTEONDO – VICTOR ZABALA'. *Deba Informacion*, 20 February 2014, debainformacion.blogspot.com/2014/02/arteondo-victor-zabala.html.
[154]John Walton, 'Sport and the Basques', *Journal of Historical Sociology* 24, no. 4 (2011): 451–71.
[155]Fernando Molina and Pedro J. Oiarzabal, 'Basque-Atlantic shores: Ethnicity, the nation-state and the diaspora in Europe and America (1808–98)', *Ethnic and Racial Studies* 32 (2009): 698–715.

a much broader sense of Basque identity.[156] Either Scottish or Basque cultures could have provided a framework for global sport or practice but the broader 'smoothening' or 'emptying' process that globalized judo, gymnastics or physical culture did not occur. Logistical issues may have been cited, but the 1900 Paris Olympics showed how global competitions could have arisen. Likewise, it is not that this was an unknown practice with no real lineage. In some instances, it dated hundreds of years, if not more. It was, and remained, a local practice.

Swinging heavy clubs

Writing in *Health & Strength* magazine in 1951, W. A. Pullum described Professor Harrison and classed him as one of the spectacles of the nineteenth century. There was, however, a curio in Pullum's writings. How did a spectacle so domineering as Harrison's disappear?[157] Harrison was different. While others swung the light clubs previously discussed, Harrison swung large clubs, which he described as *mugdars*. These clubs weighed 47 lbs and Harrison swung two as part of his act.[158] Harrison's performances were more like the Indian and Persian ones which initially pressed British physicians and troops to swing clubs. Even the name denoted its Indian origins, albeit Harrison created an Anglicized version of the *jori* or *muggah*. Pullum's writing noted that there was a time when Harrison's performances 'drew big, intensely interested crowds'.[159] Harrison was a globally famous individual. He received accolades from reigning British monarch Queen Victoria after he impressed her with his strength and his books on club-swinging sold on two continents. Such was Harrison's intrigue that the *New York Clipper* sent a reporter from New York to Harrison's tavern in England to report on the Professor.[160] For centuries, individuals in India and Persia swung heavy clubs for exercise, military training and as part of a socio-religious practice. Lightweight club-swinging did not become a pastime until the nineteenth century. As it rose in popularity, heavy club-swinging declined in use. This was the case even in India, and due to the British military, it is likely more Indian men swung light clubs than traditional heavy clubs.[161]

And yet quirks like Harrison existed. Likewise, we know that people in Europe, North America and Oceania were familiar with heavy club-swinging.

---

[156]Carrie Douglass, *Bulls, bullfighting, and Spanish identities* (University of Arizona Press, 1999), 153.
[157]W.A. Pullum, 'Random recollections', *Health and Strength*, 27 December (1951), 24–5.
[158]Ibid.
[159]Ibid.
[160]'Sights in London: Reminiscences of a trip to England', *The New York Clipper*, 12 September 1863.
[161]Conor Heffernan, *Indian club-swinging and the Birth of global fitness: Mugdars, masculinity and marketing* (Bloomsbury, 2023), 127–60.

Todd's research on George Barker Windship, the mid-nineteenth-century physician who promoted heavy weight-training, recorded a 137 lbs Indian club in Windship's gym.[162] How Windship came to use it, where he purchased it and why he wanted it are all lost to time. Nevertheless, its very existence in America during this time is similar in a sense to the use of stone-lifting at the Paris Olympics. It showed a potential for a potential globalization. Likewise, Todd notes that the term *mugdah* (or 'mugdaugh') is listed in *Dewitt's Athletics Exercises for Health and Strength* published in 1870.[163] Sporadic pockets of heavy club-swingers existed but the practice did not become globalized in the sense of a regular and recognized practice. Why? Performing in the 1850s and 1860s, Harrison can be considered to be an early strongman performer. In Europe, Felice Napoli (1821–87) toured countries impressing individuals with his strongman act. One of Napoli's admirers was Louis Durlacher or Professor Atilla the strongman who came to mentor Eugen Sandow. From Felice to Sandow, we find a strongman lineage and the transfer of knowledge around physical culture practices. Harrison did not enjoy a similar influence. When he died, there were few, if any, heavy club-swinging enthusiasts.[164] Harrison had a global fame, operated at a point when physical culture was beginning to monetize, albeit tentatively, and had an impressive physique. He even boasted the clichéd transformation story. When the *Illustrated London News* published a piece on Harrison in the early 1850s, they celebrated his progression from struggling with seven-pound clubs to his forty-seven-pound iterations.[165] Still, Harrison and heavy club-swinging faded from memory, effectively disappearing from the global fitness environment before the Great War.[166] Why did it fail to 'catch' onto the broader wave of global fitness?

Somewhat perversely, it is useful to begin in England. It was England where Indian club-swinging, using light clubs, was globalized. English texts were read and translated around the world, and military officers were vital in the spread of club-swinging around Europe. It is England where Harrison became the first European and white strongman to wield heavy clubs in a serious way. While there is evidence of British men attempting to swing heavy clubs and Persian *meels* at the beginning of the nineteenth century, this was done in military camps.[167] Harrison represented a change. He was someone who used the clubs divorced from their origins. Likewise, Harrison

---

[162]Jan Todd, 'Strength is health: George Barker windship and the first American weight-training boom', *Iron Game History* 3 (1993): 6.
[163]Jan Todd, 'From milo to milo: A history of barbells, dumbells, and Indian clubs', *Iron Game History* 3, no. 6 (1995): 4–16.
[164]Heffernan, *Indian Club-swinging* ... , 106.
[165]'Professor Harrison', *The Illustrated London News*, 14 August 1852.
[166]Jason Shurley, Jan Todd and Terry Todd, *Strength coaching in America: A history of the innovation that transformed sports* (University of Texas, 2019), 96.
[167]Mountstuart Elphinstone, *An account of the kingdom of Caubul and its dependencies in Persia, Tartary, and India* (Longman, 1815), 263–4.

FIGURE 5.3 Harrison's first image in *The Illustrated London News*.[168]

did not come from a military background, had never been to India and only became aware of the practice after an exhibition by Indian strongmen in England. He serves as a fascinating starting point for the practice of heavy club-swinging.

Surveying English texts prior to Harrison's 1851 article in the *Illustrated London News*, there is little evidence of sustained interest in medical or military journals promoting heavy club-swinging outside of occasional commentaries about the 'mugdar'.[169] Turning to Harrison's 1865 book, *Indian Clubs, Dumb-Bells, and Sword exercises*, the preface listed the Rajah

---

[168]'Professor Harrison', *The Illustrated London News*.
[169]Heffernan, *Indian Club-swinging ...* , 95–126.

of Coorg, Prince of Oude and King of Scinde as Indian representatives impressed by his club-swinging.[170] Harrison's book instructed men on how they too, could swing heavy clubs. It represented one of the first times trainees were encouraged to swing heavy clubs. It is funny to note that Indian practices were only commented on in passing by Harrison. At one point, he noted the Indian practice of sometimes throwing clubs into the air and catching them but labelled this as performative rather athletic.[171]

Harrison's popularity briefly prompted the emergence of 'copycat' entertainers in Britain and the United States. In 1862, 'Professor Gregory' began performing with large clubs around Britain and there is evidence of similar copycats emerging.[172] Likewise, in 1861, William Wood submitted a sketching to the *New York Clipper* which mimicked Harrison's pose from the *Illustrated London News* some years previously.[173] Soon after, the *Clipper* published an illustration of 'Mr. Montgomery' exercising with dumbbells and challenging Harrison.[174] Copycats did not develop into practitioners, and not at a larger scale.

Within the Anglophone world, a few books encouraged the use of heavy club-swinging. One example was Lemaire's 1889 *Indian Clubs and How to Use Them*. A member of the German Gymnastic Society, Lemaire boasted being able to use clubs weighing 40 lbs.[175] Lemaire's gymnasium did encourage some form of heavy club-swinging but there is no indication that others took up heavy club-swinging. While it is possible to point at a handful of books which mentioned heavy club-swinging, there were dozens advocating for light club-swinging during this period. Evidence of this is Lemaire's attempts to 'convince unbelievers' about heavy clubs.[176] This, in a sentence, typified the challenges surrounding heavy club-swinging as a globalized practice. Occasional pockets opened outside of India and Persia but there was little in the way of a sustained practice. There was one other element of note in Lemaire's text. He recorded his disgust at a prominent clubmaker who told him about a fraudulent heavy-club he produced.[177] Made to be large and intimidating, the club appeared to weigh anywhere from 45 to 100 lbs. The actual weight was no more than 3 lbs and Lemaire was convinced that strongmen were using the device to trick audiences.

Lemaire's suspicions were not unfounded. Gus Hill (1858–1937), an American performer, was known for using fraudulent clubs. Despite being a respected club-swinging athlete, Hill was far more adept at promotions. When promoting his shows in a new town, it was common for Hill to leave

---

[170]Professor Harrison, *Indian Clubs, Dumb-Bells and Sword exercises* (Henry Lea, 1868), 41.
[171]Ibid., 14.
[172]'The Celebrated Indian Club Exercise', *Congleton and Macclesfield Mercury*, 9 August 1862.
[173]Ibid., 96.
[174]'Young America', *The New York Clipper*, 17 May 1856.
[175]E. Ferdinand Lemaire, *Indian Clubs and how to use them* (Iliffe and Son, 1889), 9.
[176]Ibid., 1–12.
[177]Ibid., 15–20.

heavy clubs in places of prominence with an invitation for locals to lift them. When Hill returned to retrieve his clubs he would subtly lower the weight by removing internal weights stored in the clubs and casually lift them.[178] Even his vaudeville posters boasted heavy clubs, supposedly weighing 150 lbs, a weight which would have been a near physical impossibility for the light athlete. The heavy club was great for showmen but did not attract individual trainees in the Western world. Remember that heavy weight training was often discouraged by Anglophone physicians. Now add in the fact that heavy club-swinging was cumbersome. Additionally where could one get one made? Lemaire's book, written at club-swinging's height in Britain, noted the difficulty one faced in making heavy clubs.[179]

Returning, briefly, to Harrison, he was exposed to heavy clubs at some point in the 1840s when he attended a demonstration by Indian practitioners. The nineteenth century was a period wherein European and Western eyes often enjoyed, and through their enjoyment demanded, a regular supply of 'exotic' exhibitions. At times, such events were celebrations for new technologies, such as The Great Exhibition in London held in 1851 or various World Fairs held in Europe, North America or Oceania.[180] Such events brought entrepreneurs, academics, explorers and scientists together to demonstrate technological advances or different cultures. The intersection between physical culture and World Fairs is usually discussed in passing with reference to Sandow's appearance in Chicago in 1893. Or, prior to this, the 1851 Great Exhibition in London which, Budd noted, was critical in shaping fitness goals around Greco-Roman ideals.[181]

The Great Exhibition, in London, was done to celebrate *pax Britannica* and as a testimony to the century's technological advancements. Within the Exhibition halls was an Indian display which included Hindu athletes swinging heavy clubs in conjunction with their callisthenic regimes. Such displays were not removed from the smaller show Harrison encountered some decades previous.[182] Within India, a series of exhibitions were held in Lucknow and Calcutta, containing 'mugdars' which were reported back in London. There was also a lot to be said for the travelling show.[183] A remarkable exhibition, captured in still image, came in 1896 when the India and Ceylon Exhibition appeared in London.[184] The unnamed 'jori' swinger, shown below, performed prowess, a traditional, heavy, club.

---

[178]Heffernan, *Indian Club-swinging* ... , 127–40.
[179]Lemaire, *Indian Clubs* ... , 23–40.
[180]Heffernan, *Indian Club-swinging* ... , 150–1.
[181]Michael Anton Budd, *The sculpture machine: Physical culture and body politics in the age of empire* (New York University Press, 1997), 11.
[182]Heffernan, *Indian Club-swinging* ... , 150–1.
[183]Lucknow University, *Canning college, Lucknow exhibition, 1885 catalogue of departments* (London Printing Press, 1885), 96; *Official report of the Calcutta international exhibition, 1883–84* (Bengal Secretariat Press, 1885), 350.
[184]From Author's Collection.

FIGURE 5.4 Club swinger at the 1896 India and Ceylon Exhibition.[185]

Exhibitions did not have to be 'live' in order to be impactful. Owing to the power of the printed world and illustration, Indian exhibitions were reported on globally. A striking example of this came in 1860 when the *Illustrated London News* printed the below image with the accompanying observation that club-swinging represented 'one of the most effectual athletic exercises known anywhere in common use throughout India'.[186]

The image, and observation, came six years before American Sim Kehoe published his club-swinging book.[187] In his introduction, Kehoe referred to an unnamed British officer and of the clubs before taking, verbatim, passages written in the *Illustrated London News*.[188] Whether or not the newspaper or

---

[185]Ibid.
[186]'Callisthenic exercises in India', *Illustrated London News*, 18 February 1860.
[187]Simon D. Kehoe, *The Indian Club exercise: With explanatory figures and positions* (Dick&Fitzgerald, 1866).
[188]Ibid., 4–5.

FIGURE 5.5 Club swingers in India, c. 1860.[189]

any of its contributors had been to India and seen this exhibition is beyond the point, the ripple effect of the illustration was clear. Real or not, it raised awareness of the practice, at a global, but certainly transnational, scale.

The manner in which the exhibitions were written about and presented mattered. Whereas Harrison used fetes, gymnasiums displays to show his strength, not to mention countless newspaper articles and illustrations, Indian men were exhibited as cultural curios, often behind exhibition displays. They were physically and culturally separated from Western eyes and the language used was one of colonialism. It was not uncommon for such clubs to be confused with 'war clubs' or for their histories to be muddled with orientalist ideas about 'primitive cultures'.[190] The physical strength exhibited by club swingers in Western media was often treated as an anachronism to Western modernity. It is interesting to contrast this with

---

[189]Ibid.
[190]Ibid.

other colonial subjects. When a New Zealand rugby team toured Britain in the early 1900s, many praised their skill and stature to the point of using it as an example for how degenerated the British race had become.[191] Rarely, if ever, were such discourses applied to club swingers. Their race and position within the colonial hierarchy seemed to disqualify them from a global transfer. Some may argue that polo, a distinctly Indian pastime, was globalized through British hands in the nineteenth century. The difference between polo and club-swinging was that Indian clubs *were* globalized, but only the lightweight versions which were distinctly Westernized.[192]

What about competition? Surely this could have globalized club-swinging? Stone-lifting and certainly weightlifting boasted competitions during this period, however varied the rules. Imy previously noted the practice of Indian soldiers challenging British men to heavy club-swinging competitions as an informal, and playful, test of masculinity.[193] A century before, Mountstuart Elphinstone praised one English soldier for successfully performing 600 *dands* (a form of push up) followed by club-swinging after being challenged by an Indian soldier. Elphinstone finished his writing with the observation that they [Indian clubs] are one of the best inventions which Europe could borrow from the East ....[194] Critically, Elphinstone was referring to heavy club-swinging. Competition can be a powerful driver of globalization, especially in a sporting context. In the case of heavy club-swinging, there were several instances in the early twentieth century which left no tangible impact.

Chapter 2 briefly discussed the rise of the Hindu mela in India during the latter half of the nineteenth century. The mela marked an intensification of Hindu physical culture and an explicit, eventually global, effort by Hindu nationalists to dispute colonial claims about their inferiority.[195] Part of this manifested itself in wrestling matches between Indian wrestlers and those based in Europe. Two such wrestlers, Buttan Singh and Gama the Great, warrant our attention. Both toured Britain during the early 1900s, and Singh later settled in Australia. In Britain and Australia, Singh was famous for swinging clubs weighing over 100 lbs. In 1909, *The Era* in England noted a music hall program which included the 'Hindoo' athlete Singh 'whose swinging of heavy Indian clubs causes much interest'.[196] Shaw Desmond, a British art critic who admired Singh, gushingly wrote around this time

---

[191] John Nauright, 'Sport, manhood and empire: British responses to the New Zealand rugby tour of 1905', *The International Journal of the History of Sport* 8 (1991): 239–55.
[192] Patrick McDevitt, 'The king of sports: Polo in late Victorian and Edwardian India', *The International Journal of the History of Sport* 20 (2003): 1–27.
[193] Imy, 'Fascist yogis ... '.
[194] Elphinstone, *An Account of ...* , 263–4.
[195] Amitava Chatterjee, 'From courtyard sport to competitive sport', *Sport in Society* 18 (2015): 1–16.
[196] Heffernan, *Indian Club-swinging*, 171–4.

that Singh's strength was inconceivable.[197] In *Health & Strength*, Singh's strength was noted regularly great during his tour.[198] A common piece of rhetoric was that such clubs were out of the ordinary in a British context and the strength needed to yield them was beyond belief. This was echoed in Australia where Singh settled in the early 1900s. What seemed to further individual's incredulity with Singh's clubs was his small stature.[199]

One of Singh's contemporaries was Ghulam Mohammad Baksh Butt (Gama the Great) who toured Britain in the early 1900s where he defeated a series of elite wrestlers. One of the finest wrestlers of his generation, Gama's strength and endurance were legendary. That it is still reported that Gama lifted a 1,200-kilogram stone – to be clear an absolute impossibility – is testament to how strong people believed he was.[200] What is undeniable is that he was a well-conditioned athlete who was a master of their craft. Percy Longhurst, a British self-defence coach, wrote of Gama's tour in Britain in the early 1910s. In *Health & Strength*, Longhurst recalled sneaking into Gama's training facility with some fellow physical culturists to spy on Gama's training.[201] The men stood in wonder as the wrestler went through thousands of repetitions in bodyweight exercises. Gama was firmly associated with a distinct form of wrestling training, which centred on bodyweight exercises and club-swinging.[202] Alter notes that during the Prince of Wales' tour of India in 1922, he presented Gama with a silver mace in recognition of his successes. This honour was repeated later when Gama faced a long-time rival Stanislaus Zbyszko in 1927.[203] That individuals understood the social importance of the heavy mace, often confused with the heavy club, showed the global awareness of what the practice was, especially among wrestlers.

What, then, of the Indian context? From a sporting point of view, the practice of heavy club-swinging did not become an organized and competitive sport in India until the 1980s. Prior to this point, it was an ongoing practice in gymnasium spaces, albeit in a disjointed manner. For our period, we know that heavy club-swinging, be it *joris, gadas* or *maces*, continued to be used in military camps and *akharas* although the extent to which it was done paled in comparison to the institutional military forms done with light-clubs. The introduction of light club-swinging in the 1860s by the British military impacted the popularity of heavy club-swinging which was a more restricted practice. Military club-swinging also trickled out to Indian schools and gyms.

---

[197]Ibid.
[198]Ibid.
[199]'Sikh who downed world's best', *The Daily News*, 13 August 1929, 5.
[200]Joseph Alter, 'Subaltern bodies and nationalist physiques: Gama the great and the heroics of Indian wrestling', *Body & Society* 6 (2000): 45–72.
[201]Percy Longhurst, 'On Gama', *Health and Strength*, 4 May (1935), 21–4.
[202]Alter, 'Subaltern bodies ... '.
[203]Abhijit Gupta, 'Cultures of the body in colonial Bengal', *The International Journal of the History of Sport* 29 (2012): 1687–700.

How did this fit within a broader physical culture context? As per Alter, it would be incorrect to see traditional *jori* swinging as a practice untouched by globalization.[204] During the latter half of the nineteenth century, Indian physical culture underwent three seismic introductions in the introduction of British military gymnastics, the proliferation of YMCA missions in India and the growing importance of Swedish gymnastics. Such factors added a new level of rigidity to Indian physical culture, forcing some elements to, in essence, join the Western physical culture movement. Singleton previously traced the influence that Swedish drill, in particular, had on yoga postures. Alter noted that although the muscular Christian zeal underpinning Western physical culture systems did not mesh well with the nationalism attached to Indian physical culture, the latter often transformed itself by appropriating certain foreign practices.[205] Alter cited *kabaddi*, a contact sport, which transformed from a rural practice to highly regimented sport as one such example as well as the emergence of multiple 'professors' of physical culture in India during this period.[206]

Heavy club-swinging was, in Alter's mind, somewhat influenced by this broader mixing of systems. A particularly interesting example of this can be found in D.C. Mujumdar's 1950 publication the *Encyclopedia of Indian Physical Culture*. Mujumdar was the editor of *Vyayam Dnyankosh,* an inter-war Indian physical culture periodical. *Vyayam* was one of the largest magazines of its era.[207] Its core focus was on promoting Indian physical cultures. One issue in 1939 noted the use of *gadas* by wrestlers to strength their bodies.[208] Conceding that the practice was not widely used in the Maharashtra region, it was described as a traditional exercise which still held relevancy for athletes. One year earlier, in 1938, more descriptions were given of the gada, then described as an effective but unpopular training tool.[209] The same edition included images of a small child next to the *gada* as a sort of rousing encouragement for exercisers to take to the practice. Importantly, images and instructions were complimented by texts on British clubs. One edition opened with an image of light-clubs being used before promoting traditional physical culture practices in later articles.[210] A lot of Mujumdar's texts were subsequently collected in his 1950 *Encyclopaedia*

---

[204]Joseph Alter, 'Indian clubs and colonialism: Hindu masculinity and muscular Christianity,' *Comparative Studies in Society and History* 46, no. 3 (2004): 497–534.
[205]Ibid.
[206]Ibid.
[207]Ronojoy Sen, *Nation at play: A history of sport in India* (Columbia University Press, 2015), 19–24.
[208]Karandikar (Mujumdar), Dattatraya Chintaman, ed. *Vyayamgyankosh Khand 5* (Baroda: Shriramvijay Press, 22 October 1939), 1.
[209]Karandikar (Mujumdar), Dattatraya Chintaman, ed. *Vyayamgyankosh Khand 4* (Baroda: Shriramvijay Press, 20 May 1938), 17–19.
[210]Karandikar (Mujumdar), Dattatraya Chintaman, ed. *Vyayamgyankosh Khand 5*.

wherein *gada*, and club-swinging were included in body-building exercises in a mix of Western and Indian physical cultures.[211] Once more British clubs were included and presented uncritically alongside heavy clubs.

What then can be said about heavy club-swinging in India? It existed but was rarely a popular practice. Its social status was valued among some and it is telling that when colonial administrators held exhibitions in Lucknow and Calcutta during the 1880s, they included *mugdars* and/or *gadas* as a sign of traditional physical culture.[212] Likewise, travel diaries exist detailing the swinging exhibitions of Indian men but this was hardly widespread. The same goes incidentally for the Persian *meel*, which rarely seems to have ventured out of the *zurkhaneh*. Unlike other forms of traditional physical culture, heavy club-swinging emerged in other parts of the world.[213] It was known within the global physical culture community, albeit to a limited extent, and it was somewhat common for strongmen, in particular, to use it during shows. But the widespread appeal of the clubs did not manifest, even it seems, in India where they remained primarily a tool of the *akhara*. It is difficult when researching this history not to note a vague, but obvious, passing interest in heavy club-swinging among European and North American exercisers. Yes a Windship, Harrison or Hill could use them, but the general public did not. Orientalism, perhaps, played a role, so too did the association between club-swinging and muscular non-white bodies. The popularization of light club-swinging only came after the practice was association in visual cultures with white, as opposed to non-white bodies. Those of a commercial mind would undoubtedly note the difficult in manufacturing heavy clubs and in convincing people that the practice was safe. That European wrestlers did not adopt it despite Gama's success in England, and the generally positive reception that Gama and Singh's respective strength garnered shows the heavy clubs' lack of appeal. What reinforced their unattractiveness was the generally positive reception to their newer, and ersatz, light-weight comparison.

Conclusion

Weightlifting and stone-lifting cultures became global practices in the twentieth century. In the case of weightlifting, regional tensions were resolved in the interwar period, leading to the sport's formalization. With stone-lifting, the latter half of the twentieth century was a time when it sportified to a greater extent. The past two decades have been interesting

---

[211]Conor Heffernan, 'What's wrong with a little swinging? Indian clubs as a tool of suppression and rebellion in post-rebellion India,' *The International Journal of the History of Sport* 34, no. 7–8 (2017): 554–77.
[212]Lucknow University, *Canning college*, 96; *Official Report of the Calcutta ...* , 350.
[213]Heffernan, *Indian Club-swinging ...* , 106–16.

in that a global tourism trade has opened which allows stones to remain in situ, while simultaneously being 'emptied' and reimagined by travelling strength tourists. For others, however, stone-lifting has been commodified through the production of stone-lifting equipment. Heavy club-swinging, however, continues to remain a distinctly Indian, Iranian and Pakistani practice.[214] Club-swinging competitions do exist, and the practice remains popular in some gyms but it remains a domestic endeavour. Looking to the nineteenth century, each of these practices was regionalized at a time when other movements were globalized. Why this was the case varied depending on the practice in question but there are three key themes worth discussing. First that weightlifting, stone-lifting and club-swinging all had glimpses or moments of potential globalization during the nineteenth century. Weightlifting, and the failed attempts to federalize it, had the most obvious examples of this but stone-lifting and club-swinging were known on the global stage. There were opportunities to build momentum which were not taken. This leads to the second point which is the randomness, to an extent, of global fitness. Lifting stones or swinging heavy-clubs may seem odd but is it any stranger than lifting dumbbells or doing judo? Obviously some practices fit easier into national narratives and global trade but it is important to stress that those practices that did globalize were far from predetermined. Even in weightlifting, there is no reason why continental and French styles should have clashed or that organizers bickered. Historical quirks need to be accounted for. 'Failure' to globalize does not represent a failure in the practices. Rather than viewing global fitness as a story of winners and losers, it is better to conceptualize it as a story of ripples. Some activities, like judo, yoga or physical culture, rippled throughout the world. Others, like stone-lifting, created fewer ripples but both activities were still part of the same pool. In a less laboured explanation, it is important to draw back to the first chapter and the argument that strength and fitness behaviours seem to be culturally significant across societies. During the nineteenth century, some practices were more porous than others.

---

[214]Ibid., 226–34.

Conclusion

In 1901 Ray Lankester, curator of London's Natural History Museum, approached Eugen Sandow with a proposition. Lankester was interested in commissioning a series of statues of 'perfect types' for each race. Sandow, naturally, was a perfect emblem of the white race. Sandow agreed and flexed his muscles while plaster was applied to his body. The result, for many, was grotesque. The cast was out of proportion with Sandow's body, and there were supposedly complaints about Sandow's exposed genitalia. The statue was hidden, tucked away in the Museum's archives and forgotten about for several decades. At the time of writing, the statue has been broken into various parts, fragments of a bygone age. Sandow's forgotten and fragmented statue serves as a metaphor for nineteenth-century fitness.[1] The zeal behind the practices discussed in this book has been forgotten, tucked away in the cultural psyche of nations but their presence lingers on. Physical culture, in the nineteenth century, represented a broad church encompassing everything from self-defence and spirituality to muscle-building and anti-aging. These terms have now splintered into distinct groups and pastimes. Even something as simple as lifting weights can be done for bodybuilding, weightlifting or powerlifting, among other labels. The term 'yoga' is unsuitably vague nowadays for practitioners who may prefer to specify the school, lineage and practice. In a sense, the world of modern fitness is completely different from the nineteenth century. And yet it's not.

A point of ongoing, contention for pre-modernists is the fuzzy line historians often draw between pre-modern and modern worlds.[2] Studying physical culture, however, there is a clear 'before' and 'after' period. This being the nineteenth century. The catalyst for this change was the globalization of fitness practices and the commerce which fuelled it. This book focused on two core issues. Why did this happen? And, what was the impact? The why

---

[1]Constance Crompton, 'Eugen Sandow (1867–1925)', *Victorian Review* 37 (2011): 37–41.
[2]Allen Guttmann, 'The development of modern sports', in Jay Coakley and Eric Dunning (eds.), *Handbook of Sports Studies* (Sage, 2000), 248–59.

is always easier than the what. Why did this happen? One can, and indeed this book did, point to Empire, industrialization, military and educational policies, rising commerce and growing medical concerns. It's a neat narrative but one which holds. Equally critical, and a point often missed by historians including myself, is that for some, exercise was fun. This is reductive but one cannot discount it. Sport globalized during this period and wouldn't have done so if some didn't find joy in it.[3] 'Macro' factors globalized physical culture, but it was individuals who found meaning in it. For some, physical culture became all-encompassing, impacting how they ate, slept and moved. The 'why' factors intensified during the twentieth century and especially so in the past four decades, but it is clear that fitness was globalized during the nineteenth century.

What impact did this have? Looking at the broader context during the nineteenth century, fitness became a state-mandated requirement in many countries. How soldiers, and students, trained was formalized and systematized. Furthermore, there was an unanimity of movement to the extent that schoolchildren in Germany used the same *Turnverein* methods as those in the United States. Or, better yet, Japanese soldiers used the same Swedish exercises as those in Britain. For this to happen nations, and officials, had to agree on a framework for what a body is, how it should be developed and how it responded to exercise. Yes, some activities remained regionalized, but far more became global systems. State-mandated fitness was informed by broad, and attractive, ideas about modernity in the nineteenth century. Physical culture was, in many respects, a reaction against modernity in different forms.

Returning to Japan, the Meiji governments adopted European physical cultures to keep pace with modernity. In Britain, physical culture was used to protect citizens against modernity's deleterious effects. Nevertheless, both shared a belief that fitness took a heightened meaning in a new age. Accompanying such discourses was a steady dose of race science and fears about the purity of future generations. Such discourses existed elsewhere, but where else could race scientists experiment with body 'perfection' other than physical culture? That Herbert Spencer, the man who coined the term eugenics, was a gleeful spectator at Sandow's 1901 Great Competition is proof of how these worlds intersected.[4] The impact of 'global' fitness also extended to how individuals consumed fitness. This was the century when books, magazines, supplements and equipment became commonplace. Doing physical culture often meant purchasing products and, as commerce became more widespread, so did predatory practices and half-truths around

---

[3]Paul Rouse, 'The sporting world and the human heart: Ireland, 1880–1930', *Irish Studies Review* 27 (2019): 309–24.
[4]Conor Heffernan, 'The best developed man in Great Britain and Ireland? Eugen Sandow and the commercialization of Eugenics in Twentieth-Century Britain', *Journal of Victorian Culture* 28 (2023): 302–20.

fitness. These half-truths about perfecting one's body to perfect one's life, of miraculous transformations and inconceivable outcomes continue to exist as fragments in the modern-age. At a broad level, the impact of this transformation was profound. It created a baseline which traversed borders and changed how entire nation's thought about the body. But what of the individual?

This book has, in a sense, been a continuation of George Mosse's 1996 work *The Image of Man*.[5] I encountered this book as an undergraduate desperate to know how others studied the body. Mosse's argument that the nineteenth century witnessed the birth of a 'national stereotype' continues to dominate my thinking in many respects. Mosse found in European societies the discursive creation of a manliness trope which was distinct to each nation. Despite the differences between male behaviour in France versus Germany versus Britain, Mosse stressed the power stereotypes had in political, social and medical discourses. Where Mosse stressed the overarching strength of such a concept, he was skillful enough to note national differences. Across societies, however, the body and its beauty or strength, proved a common theme.[6] At an individual level, the nineteenth century witnessed a fitness stereotype which proved deeply rigid move across nations. Although the discourses for why such a body was needed varied across nations, a global consensus began to form around the 'right' kind of body. Thus many individuals took to physical culture out of enjoyment or obligation. What impact did this have on the individual?

Physical culture practices changed how many individuals interacted with or understood their bodies. Routinized exercise forced individuals to move their bodies in ways that would have been alien just a half-century before. Likewise physical culture allowed individuals to express their bodies in new ways. It democratized the body's movement. Return, for a moment, to Sandow. In 1898 he announced the hosting of a physical culture competition. Within a year his magazine was filled with pictures of half-naked men flexing their muscles. This was not presented as a lewd act but a respectable behaviour. Turn next to Sandow's contemporary, gym owner Joseph Szalay, whose gym was home to countless men competing in weightlifting competitions and being celebrated for doing so.[7] Such individuals were not celebrities but attained a status, and a platform, based on their physiques. Next, think of Friedrich Ludwig Jahn's open air gymnasiums in Prussia, where members of the public came to be amazed by Jahn's students. Fitness, and the expression of fitness, took on a new meaning and outlet. It became public in a tangible way.

---

[5]George Mosse, *The image of man: The creation of modern masculinity* (Oxford: Oxford University Press, 1998).
[6]Kathleen Canning, 'The body as method? Reflections on the place of the body in gender history', *Gender & History* 11 (1999): 499–513.
[7]Heffernan, 'The Best Developed Man … ?'

Something I grapple with as a historian is the impact physical culture had on people's bodies. The globalization of physical culture meant the transformation of millions of physiques over the course of the century. That is remarkable. The frame, musculature and strength of millions of men and women were impacted. For those in disbelief, a simple and I promise, scientific, experiment will suffice. Hold this book in one hand and lift it upwards towards your shoulders one hundred times, do this for thirty days and report back on how your arm looks and feels after that period. It will have developed physically. This is a silly example, unless of course it resonates, but the underlying principle holds. Purposive exercise changes the body. It makes the muscles leaner, harder and/or larger. This is not the ramblings of a historian, but observable phenomena long noted by scientists.[8] Some will experience rapid physical transformations, others less so but the basic idea that exercise changes how the body looks, feels and moves is powerful. During the nineteenth century there was a revolution in how millions of bodies developed and, critically, how we came to globally understand what a fit body looked like. Unlike previous centuries when one's physique was the product of nutrition, genetics and physical labour, during the nineteenth century systematized training programmes were created and used around the world. The body was divided into arms, backs, legs, trunks and chests, each of which was given specialized exercises. Some, as I have written elsewhere, left photographs of their transformations, even writing testimonies as to how different they felt thanks to exercise.[9] Others did not, and the silent majority of soldiers and schoolchildren is an important group to hold.

Was this a universal good? Of course not. Foucauldian scholars have long critiqued exercise as a means of disciplining bodies and inculcating in trainees the idea of subservient discipline.[10] There is also, of course, an imperial element to this. Walsh's work on nineteenth-century gymnastics in the United States used a theatre studies lens to examine how workouts were used to reinforce a sense of white-ness.[11] One cannot discuss global fitness without the power of Western ideas of perfection. Sandow became a global beauty emblem to the extent that well into the interwar period, Indian physical culturists referred to him as an ideal body.[12] Prior to Sandow

---

[8]Brad Schoenfeld, 'The mechanisms of muscle hypertrophy and their application to resistance training', *The Journal of Strength & Conditioning Research* 24 (2010): 2857–72.
[9]Conor Heffernan, 'Body projects as a historical phenomenon: Irish physical culture and the body as process', *Rethinking History* 24 (2020): 417–41.
[10]Genevieve Rail and Jean Harvey, 'Body at work: Michel Foucault and the sociology of sport', *Sociology of Sport Journal* 12 (1995): 164–79.
[11]Shannon Walsh, *Eugenics and physical culture performance in the progressive era: Watch Whiteness Workout* (Springer, 2020).
[12]Carey Watt, 'Cultural exchange, appropriation and physical culture: Strongman Eugen Sandow in colonial India, 1904–1905', *The International Journal of the History of Sport* 33 (2016): 1921–42.

it was Swedish and German ideas around perfect, implicitly white, bodies which informed practices. The physical transformations effected, often done implicitly or explicitly along Western lines, are clearly problematic. This is doubly so in the realm of military gymnastics in Empires where gymnastics was very much imposed upon colonial bodies and used as a disciplinary tool. In recreational circles, globally, physical culture oftentimes had an air of empowerment or self-efficacy. To that end, innumerable testimonies into British, French and American physical culture magazines spoke of the joy exercise brought to readers' lives and their pride in their transformation. It is simply impossible to disconnect one from the other and instead it is more useful to consider the one element they shared: physical transformations.

This book has centred on three arguments. First that health and exercise have, across time, held importance in many cultures. In Chapter 1 an argument was made that these traits may even be viewed as essential parts of what it means to be human. John Huizinga initiated the study of play along similar lines, helping to spur countless generations of those studying sport and leisure.[13] Purposive exercise is not spontaneous play. It is often regimented and requires planning. There are playful elements to strength, but it is often formal. It is not spontaneous, but is socially significant. As Chapter One tried to show, religious, medical, military and educational texts from the ancient world to the modern one have often included passages about physical culture's value. Studying the *long durée* of fitness was an important part of this book because so many authors in the nineteenth century made reference to the past. This past ranged anywhere from the Enlightenment period to the ancient gymnasiums of Athens. Yes, it is possible to arbitrarily cut off the long nineteenth century from that which went before, but doing so does a disservice to the cultural scripts many physical culturists drew from.

Chapter 2 examined what happened when local physical culture practices, culturally significant to India and Japan, left their origins and entered the global marketplace of fitness. The three processes studied (club-swinging, yoga and judo) underwent the same transformation once used outside of their homes. This was the 'emptying' process previously used by Alter to examine how and why a traditional Indian practice like club-swinging became a global phenomenon with little connection to its roots.[14] As per Alter, such activities were stripped of their original origins and refilled with new, globally attractive, meanings. In club-swinging, the objects themselves and their cultural significance were altered.[15] Yoga underwent a more

---

[13] Robert Anchor, 'History and play: Johan Huizinga and his critics', *History and Theory* 17 (1978): 63–93.
[14] Joseph Alter, 'Indian clubs and colonialism: Hindu masculinity and muscular Christianity', *Comparative Studies in Society and History* 46 (2004): 497–534.
[15] Ibid.

nuanced change.[16] Some of its origins were kept as a means of stressing its originality and value. The system hybridized and became a globalized practice which, depending on the yoga school in question, was influenced by physical culture. Judo underwent a similar change. Part of the Meiji fetishization for modernity, as well as originator Kano's interest in the Muscular Christian and Olympic movements, judo tapped into a broader global pathway interested in protection and self-defence, especially for the weak. As per the other practices, knowledge was spread through books and trainers which travelled to far-flung regions to preach a gospel of the body. Indian clubs, yoga and judo were disparate practices but shared two commonalities. Regardless of which version was used their longevity and histories were often commented on or alluded to. All were brought into the physical culture movement, a point which highlights just how broad the term physical culture was.

Accepting the exercise has long held importance, the book's second premise was that something happened at an institutional level during the nineteenth century. That 'something' was an active powerful adoption of physical culture by militaries and schools globally. As militaries and schools placed gymnastic programmes into scheduled activities, millions of people were exposed to exercise. The delivery may have been substandard, or misguided, but this formalization of exercise occurred *en masse*. This elevated the global consciousness of exercises and movements but also solidified practices which exist to this day. Chapter 3 examined this institutionalization with reference to militaries and schools. Here three systems were taken as dominant forms. They were the Turnverin system, the Ling system and the later British system. Combined these systems accounted for many trainees' experiences in militaries, police forces and schools, or, in some cases, served as inspiration for other systems. Other gymnastics and physical culture practices existed and arose during this period, but none matched these systems' scope. Institutional physical culture can be understood as physical culture 'imposed from above' rather than organically undertaken. It was a pre-requisite to being part of an institution and was a mandatory experience. The length and breadth of exercise here were jaw-dropping. Educators and trainers cited philosophers like Rousseau or Locke to bolster their system's importance. Books were translated and published in serials, monographs and snippets. The pace and depth of knowledge exchange, combined with a movement of peoples around the world, facilitated global physical cultures. Was it all bad? After all, compulsory PE brings us ideas of schoolchildren or military personnel labouring away with broken spirits. Some found enjoyment and value in it. McNeill wrote an entire book on the concept

---

[16]Mark Singleton, *Yoga body: The origins of modern posture practice* (Oxford University Press, 2010).

of 'muscular bonding' borne from these activities.¹⁷ What is critical is that institutional regimes were always done with a theoretical body in mind. The systems were expected to produce a certain kind of health and physique. There was, in a global context, a quantification of fitness which narrowed physiques, and ideas about fitness, into a tight bottleneck of acceptable versus unacceptable bodies.

The third idea put forward here was that physical culture commerce was transformative. Recreational physical culture, as expressed in the 'physical culture' movement was predicated on the idea that a product could guarantee health. Exercise books, magazines, photographs, supplements, equipment and a host of other products were sold with implicit and explicit promises of physical perfection. Informally organized, the commodity market, which included the movement's 'celebrities' be they Sandow, Sandwina, or anyone else, marched across borders and minds. Where institutional physical culture was imposed from above, recreational physical culture was premised on the individual. Often one had to literally 'buy in' to the practice. Predominately a European and North American phenomenon, in terms of its highest clustering, this commerce moved to foreign markets where it supplanted domestic ideas or provided inspiration for local copy-cats. One can view this as positive or negative, but it was a transformation. The scale of commerce in the nineteenth century was unprecedented and impacted individual and societal ideas about health. Its echoes, or fragments, continue to be found in the present day in the 'sick to strong' discourses or the idealized body types still used to sell products.

Where to go from here? In 2022 I published an article on the present condition of physical culture histories.¹⁸ During the 1990s, it was possible to count on one hand, the number of individuals writing on this field. Three decades later and the field has experienced a moderate, but clear, boom. This was driven by the increased presence fitness has in contemporary lives. There is a danger that histories of fitness and physical culture date themselves from the 1970s and 1980s when a further intensification in fitness practices, one more recognizable perhaps, occurred.¹⁹ Likewise there is a danger, and one I have fallen into, with dating physical culture and modern fitness to Sandow's generation. This book has been a professional cry for help. More needs to be done on the nineteenth-century and before. Furthermore, more needs to be done to connect the various national histories which are being produced. There is good work being done on physical culture, but more needs to be done. Physical culture was never a national phenomenon.

---

¹⁷William McNeill, *Keeping together in time: Dance and drill in human history* (Harvard University Press, 1997).
¹⁸Conor Heffernan, 'State of the field: Physical culture', *History* 107 (2022): 143–62.
¹⁹Rachel Louise Moran, *Governing bodies: American politics and the shaping of the modern physique* (University of Pennsylvania Press, 2018); Natalia Mehlman Petrzela, *Fit Nation* (University of Chicago Press, 2022).

It was always attached to global ideas and, indeed, markets. It is not enough to study American, Irish, German, French, Indian, etc., physical culture without trying to connect to the global elements which fuelled it. A singular hope for this book is that it can spark such debates by either providing a framework for further study or a strawman viciously picked apart by researchers determined to prove it wrong. Perhaps some could extend it into the period of the Great War (1918–39) and beyond?

Happy being an architect of my own destruction, three clear areas that need more attention are race, commerce and medicine. We need to know more about the non-white experience of physical culture, especially in Asia and Africa. Cleophas' work on interwar South Africa as well as Bromber's work on Ethiopia has provided some clues as to how non-European trainees created nuanced and conflicting ideas about their place within physical culture.[20] Likewise work on Asian physical culture, conducted by Morris, Creak and Brownell has drawn out tensions between local and international ideals but more scholars, working on more nations, can help us understand the limits of physical culture communities.[21] I am compelled to learn more about the experiences of those who experienced institutional physical culture regimes as well as those non-European or North American physical culturists who submitted images to physical culture magazines which often dealt with them at a distance. I return to K.V. Iyer's letters to Mark Berry in the 1930s which expressed Iyer's Vedantic worldview alongside his appreciation of the classical Grecian form. How many others balanced differing cultures in their body regimes?[22]

More needs to be done on physical culture commerce. There are a handful of studies examining the role of physical culture entrepreneurs which traced their socio-cultural histories and biographies but we are missing numbers. Mike Cronin asked some years ago why sport historians stopped counting?[23] In the case of entrepreneurs, and their products, we need more information on the cost of products, how they varied across countries and how new products were brought to market. This is a tall, but not an unfair, ask as a great deal of information is available in the public domain. Likewise, we need

---

[20]Francois Cleophas, *Physical education and physical culture in South Africa, 1837–1966* (Springer, 2024); Katrin Bromber, *Sports and modernity in late imperial ethiopia* (Boydell & Brewer, 2022).

[21]Andrew Morris, *Marrow of the nation: A history of sport and physical culture in Republican China* (University of California Press, 2004); Simon Creak, *Embodied nation: Sport, masculinity, and the making of modern Laos* (University of Hawaii Press, 2017); Susan Brownell, *Training the body for China: Sports in the moral order of the People's Republic* (University of Chicago Press, 1995).

[22]Aishwarya Ramachandran and Conor Heffernan, 'Building the transnational "Body Beautiful" – KV Iyer and the circulation of bodybuilding practices between India and the United States', *Sport History Review* 52 (2021): 279–97.

[23]Mike Cronin, 'What went wrong with counting? Thinking about sport and class in Britain and Ireland'. *Sport in History* 29 (2009): 392–404.

information on the readership of physical culture magazines. Magazines often published circulation figures and, in issues, welcomed submissions from readers from around the world. Quantified such information would add a structural basis to global and domestic physical culture. Such information is vital to quantify physical culture in a substantive way.

Finally, there is the issue of medicine, or specifically, the history of medicine. Is the history of physical culture a history of medicine? Historians of medicine have long noted the role physical culturists played in understandings of health.[24] Likewise, physical culture historians have noted the role physicians had in legitimizing physical culture. The problem, thus far, is that such observations have tended to exist on the margins in disciplinary bunkers. We have yet to see the history of physical culture situated within the broader history of nineteenth-century medicine. Such a work could explain the role understandings of hygiene, physiology and psychiatry played in how physical culture was marketed by entrepreneurs, understood by physicians and explained in individual's behaviours. This is to say nothing of the need for a fuller understanding of the role physical culture played in popularizing alternative or unorthodox medical procedures. Additionally, a great deal could be gained from examining the role colonial and military physicians played in the development of institutional gymnastics globally.

I hope this book has kindled in others the fascination I have in the development of physical culture. This is a vibrant story whose developments continue to dictate the course of individual, and international, health practices. Unlike Sandow's statue, broken away and hidden from view, it is possible to access it every time someone lifts a weight, moves into a downward dog, or stretches a tight muscle. It is a history we can read, but one we can feel through our very bodies. In 2022 I implored scholars to continue working on, and uncovering, the history of physical culture.[25] I end with the same call to arms. My hope, in reading this book, is that some will continue this study of the nineteenth century, tell us more about those who brought practices with them across borders and, ultimately, shine a light on the bodies which were impacted most.

---

[24]Dorothy Porter, *Medicine in the twentieth-century* (Taylor & Francis, 2020), 201–16.
[25]Heffernan, 'State of ... '.

BIBLIOGRAPHY

Primary Sources

Archives

Archive.org
Bibliothèque nationale de France
British Library
British Newspaper Archives
Digital Commonwealth
H. J. Lutcher Stark Center for Physical Culture and Sport Studies
Munich Digitisation Centre
National Archives, London
National Library of Congress
Newspapers.com
Royal Archives, London
Royal Army Physical Training Corps Museum, Aldershot
Wellcome Collection Archive
Wiki Commons

Magazines and Newspapers

Belfast Commercial Chronicle
Birmingham Mail
Bloomberg News
Caledonian Mercury
Congleton and Macclesfield Mercury
GQ Magazine
Health and Strength
Illustrated London News
Internationale Illustrierte Athleten Zeitung
Iron Game History
New Times
Pall Mall Gazette
Pearson's Magazine
Physical Culture
Physical Culture Study
Sandow's Magazine of Physical Culture
Sunday World

The Daily News
The Morning Post
The National Police Gazette
The New York Clipper
The Royal Magazine
The Sketch
The Sporting Life
The Strand
The Tatler
Times Herald
Tokyo Times
Vanity Fair

Monographs and Articles

Amorós, Francisco, *Gymnase Normal, Militaire Et Civil, Idée Et État De Cette Institution Au Commencement De L'année 1821* (Imprimerie, 1821).

Amoros, Francisco, *Manuel D'éducation Physique, Gymnastique Et Morale* (Roret, 1830).

Anderson, Lieutenant, *A Series of Exercises for the Regulation Clubs* (War Office, 1863).

Bankier, William, *Ju-jitsu: What It Really Is* (Health Promotion, 1905).

Brett, Frederick Harrington, *A Practical Essay on Some of the Principal Surgical Diseases of India* (Thacker, 1840), 42.

Checkley, Edwin, *A Natural Method of Physical Training* (Scholar's Choice, 1895).

Checkley, Edwin, *A Natural Method of Physical Training: Making Muscle and Reducing Flesh without Dieting Orpparatus* (Bryant, 1892).

Clias, Peter Heinrich, *Anfangsgründe Der Gymnastik Oder Turnkunst* (Burgdorfer, 1816).

Clias, Peter Heinrich, *An Elementary Course of Gymnastic Exercises: Intended to Develope and Improve the Physical Powers of Man*, (Sherwood, Gilbert, and Piper, 1825)

Clias, Peter Heinrich, *Gymnastique Élémentaire Ou Cours Analytique Et Gradué ...* (Colas, 1819).

Darwin, Charles, *The Descent of Man and Selection in Relation to Sex* (Modern Library, 1871).

Delafield, Richard, *Report on the Art of War in Europe in 1854, 1855, 1856* (Bowerman, 1860).

Desbonnet, Edmond and David Chapman, *The Kings of Strength: A History of All Strong Men from Ancient Times to Our Own* (McFarland, 2022).

Duhesme, Guillaume Philibert, *Essai Sur L'infanterie Légère, Ou Traité Des Petites Opérations De La Guerre, À L'usage Des Jeunes Officiers: Avec Cartes Et Plans* (Michaud, 1814).

Elphinstone, Mountstuart, *An Account of the Kingdom of Caubul and Its Dependencies in Persia, Tartary, and India* (Longman, 1815).

Eugen Sandow Patent Spring Grip Dumbbells (1910).

Guts Muths, Johann Christoph Friedrich, *Gymnastik Für Die Jugend: Enthaltend Eine Praktische Anweisung Zu Leibesübungen: Ein Beytrag Zur Nöthigsten Verbesserung Der Körperlichen Erziehung* (HMSO, 1793).

Guts Muths, Johann Christoph Friedrich, *Turnbuch Für Die Söhne Des Vaterlandes* (Wilmans, 1817),

Guts Muths, Johann Christoph Friedrich and Christian Gotthilf Salzmann, *Gymnastics for Youth: Or a Practical Guide to Healthful and Amusing Exercises for the Use of Schools* (Byrne, 1803).

Hackenschmidt, George, 'European corner: How I met Dr. Krajewsky', *Iron Game History* 1 (1990): 13.

Hackenschmidt, George, *The Way to Live: Health & Physical Fitness* (Health & Strength, 1908).

Hague, William Grant, *The Eugenic Mother and Baby: A Complete Home Guide* (Hauge, 1913).

Hancock, H. Irving, *The High School Freshmen* (CreateSpace, 2015).

Hancock, H. Irving, *The Physical Culture Life: A Guide for All Who Seek the Simple Laws of Abounding Health* (Putnam, 1905).

Harrison, Professor, *Indian Clubs, Dumb-Bells and Sword Exercises* (Lea, 1868).

Her Majesty's Office, *Official Report of the Calcutta International Exhibition, 1883–84* (Bengal Secretariat Press, 1885).

HMSO, *Army Medical Report: Statistical, Sanitary and Medical Reports for the Year 1860* (Harrison & Co, 1862).

HMSO, *Royal Commission Appointed to Inquire into the Sanitary Condition of the Army, Report of the Commissioners Appointed to Inquire into the Regulations Affecting the Sanitary Condition of the Army, The Organization of Military Hospitals, and the Treatment of the Sick and Wounded* (HMSO, 1858).

Inch, Thomas, *Scientific Weight Lifting* (Health & Strength, 1905).

Irving, Hancock, H. and Katsukuma Higashi, *The Complete Kano Jiu-Jitsu* (Putnam, 1905).

Jones, A. Wallace, *Fifty Exercises for Health & Strength* (Gale and Polden, c. 1908), 9.

Jowett, George F., *The Strongest Man That Ever Lived* (Your Physique, 1949).

Kehoe, Simon D., *The Indian Club Exercise: With Explanatory Figures and Positions: Photographed from Life: Also, General Remarks on Physical Culture: Illustrated with Portraitures of Celebrated Athletes* (Dick & Fitzgerald, 1866).

Krause, Johann Heinrich, *Die Gymnastik und Agonistik der Hellenen* (Barth, 1841).

Kunze, Julius, *Die Gymnastik. Faßliche Anleitung zu gymnastischen Übungen; enthaltend das Turnen, Schlittschuhlaufen, Schwimmen, Rudern, Reiten, Fahren, Schießen, Jagen; Nach Walker bearbeitet von Julius Kunze* (Verlags, 1846).

Laisné, Napoléon, *Gymnastique des demoiselles. Ouvrage destiné aux mères de famille et contenant la description des exercices avec la construction et le prix des instruments* (Typographie Walder, 1854).

Ling, P.H., *Reglemente För Gymnastik* (Granbergs Trycker, 1836).

Ling, Per Henrik and Hg Rothstein, *Die Gymnastik, Nach Dem Systeme Des Schwedischen Gumnasiarchen* (Schroeder, 1847).

Logan, James, *The Scotish Gaël, or, Celtic Manners: As Preserved among the Highlanders ...* (Marsh, Capen & Lyon, 1833).

Lucknow University, *Canning College, Lucknow Exhibition, 1885 Catalogue of Departments A & B. Held in Canning College, Kaisar Bagh* (Printing Press, 1885).

Macfadden, Bernarr and Marion Malcolm, *Health–Beauty–Sexuality, from Girlhood to Womanhood: Plain Advice to Girls That Will Be Found Invaluable as They Grow from Girlhood into Womanhood* (Physical Culture, 1904).
Macfadden, Marguerite, *Physical Culture for Babies* (Physical Culture, 1904).
Maclaren, Archibald, 'Military Gymnasia', *Royal United Services Institution. Journal* 8 (1864): 217–30.
Maclaren, Archibald, *A Military System of Gymnastic Exercises for the Use of Instructors* (Adjutant-General's Office, 1862).
Maclaren, Archibald, *Physical Education* (Clarendon, 1895)
Maclaren, Archibald, *Training, in Theory and Practice* (Macmillan, 1874).
Madan, Martin, *A New and Literal Translation of Juvenal and Persius: With Copious Explanatory Notes, by Which These Difficult Satirists Are Rendered Easy and Familiar to the Reader* (Tegg, 1829).
Maxick, *Great Strength by Muscle-control* (Health & Strength, 1913).
Maxick, *Muscle Control, or Body Development by Will-Power* (Seymour & Co, 1913).
Miles, Eustace, *The Eustace Miles System of Physical Culture: With Hints as to Diet* (Health & Strength, 1907).
Mujumdar, D.C., *Encyclopaedia of Indian Physical Culture* (Mujumdar, 1950), 614
Muller, J.P., *My Breathing System* (McKay, 1914).
Muller, J.P., *My System: 15 Minutes of Exercise a Day for Health's Sake* (Athletic Publications, c. 1935).
Muller, J.P., *My System for Ladies-15 Minutes' Exercise a Day for Health's Sake* (Read Books, 2011).
Ondeano, Amoros y, *Manuel d'éducation physique, gymnastique et morale* (Paris, 1834)
Ramacharaka, Yogi, *Hatha Yoga; or, the Yogi Philosophy of Physical Well-Being, with Numerous Exercises, etc* (Yoga Publication Society, 1904).
Renatus, Flavius Vegetius, *The Military Institutions of the Romans* (Lulu.Com, 2017).
Roth, Mathias and Per Henrik Ling, *The Gymnastic Free Exercises of Ph Ling* (Ticknor, Reed And Fields, 1853).
Rothstein, Hugo, *Die Geräth-Uebungen und Spiele aus der pädagogischen Gymnastik* (Schroeder, 1862).
Rothstein, Hugo and Pehr Henrik Ling, *The Gymnastic Free Exercises of Ph Ling: A Systemized Course of Gymnastics without Apparatus* (Groombridge, 1853).
Rousseau, Jean-Jacques, *Of the Social Contract and Other Political Writings* (Penguin, 2012).
Rousseau, Jean-Jacques, *Rousseau: The Social Contract and Other Later Political Writings* (Cambridge University Press, 2018).
Rousseau, Jean-Jacques and William Payne, *Rousseau's Emile or Treatise on Education* (Appleton, 1893).
Sandow, Eugen, *The Gospel of Strength according to Sandow* (Sandow, 1902).
Sandow, Eugen, *Sandow on Physical Training: A Study in the Perfect Type of the Human Form ...* (Tait, 1894).
Sandow, Eugen, *Strength and How to Obtain It* (Gale & Polden, 1897).
Saxon, Arthur, *The Development of Physical Power* (Health & Strength, 1906).
Stebbins, Genevieve, *Dynamic Breathing and Harmonic Gymnastics: A Complete System of Psychical, Aesthetic and Physical Culture* (Werner, 1893).

Stebbins, Genevieve, *The Genevieve Stebbins System of Physical Training* (Werner, 1899).
Stolz, Albert, *Mannesschönheit durch gesunde körperliche Ausbildung. Mit 112 Kunstdruckbildern und 23 Abbildungen im Text* (Taschenbuch, 1912).
Swoboda, Alois, *Swoboda System of Conscious Evolution of Mind and Body* (Swoboda, 1914).
Toepoel, Pieter, *Het origineele Ju Jutsu* (Van de Ven, Baarn, 1919).
Vasu, S.C., *The Gheranda Sanhita* (Tatva-Vivechaka, 1895).
Vivekananda, Swami, *Complete Works of Swami Vivekananda* (Partha Sinha, 2019), 76.
Vivekananda, Swami, *The Complete Works of Swami Vivekananda, Addresses at the Parliament of Religions, Karma-Yoga, Raja-Yoga, Lectures and Discourses* (Discovery, 2017),
Vivekananda, Swami, *The Indispensable Vivekananda: An Anthology for Our Times* (Orient, 2006),
Walker, Donald, *British Manly Exercises: In Which Rowing and Sailing Are Now First Described, and Riding and Driving Are for the First Time Given in a Work of This Kind ...* (Hurst, 1835).
Walker, Donald, *Exercises for Ladies; Calculated to Preserve and Improve Beauty, etc* (Hurst, 1836).
Walker, Donald, *Games and Sports: Being an Appendix to Manly Exercises and Exercises for Ladies* (Hurst, 1837).
Watts, Diana, *The Renaissance of the Greek Ideal* (Stoke, 1914).
Watts, Emily, *Fine Art of Jujutsu* (William Heinemann, 1906).

Secondary Sources

Monographs

Allen, Barbara. *Animals in Religion: Devotion, Symbol and Ritual*. Reaktion Books, 2016
Allmand, Christopher. *The De re militari of Vegetius: The Reception, Transmission and Legacy of a Roman Text in the Middle Ages*. Cambridge University Press, 2011.
Alter, J.S. *Gandhi's Body: Sex, Diet, and the Politics of Nationalism*. University of Pennsylvania Press, 2011.
Alter, J.S. *The Wrestler's Body: Identity and Ideology in North India*. University of California Press, 1992.
Alter, J.S. *Yoga in Modern India: The Body between Science and Philosophy*. Princeton University Press, 2005.
Anderson, Benedict. *Imagined Communities: Reflections on the Origin and Spread of Nationalism*. Verso, 1991.
Asprey, Robert. *The Rise of Napoleon Bonaparte*. Hachette, 2008.
Balme, Christopher. *The Globalization of Theatre 1870–1930: The Theatrical Networks of Maurice Bandmann*. Cambridge University Press, 2020.
Banerjee, Sikata. *Make Me a Man!: Masculinity, Hinduism, and Nationalism in India*. State University of New York Press, 2012.

Banhatti, Gopal Shrinivas. *Life and Philosophy of Swami Vivekananda*. Atlantic Publishers, 1995.
Bayly, Christopher Alan. *The Birth of the Modern World, 1780–1914: Global Connections and Comparisons*. Blackwell, 2004.
Bayly, Christopher Alan. *Remaking the Modern World 1900–2015: Global Connections and Comparisons*. Wiley & Sons, 2018.
Black, Jonathan. *Making the American Body: The Remarkable Saga of the Men and Women Whose Feats, Feuds, and Passions Shaped Fitness History*. University of Nebraska Press, 2013.
Blanning, Tim. *Frederick the Great: King of Prussia*. Penguin, 2015.
Bloom, Peter. *French Colonial Documentary: Mythologies of Humanitarianism*. University of Minnesota Press, 2008.
Bogdanovic, Nikolai. *Fit to Fight: A History of the Royal Army Physical Training Corps 1860–2015*. Bloomsbury, 2017.
Bonadonna, Reed. *Soldiers and Civilization: How the Profession of Arms Thought and Fought the Modern World into Existence*. Naval Institute Press, 2017.
Bonner, Mike. *The Composite Guide to Strongman Competition*. Chelsea House, 2000.
Bourke, Joanna. *Working Class Cultures in Britain, 1890–1960: Gender, Class and Ethnicity*. Routledge, 2008.
Bowman, Paul. *The Invention of Martial Arts: Popular Culture between Asia and America*. Oxford University Press, 2021.
Bradford, Alfred. *With Arrow, Sword, and Spear*. Bloomsbury, 2000.
Braudy, Leo. *The Frenzy of Renown: Fame & Its History*. Oxford University Press, 1986.
Brekke, Torkel. *Makers of Modern Indian Religion in the Late Nineteenth-Century*. Oxford University Press, 2002.
Bromber, Katrin. *Sports and Modernity in Late Imperial Ethiopia*. Boydell & Brewer, 2022.
Brownell, Susan. *Training the Body for China: Sports in the Moral Order of the People's Republic*. University of Chicago Press, 1995.
Budd, M.A. *The Sculpture Machine: Physical Culture and Body Politics in the Age of Empire*. New York University Press, 1997.
Cantor, Geoffrey. *Religion and the Great Exhibition of 1851*. Oxford University Press, 2011.
Chaline, Eric. *The Temple of Perfection: A History of the Gym*. Reaktion, 2015.
Challis, Debbie. *The Archaeology of Race: The Eugenic Ideas of Francis Galton and Flinders Petrie*. A&C Black, 2013.
Chandler, David. *The Campaigns of Napoleon*. Simon & Schuster, 2009.
Chapman, David. *Sandow the Magnificent: Eugen Sandow and the Beginnings of Bodybuilding*. University of Illinois Press, 1994.
Chow, Broderick. *Physical Culture and the Performance of Masculinity*. Northwestern University Press, 2024.
Clarke, J.J. *Oriental Enlightenment: The Encounter between Asian and Western Thought*. Routledge, 1997.
Cleophas, Francois Johannes. *Physical Education and Physical Culture in South Africa, 1837–1966*. Springer, 2024.
Collins, Tony. *Rugby's Great Split: Class, Culture and the Origins of Rugby League Football*. Routledge, 2012.

Conrad, Sebastian. *What Is Global History?* Princeton University Press, 2017.
Creak, Simon. *Embodied Nation: Sport, Masculinity, and the Making of Modern Laos.* University of Hawaii Press, 2017.
Crossley, Pamela Kyle. *What Is Global History?* Polity, 2008.
Daley, Caroline. *Leisure and Pleasure: Reshaping and Revealing the New Zealand Body 1900–1960.* Auckland University Press, 2013.
De La Peña, Carolyn Thomas. *The Body Electric: How Strange Machines Built the Modern American.* New York University Press, 2003.
De Michelis, Elizabeth. *A History of Modern Yoga.* A&C Black, 2005.
Deutsch, Ronald. *The Nuts among the Berries.* Ballantine, 1967.
Donaldson, E.A. *The Scottish Highland Games in America.* Pelican, 1999.
Dorson, R.M. *Folk Legends of Japan.* Tuttle, 2012.
Douglass, C.B. *Bulls, Bullfighting, and Spanish Identities.* University of Arizona Press, 1999.
Duke, Benjamin. *The History of Modern Japanese Education: Constructing the National School System, 1872–1890.* Rutgers University Press, 2009.
Dunkle, Roger. *Gladiators: Violence and Spectacle in Ancient Rome.* Routledge, 2013.
Foxen, Anya. *Biography of a Yogi: Paramahansa Yogananda and the Origins of Modern Yoga.* Oxford University Press, 2017.
Foxen, Anya. *Inhaling Spirit: Harmonialism, Orientalism, and the Western Roots of Modern Yoga.* Oxford University Press, 2020.
Gebhardt, Nicholas. *Vaudeville Melodies: Popular Musicians and Mass Entertainment in American Culture, 1870–1929.* University of Chicago Press, 2017.
Gilbert, Pamela. *Citizen's Body.* Ohio State University Press, 2007.
Gilman, Sander. *Stand Up Straight!: A History of Posture.* Reaktion, 2018.
Godfrey, Emelyne. *Femininity, Crime and Self-Defence in Victorian Literature and Society: From Dagger-Fans to Suffragettes.* Routledge, 2012.
Godfrey, Emelyne. *Masculinity, Crime and Self-Defence in Victorian Literature: Duelling with Danger.* Springer, 2010.
Goldberg, Elliott. *The Path of Modern Yoga: The History of an Embodied Spiritual Practice.* Simon & Schuster, 2016.
Golden, Mark. *Sport and Society in Ancient Greece.* Cambridge University Press, 1998.
Griffith, R.M. *Born Again Bodies: Flesh and Spirit in American Christianity.* University of California Press, 2004.
Guttmann, Allen. *From Ritual to Record: The Nature of Modern Sports.* Columbia University Press, 1978.
Guttmann, Allen. *The Olympics: A History of the Modern Games.* University of Illinois Press, 2002.
Hague, William Grant. *The Eugenic Mother and Baby: A Complete Home Guide.* Hague, 1913.
Haley, Bruce. *The Healthy Body and Victorian Culture.* Harvard University Press, 1978.
Hampton, Jean. *Hobbes and the Social Contract Tradition.* Cambridge University Press, 1986.
Harrison, Mark. *Public Health in British India: Anglo-Indian Preventive Medicine 1859–1914.* Cambridge University Press, 1994.

Hartmann, Heinrich. *The Body Populace: Military Statistics and Demography in Europe before the First World War.* MIT, 2019.
Hayes, Bill. *Sweat: A History of Exercise.* Bloomsbury, 2022.
Heffernan, Conor. *Indian Club-Swinging and the Birth of Global Fitness: Mugdars, Masculinity and Marketing.* Bloomsbury, 2023.
Hobsbawm, Eric. *Age of Empire: 1875–1914.* Hachette, 2010.
Hofmann, Annette R. *Turnen and sport.* Verlag, 2004.
Hofschröer, Peter. *Leipzig 1813: The Battle of the Nations.* Bloomsbury, 2012.
Holt, Richard. *Sport and the British: A Modern History.* Oxford University Press, 1990.
Huang, Fuhua and Fan Hong. *A History of Chinese Martial Arts.* Routledge, 2018.
Hunt, William. *Body Love: The Amazing Career of Bernarr Macfadden.* Popular Press, 1989.
Irokawa, Daikichi. *The Culture of the Meiji Period.* Princeton University Press, 1985.
Jackson, Ashley. *The British Empire.* Oxford University Press, 2013.
Jansen, Marius. *The Making of Modern Japan.* Harvard University Press, 2002.
Johnson, David. *Buying Gay: How Physique Entrepreneurs Sparked a Movement.* Columbia University Press, 2019.
Kent, Graeme. *The Strongest Men on Earth: When the Muscle Men Ruled Show Business.* Biteback, 2012.
Keys, Barbara. *Globalizing Sport.* Harvard University Press, 2013.
Kirk, David. *Defining Physical Education: The Social Construction of a School Subject in Postwar Britain.* Routledge, 2012.
Kline, Wendy. *Building a Better Race: Gender, Sexuality, and Eugenics from the Turn of the Century to the Baby Boom.* University of California Press, 2001.
Lynn, John. *Battle: A History of Combat and Culture.* Hachette, 2009.
Macdonald, Charlotte. *Strong, Beautiful and Modern: National Fitness in Britain, New Zealand, Australia and Canada, 1935–1960.* UBC Press, 2013.
Mansfield, Stephen. *Japanese Stone Gardens: Origins, Meaning, Form.* Tuttle, 2012.
Manzenreiter, Wolfram. *Sport and Body Politics in Japan.* Routledge, 2013.
Martschukat, Jürgen. *The Age of Fitness.* Wiley & Sons, 2021.
McKenzie, Shelly. *Getting Physical: The Rise of Fitness Culture in America.* University Press of Kansas, 2016.
McNeill, William. *Keeping Together in Time: Dance and Drill in Human History.* Harvard University Press, 1997.
Misra, Nityananda. *Kumbha: The Traditionally Modern Mela.* Bloomsbury Publishing, 2019.
Mokyr, Joel. *A Culture of Growth: The Origins of the Modern Economy.* Princeton University Press, 2016.
Moran, Rachel Louise. *Governing Bodies: American Politics and the Shaping of the Modern Physique.* University of Pennsylvania Press, 2018.
Morris, Andrew. *Marrow of the Nation: A History of Sport and Physical Culture in Republican China.* University of California Press, 2004.
Mosse, George. *The Image of Man: The Creation of Modern Masculinity.* Oxford University Press, 1998.
Murray, Stuart. *Sports Diplomacy: Origins, Theory and Practice.* Routledge, 2018.
Nolte, Claire. *The Sokol in the Czech Lands to 1914: Training for the Nation.* Springer, 2002.

Petrzela, Natalia Mehlman. *Fit Nation*. University of Chicago Press, 2022.
Poskett, James. *Materials of the Mind: Phrenology, Race, and the Global History of Science, 1815–1920*. University of Chicago Press, 2019.
Prabucki, Bartosz. *Traditional Sports and Games in the Contemporary World*. Cambridge Scholars, 2022.
Presner, Todd Samuel. *Muscular Judaism: The Jewish Body and the Politics of Regeneration*. Routledge, 2007.
Pronger, Brian. *Body Fascism: Salvation in the Technology of Physical Fitness*. University of Toronto Press, 2002.
Putney, Clifford. *Muscular Christianity: Manhood and Sports in Protestant America, 1880–1920*. Harvard University Press, 2009.
Qaradawi, Yusuf. *Islam: An Introduction*. The Other Press, 2010.
Ravina, Mark. *To Stand with the Nations of the World*. Oxford University Press, 2017.
Recas, Lucio Doncel. *Harri-Jasotze: Levantamiento de piedras en Euskadi y Navarra*. Vision Libros, 2021.
Reel, Guy. *National Police Gazette and the Making of the Modern American Man, 1879–1906*. Springer, 2006.
Roach, Randy. *Muscle, Smoke & Mirrors*. Openhouse, 2008.
Rouse, Wendy. *Her Own Hero*. New York University Press, 2017.
Roy, Tirthankar and Prasenjit Saha. *Wondrous Wrestlers*. Boibishwa, 2024.
Ruyter, Nancy. *The Cultivation of Body and Mind in Nineteenth-Century American Delsartism*. Bloomsbury, 1999.
Sandage, Scott. *Born Losers: A History of Failure in America*. Harvard University Press, 2005.
Scott, James. *The Art of Not Being Governed: An Anarchist History of Upland Southeast Asia*. Yale University Press, 2009.
Sen, Ronojoy. *Nation at Play: A History of Sport in India*. Columbia University Press, 2015.
Shephard, Roy. *An Illustrated History of Health and Fitness, from Pre-History to Our Post-Modern World*. Springer, 2015.
Shepherd, John. *The Crimean Doctors: A History of the British Medical Services in the Crimean War*. Liverpool University Press, 1991.
Shurley, Jason, Jan Todd and Terry Todd. *Strength Coaching in America: A History of the Innovation That Transformed Sports*. University of Texas Press, 2019.
Singleton, Mark. *Yoga Body: The Origins of Modern Posture Practice*. Oxford University Press, 2010.
Sirvent, Rafael Fernández. *Francisco Amorós Y Los Inicios De La Educación Física Moderna: Biografía De Un Funcionario Al Servicio De España Y Francia*. Universidad De Alicante, 2005.
Stevens, John. *The Way of Judo: A Portrait of Jigoro Kano and His Students*. Shambhala, 2013.
Streets, Heather. *Martial Races: The Military, Race and Masculinity in British Imperial Culture, 1857–1914*. Manchester University Press, 2004.
Sublette, Ned and Constance Sublette. *The American Slave Coast: A History of the Slave-Breeding Industry*. Chicago Review Press, 2015.
Sussman, Herbert. *Victorian Technology: Invention, Innovation, and the Rise of the Machine*. Bloomsbury, 2009.
Sutcliffe, Adam. *What Are Jews For?: History, Peoplehood, and Purpose*. Princeton University Press, 2020.

Taylor, Matthew. *World of Sport: Transnational and Connected Histories*. Taylor & Francis, 2024.
Thomas, Helen. *Dance, Modernity and Culture*. Routledge, 2003.
Thomas, James Edward. *Modern Japan: A Social History since 1868*. Routledge, 2014.
Todd, Jan. *Physical Culture and the Body Beautiful: Purposive Exercise in the Lives of American Women, 1800–1870*. Mercer University Press, 1998.
Trentmann, Frank. *Empire of Things*. Penguin UK, 2016.
Verbrugge, Martha. *Active Bodies: A History of Women's Physical Education in Twentieth-Century America*. Oxford University Press, 2012.
Vertinsky, Patricia. *The Eternally Wounded Woman: Women, Doctors, and Exercise in the Late Nineteenth-Century*. Manchester University Press, 1990.
Vigarello, Georges. *The Metamorphoses of Fat: A History of Obesity*. Columbia University Press, 2013.
Wacquant, Loïc. *Body & Soul: Notebooks of an Apprentice Boxer*. Oxford University Press, 2006.
Waller, David. *The Perfect Man: The Muscular Life and Times of Eugen Sandow, Victorian Strongman*. Victorian Secrets, 2011.
Walsh, Shannon. *Eugenics and Physical Culture Performance in the Progressive Era: Watch Whiteness Workout*. Springer, 2020.
Washington, Peter. *Madame Blavatsky's Baboon: A History of the Mystics, Mediums, and Misfits Who Brought Spiritualism to America*. Schocken, 1996.
Watt, Carey. *Strongman Eugen Sandow's World Tour of 1904–1905: The 'Perfect Man' in Colonial India and Afro-Asia*. Anthem Press, 2025.
Webster, David. *Donald Dinnie: The First Sporting Superstar*. Ardo Pub., 1999.
Webster, David. *The Iron Game*. Geddes, 1976.
Webster, David. *Sons of Samson*. Ironmind, 1993.
Webster, David. *Sons of Samson II*. Ironmind, 1998.
Wedemeyer-Kolwe, Bernd. *Der Athletenvater Theodor Siebert (1866–1961) eine Biographie zwischen Körperkultur, Lebensreform und Esoterik*. Klatt, 1999.
Wedemeyer-Kolwe, Bernd. *'Der neue Mensch': Körperkultur im Kaiserreich und in der Weimarer Republik*. Königshausen & Neumann, 2004.
Weiner, Michael. *Race and Migration in Imperial Japan*. Routledge, 2013.
Weiss, Richard. *The American Myth of Success: From Horatio Alger to Norman Vincent Peale*. University of Illinois Press, 1969.
Westney, D.E. *Imitation and Innovation: The Transfer of Western Organizational Patterns to Meiji Japan*. Harvard University Press, 1987.
Whorton, James. *Crusaders for Fitness: The History of American Health Reformers*. Princeton University Press, 1982.
Williams, David Lay. *Rousseau's Platonic Enlightenment*. Penn State Press, 2010.
Willoughby, David. *The Super Athletes*. Barnes, 1970.
Wokler, Robert. *Rousseau*. Oxford University Press, 2001.
Woycke, James. *Esprit de Corps: A History of North American Bodybuilding*. Self-Published, 2016.
Zweiniger-Bargielowska, Ina. *Managing the Body: Beauty, Health, and Fitness in Britain 1880–1939*. Oxford University Press, 2010.

Academic Articles

Abe, Ikuo, Yasuharu Kiyohara and Ken Nakajima, 'Sport and physical education under fascistization in Japan', *InYo: Journal of Alternative Perspectives* 9 (2000): 1–25.

Agehananda, Bharati, 'The Hindu renaissance and its apologetic patterns', *Journal of Asian Studies. Association for Asian Studies* 29 (1970): 267–87.

Allred, Brian, 'Working out your salvation and just working out', *Mid-America Journal of Theology* 29 (2018): 173–81.

Alter, Joseph, 'Indian clubs and colonialism: Hindu masculinity and muscular Christianity', *Comparative Studies in Society and History* 46 (2004): 497–534.

Alter, Joseph, 'The sannyasi and the Indian wrestler: The anatomy of a relationship', *American Ethnologist* 19 (1992): 317–36.

Alter, Joseph, 'Somatic nationalism: Indian wrestling and militant Hinduism', *Modern Asian Studies* 28 (1994): 557–88.

Alter, Joseph, 'Subaltern bodies and nationalist physiques: Gama the great and the heroics of Indian wrestling', *Body & Society* 6 (2000): 45–72.

Alter, Joseph, 'Yoga and physical education: Swami Kuvalayananda's Nationalist project', *Asian Medicine* 3 (2007): 20–36.

Amgarten, Evelise, 'Between gymnastics and sport: Education of the body and preservation of identity in German-Brazilian gymnastics societies', *Educação Em Revista* 35 (2019): E217174.

Anchor, Robert, 'History and play: Johan Huizinga and his critics', *History and Theory* 17 (1978): 63–93.

Andreasson, Jesper and Thomas Johansson, '"Doing for group exercise what McDonald's did for hamburgers": Les Mills, and the fitness professional as global traveller', *Sport, Education and Society* 21 (2016): 148–65.

Andreasson, Jesper and Thomas Johansson, 'The fitness revolution: Historical transformations in the global gym and fitness culture', *Sport Science Review* 23 (2014): 91–112.

Appadurai, Arjun, 'Commodities and the politics of value', In *Interpreting objects and collections*, edited by Susan Pearce, 76–91. Routledge, 2012.

Appadurai, Arjun, 'Disjuncture and difference in the global cultural economy', *Theory, Culture & Society* 7 (1990): 295–310.

Appadurai, Arjun, 'Grassroots globalization and the research imagination', *Public Culture* 12 (2000): 1–20.

Armstrong, Jerome, 'Uncovering Vyāyāma in Yoga', *Journal of Yoga Studies* 4 (2023): 271–302.

Arnoldy, Ashton Kohl, 'Genevieve Stebbins and the philosophical roots of somatics', *Journal of Dance & Somatic Practices* 14 (2022): 23–33.

Assmann, Alice Beatriz, Carolina Fernandes Da Silva and Janice Zarpellon Mazo, 'German-Brazilian women in Turnen at the beginning of the twentieth-century', *The International Journal of the History of Sport* 39 (2022): 536–56.

Baczko, Bronislaw, 'The social contract of the French: Sieyès and Rousseau', *The Journal of Modern History* 60 (1988): S98–S125.

Badyna, Piotr, 'Were the natural sciences global in the 19th century? The case of Charles Darwin', In *Interpreting Globalization*, edited by L Koczanowicz, 80–90. Brill, 2021.

Bailey, Peter, 'Conspiracies of meaning: Music-hall and the knowingness of popular culture', *Past & Present* 144 (1994): 138–70.

Baker, William, 'To pray or to play? The YMCA question in the United Kingdom and the United States, 1850–1900', *The International Journal of the History of Sport* 11 (1994): 42–62.

Baker, William, 'William Webb Ellis and the origins of rugby football: The life and death of a Victorian myth', *Albion* 13 (1981): 117–30.

Batchelor, Robert, 'Thinking about the gym: Greek ideals, Newtonian bodies and exercise in early eighteenth-century Britain', *Journal for Eighteenth-Century Studies* 35 (2012): 185–97.

Beckwith, Kim and Jan Todd, 'Requiem for a strongman: Reassessing the career of Louis Attila', *Iron Game History* 7 (2002): 42–55.

Beckwith, Kim and Jan Todd, 'Strength: America's first muscle magazine, 1914–1935', *Iron Game History* 9 (2005): 11–28.

Behringer, Wolfgang, 'The invention of sports: Early modern ball games', In *Sports and physical exercise in early modern culture*, edited by Rebekka von Mallinckrodt and Angela Schattner, 21–47. Routledge, 2017.

Betts, John, 'Mind and body in early American thought', *The Journal of American History* 54 (1968): 787–805.

Bloch, Jean, 'Rousseau's reputation as an authority on childcare and physical education in France before the revolution', *Paedagogica Historica* 14 (1974): 5–33.

Bloomfield, Anne, 'Martina Bergman-Osterberg (1849–1915): Creating a professional role for women in physical training', *History of Education* 34 (2005): 517–34.

Bonde, Hans, 'Farmers' gymnastics in Denmark in the late nineteenth and early twentieth centuries: A semiotic analysis of exercise on moral action', *The International Journal of the History of Sport* 10 (1993): 193–214.

Bonde, Hans, 'From hygiene to salvation: JP Muller, international advocate of gymnastics', *The International Journal of the History of Sport* 26 (2009): 1357–75.

Bonde, Hans, 'The time and speed ideology: 19th century industrialisation and sport', *The International Journal of the History of Sport* 26 (2009): 1315–34.

Bonini, Gherardo, 'London: The cradle of modern weightlifting', *Sports Historian* 21 (2001): 56–70.

Bonzom, Alice, '"If you want to earn some time, throw a policeman!": Suffragettes and self-defence in Edwardian Britain', *Caliban* 62 (2019): 31–54.

Bordelon, Suzanne, 'Embodied ethos and rhetorical accretion: Genevieve Stebbins and the Delsarte system of expression', *Rhetoric Society Quarterly* 46 (2016): 105–30.

Bossenga, Gail, 'Origins of the French revolution', *History Compass* 5 (2007): 1294–337.

Brantlinger, Patrick, 'Kipling's "The white man's burden" and its afterlives', *English Literature in Transition, 1880–1920* 50 (2007): 172–91.

Brauer, Fae, 'Virilizing and valorizing homoeroticism: Eugen sandow's queering of body cultures before and after the wilde trials', *Visual Culture in Britain* 18 (2017): 35–67.

Briggs, Austin, 'The mismeasure of bloom: Sandow, folklore, scientific racism, eugenics', *James Joyce Quarterly* 59 (2022): 597–615.

Brodin, Harald, 'Per Henrik Ling and his impact on gymnastics', *Svensk Medicinhistorisk Tidskrift* 12 (2008): 61–8.

Brough, David, 'Self-defence with a walking-stick: Revisited', *Martial Arts Studies* 11 (2021): 101–9.

Brough, David, 'The golden square dojo and its place in British Jujutsu history', *Martial Arts Studies* 10 (2020): 66–72.

Brühwiler, Ingrid, 'In-between "Swedish Gymnastics" and "Deutsche Turnkunst"', *Nordic Journal of Educational History* 4 (2017): 71–84.
Bryant, Rachel, 'World trends in physical education', *Journal of the American Association for Health, Physical Education, and Recreation* 21 (1950): 32–3.
Buck, Josh, 'Louis Cyr and Charles Sampson: Archetypes of vaudevillian strongmen', *Iron Game History* 5 (1998): 18–28.
Cain, Peter and Anthony Hopkins, 'The political economy of British expansion overseas, 1750–1914', *The Economic History Review* 33 (1980): 463–90.
Cairus, José, 'Modernization, nationalism and the elite: The genesis of Brazilian jiu-jitsu, 1905–1920', *Revista tempo e argumento* 3 (2011): 100–21.
Callan, Mike and Slaviša Bradić, 'Historical development of Judo', In *The science of Judo*, edited by Mike Callan, 7–13. Routledge, 2018.
Callan, Mike, Conor Heffernan and Amanda Spenn, 'Women's Jūjutsu and Judo in the early twentieth-century', *The International Journal of the History of Sport* 35 (2018): 530–53.
Campbell, James, 'Training for sport is training for war': Sport and the transformation of the British army, 1860–1914', *The International Journal of the History of Sport* 17 (2000): 21–58.
Canning, Kathleen, 'The body as method? Reflections on the place of the body in gender history', *Gender & History* 11 (1999): 499–513.
Carter, Andy, 'At home at Oxbridge': British views of ancient Greek sport 1749–1974', *Sport in History* 41 (2021): 280–307.
Carter, John Marshall, 'Muscular Christianity and its makers: Sporting monks and churchmen in Anglo-Norman society, 1000–1300', *The International Journal of the History of Sport* 1 (1984): 109–24.
Chalhoub, Sidney, 'The politics of silence: Race and citizenship in nineteenth-century Brazil', *Slavery and Abolition* 27, no. 1 (2006): 73–87.
Chatterjee, Amitava, 'From courtyard sport to competitive sport: Evolution of wrestling in colonial Bengal', *Sport in Society* 18 (2015): 1–16.
Chatterjee, Amitava and Souvik Naha, 'The muscular monk: Vivekananda, sports and physical culture in colonial Bengal', *Economic and Political Weekly* (2014): 25–9.
Chisholm, Ann, 'The disciplinary dimensions of nineteenth-century gymnastics for us women', *The International Journal of the History of Sport* 24 (2007): 432–79.
Chisholm, Ann, 'Gymnastics and the reconstitution of republican motherhood among true women of civic virtue, 1830–1870', *The International Journal of the History of Sport* 23, no. 8 (2006): 1275–313.
Clarkson, Priscilla and Mary Dedrick, 'Exercise-induced muscle damage, repair, and adaptation in old and young subjects', *Journal of Gerontology* 43 (1988): M91–M96.
Clendinnen, Inga, 'The cost of courage in Aztec society', *Past & Present* 107 (1985): 44–89.
Combeau-Mari, Evelyne, 'Colonial sport in Madagascar 1896–1960', *The International Journal of the History of Sport* 28 (2011): 1557–65.
Combeau-Mari, Evelyne, 'Sport in the French colonies (1880–1962): A case study', *Journal of Sport History* 33 (2006): 27–57.
Connell, R.W. and James Messerschmidt, 'Hegemonic masculinity: Rethinking the concept', *Gender & Society* 19 (2005): 829–59.

Conrad, Sebastian, 'Globalizing the beautiful body: Eugen sandow, bodybuilding, and the ideal of muscular manliness at the turn of the twentieth-century', *Journal of World History* 32 (2021): 95–125.

Corbera Castellanos, Roger and Josep Monserrat-Molas, 'Potentia eximia & excellentia facultatum: The elation between liberty and power from the Leviathan to De Homine', *British Journal for the History of Philosophy* 32 (2024): 65–78.

Costa, Mg Da, João Marcos Perelli and Leonardo Mataruna-Dos-Santos, 'História Da Ginástica No Brasil: Da Concepção E Influência Militar Aos Nossos Dias', *Navigator: Subsídios Para A História Marítima Do Brasil. Rio De Janeiro* 12 (2016): 63–75.

Crompton, Constance, 'Eugen Sandow (1867–1925)', *Victorian Review* 37 (2011): 37–41.

Cronin, Mike, 'What went wrong with counting? Thinking about sport and class in Britain and Ireland', *Sport in History* 29 (2009): 392–404.

Cynarski, Wojciech, 'Three patterns of group relations in martial arts schools', *Studies in Sport Humanities* 19 (2016): 54–9.

Daley, Caroline, 'Selling Sandow: Modernity and leisure in early twentieth-century New Zealand', *New Zealand Journal of History* 34 (2000): 241–61.

Daley, Caroline, 'The strongman of eugenics, Eugen Sandow', *Australian Historical Studies* 33 (2002): 233–48.

Dalen, D.B. Van, 'The idea of history of Physical Education during the middle ages', In *Sport & physical education in the Middles Ages*, edited by Earle Zeigler, xx. Bloomington, 2006.

Dark, Kimberly, 'Exposure and erasure: Fat kids in gym class, fat adults as athletes', *Fat Studies* 8 (2019): 127–34.

Deimary, Nima and Mohammad Mohammadi, 'Investigating the impact of ancient and heroic rituals on formation of Zurkhaneh architecture in Iran', *American International Journal of Research in Humanities, Arts and Social Sciences* 20 (2017): 40–5.

Delheye, Pascal, Thomas Ameye and Stijn Knuts, 'Expansionism, physical education and Olympism: Common interests of king leopold II of Belgium, Cyrille Van Overbergh and Pierre De Coubertin (1894–1914)', *The International Journal of the History of Sport* 31 (2014): 1158–77.

Demirel, Duygu Harmandar and Ibrahim Yildiran, 'The philosophy of physical education and sport from ancient times to the enlightenment', *European Journal of Educational Research* 2 (2013): 191–202.

Dencker, Berit Elisabeth, 'Popular gymnastics and the military spirit in Germany, 1848–1871', *Central European History* 34 (2001): 503–30.

Duncan, Samuel, 'The spirit of play: Fun and freedom in the professional age of sport', *Sport, Ethics and Philosophy* 16 (2022): 281–99.

Dyreson, Mark, 'Globalizing the nation-making process: Modern sport in world history', *The International Journal of the History of Sport* 20 (2003): 91–106.

Edgren, Robert, 'The fearful art of Jiu Jitsu', *Journal of Combative Sport*, March (2000). Available at https://ejmas.com/jcs/jcsart_edgren1_0300.htm.

Eichberg, Henning, 'Body culture and democratic nationalism: "Popular Gymnastics" in nineteenth-century Denmark', *The International Journal of the History of Sport* 12 (1995): 108–24.

Eisen, George, 'Physical activity, physical education and sport in the old testament', *Canadian Journal of History of Sport & Physical Education* 6 (1975): 44–65.

Eisenberg, Christiane, 'Charismatic nationalist leader: Turnvater Jahn', in *European Heroes*, edited by Pierre Lanfranchi, Richard Holt and J.A. Mangan, 14–27. Routledge, 2013.

Ercan, Sabriye and Aydan Örsçelik, 'Avicenna's perspective of exercise: Content analysis of the "Canon of Medicine"', *Mersin Üniversitesi Tıp Fakültesi Lokman Hekim Tıp Tarihi ve Folklorik Tıp Dergisi* 12 (2022): 483–92.

Fair, John, 'Eugen Sandow and eugenics', *Sport in History* 44 (2024): 56–77.

Fair, John, 'The iron game and capitalist culture: A century of American weightlifting in the Olympics, 1896–1996', *The International Journal of the History of Sport* 15 (1998): 18–19.

Fair, John, 'Katie Sandwina: Hercules can be a lady', *Iron Game History* 9 (2005): 4–7

Fair, John, 'The tragic history of the military press in Olympic and world championship competition, 1928–1972', *Journal of Sport History* 28 (2001): 345–74.

Fischer-Tiné, Harald, 'Fitness for modernity? The YMCA and physical-education schemes in late-colonial South Asia (circa 1900–40)', *Modern Asian Studies* 53 (2019): 512–59.

Forbes, Clarence A., 'Expanded uses of the Greek gymnasium', *Classical Philology* 40 (1945): 32–42.

Freedman, Estelle, '"Crimes which startle and horrify": Gender, age, and the racialization of sexual violence in White American newspapers, 1870–1900', *Journal of the History of Sexuality* 20 (2011): 465–97.

Fuld, Leonhard Felix, 'Physical education in Greece and Rome', *American Physical Education Review* 12 (1907): 1–14.

Galton, D.J., 'Eugenics: Some lessons from the past', *Reproductive BioMedicine* 10 (2005): 133–6.

Gänger, Stefanie, 'Circulation: Reflections on circularity, entity, and liquidity in the language of global history', *Journal of Global History* 12 (2017): 303–18.

García, Raúl Sánchez and Antonio Rivero Herraiz, '"Governmentality" in the origins of European female PE and sport: The Spanish case study (1883–1936)', *Sport, Education and Society* 18 (2013): 494–510.

Gauthier, Philippe, 'Notes on the role of the gymnasion in the Hellenistic city', *Greek Athletics* (2010): 87–101.

Gelders, Raf and S.N. Balagangadhara, 'Rethinking orientalism: Colonialism and the study of Indian traditions', *History of Religions* 51 (2011): 101–28.

Giessing, Jurgen and Jan Todd, 'The origins of German bodybuilding: 1790–1970', *Iron Game History* 9 (2005): 14.

Gilman, Sander, 'Muscular Judaism: The Jewish body and the politics of regeneration', *Monatshefte* 100 (2008): 320–1.

Gluck, Carol, 'Japan's constitution across time and space', *Colum. J. Asian L* 33 (2019): 41.

Godfrey, Emelyne, 'Urban heroes versus folk devils: Civilian self-defence in London (1880–1914)', *Crime, Histoire & Sociétés/Crime, History & Societies* 14 (2010): 5–30.

Goellner, Silvana Vilodre, Sebastião Josué Votre and Maria Claudia Brandão Pinheiro, 'Strong mothers make strong children', *Sport, Education and Society* 17 (2012): 555–70.

Goodwin, Christopher Thomas, 'Surviving crisis: The Napoleonic Upheavals and the "Time of the French" as cultural Trauma in Prussia, 1806–1812', *War & Society* 41 (2022): 1–20.

Gosling, F.G. and Joyce Ray, 'The right to be sick: American physicians and nervous patients, 1885–1910', *Journal of Social History* 20 (1986): 251–67.

Gotter, Ulrich, 'Cultural differences and cross-cultural contact: Greek and Roman concepts of power', *Harvard Studies in Classical Philology* 104 (2008): 179–230.

Granjel, Luis Sánchez, 'La obra de un médico giennense: Cristóbal Méndez', *Seminario médico* 42 (1990): 13–36.

Gregson, Keith and Mike Huggins, 'Sport, music-hall culture and popular song in nineteenth-century England', *Culture, Sport Society* 2 (1999): 82–102.

Guedes, Claudia, '"Changing the cultural landscape": English engineers, American missionaries, and the YMCA bring sports to Brazil–the 1870s to the 1930s', *The International Journal of the History of Sport* 28 (2011): 2594–608.

Gupta, Abhijit, 'Cultures of the body in colonial Bengal: The career of Gobor Guha', *The International Journal of the History of Sport* 29 (2012): 1687–700.

Gupta, Kshama and Prasad Mamidi, 'Pushpitakam of Charaka Indriya sthana–An explorative study', *Int J Ayu Alt Med* 7 (2019): 176–82.

Hadas, Miklós, 'Gymnastic exercises, or "work wrapped in the gown of youthful joy": Masculinities and the civilizing process in 19th century hungary', *Journal of Social History* (2007): 161–80.

Hagedorn, Nancy, 'A Friend to go between them: The interpreter as cultural broker during Anglo-Iroquois councils, 1740–70', *Ethnohistory* (1988): 60–80.

Hardy, Stephen, 'Entrepreneurs, organizations, and the sport marketplace: Subjects in search of historians', *Journal of Sport History* 13, no. 1 (1986): 14–33.

Hardy, Stephen, 'The medieval tournament: A functional sport of the upper class', *Journal of Sport History* 1 (1974): 91–105.

Harris, Susan, 'Kipling's the white man's Burden'and the British newspaper context, 1898–1899', *Comparative American Studies: An International Journal* 5 (2007): 243–63.

Hashimoto, Yorimitsu, 'Soft power of the soft art: Jiu-jitsu in the British empire of the early 20th century', *Questioning Oriental Aesthetics and Thinking* 38 (2011): 69–80.

Hay, Alexander, 'The art and politics of fence: Subtexts and ideologies of late 16th century fencing manuals', *Martial Arts Studies* 1 (2015): 60–71.

Head, Keith and Thierry Mayer, 'What separates us? Sources of resistance to globalization', *Canadian Journal of Economics/Revue canadienne d'économique* 46 (2013): 1196–231.

Heffernan, Conor, 'All muscle and no brains?: Contextualizing the fitness entrepreneur in sport history', *Sporting Traditions* 39 (2022): 13–32.

Heffernan, Conor, 'The best developed man in Great Britain and Ireland? Eugen Sandow and the commercialization of eugenics in twentieth-century Britain', *Journal of Victorian Culture* 28 (2023): 302–20.

Heffernan, Conor, 'Body projects as a historical phenomenon', *Rethinking History* 24 (2020): 417–41.

Heffernan, Conor, 'Born swinging': Tom Burrows and the forgotten art of endurance club-swinging', *Sport in History* 39 (2019): 45–73.

Heffernan, Conor, 'Desirable bodies and Eugen Sandow's curative institute in Edwardian England', *Social History of Medicine* 35 (2022): 195–216.

Heffernan, Conor, '"An elegant and able practitioner." Marian Mason and the rise of women's Calisthenics in nineteenth-century Britain', *Sport in History* (2024): 1–17.

Heffernan, Conor, 'Fitness and fun that's not just for mum: The women's league of health and beauty in 1930s Ireland', *Women's History Review* 28 (2019): 1017–22.

Heffernan, Conor, 'Hearts and muscles: Emotional communities and physical culture magazines in 1900s Ireland', *Gender & History* 33 (2021): 129–48.

Heffernan, Conor, 'Indian club-swinging in the early Victorian period', *Sport in History* 37, no. 1 (2017): 95–120.

Heffernan, Conor, 'The Irish Sandow school: Physical culture competitions in fin-de-siècle Ireland', *Irish Studies Review* 27 (2019): 402–21.

Heffernan, Conor, 'The lift seen around the world: Hafþór Björnsson and legitimacy in strongman', In *'Time Out': Sport and the CoronalLockdown*, edited by Jüörg Krieger, April Henning, Lindsay Parks Pieper and Paul Dimeo, 1–20. CommonGround, 2021.

Heffernan, Conor, 'State of the field: Physical culture', *History* 107 (2022): 143–62.

Heffernan, Conor, 'Superfood or superficial? Plasmon and the birth of the supplement industry', *Journal of Sport History* 47 (2020): 243–62.

Heffernan, Conor, '"A strong woman's troubles": Victorina and the strong woman in Victorian Britain', *Women's History Review* 30 (2021): 354–74.

Heffernan, Conor, 'Truly muscular Gaels? W.N. Kerr, physical culture and Irish masculinity in the early twentieth-century', *Sport in History* 41 (2021): 1–24.

Heffernan, Conor, 'Uncovering the history of William L. Murray, bodybuilding's first champion', *Iron Game History* 16 (2022): 13–24.

Heffernan, Conor, 'What's wrong with a little swinging? Indian clubs as a tool of suppression and rebellion in post-rebellion India', *The International Journal of the History of Sport* 34 (2017): 554–77.

Heffernan, Conor and Conor Curran, 'Much ado about nothing?: The problems of Irish physical education, 1820–1920', *Sporting Traditions* 37 (2020): 65–86.

Heggie, Vanessa, 'Lies, damn lies, and Manchester's recruiting statistics: Degeneration as an "urban legend" in Victorian and Edwardian Britain', *Journal of the History of Medicine and Allied Sciences* 63 (2008): 178–216.

Higgs, Robert, 'Muscular christianity, holy play, and spiritual exercises: Confusion about Christ in sports and religion', *Aethlon* 1 (1983): 59.

Hjarvard, Stig, 'The mediatization of religion: A theory of the media as agents of religious change', *Northern Lights: Film & Media Studies Yearbook* 6 (2008): 9–26.

Hlinak, Matt, 'Judo comes to California: Judo vs. Wrestling in the American West, 1900–1920', *Journal of Asian Martial Arts* 18 (2009): 8–20.

Hohendahl, Peter Uwe, 'The new man: Theories of masculinity around 1800', *Goethe Yearbook* 15 (2008): 187–215.

Holmberg, Oswald, 'Per Henrik Ling: His life and gymnastic principles', *Physical Educator* 1 (1940): 77–80.

Horlacher, Rebekka, 'The emergence of physical education as a subject for compulsory schooling in the first half of the nineteenth-century: The case of Phokion Heinrich Clias and Adolf Spiess', *Nordic Journal of Educational History* 4 (2017): 13–30.

Imy, Kate, 'Fascist yogis: Martial bodies and Imperial Impotence', *Journal of British Studies* 55 (2016): 320–43.
Insom, Surachet, 'The Bible and health: The miracle of healing', *Human Behavior, Development & Society* 24 (2023): 71–80.
Jafarlou, Hamid Reza Safari, Azim Jabareh Naserou and Mohammad Hossein Ghorbani, 'Koshti/Wrestling: A victory key for heroes in Shahnameh', *Sport, Ethics and Philosophy* 15 (2021): 522–45.
Jarvie, Grant, 'Highland gatherings, balmorality, and the glamour of backwardness', *Sociology of Sport Journal* 9 (1992): 167–78.
Kaimakamis, Vasilis, George Dallas, Panagiotis Stefanidis and George Papadopoulos, 'The spread of gymnastics in Europe and America by pedagogue-gymnasts during the first half of the 19th century', *Science of Gymnastics Journal* 3 (2011): 49–60.
Kaur, Lakhveer and Rajesh Chander, 'Ancient Indian sports: A historical analysis', *International Journal of Humanities* 3 (2015): 75–8.
Kerr, Douglas, 'The straight left: Sport and the nation in Arthur Conan Doyle', *Victorian Literature and Culture* 38 (2010): 187–206.
Khan, Wasim, Asif Ali, Salahuddin Khan and Naveed Yazdani, 'Islamic perspective regarding the promotion of health and participation in sports activities', *Journal of Islamic Thought and Civilization* 10 (2020): 364–74.
King, Helen, 'Comparative perspectives on medicine and religion in the ancient world', *Religion, Health, and Suffering* (1999): 276–94.
Kirk, David, 'Physical culture, physical education and relational analysis', *Sport, Education and Society* 4 (1999): 63–73.
Kirk, David, 'Physical education and regimes of the body', *The Australian and New Zealand Journal of Sociology* 30 (1994): 165–77.
Kizar, Oktay, 'The place of sports in the light of Quran, Hadiths and the opinions of the Muslim scholar in Islam', *Universal Journal of Educational Research* 6 (2018): 2663–8.
Komlos, John and Francesco Cinnirella, 'European heights in the early 18 th century', *Vswg: Vierteljahrschrift Für Sozial-Und Wirtschaftsgeschichte* (2007): 271–84.
Kotteck, Samuel S., 'Physical exercise and training in ancient Jewish Lore', *Iron Game History* 4 (1996): 19–20.
Kowner, Rotem, 'Lighter than yellow, but not enough': Western discourse on the Japanese 'Race', 1854–1904', *The Historical Journal* 43 (2000): 103–31.
Kritikos, A., A. Bekiari, N. Nikitaras, K. Famissis and K. Sakellariou, 'Hippocrates' counselling with regard to physical exercise, gymnastics, dietetics and health', *Irish Journal of Medical Science* 178 (2009): 377–83.
Kruger, Arnd and Akira Ito, 'On the limitations of Eichberg's and Mandell's theory of sports and their quantification in view of Chikaraishi', *Stadion* 3 (1990): 103–13.
Krüger, Michael, 'Body culture and nation building: The history of gymnastics in Germany in the period of its foundation as a nation-state', (1996): 409–17.
Krüger, Michael, 'History of sports medicine in Germany: Some preliminary reflections on a complex research project', *Historical Social Research/Historische Sozialforschung* (2015): 338–45.
Kumar, Ashok, 'Status of education system in ancient Indian society', *International Multidisciplinary Research Journal* 4 (2017): 1–3.

Kumar, Jatinder and Abhishek Magotra, 'Role of Vyayama (Exercise) in maintenance of health-An Ay', *Journal of Ayurveda and Integrated Medical Sciences* 5 (2020): 489–93.

Kyle, Donald, 'Decker on sport in pharaonic egypt: Recreations and rituals, combats and ceremonies, agonism – and athletics? Sports and games of ancient Egypt', *Sport History Review* 24 (1993): 75–83.

Leblanc, Hélène and Franck Cinato, 'Scholastic clues in two Latin fencing manuals: Bridging the gap between medieval and renaissance cultures', *Acta Periodica Duellatorum* 11 (2023): 39–63.

Lennartz, Karl, 'The 2nd international Olympic games in athens 1906', *Journal of Olympic History* 10 (2002): 3–24.

Leonard-Fleckman, Mahri, 'Samson and our reactions to the strongman', *Word and World* 37 (2017): 217–25.

Leonard, Fred Eugene, 'The beginnings of modern physical training in Europe', *American Physical Education Review* 9 (1904): 96.

Leonard, Fred Eugene, 'Friedrich Ludwig Jahn, and the development of popular gymnastics (Vereins-Turnen) in Germany. Ii', *American Physical Education Review* 10 (1905): 1–19.

Leonard, Hugh and Katsukuma Higashi, 'American wrestling vs. juJitsu', *The Cosmopolitan* 39 (1905): 33–42.

Levett, Geoffrey, 'Degenerate days: Colonial sports tours and British manliness 1900–1910', *Sport in History* 38 (2018): 46–74.

Levine, James, 'Non-exercise activity thermogenesis (Neat)', *Nutrition Reviews* 62 (2004): S82–S97.

Lim, Peng Han and Mohd Salleh Aman, 'The origins and development of athletics among the military, European and migrant communities in nineteenth-century Singapore, 1819–1899', *The International Journal of the History of Sport* 31 (2014): 652–73.

Lock, Margaret, 'Cultivating the body: Anthropology and epistemologies of bodily practice and knowledge', *Annual Review of Anthropology* (1993): 133–55.

Luger, Jason, 'God's viral warriors: Christian nationalism, masculinity, and the representation of self', *Journal of Bodies, Sexualities, and Masculinities* 5 (2024): 35–58.

Lundvall, Suzanne, 'From Ling gymnastics to sport science: The Swedish school of sport and health sciences, Gih, from 1813 to 2013', *The International Journal of the History of Sport* 32 (2015): 789–99.

Lutz, Rolland Ray, 'Father Jahn and his teacher-revolutionaries from the German student movement', *The Journal of Modern History* 48 (1976): 1–34.

Lynch, Kelly Jean, 'Aesthetic dance as woman's culture in America at the turn of the twentieth-century', *Feminist Modernist Studies* 5 (2022): 247–60.

Maertens, Eppo, 'Polanyi's double movement: A critical reappraisal', *Social Thought & Research* (2008): 129–53.

Mahapatra, Achintya, 'Warfare and military history in ancient India–A case study', *RES MILITARIS* 13 (2023): 5649–53.

Malamitsi-Puchner, Ariadne, 'Recommendations of ancient Greek and byzantine physicians and philosophers on perinatal nutrition and care', *Acta Paediatrica* 110 (2021): 2344–7.

Mangan, James Anthony, 'Christ and the imperial games fields: Evangelical athletes of the Empire', *The International Journal of the History of Sport* 1 (1984): 184–201.

Mangan, J.A. and Frank Galligan, 'Militarism, drill and elementary education: Birmingham nonconformist responses to conformist responses to the teutonic threat prior to the great war', *The International Journal of the History of Sport* 28 (2011): 568–603.

Markel, Howard, 'Worldly approaches to global health: 1851 to the present', *Public Health* 128 (2014): 124–8.

Markovits, Stefanie, 'Rushing into print: Participatory journalism during the Crimean War', *Victorian Studies* 50 (2008): 559–86.

Martin, Bernd and Peter Wetzler, 'The German role in the modernization of Japan – the pitfall of blind acculturation', *Oriens Extremus* (1990): 77–88.

Mayencourt, Gil, 'The Gymnast and the Shepherd: The invention of a national games' tradition in Switzerland', *The International Journal of Sport and Society* 13 (2022): 1–21.

Mayr, Ernst, 'Lamarck revisited', *Journal of the History of Biology* (1972): 55–94.

McCartney, Patrick, 'Poles apart? From wrestling and Mallkhāmb to Pole Yoga', *Journal of Yoga Studies* 4 (2023): 215–70.

McDevitt, Patrick, 'The king of sports: Polo in late Victorian and Edwardian India', *The International Journal of the History of Sport* 20 (2003): 1–27.

Mcintosh, Peter, 'Hieronymus mercurialis "De Arte Gymnastica"', *The International Journal of the History of Sport* 1 (1984): 73–84.

Mcneill, William, 'The rise of the West after twenty-five years', *Journal of World History* 1 (1990): 1–21.

Menze, Ernest, 'Friedrich Ludwig Jahn', *Yearbook of German-American Studies* 49 (2014): 101–14.

Merkel, Udo, 'The politics of physical culture and German nationalism: Turnen versus English sports and French olympism, 1871–1914', *German Politics & Society* 21, no. 67 (2003): 69–96.

Miller, Peter, 'The imaginary antiquity of physical culture', *The Classical Outlook* 93 (2018): 21–31.

Minuzzi, Sabrina, '15th-century practical medicine in print: Beyond the profession, towards the miscere utile dulci', *Nuncius* 36 (2021): 199–263.

Moenig, Udo and Kim Minho, 'The invention of Taekwondo tradition, 1945–1972: When mythology becomes' history', *Acta Koreana* 19 (2016): 131–64.

Mohammadi, Mohammad, Bisotoon Azizi and Nima Deimary, 'The role of ancient sports and Zurkhaneh in ethical promoting and religious virtues', *Sport, Ethics and Philosophy* 17 (2023): 162–71.

Molina, Fernando and Pedro J. Oiarzabal, 'Basque-Atlantic Shores: Ethnicity, the nation-state and the diaspora in Europe and America (1808–98)', *Ethnic and Racial Studies* 32 (2009): 698–715.

Mondal, Samiran, 'Exercise science in the ancient India', *Special Feature: Exercise and Science in Ancient Times* 8 (2016): 71.

Moore, Katharine, 'A neglected imperialist: The promotion of the British Empire in the writing of John Astley Cooper', *The International Journal of the History of Sport* 8 (1991): 256–69.

Moore, Louis, 'Fit for citizenship: Black sparring masters, gymnasium owners, and the white body, 1825–1886', *The Journal of African American History* 96 (2011): 448–73.

Morais, Dominic, 'Branding iron: Eugen Sandow's "modern" marketing strategies, 1887–1925', *Journal of Sport History* 40 (2013): 193–214.

Morton, Desmond, 'The cadet movement in the moment of Canadian militarism, 1909–1914', *Journal of Canadian Studies* 13 (1978): 56–68.

Moser, Jeffrey, 'Why cauldrons come first', *Journal of Art Historiography* 11 (2014): 1–5.

Mosse, George, 'Racism and nationalism', *Nations and Nationalism* 1 (1995): 163–73.

Mouratidis, John, 'Heracles at Olympia and the exclusion of women from the ancient Olympic games', *Journal of Sport History* 11 (1984): 41–55.

Mouratidis, John, 'Nero: The artist, the athlete and his downfall', *Journal of Sport History* 12 (1985): 5–20.

Mukhopadhyay, Mriganka, 'The occult and the orient: The theosophical society and the socio-religious space in colonial India', *Presidency Historical Review* 1 (2015): 9–37.

Murtha, Ryan, Conor Heffernan and Thomas Hunt, 'Building American supermen? Bernarr MacFadden, Benito Mussolini and American fascism in the 1930s', *Sport in Society* 24 (2021): 1941–55.

Nakajima, Tetsuya and Lee Thompson, 'Judo and the process of nation-building in Japan: Kanō Jigorō and the formation of Kōdōkan judo', *Asia Pacific Journal of Sport and Social Science* 1 (2012): 97–110.

Nauright, John, 'Sport, manhood and empire: British responses to the New Zealand rugby tour of 1905', *The International Journal of the History of Sport* 8 (1991): 239–55.

Ndee, Hamad, 'Germany and Eastern Africa: Gymnastics in Germany in the nineteenth-century and the diffusion of German Gymnastics into German East Africa', *The International Journal of the History of Sport* 27 (2010): 820–44.

Neely, Alan, 'The parliaments of the world's religions: 1893 and 1993', *International Bulletin of Missionary Research* 18 (1994): 60–4.

Niehaus, Andreas, 'Kano Jigoro–The "Father of the Olympic movement" in Japan', *Journal of Olympic History* 29 (2021): 6–17.

Noble, Denis, 'Charles Darwin, Jean-Baptiste Lamarck, and 21st century arguments on the fundamentals of biology', *Progress in Biophysics and Molecular Biology* 153 (2020): 1–4.

Nomikos, Nikitas, C. Trompoukis, Chris Lamprou and G. Nomikos, 'The role of exercise in Hippocratic Medicine', *American Journal of Sports Science and Medicine* 4 (2016): 115–19.

Nordlund, Alexander M., 'A war of others: British war correspondents, orientalist discourse, and the Russo-Japanese War, 1904–1905', *War in History* 22 (2015): 28–46.

Nye, Joseph, 'Soft power', *Foreign Policy* 80 (1990): 153–71.

O'Hagan, Lauren Alex, 'Flesh-formers or fads? Historicizing the contemporary protein-enhanced food trend', *Food, Culture & Society* (2021): 1–24.

O'Hanlon, Rosalind, 'Military sports and the history of the martial body in India', *Journal of the Economic and Social History of the Orient* 50 (2007): 490–523.

Okada, Kei, 'Jiu-Jitsu beats bodybuilders: British experience of Fad for Jiu-Jitsu and "Physical culture" from late 19th to the early 20th century', *Japan Journal of Sport Anthropology* 2004 (2005): 27–43.

Oppong, Steward Harrison, 'Religion and identity', *American International Journal of Contemporary Research* 3 (2013): 10–16.

Ozerkevich, Rachel, 'Retouched and remarkable: Female athletes in la culture physique (1904) as historical and visual documentation', *Sport History Review* 1 (2023): 1–20.
Ozerkevich, Rachel and Conor Heffernan, 'Physical culture, posing, and the medium of fitness magazines', *Early Popular Visual Culture* (2024): 1–22.
Parikh, Rachel, 'Yoga under the Mughals: From practice to paintings', *South Asian Studies* 31 (2015): 215–36.
Park, Roberta, 'Concern for health and exercise as expressed in the writings of 18th century physicians and informed laymen', *Research Quarterly. American Alliance for Health, Physical Education and Recreation* 47 (1976): 756–67.
Park, Roberta, 'Concern for the physical education of the female sex from 1675 to 1800 in France, England, and Spain', *Research Quarterly. American Alliance for Health, Physical Education and Recreation* 45 (1974): 104–19.
Park, Roberta, 'Health, exercise, and the biomedical impulse, 1870–1914', *Research Quarterly for Exercise and Sport* 61 (1990): 126–40.
Park, Roberta, 'Muscles, symmetry and action:" Do you measure up?"' *The International Journal of the History of Sport* 24 (2007): 1604–36.
Park, Roberta, 'Physiologists, physicians, and physical educators', *Journal of Sport History* 14 (1987): 28–60.
Park, Roberta, 'Sharing, arguing, and seeking recognition', *The International Journal of the History of Sport* 25 (2008): 519–48.
Parrott, Matthew, John Ruyak and Gary Liguori, 'The history of exercise equipment', *ACSM's Health & Fitness Journal* 24 (2020): 5–8.
Pasca, Maria, 'The Salerno school of medicine', *American Journal of Nephrology* 14 (1994): 478–82.
Pate, Russell R., 'The evolving definition of physical fitness', *Quest* 40 (1988): 174–9.
Paul, Joan, 'The health reformers: George Barker Windship and Boston's strength seekers', *Journal of Sport History* 10 (1983): 41–57.
Pearson, M.N., 'Recreation in Mughal India', *The International Journal of the History of Sport* 1 (1984): 335–50.
Pfister, Gertrud, 'Colonialism and the enactment of German identity – "Turnen" in South West Africa', *Journal of Sport History* 33 (2006): 59–83.
Pfister, Gertrud, 'Cultural confrontations: German Turnen, Swedish gymnastics and English sport–European diversity in physical activities from a historical perspective', *Culture, Sport, Society* 6 (2003): 61–91.
Pfister, Gertrud, 'The medical discourse on female physical culture in Germany in the 19th and early 20th centuries', *Journal of Sport History* 17 (1990): 183–98.
Phor, Rajesh Kumar, 'Historical analysis of physical activities and sports in ancient India', *Purva Mimaansa* 12 (2021): 132–40.
Pieterse, Jan Nederveen, 'Periodizing globalization: Histories of globalization', *New Global Studies* 6 (2012): 7–30.
Plock, Vike Martina, 'A feat of strength in "Ithaca"', *Journal of Modern Literature* 30 (2006): 129–39.
Pollack, Benjamin and Janice Todd, 'Before Charles Atlas: Earle Liederman, the 1920s king of mail-order muscle', *Journal of Sport History* 44 (2017): 399–420.
Polo-Martín, Bárbara and César Ducruet, 'Coupled connectivity in the global complex network: The case of United Kingdom (1880–1925)', *Applied Network Science* 9 (2024): 15.

Porter, Dilwyn, 'Opportunistic, parasitic, strategic, symbiotic: Entrepreneurship and the business of sport', *The International Journal of the History of Sport* 35 (2018): 641–58.

Potter, Simon and Jonathan Saha, 'Global history, imperial history and connected histories of empire', *Journal of Colonialism and Colonial History* 16 (2015): 1–35.

Presner, Todd Samuel, 'Clear heads, solid stomachs, and hard muscles', *Modernism/Modernity* 10 (2003): 269–96.

Quin, Grégory, 'A professor of gymnastics in hospital. Napoléon Laisné (1810–1896) introduce gymnastics at the «Hôpital Des Enfants Malades»', *Staps* 4 (2009): 79–91.

Quin, Grégory and Anaïs Bohuon, 'Muscles, nerves, and sex: The contradictions of the medical approach to female bodies in movement in France, 1847–1914', *Gender & History* 24 (2012): 172–86.

Rail, Genevieve and Jean Harvey, 'Body at work: Michel Foucault and the sociology of sport', *Sociology of Sport Journal* 12 (1995): 164–79.

Ramachandran, Aishwarya and Conor Heffernan, 'Building the transnational "Body Beautiful" – KV Iyer and the circulation of bodybuilding practices between India and the United States', *Sport History Review* 52 (2021): 279–97.

Reicher, Dieter, 'Nationalistic German gymnastic movements and modern sports: Culture between identity and habitus', *Historical Social Research/Historische Sozialforschung* 45 (2020): 207–25.

Reid, Heather, 'Was the Roman gladiator an athlete?' *Journal of the Philosophy of Sport* 33 (2006): 37–49.

Rhea, Matthew R., Brent A. Alvar, Lee N. Burkett and Stephen D. Ball, 'A meta-analysis to determine the dose response for strength development', *Medicine & Science in Sports & Exercise* 35, no. 3 (2003): 456–64.

Rosselli, John, 'The self-image of effeteness: Physical education and nationalism in nineteenth-century Bengal', *Past & Present* 86 (1980): 121–48.

Rost, R. and W. Hollmann, 'Athlete's heart-a review of its historical assessment and new aspects', *International Journal of Sports Medicine* 4 (1983): 147–65.

Rouse, Paul, 'The sporting world and the human heart: Ireland, 1880–1930', *Irish Studies Review* 27 (2019): 309–24.

Rouse, Wendy, 'Jiu-Jitsuing Uncle Sam: The Unmanly art of Jiu-Jitsu and the yellow peril threat in the progressive era United States', *Pacific Historical Review* 84 (2015): 448–77.

Rouse, W. and B. Slutsky, 'Empowering the physical and political self: Women and the practice of self-defense, 1890–1920', *The Journal of the Gilded Age and Progressive Era* 13 (2014): 470–99.

Ruyter, Nancy Lee Chalfa, 'American Delsartism: Precursor of an American dance art', *The International Journal of the History of Sport* 26 (2009): 2015–30.

Saint-Martin, Jean and Michaël Attali, 'The Joinville school and the institutionalization of a French-style physical education, 1852–1939', *The International Journal of the History of Sport* 32 (2015): 740–53.

Balaneskovic, Saša, 'Hua Tuo's Wu Qin Xi (Five Animal Frolics) movements and the logic behind it', *Chinese Medicine and Culture* 1 (2018): 127–34.

Sato, Shohei, 'The sportification of judo: Global convergence and evolution', *Journal of Global History* 8 (2013): 299–317.

Scarpa, Stefano and Attilio Nicola Carraro, 'Does christianity demean the body and Deny the value of sport?–A provocative Thesis', *Sport, Ethics and Philosophy* 5 (2011): 110–23.

Scharagrodsky, Pablo Ariel, 'Girls, women and physical activity in Argentina: Past and present', *Sport Science & Physical Education Bulletin* 72 (2017): 29–36.

Schoenfeld, Brad, 'The mechanisms of muscle hypertrophy and their application to resistance training', *The Journal of Strength & Conditioning Research* 24 (2010): 2857–72.

Secord, James, 'Knowledge in transit', *Isis* 95 (2004): 654–72.

Selinger, Vyjayanthi R., 'The sword trope and the Birth of the Shogunate: Historical metaphors in Muromachi Japan', *Japanese Language and Literature* 43 (2009): 55–81.

Selvamani, P., 'Gurukul system-an ancient educational system of India', *International Journal of Applied Social Science* 6 (2019): 1620–22.

Seyferth, Giralda, 'The diverse understandings of foreign migration to the South of Brazil (1818–1950)', *Vibrant: Virtual Brazilian Anthropology* 10 (2013): 118–62.

Shilling, Chris and Tanya Bunsell, 'The female bodybuilder as a gender outlaw', *Qualitative Research in Sport and Exercise* 1 (2009): 141–59.

Showalter, Dennis E., 'Caste, skill, and training: The evolution of cohesion in European armies from the Middle Ages to the sixteenth century', *The Journal of Military History* 57 (1993): 407–30.

Shrimali, Krishna Mohan, 'Knowledge transmission: Processes, contents and apparatus in early India', *Social Scientist* 39 (2011): 3–22.

Siahpoosh, M.B., M. Ebadiani, GhR Shah Hosseini, M.M. Isfahani, A. Nikbakht Nasrabadi and H. Dadgostar, 'Avicenna the first to describe diseases which may be prevented by exercise', *Iranian Journal of Public Health* 41 (2012): 98–104.

Siebenga, Rianne, 'Colonial India's "Fanatical Fakirs" and their popular representations', *History and Anthropology* 23 (2012): 445–66.

Smith, Elise, '"Why do we measure mankind?" Marketing anthropometry in late-victorian Britain', *History of Science* 58 (2020): 142–65.

Smith, J. Andy, Tammy Greer, Timothy Sheets and Sheree Watson, 'Is there more to yoga than exercise?' *Alternative Therapies in Health & Medicine* 17 (2011): 22–9.

Snook, George, 'The history of sports medicine', *The American Journal of Sports Medicine* 12 (1984): 252–4.

Solberg, Sarah, 'International: The highland games', *Journal of Health, Physical Education, Recreation* 45 (1974): 19–21.

Spears, Betty, 'A perspective of the history of women's sport in ancient Greece', *Journal of Sport History* 11 (1984): 32–47.

Staurowsky, Ellen, 'ABC sports: The rise and fall of network sports television', *International Journal of Sport Communication* 13 (2020): 275–8.

Stavrakakis, N. and E. Albanidis, 'The therapeutic use of sport during the Byzantine period', *Archives of Hellenic Medicine/Arheia Ellenikes Iatrikes* 32 (2015): 95–101.

Steinitz, Lesley, 'Transforming Pig's wash into health food: The construction of skimmed milk protein powders', *Global Food History* (2021): 1–34.

Stieglitz, Olaf, '"Mentally superior children are born of physically superior people": Bernarr Macfadden's "physical culture" world and the influence of

eugenic thought in American fitness culture, 1900S–1930S', *Amerikastudien* 17 (2019): 241–64.
Sundaram, Jomo Kwame, 'Globalization, imperialism and its discontents', *Inter-Asia Cultural Studies* 15 (2014): 17–24.
Szymanski, Stefan, 'A theory of the evolution of modern sport', *Journal of Sport History* (2008): 1–32.
Thomas, Ajay Jacob, 'Reconfiguring colonial hierarchies', *The Indian Economic & Social History Review* 59 (2022): 171–98.
Tipton, Charles M., 'Antiquity to the early years of the 20th century', *History of Exercise Physiology* (2014): 3–32.
Tipton, Charles M., 'The history of "Exercise is Medicine" in ancient civilizations', *Advances in Physiology Education* 38 (2014): 109–17.
Tipton, Charles M., 'Susruta of India, an unrecognized contributor to the history of exercise physiology', *Journal of Applied Physiology* 104 (2008): 1553–6.
Tlustý, Tomáš, 'The American YMCA and its physical education program–first steps to world expansion', *Studies in Sport Humanities* 20 (2016): 39–47.
Todd, Jan, 'As men do walk a mile, women should talk an hour …. Tis their exercise and other pre-enlightenment thought on women and purposive training', *Iron Game History* 7 (2002): 56–70.
Todd, Jan, 'Bernarr Macfadden: Reformer of feminine form', *Journal of Sport History* 14 (1987): 61–75.
Todd, Jan, 'The classical ideal and its impact on the search for suitable exercise: 1774–1830', *Iron Game History* 2 (1992): 7.
Todd, Jan, 'Center ring: Katie Sandwina and the construction of celebrity', *Iron Game History* 10 (2007): 29–33.
Todd, Jan, 'From milo to milo: A history of barbells, dumbbells, and Indian clubs', *Iron Game History* 3 (1995): 10.
Todd, Jan, 'Reflections on physical culture: Defining our field and protecting its integrity', *Iron Game History*, 13 (2015): 2–8
Todd, Jan, 'The strength builders: A history of barbells, dumbbells and Indian clubs', *The International Journal of the History of Sport* 20 (2003): 65–90.
Todd, Jan, 'Strength is health: George Barker Windship and the first American weight-training boom', *Iron Game History* 3 (1993): 6.
Todd, Jan, Joe Roark and Terry Todd, 'A briefly annotated bibliography of English language serial publications in the field of physical culture', *Iron Game History* 1 (1991): 25–40.
Todd, Terry, 'The Arnold strength summit', *Iron Game History* 7 (2002): 4–5.
Todd, Terry and Spencer Maxcy, 'Muscles, memory: And George Hackenschmidt', *Iron Game History* 2 (1992): 10–15.
Todd, Terry and John Hoberman, 'Yearning for muscular power', *Iron Game History* 9 (2007): 24.
Tosato-Rigo, Danièle, 'In the shadow of Emile: Pedagogues, paediatricians, physical education, 1686–1762', *Studies in Philosophy and Education* 31 (2012): 449–63.
Trangbaek, Else, 'Discipline and emancipation through sport: The pioneers of women's sport in Denmark', *Scandinavian Journal of History* 21 (1996): 121–34.
Trenson, Steven, 'Buddhism and martial arts in premodern Japan: New observations from a religious historical perspective', *Religions* 13 (2022): 440.

Tröhler, Daniel, 'Shaping the national body: Physical education and the transformation of German nationalism in the long nineteenth-century', *Nordic Journal of Educational History* 4 (2017): 31–45.

Valdameri, Elena, 'Training female bodies for New India: Women's physical education between global trends and local politics in colonial South Asia, c. 1900–1939', *The International Journal of the History of Sport* 39 (2022): 1240–64.

Vamplew, Wray, 'Products, promotion, and (possibly) profits: Sports entrepreneurship revisited', *Journal of Sport History* 45 (2018): 183–201.

Vertinsky, Patricia, 'Transatlantic traffic in expressive movement: From Delsarte and Dalcroze to Margaret H'Doubler and Rudolf Laban', *The International Journal of the History of Sport* 26 (2009): 2031–51.

Vertinsky, Patricia and Aishwarya Ramachandran, 'The "Y" goes to India', *Journal of Sport History* 46 (2019): 363–79.

Wallhead, Tristan and Mary O'Sullivan, 'Sport education: Physical education for the new millennium?' *Physical Education and Sport Pedagogy* 10 (2005): 181–210.

Walton, John, 'Sport and the basques: Constructed and contested identities, 1876–1936', *Journal of Historical Sociology* 24 (2011): 451–71.

Wanneberg, Pia Lundquist, 'Gymnastics as remedy: A study of nineteenth-century Swedish medical gymnastics', *Athens Journal of Sports* 5 (2018): 33–52.

Watt, Carey, 'Cultural exchange, appropriation and physical culture: Strongman Eugen Sandow in colonial India, 1904–1905', *The International Journal of the History of Sport* 33 (2016): 1921–42.

Weber, Eugen, 'Gymnastics and sports in Fin-De-Siècle France: Opium of the classes?' *The American Historical Review* 71 (1971): 70–98.

Wedemeyer, Bernd and Anthony Haywood (translator), 'Bodybuilding in Germany in the late nineteenth and early twentieth centuries', *Iron Game History* 3 (1994): 4–7.

Westberg, Johannes, 'Adjusting Swedish gymnastics to the female nature', *Espacio, Tiempo Y Educación* 5 (2018): 261–79.

Westberg, Johannes, 'Girls' gymnastics in the service of the nation: Educationalisation, gender and Swedish gymnastics in the mid-nineteenth-century', *Nordic Journal of Educational History* 4 (2017): 47–69.

Whorton, James, '"Athlete's heart": The medical debate over athleticism, 1870–920', *Journal of Sport History* 9 (1982): 30–52.

Williams, Craig, 'The rhetoricity of gender and the ideal of mediocritas in vitruvius's de architectura', *Arethusa* 49 (2016): 245–6.

Wilms, Sabine, 'Nurturing life in classical Chinese medicine: Sun Simiao on healing without drugs, transforming bodies and cultivating life', *JCM* 93 (2010): 5–13.

Winett, Richard and Ralph Carpinelli, 'Potential health-related benefits of resistance training', *Preventive Medicine* 33 (2001): 503–13.

Wood, Aaron, 'Eugen Sandow: Performing new masculinities', *Eidos. A Journal for Philosophy of Culture* 5 (2021): 21–38.

Wooyeal, Paik and Daniel A. Bell, 'Citizenship and state-sponsored physical education: Ancient Greece and ancient China', *The Review of Politics* 66 (2004): 7–34.

Yabu, Kotaro, 'Diffusion of judo in the United States during the Russo-Japanese War: Aiming to overcome the' match-based historical view', *Martial Arts Studies* 6 (2018): 41–51.
Young, Iris Marion, 'Throwing like a girl: A phenomenology of feminine body comportment motility and spatiality', *Human Studies* 3 (1980): 137–56.
Zarnowski, Frank, 'The amazing Donald Dinnie: The nineteenth-century's greatest athlete', *Iron Game History* 5 (1998): 3–11.
Zarrilli, Phillip, 'Toward a phenomenological model of the actor's embodied modes of experience', *Theatre Journal* 56 (2004): 653–66.
Zweiniger-Bargielowska, Ina, 'The culture of the abdomen: Obesity and reducing in Britain, circa 1900–1939', *Journal of British Studies* 44 (2005): 239–73.
藪耕太郎, and ヤブコウタロウ. 'Did the Japanese dream of a muscular body?: Western style of physical training in the Meiji era', 仙台大学紀要 50 (2018): 1–9.

Chapters in Edited Collections

Alter, Joseph, 'Yoga at the Fin de Siècle: Muscular Christianity with a "Hindu" twist', In *Muscular Christianity and the colonial and post-colonial world*, edited by John Macaloon, 59–76. Routledge, 2013.
Atkinson, Mike, 'Norbert Elias and the body', In *Routledge handbook of body studies*, edited by Bryan Turner, 62–74. Routledge, 2012.
Baas, Michiel, 'Muscles, masculinity and middle classness', In *Routledge handbook of contemporary India*, edited by Knut Jacobsen, 444–56. Routledge, 2016.
Bayly, C.A., 'From archaic globalization to international networks, circa 1600–2000', In *Interactions: Transregional perspectives on world history*, edited by Jerry H. Bentley, Renate Bridenthal and Anand Yang, 14–15. University of Hawaii Press, 2005.
Bayly, C.A., 'Introduction: The connected world of empires', In *Modernity and culture from the mediterranean to the Indian Ocean, 1890–1920*, edited by Christopher A. Bayly and Leila Fawaz, 1–27. Columbia University Press, 2002.
Berryman, Jack, 'Exercise and the medical tradition from hippocrates through Antebellum America: A review essay', In *Sport and exercise science: Essays in the history of sports medicine*, edited by Jack Berryman and Roberta Park, 3–15. University of Illinois Press, 1992.
Bonini, Gherardo, 'Weightlifting', In *Routledge handbook of global sport*, edited by John Nauright and Sarah Zipp, 392–3. Routledge, 2020.
Cavallo, Sandra and Tessa Storey, 'Regimens, authors and readers: Italy and England compared', In *Conserving health in early modern culture*, edited by Sandra Cavallo and Tessa Storey, 23–52. Manchester University Press, 2017.
Collins, Tony, 'Sport and physical culture at the edges of the imperial project', In *Critical reflections on physical culture at the edges of empire*, edited by Francois Cleophas, 209–13. African Sun, 2021.
Doak, Kevin 'National identity and nationalism', In *A companion to Japanese history*, edited by William Tsutsui, 528–44. Wiley, 2007.
Frühstück, Sabine and Wolfram Manzenreiter, 'Neverland lost: Judo cultures in Austria, Japan, and elsewhere struggling for cultural hegemony at the Vienna

Budokan', In *Globalizing Japan*, edited by Harumi Befu and Sylvie Guichard-Anguis, 91–115. Routledge, 2003.

Guttmann, Allen, 'The development of modern sports', In *Handbook of sports studies*, edited by Jay Coakley and Eric Dunning, 248–59. Sage, 2000.

Guttmann, Allen and Lee Thompson, 'Educators, imitators, modernizers: The arrival and spread of modern sport in Japan', In *Europe, sport, World*, edited by J.A. Mangan, 23–48. Routledge, 2013.

Hoffmann, Annette and Gertrud Pfister, 'Tunen – A forgotten movement culture: Its beginnings in Germany and diffusion in the United States', In *Turnen and sport*, edited by Annette R. Hoffmann, 11–24. Waxmann Verlag, 2004.

Hoornstra, David 'Boucicaut fils and the Great Hiatus: Insights from the career of Jean II le Meingre, called Boucicaut', In *The hundred years war (Part III)*, edited by L.J. Andrew Villalon and Donald J. Kagay, 105–44. Brill, 2013.

Hurst, C. 'Kendo', In *Martial arts of the world*, edited by T. Green, 249–54. Clio, 2001.

Ichiba, Toshiyuki, 'Traces of German Turnen in Japan', In *Turnen around the World*, edited by Annette Hoffman and G. Pfister, 275–80. Lexington, 2023.

Iser, Wolfgang, 'Interaction between text and reader', In *Readers and reading*, edited by Andrew Bennett, 20–31. Routledge, 2014.

Johar, Navtej Singh, 'The contemplative spectator: Seeing as a mode of stilling mind', In *Movements of interweaving*, edited by Gabriele Brandstetter, Gerko Egert and Holger Hartung, 321–42. Routledge, 2018.

Kirk, David, 'Physical education: A gendered history', In *Gender and physical education*, edited by Dawn Penney, 36–50. Routledge, 2002.

Kyle, Donald, 'Greek female sport: Rites, running, and racing', In *A companion to sport and spectacle in Greek and Roman antiquity*, edited by Paul Christesen and Donald Kyle, 258–75. Wiley, 2013.

Lempa, Heikki, 'The body in motion: The image of man in physical education in late eighteenth-century Schnepfenthal', In *Anatomy of the medical image*, edited by Axel Fliethmann and Christiane Weller, 95–111. Brill, 2021.

Macaloon, John 'Introduction: Muscular Christianity after 150 years', In *Muscular christianity and the colonial and post-colonial world*, edited by John Macaloon, xi–xxiv. Routledge, 2013.

Mangan, J.A. and Hamad Ndee, 'Military Drill – rather more than "brief and Basic": English elementary schools and English Militarism', In *Militarism, sport, Europe*, edited by J.A. Mangan, 67–99. Routledge, 2004.

Matsunami, Minoru. 'Traditional sport in Japan', In *The Palgrave handbook of leisure theory*, edited by Karl Spracklen, Brett Lashua, Erin Sharpe and Spencer Swain, 169–86. Palgrave, 2017.

Molli, Giovanna Baldissin. 'The sculpted body: Interferences between beauty and anatomy', In *Introduction to medical humanities: Medicine and the Italian artistic heritage*, edited by Renzo Pegoraro, Luciana Caenazzo and Lucia Mariani, 69–89. Springer, 2022.

Nagai, Michio, 'Westernization and Japanization: The early Meiji transformation of education', In *Tradition and modernization in Japanese culture*, edited by Donald Shively, 35–76. Princeton University Press, 1971.

Naul, Roland. 'History of sport and physical education in Germany, 1800–1945', In *Sport and physical education in Germany*, edited by Ken Hardman and Roland Naul, 15–27. Routledge, 2005.

Newcombe, Suzanne. 'Yoga in Europe', In *Handbook of Hinduism in Europe*, edited by Knut Jacobsen and Ferdinando Sardella, 555–87. Brill, 2020.

Peattie, Mark, 'Japanese attitudes toward colonialism, 1895–1945', In *The Japanese colonial empire 1895–1945*, edited by Ramon Myers and Mark Peattie, 80–127. Princeton University Press, 1984.

Robertson, Roland, 'Glocalization: Time-space and homogeneity-heterogeneity', In *Global Modernities/Sage*, edited by Mike Featherstone, Scott Lash and Roland Robertson, 25–44. Sage Publications, 1995.

Robertson, Roland, 'Social theory, cultural relativity, and the problem of globality', In *Sociology of globalization*, edited by Keri Iyall Smith, 61–7. Routledge, 2018.

Schattner, Angela, 'Putting sports in place', In *Sports and physical exercise in early modern culture*, edited by Rebekka von Mallinckrodt and Angela Schattner, 65–85. Routledge, 2017.

Scott, Michael, 'The social life of Greek athletic facilities (other than stadia)', In *A Companion to sport and spectacle in Greek and Roman Antiquity*, edited by Paul Christesen, 295–308. Wiley, 2013.

Singleton, Mark, 'Yoga and physical culture: Transnational history and blurred discursive contexts', In *Routledge handbook of contemporary India*, edited by Knut Jacobsen, 172–84. Taylor & Francis, 2015.

Speak, Mike, 'China in the modern world', In *Sport and physical education in China*, edited by Robin Jones and Jim Riordan. Routledge, 1999.

Speak, Mike, 'Recreation and sport in Ancient China: Primitive society to AD 960', In *Sport and physical education in China*, edited by Robin Jones and James Riordan, 40–57. Routledge, 2002.

Spenn, Amanda, 'A history of women in judo', In *Women in Judo*, edited by Mike Callan, 5–16. Routledge, 2021.

Taube, Karl, Marc Zender, Heather Orr and Rex Koontz, 'American gladiators: Ritual boxing in ancient Mesoamerica', In *Blood and beauty: Organized violence in the art and archaeology of Mesoamerica and Central America*, edited by Heather Orr and Rex Koontz, 161–220. Cotsen Institute, 2009.

Thorlindsson, Thorolfur and Vidar Halldorsson, 'The roots of Icelandic physical culture and sport in the Saga age', In *The Nordic Model and physical culture*, edited by Mikkel Tin, Frode Telseth, Jan Ove Tangen and Richard Giulianotti, 101–16. Routledge, 2019.

Tipton, Charles, 'Historical perspective: The antiquity of exercise, exercise physiology and the exercise prescription for health', In *Nutrition and fitness: Cultural, genetic and metabolic aspects*, edited by A.P. Simopoulos, 218–22. Karger Publishers, 2008.

Watt, Carey, 'Physical culture and the body in colonial India, c. 1800–1947', In *Routledge handbook of the history of Colonialism in South Asia*, edited by Harald Fischer-Tiné and Maria Framke, 345–58. Routledge, 2021.

Wichmann, Angela, 'Diversity versus unity: A comparative analysis of the complex roots of the World Gymnaestrada', In *Global perspectives on sport and physical cultures*, edited by Annette Hofmann, Gerald Gems and Maureen Smith, 113–28. Routledge, 2018.

Dissertations

Beckwith, K.A. 'Building strength: Alan Calvert, the Milo Bar-bell Company, and the modernization of American weight training', University of Texas at Austin, 2006.

Carter, Andrew Kerr. 'Games, Greek and pluck: Athleticism, classicism and elite British education, 1850–1914', Manchester Metropolitan University, 2023.

Cleophas, Francois Johannes. 'Physical education and physical culture in the Coloured community of the Western Cape, 1837–1966', Stellenbosch University, 2009.

Kavvadia, Maria. 'Making medicine in post-tridentine Rome: Girolamo Mercuriale's "De Arte Gymnastica": A different reading of the book', European University Institute, 2015.

Kodya, Mark. 'An exploration of the history of weightlifting as a reflection of the major socio-political events and trends of the 20th century', State University of New York Empire State College, 2005.

Maranhão, Tiago Fernandes de Albuquerque. 'Molding the body, forging the Nation: Race, physical culture, and the shaping of Brazil (1822–1930)', Vanderbilt University, 2020.

Schöler, Julia Helene. 'Über Die Anfänge Der Schwedischen Heilgymnastik In Deutschland: Ein Beitrag Zur Geschichte Der Krankengymnastik Im 19. Jahrhundert', Universität Münster, 2005.

Underwood, Chloe Louise. 'Exercising virtue: The physical reform of the leisured elite in eighteenth-century France', University of Warwick, 2001.

Zhang, Huijie. 'Missionary schools, the YMCA and the transformation of physical education and sport in modern China (1840–1937)', University of Western Australia, 2015.

Websites

Auñamendi Eusko Entziklopedia
IronMind
Physical Culture Study
Playing Pasts

INDEX

Academy, the 38–9
Agehananda, Bharati 62
agoge system 47
akhara 26–7, 50, 56, 201, 203
Alter, Joseph 10, 27, 51, 68
Amateur-Athleten-Weltunion (Amateur Athletic World Union) 180–2
American Alliance for Health and Physical Education (AAHPE) 130
Amorós y Ondeano, Francisco 108–9
   Gymnase civil français 108
   Gymnase Normal Militaire 109
   Noveau manuel complet d'éducation physique 61, 63
Anderson, Benedict 158
Anderson, Lieutenant, *A Series of Exercises for the Regulation Clubs* 61–2
Andry, Nicolas, *Orthopédie* 57
archery 23, 42, 44, 46, 48
Aristotle 30, 39
Arizmendi, Francisco 191
ashraf class 44
Atilla, Louis 133–4, 152, 194
Atilla's gymnasium 152
Atkinson, William Walker 78–80
Avicenna 32–3, 36

Bader, M. Josef 176
Balagangadhara, S. N. 70
Bälz, Erwin 91
Bankier, William (Apollo) 81, 87
Barrenstreit ('parallel bar dispute') 111
Barton-Wright, Edward 85–7
Basedow, Johann Bernhard 99–100
   Das Ekmentarwerk 99
   Philanthropium 99–100

Basu, Shanker 78
Beaujeu, Monsieur 119–20
Belfast Commercial Chronicle 190
Bell, Daniel A. 41
Benkei, Saitō Musashibō 26
Berry, Mark 156, 212
Bhagavad Gita 20, 23, 72
bikini mosaic (forms of physical culture) 39–40
Birmingham Mail 178
Bittor Zabala ('Arteondo') 192
Blavatsky, Helena 70
Bloom, Leopold (fictional character) 5, 136
Blundell, John 34
body/bodies
   and the barbell 137
   boys and girls 119–20
   and emotional expression 74
   global 6–8, 55, 93–4, 96, 115, 118, 130, 168, 173
   ideals 2, 33, 55, 62, 93
   implicitly 5
   as machine 105
   martial and non-martial 115
   politics 126
   types 10
   white and non-white 9–10, 124
bodybuilding 15, 34, 133, 135, 145, 167, 205
bodyweight exercises 11, 137, 179, 201
Bonde, Hans 166
Book of Samuel 20–1
Bourdieu, Pierre, *habitus* 5, 7
Bourke, Joanna 140
Braudy, Leo 134
Brazil 91–2, 116–17

Brett, Frederick Harrington, *A Practical Essay on Some of the Principal Surgical Diseases of India* 57–8, 70
British military 12–13, 57, 60–2, 66, 78, 80, 106, 113, 141, 193, 201–2
Brunton, Thomas Lauder 88
Buddha 71
Budd, Michael Anton 157, 197
Burrows, Tom 1, 66–7, 158
Byzantine physicians 31

Cairus, José 92
Caledonian Mercury 190
Calvert, Alan 143, 149, 168, 188
Campbell, James 60
capoeira 92
Carraro, Attilio Nicola 21
La Casa Giocosa (house of joy) 43
Centennial Exhibition (1876) 143
Central Gymnastic Institute 60, 110
Chapman, David 147–8
Charaka 29
charioteering 42, 48
Chicago World Fair (1893) 147
Chikaraishi stone-lifting 25–6
Choudhury, Bikram 78
Cinato, Franck 50
Cleophas, Francois 212
Clias, Peter Heinrich 57, 60, 107–9, 111, 119
    Anfangsgrnde der Gymnasik oder Turnkunst 107–8
club-swinging 10–12, 23, 54–68, 70, 80–1, 85, 91–3, 111, 113–14, 120, 135, 147, 173, 193–8, 200–4, 209
colonialism and fitness 4, 55, 116, 199
commodification of fitness 135, 157, 168
Conrad, Sebastian 3, 7, 10, 54, 133
Cooper, John Astley 177
Coubertin, Pierre de 177, 190
Coulson, William, *On Deformities of the Chest* 59
Crimean War 60–1, 111–12
Cronin, Mike 212
cuāuhocēlōtl warrior class 48–9

cultural transfer 39–40
La Culture Physique 143, 158, 160
Curtis, Edward Ely 106–7
Cyr, Louis 144–5, 175, 186

Da Costa, Mg 117
da Feltre, Vittorino 43–4
Darwin, Charles 126–7
da Verona, Guarino 43–4
David (biblical) 20–1
David (Old Testament) 20–1
deepening process 4, 12, 14, 55, 71, 114, 167, 189
Delafield, Richard 112
Denmark 104–5, 119, 121–2, 127
Desbonnet, Edmond 142–4, 149, 152, 179, 188
Desmond, Shaw 200–1
Deutscher Athleten-Verband 176
ding (heavy cauldron) lifting 25
Dinnie, Donald 185
Donaldson, Emily Ann 189

École de Joinville (military school) 60, 109
Eisen, George 20–1
Elliot, Launceston 178
Elphinstone, Mountstuart 200
Empire of Things 13, 135, 146–56
Encyclopaedia of Indian Physical Culture 63
Euler, Carl 110–11
European gymnastics 95, 97–8, 114, 116–18, 152
exercise
    for fighting 46–51
    as medicine 28–36
    and physical education 36–45
    and religious practices 19–28

Fair, John 174
Faruqui, Munis Daniyal 44
Fédération Internationale Haltérophilie (FIH) 183
fighting, exercise for 46–51
fitness
    colonialism and 4, 55, 116, 199
    and commerce 5, 8, 13, 63, 68, 147–8, 151, 205–6, 211–12

and Empire 4, 12–13, 27, 31, 39, 44, 47–9, 111–15, 123, 128, 140–2, 146–56, 161, 167, 188
entrepreneurship 8–9, 13, 65–6, 135, 140–5, 149, 151, 161, 171, 177, 212–13
and gender 9–10, 59, 120, 122, 124–5, 145–6, 149
industry 8, 154–5, 188
print networks 135
and race 9–10, 64–5, 121, 125–7, 130, 136, 145, 167, 200, 206
as spectacle 49, 135, 193
fitness spaces
   clubs (*see also* club-swinging; Indian clubs)
      globalism 60
      heavy club-swinging 63, 65, 172–3, 193–204
      Kehoe 66
      light club-swinging 193–4, 196, 201–3
      regulation 62
      Turnverein 67
   stages 138–9, 142, 144–6, 208
Forbes, Clarence 39
Foxen, Anya 72–3
Fox, Richard 145
French Revolution 102
Fry, C. B. 150
Fujimaro, Tanaka 124
Fuld, Leonhard Felix, *American Physical Education Review* 37–8
Fyfe, Aileen 166

gadas 202–3
Galen 30–3
Galton, Francis 9, 126, 141
Gama the Great (Ghulam Muhammad) 71, 200–1, 203
Gänger, Stefanie 96
Garrud, Edith 87–8
Gelders, Raf 70
gender and fitness 9–10, 59, 120, 122, 124–5, 145–6, 149
German gymnastics 115, 118, 129–30
Ghosh, Bishnu Charan, *Muscle Control* 78

Gilbert, Pamela 178
Gilman, Sander 59–60, 118
global body 6–8, 55, 93–4, 96, 115, 118, 130, 168, 173
globalization of fitness 1–4, 6–7, 9–15, 19, 31, 36–7, 51–3, 55, 69, 81, 83, 85, 90, 92–3, 96–7, 111, 115, 122, 128, 152–3, 171–3, 177, 184, 186, 189, 194, 200, 202, 204–5, 208
glocalization 4–5
go-betweens (cultural) 54, 97
Godfrey, Emelyne 86
Goldberg, Elliott 69, 72
Goliath (biblical figure) 155
Great Exhibition, in London 128, 197
Great War 12–13, 67, 71, 76, 134, 140, 158–9, 182–3, 194, 212
Greco-Roman statues 18, 29–31, 33–4, 36, 43, 97, 145, 154, 163, 197
gurukulam education system 40–1
GutsMuths, Johann 95–6, 100–5
   Gymnastik für die Jugend ('Gymnastics for Youth') 100–1
Guttmann, Allen 190
gymnasiums 25–7, 32, 36, 38–40, 50, 63, 97, 104, 108–9, 112, 114–15, 128–9, 136, 141, 146, 151–3, 160, 196, 199, 201, 207, 209
gymnastica system 30
gymnastics 11, 20, 34, 43, 60–1, 64–7, 78. *See also* Young Men's Christian Association (YMCAs)
   and education 108–9, 121
   European 95, 97–8, 114, 116–18, 152
   German 115, 118, 129–30
   institutionalization of 118–21, 136, 165, 213
   Ling 75, 78, 106, 111, 121
   military 61, 84, 97, 106–19, 124, 130, 202, 209
   modernization of 97–106

Swedish 4, 61, 110, 115–16, 118, 202
turner system 64–5, 103–4, 109–11, 116–17, 137
Western 83, 115

Hackenschmidt, George 144, 167, 186–7
  The Way to Live 163
Hadley, Hopton 142
Hague, William Grant 166
Haley, Bruce 126–7
Hancock, Harrie Irving 90–1
Hanuman 23–4, 51
Harmonic Gymnastics 75
Harrison, James (Professor) 65, 67, 153, 193–7, 199
  Indian Clubs, Dumb-Bells, and Sword exercises 195–6
Harrison, Mark 57
Hatha Yoga 68–9, 71–2, 75, 79
Health and Strength/Health and Strength League (magazine) 66–7, 81, 87, 140, 142, 153, 156, 158–9, 167–8, 193, 201
heavy club-swinging 63, 65, 172–3, 193–204
heishiki taisō (military gymnastics) 117
Henriot 61, 63
Herakles (Hercules) 24
Herbert, Sidney 61, 112
Herodicus 30
Highland Games 25, 189–92
Hill, Gus 196–7
Hill, Samuel 89
Hippocrates 30–2
Hobbes, Thomas 98
Hoffman, Annette 64
Hornibrook, F. A., *The Culture of the Abdomen* 160–1, 168
Hua Tuo case 29
Hughes, Thomas, *Tom Brown's School Days* 127
Huizinga, John 18, 52, 209

Ibn Rushd 33
Inch, Thomas 143, 164
Indian clubs 11–12, 14, 55–6, 58, 62–5, 67, 79–80, 173, 184, 188, 194, 200. *See also* club-swinging

industrialization 4, 14, 79, 89, 96, 114, 118, 122, 126, 166, 206
Insom, Surachet 21–2
Internationaler Weltverband 182–3
International Weightlifting Federation (IWF) 174, 177, 180
Isaiah (biblical) 21
Iyer, K. V. 77, 145, 156

Jacob (biblical) 21
Jacob (Old Testament) 21
Jahn, Friedrich Ludwig 9, 11, 64, 102–5, 110–11, 116, 124, 207
  Deutsches Volkstum 103
Japan 25–6, 82–93, 116–18, 124, 191
Jensen, Viggo 178
Jesus Christ 21
Jones, Alexander Wallace 136
Jowett, George 186
Joyce, James, *Ulysses* 5, 136
judo 54–5, 81–93, 210
judokas 85, 90, 92
jujutsu/jiujitsu 81, 84–8, 90–3
Juvenal 19, 40, 49

kami 25
Kanō Jigorō, *The Complete Kano Jujitsu* 81, 84–5, 87, 90–2, 210
Katsukuma, Higashi 90–1
Kavvadia, Maria 33
Kehoe, Sim, *The Indian Club Exercise* 65–6, 198–9
Kennell, Nigel 47
Kerr, W. N. 157, 159–60
Kipling, Rudyard 85–6
Kizar, Oktay 22
koshti (wrestling) 27
Kotteck, Samuel S. 21
Kraft und Gewandtheit 179
Krajewski, Wladislaw von 179
Kramer, Owana 159
Krause, Johann Heinrich 63
Kraus, Franz 179
Krüger, Michael, *Barrenstreit* 111
Kunze, Julius von 64
Kyle, Donald 38–9

Laisné, Napoléon, *Gymnastique des demoiselles* [Ladies' Gymnastics] 63, 109
Lamarck, Jean-Baptiste, *Philosophie Zoologique* 125–6
Lankester, Ray 205
Lawrence-Levy, E. 177–8
Leblanc, Hélène 50
legitimate and illegitimate goods 9
Leland, George 124
Lemaire, E. Ferdinand, *Indian Clubs and How to Use Them* 196–7
Leonard-Fleckman, Mahri 22
Leopold II, King 115
Lewis, Dio L., *The New Gymnastics* 9, 65, 136
light club-swinging 193–4, 196, 201–3
Lightman, Bernard 166
Ling, Per Henrik 78, 104–6, 110–11, 113, 122
  Ling gymnastics 75, 78, 106, 111, 121
  Reglemente för *Gymnastik* 105
Li, Xifan 25
Locke, John, *Some Thoughts Concerning Education* 98
Logan, James, *The Scottish Gael* 191
Lyceum, the 38–9

Macfadden, Bernarr 29, 77, 141–5, 147, 149, 152, 161–4, 166–8
Macfadden, Marguerite 164
Mackaye, Steele 75
MacLaren, Archibald 60–2, 112–15
  A Military System of Gymnastic Exercises 61–2
  Physical Education 113
Maeda, Mitsuyo 92
Mahabharata 23, 27
Maimonides, *Mishneh Thora* 21
Maingre, Jean Le 51
Majumdar, Sachindra 159
Malamitsi-Puchner, Ariadne 30
Malla-Purana 50
Mason, Marian 108, 120–1
McClellan, George 112
McDonald, Charlotte 3
McGlashen Stones 184
McIntosh, Peter 33, 43

McNeill, William, *Keeping Together in Time* 6, 210–11
Meckel, Jakob 117–18
medical discourses in fitness 28–36, 42–3, 55, 57–8, 70, 120, 142, 149, 155
Meiji Japan 81–4, 117, 149, 206, 210
Méndez, Cristobal, *Libro del Exercicio* 34
Mercuriale, Hieronymus, *De Arte Gymnastica Aput Ancientes* 33–6, 59
Metcalf, Alida 54
Michelangelo 43
Miles, Eustace 150–1
military fighting 46–51
military gymnastics 61, 84, 97, 106–19, 124, 130, 202, 209
Mosse, George, *The Image of Man* 6, 207
Mueller, J. P., *My Breathing System* 164, 166–7
mugdars 193, 195, 197, 203
Mughal India 44
Muhammad, Prophet 22–3
Mujumdar, D. C. 63, 202–3
Müller, Jørgen Peter 144
Mundy, Peter 56
Murray, William 154
muscular bonding 6, 211
muscular Christianity 20, 22, 72, 114–15, 127–9, 136, 202, 210
muscular Judaism 127
Mutsuhito, Emperor 82

Nachtegall, Franz 104–5
Nagai, Michio 83
Naidu, Rama Murti 160
Napoleonic wars 56, 102–3, 108
Napoli, Felice 133, 194
The National Police Gazette 175
national stereotype 6–7, 207
Naul, Roland 111
Ndee, Hamad 115
Nehru, Motilal 71
New Times 190
New York Clipper, The 65, 153, 193, 196
Nordau, Max 21, 127

Obizzi, Marquis Luigi Monticelli 178–9
O'Hanlon, Rosalind 44
Omokaru-Ishi 26
Osahito, Emperor 82
Österberg, Madame 122
Österreichischer Athleten-Bund 176
Ouseley, William 56
Ozerkevich, Rachel 162

Pall Mall Gazette 178
Pant, Pratinidhi, *The Ten Point Way to Health* 77
Paraguayan War 117
Paris Exhibition (1889) 190
Patanjali 68, 72
Paul of Aegina 31–2
Pearson's Magazine 86
Perry, Matthew Calbraith (Perry Exhibition) 82
Pestalozzi, Johann Heinrich 109
Philibert, Guillaume 102
physical culture 135–46
  global print communities in 156–67
Physical Culture 77, 141, 157–8, 160–1, 167
physical education (PE)
  boys and girls 119
  in China 41–2, 124
  in Europe 42–5, 104
  exercise and 36–45
physical training 60, 95–6, 98, 102, 189
Pieterse, Jan Nederveen 31
pila, game of 44
pizza effect 62
Plasmon 150–1
popular culture and fitness 31, 80, 84, 93
Porter, Dilwyn 8
Poskett, James 125
powerlifting. *See* weightlifting
print networks and fitness magazines 3, 13, 133, 135, 140–3, 156
Puhlwans (Indian wrestlers) 58
Pullum, W. A. 143, 193
Pythagoras 30

Quetelet, Adolphe 107
Quintilian, *Institutio Oratoria* 39–40
Quran 22–3

race and physical culture 9–10, 64–5, 121, 125–7, 130, 136, 145, 167, 200, 206
Raja Yoga 68–9, 71, 74–5, 80
Ramakrishna 71
Ravina, Mark 83
Regimen Sanitatis 32–3
religion and fitness
  Christianity 20–2, 72, 114–15, 127–9, 136, 202
  Hinduism 23, 41, 71–2, 79, 127
  Judaism 20–1, 127
religious practices, exercise and 19–28
resistance and adaptation 17, 84, 96, 116, 145
Robertson, Roland 172
Roberts, Phoebe 88
Roosevelt, Theodore 89–90
Rothstein, Hugo 64, 110–11
Rousseau, Jean-Jacques 44–5, 95–100, 102, 119, 126, 166, 210
  Du Contrat Social 45
  Emile or On Education 45, 98–9, 119
  The Social Contract 98–9
Royal Army Physical Training Corps 61, 66, 112
Royal Gymnastic Central Institute (GCI) 105–6
The Royal Magazine 188
Russo-Japanese War 55, 82–3, 89

Salzmann, Christian Gotthilf 100
Salzmannschule Schnepfenthal (school) 100
Samson (biblical) 21–2
Sandage, Scott, *Born Losers* 171
Sandow, Eugen 1, 7, 9–11, 13, 76–7, 133–56, 160–6, 168, 175, 178, 188, 194, 197–209, 211, 213
  Gospel of Strength 164–5
  Plasmon, What is It? 151
  Sandow on Physical Training 165, 188
  Strength and How to Obtain It 141, 147, 163, 165–6
Sandow's Magazine of Physical Culture 140–1, 156, 160–1

Sandwina, Katie 144, 146, 153
Santesson, Anton 121–2
Sargent, Dudley Allen 75, 149
Saxon, Arthur 9, 144–5, 147, 154–5, 175
  The Development of Physical Power 164
Scarpa, Stefano 21
Schattner, Angela 44
Schödl, Gottfried 178, 181, 185
schoolchildren, training of 118–30
schools and military institutions 12, 30, 41–5, 50, 60, 93, 95–7, 99–100, 102–10, 116–31, 173, 188–9, 194–5, 201–2, 210
Scott, Michael 38
Secord, James 97
self-defence 2, 54–5, 81, 85–7, 89–90, 93, 201, 205, 210
serious leisure 2
Shahnameh 27
Shilling, Chris 5
Shurley, Jason 138
Sibert, Theodor 178
Sick, Max 78, 144
Simiao, Sun 32
Singh, Buttan 200–1, 203
Singleton, Mark 55, 69, 75–8, 80, 202
Spencer, Herbert 206
Spiess, Adolf 111
The Sporting Life 177
Stebbins, Genevieve, *Genevieve Stebbins System of Physical Training* 75, 79, 164
Steyrer, Hans (Bavarian Hercules) 185–7
Stokes, Michael 159
Stolz, Albert, *Mannesschönheit durch gesunde körperliche Ausbildung* 181
stone-lifting 14, 18, 25–6, 172–3, 184–94, 200, 203–4
  Basque 191–3
  Dinnie Stones 185–6
  Harri-Jasotze/Harri jasotzea 191–3
  Olympic inclusion of 187–8
  Paris Olympics (1900) 187
  Scottish 184–5, 189–91

spring-grip dumbbell 146–8, 188
Unspunnenfest 185
The Strand 160
stretching 53–5. *See also* yoga
Strongfort, Lionel 167
strongman and strongwoman performances 9, 25, 65, 76, 78, 81, 133–4, 146, 153–4, 159–60, 184, 194
sūryanamaskār ('sun salutation') pattern 77
Sushruta 28–9
Swedish gymnastics 4, 61, 110, 115–16, 118, 202
sweeping 53–5. *See also* judo
swinging 53. *See also* club-swinging
Szalay, Josef 146, 152–3, 175, 207

Tani, Yukio 86–7
Techow, Gustav 110
Tetsujiro Shidachi 85
theatres and stages 138–9, 142, 144–6, 208
Theosophical Society 70–2, 80
three Bs (biceps, beef and the *Bhagavad gita*) 72
Tipton, Charles, M. 28, 30
Todd, Jan 34, 65, 99, 119–21, 123, 136, 146, 194
Toepoel, Pieter 86
Tokio Times 189
Torrens, Henry 57–60
Tosato-Rigo, Danièle 99
transnational physical culture 45, 55, 58–9, 81
Triat, Hippolyte 63
turner system 64–5, 103–4, 109–11, 116–17, 137
Turnplatz (training space) 103
Turnverein gymnastic movement 61, 64, 67, 136, 206

Uyenishi, Sada Kazu 81, 86–7

Valdameri, Elena 124
Vamplew, Wray 8–9, 140
Vanity Fair 136
Vasu, S. C. 78
Veidlere, Julia 153

Victoria, Queen 133, 190, 193
Vigarello, Georges 7
Vitruvius, *De Architectura* 40
Vivekananda, Swami 20, 54, 68–75, 77–80. *See also Hatha Yoga; Raja Yoga*
    Delsarte system 69, 74–6, 79
Vyayam 202

Wacquant, Loïc 5
Walker, Donald 57–9, 62–5, 120–1
    British Manly Exercises 57–9, 63, 120
    Exercises for Ladies 63
Walsh, Shannon 65, 145, 208
Walton, John 192
Watt, Carey 3, 10, 76
Watts, Emily Diana, *The Fine Art of Jujitsu* 87–8
Webster, David 185
Wedemeyer, Bernd 167, 179
weightlifting 14, 50, 136–7, 173–83
    barbells and dumbbells 137–8
    clean and jerk, and the snatch 173, 179
    clean *vs.* continental 137
    contests 136–40, 144, 147
    German method 175, 177, 180
    at the Olympics 177–83
weight-training 50, 156, 194
Westernization 82–3
Whiteley, Alexander 147–8

William IV, King Frederick 109
Williams, George 128
Willis, Martin 162–3
Windship, George Barker 137, 194
Wodehouse, P. G. 135–6, 145
Wood, William 196
Wooyeal, Paik 41
World Fairs 197
World Strongest Man (WSM) contest 183–4
World Weightlifting Championships (1905, 1906) 179–81

Xenophon 47

yoga 53–5, 205. *See also Hatha Yoga; Raja Yoga*
    globalization of 69–70
    history of 69
    modern 69, 75–7, 81
    as physical culture 68–80
Yoshitsugu, Yamashita 85, 89–90
Young, Iris Marion, 'Throwing like a girl' 5
Young Men's Christian Association (YMCAs) 12, 20, 113, 119, 128–9

Zander, Gustav (machines fame) 143–4
Zeigfeld, Flo 141
zurkhaneh (gymnasium) 27–8, 32, 50, 203